Advance Praise for *Head First HTML5 Programming*

"HTML5 is the "future of the web". How many times have you heard that? If you really want to understand the family of technologies that make up HTML5, read this book! *Head First HTML5 Programming* is the definitive book on HTML5 for everyone from beginners to experienced developers."

> — **Aaron LaBerge, CEO, Fanzter Inc.**

"This book is a rollicking ride through the wild new territory of HTML5, where we are all bound to be battling scorpions for years. It takes you through basic concepts so you understand the purposes of the HTML5 design, and then into each area so you know your way around. Like all Head First books, it replaces dry recitation with lively, memorable, fact-laden bursts of information. I will always have the formal HTML5 spec web site for reference purposes, but I'd rather *learn* it lively."

> — **Ken Arnold, Design/Build Hub, Peak Impact, Inc.**

"A must have book on HTML5 which continues on the Head First tradition of being witty, fun, chocked-full of examples and wickedly smart!"

> — **Danny Mavromatis, Sr Software Architect, ABC Television Group**

"*Head First HTML5 Programming* does a great job of making sense of many of the key aspects of HTML5 in a fun, easy-to-digest manner. With its highly-visual style and numerous code samples, complex concepts like canvas and asynchronous programming are simplified and illustrated making them straightforward and engaging."

> — **Michael S. Scherotter, Principal Architect Evangelist, Microsoft Corporation**

"HTML5 is a cake with many layers of technologies. *Head First HTML5 Programming* bakes that cake, and then throws it at your face. You will consume deliciousness and rejoice."

> — **Josh Rhoades, co-founder of BrightHalf**

With *Head First HTML5 Programming*, the multiplicity of HTML5 is approached with a multiplicity in the medium that makes the hard work of learning fun.

> — **Ward Cunningham, wiki inventor**

"HTML5 is the hottest new technology for website development. Developers far and wide can't wait to put it to use to build flexible, rich media websites that also work great on tablets and smart phones. *Head First HTML5 Programming* is the best and funnest way to feed this exciting new technology to your brain. I highly recommend it!"

> — **Marianne Marck, SVP Technology, Blue Nile Inc.**

"Straightforward, informative and entertaining, *Head First HTML5 Programming* is a must for anyone wanting to get started with HTML5 or just to refresh their skills. The Head First series helps me to keep my technical skills up to date allowing me to better support my developers and projects."

— **Todd Guill, Project Manager, AllRecipes.com**

"This ain't your grandpa's DHTML! *Head First HTML5 Programming* paints a hopeful and confident picture of the future of the Web through HTML5, while empowering you to code your own ticket there. If you're seeking a definitive, accessible, and at times pretty funny guidebook to this standard, look no further."

— **Manny Otto, Web Producer and Creative**

"The authors have hit the nail on the head—JavaScript skills are the key to HTML5. Even if you've never written a JavaScript program before, they'll quickly get you up and running through a series of fun and practical projects."

— **David Powers, author of *PHP Solutions: Dynamic Web Design Made Easy***

Praise for other books from Eric Freeman & Elisabeth Robson

"This book's admirable clarity, humor and substantial doses of clever make it the sort of book that helps even non-programmers think well about problem-solving."

— **Cory Doctorow, co-editor of Boing Boing**
and author of *Down and Out in the Magic Kingdom*
and *Someone Comes to Town, Someone Leaves Town*

"I feel like a thousand pounds of books have just been lifted off of my head."

— **Ward Cunningham, inventor of the Wiki**
and founder of the Hillside Group

"This book is close to perfect, because of the way it combines expertise and readability. It speaks with authority and it reads beautifully. It's one of the very few software books I've ever read that strikes me as indispensable. (I'd put maybe 10 books in this category, at the outside.)"

— **David Gelernter, Professor of Computer Science, Yale University**
and author of *Mirror Worlds* and *Machine Beauty*

"I literally love this book. In fact, I kissed this book in front of my wife."

— **Satish Kumar**

"Beware. If you're someone who reads at night before falling asleep, you'll have to restrict *Head First HTML with CSS & XHTML* to daytime reading. This book wakes up your brain."

— **Pauline McNamara, Center for New Technologies and Education,**
Fribourg University, Switzerland

"*Head First HTML with CSS & XHTML* is a thoroughly modern introduction to forward-looking practices in Web page markup and presentation. It correctly anticipates readers' puzzlements and handles them just in time. The highly graphic and incremental approach precisely mimics the best way to learn this stuff: make a small change and see it in the browser to understand what each new item means."

— **Danny Goodman, author of *Dynamic HTML: The Definitive Guide***

"The Web would be a much better place if every HTML author started off by reading this book."

— **L. David Baron, Technical Lead, Layout & CSS, Mozilla Corporation**
http://dbaron.org/

"*Head First HTML with CSS & XHTML* teaches you how to do things right from the beginning without making the whole process seem overwhelming. HTML, when properly explained, is no more complicated than plain English, and they do an excellent job of keeping every concept at eye-level."

— **Mike Davidson, President & CEO, Newsvine, Inc.**

Other O'Reilly books by Eric Freeman and Elisabeth Robson

Head First Design Patterns

Head First HTML with CSS and XHTML

Other related books from O'Reilly

HTML5 Up and Running

HTML5 Canvas

HTML5: The Missing Manual

HTML5 Geolocation

HTML5 Graphics with SVG and CSS3

HTML5 Forms

HTML5 Media

Other books in O'Reilly's *Head First* series

Head First C#

Head First Java

Head First Object-Oriented Analysis and Design (OOA&D)

Head First HTML with CSS and XHTML

Head First Design Patterns

Head First Servlets and JSP

Head First SQL

Head First Software Development

Head First JavaScript

Head First Ajax

Head First Rails

Head First PHP & MySQL

Head First Web Design

Head First Networking

Head First iPhone and iPad Development

Head First jQuery

Head First
HTML5 Programming
building web apps with javascript

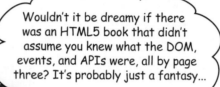

Wouldn't it be dreamy if there was an HTML5 book that didn't assume you knew what the DOM, events, and APIs were, all by page three? It's probably just a fantasy...

Eric Freeman
Elisabeth Robson

O'REILLY®

Beijing • Cambridge • Köln • Sebastopol • Tokyo

Head First HTML5 Programming

by Eric Freeman and Elisabeth Robson

Printed in the United States of America.

Published by O'Reilly Media, Inc., 1005 Gravenstein Highway North, Sebastopol, CA 95472.

O'Reilly Media books may be purchased for educational, business, or sales promotional use. Online editions are also available for most titles (*http://my.safaribooksonline.com*). For more information, contact our corporate/institutional sales department: (800) 998-9938 or *corporate@oreilly.com*.

Series Creators:	Kathy Sierra, Bert Bates
Editor:	Courtney Nash
Design Editor:	Louise Barr
Cover Designer:	Karen Montgomery
Production Editor:	Kristen Borg
Indexer:	Ellen Troutman
Proofreader:	Nancy Reinhardt

Printing History:

October 2011: First Edition.

No gumballs were harmed in the making of this book.

ISBN: 978-1-449-39054-9

[M]

To Steve Jobs, who hyped HTML5 to the point where this book should sell a zillion copies...

And to Steve Jobs, because he's our hero.

Authors of Head First HTML5 Programming

Eric Freeman

Elisabeth Robson

Eric is described by Head First series co-creator Kathy Sierra as "one of those rare individuals fluent in the language, practice, and culture of multiple domains from hipster hacker, corporate VP, engineer, think tank."

Professionally, Eric recently ended nearly a decade as a media company executive—having held the position of CTO of Disney Online & Disney.com at The Walt Disney Company. Eric is now devoting his time to WickedlySmart, a startup he co-created with Elisabeth.

By training, Eric is a computer scientist, having studied with industry luminary David Gelernter during his Ph.D. work at Yale University. His dissertation is credited as the seminal work in alternatives to the desktop metaphor, and also as the first implementation of activity streams, a concept he and Dr. Gelernter developed.

In his spare time, Eric is deeply involved with music; you'll find Eric's latest project, a collaboration with ambient music pioneer Steve Roach, available on the iPhone app store under the name Immersion Station.

Eric lives with his wife and young daughter on Bainbridge Island. His daughter is a frequent vistor to Eric's studio, where she loves to turn the knobs of his synths and audio effects. Eric's also passionate about kids education and nutrition, and looking for ways to improve them.

Write to Eric at eric@wickedlysmart.com or visit his site at http://ericfreeman.com.

Elisabeth is a software engineer, writer, and trainer. She has been passionate about technology since her days as a student at Yale University, where she earned a Masters of Science in Computer Science and designed a concurrent, visual programming language and software architecture.

Elisabeth's been involved with the Internet since the early days; she co-created the award-winning Web site, The Ada Project, one of the first Web sites designed to help women in computer science find career and mentorship information online.

She's currently co-founder of WickedlySmart, an online education experience centered on web technologies, where she creates books, articles, videos and more. Previously, as Director of Special Projects at O'Reilly Media, Elisabeth produced in-person workshops and online courses on a variety of technical topics and developed her passion for creating learning experiences to help people understand technology. Prior to her work with O'Reilly, Elisabeth spent time spreading fairy dust at The Walt Disney Company, where she led research and development efforts in digital media.

When not in front of her computer, you'll find Elisabeth hiking, cycling or kayaking in the great outdoors, with her camera nearby, or cooking vegetarian meals.

You can send her email at beth@wickedlysmart.com or visit her blog at http://elisabethrobson.com.

Table of Contents (Summary)

Table of Contents (the real thing)

Intro

Your brain on HTML5 Programming. Here *you* are trying to *learn* something, while here your *brain* is doing you a favor by making sure the learning doesn't *stick*. Your brain's thinking, "Better leave room for more important things, like which wild animals to avoid and whether naked snowboarding is a bad idea." So how *do* you trick your brain into thinking that your life depends on knowing HTML5 and JavaScript?

1

getting to know HTML5

Welcome to Webville

HTML has been on a wild ride. Sure, HTML started as a mere markup language, but more recently HTML's put on some major muscle. Now we've got a language tuned for building true web applications with local storage, 2D drawing, offline support, sockets and threads, and more. The story of HTML wasn't always pretty, and it's full of drama (we'll get to all that), but in this chapter, we're first going to go on a quick joyride through Webville to get sense for everything that goes into "HTML5." Come on, hop in, we're headed to Webville, and we're going to start by going from zero to HTML5 in 3.8 pages (flat).

introducing JavaScript and the DOM

2 A Little Code

JavaScript is going to take you to new places. You already know all about HTML markup (otherwise known as *structure*) and you know all about CSS style (otherwise known as *presentation*), but what you've been missing is JavaScript (otherwise known as *behavior*). If all you know about are structure and presentation, sure, you can create some great-looking pages, but they're still *just pages*. When you add behavior with JavaScript, you can create an interactive experience; or, even better, you can create full blown web applications. Get ready to add the most interesting and versatile skill in your web toolkit: JavaScript and programming!

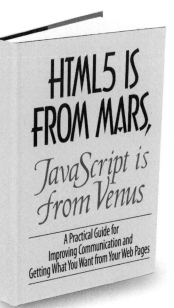

events, handlers and all that jazz

A Little Interactivity

3

You still haven't reached out to touch your user.

You've learned the basics of JavaScript but can you get interactive with your users? When pages respond to user input, they aren't just documents anymore, they're living, reacting applications. In this chapter you're going to learn how to handle one form of user input (excuse the pun), and wire up an old-fashioned HTML <form> element to actual code. It might sound dangerous, but it's also powerful. Strap yourself in, this is a fast moving to-the-point-chapter where we go from zero to interactive app in no time.

javascript functions and objects

Serious JavaScript

4

Can you call yourself a scripter yet? Probably—you already know your way around a lot of JavaScript, but who wants to be a scripter when you can be a programmer? It's time to get serious and take it up a notch—it's time you learn about **functions** and **objects**. They're the key to writing code that is more powerful, better organized and more maintainable. They're also heavily used across HTML5 JavaScript APIs, so the better you understand them the faster you can jump into a new API and start ruling with it. Strap in, this chapter is going to require your undivided attention...

making your html location aware

5 Geolocation

Wherever you go, there you are. And sometimes knowing where you are makes all the difference (especially to a web app). In this chapter we're going to show you how to create web pages that are **location aware**—sometimes you'll be able to pin point your users down to the corner they're standing on, and sometimes you'll only be able to determine the area of town they're in (but you'll still know the town!). Heck, sometimes you won't be able to determine anything about their location, which could be for technical reasons, or just because they don't want you being so nosy. Go figure. In any case, in this chapter we're going to explore a JavaScript API: Geolocation. Grab the best location-aware device you have (even if it's your desktop PC), and let's get started.

talking to the web

Extroverted Apps

6

You've been sitting in your page for too long. It's time to get out a little, to talk to web services, to gather data and to bring it all back so you can build better experiences mixing all that great data together. That's a big part of writing modern HTML5 applications, but to do that you've got to *know how* to talk to web services. In this chapter we're going to do just that, and incorporate some data from a real web service right in your page. And, after you've learned how to do that you'll be able to reach out and touch any web service you want. We'll even fill you in on the hippest new lingo you should use when talking to web services. So, come on, you're going to use some more APIs, the communications APIs.

Watch out for the cliffhanger in this chapter!

bringing out your inner artist

The Canvas

HTML's been liberated from being just a "markup" language. With HTML5's new canvas element you've got the power to create, manipulate and destroy *pixels*, right in your own hands. In this chapter we'll use the canvas element to bring out your inner artist—no more talk about HTML being all semantics and no presentation; with canvas we're going to paint and draw with color. Now it's *all* about presentation. We'll tackle how to place a canvas in your pages, how to draw text and graphics (using JavaScript of course), and even how to handle browsers that don't support the canvas element. And canvas isn't just a one-hit wonder; you're going to be seeing a lot more of canvas in other chapters in this book.

A new HTML5 startup is just waiting for you to get it off the ground!

not your father's tv

Video... with special guest star "Canvas"

8

We don't need no plug-in.
After all, video is now a first-class member of the HTML family—just throw a <video> element in your page and you've got instant video, even across most devices. But video is *far more* than *just an element*, it's also a JavaScript API that allows us to control playback, create our own custom video interfaces and integrate video with the rest of HTML in totally new ways. Speaking of *integration*... remember there's that *video and canvas connection* we've been talking about—you're going to see that putting video and canvas together gives us a powerful new way to *process video* in real time. In this chapter we're going to start by getting video up and running in a page and then we'll put the JavaScript API through its paces. Come on, you're going to be amazed what you can do with a little markup, JavaScript and video & canvas.

Tune in to Webville TV...

storing things locally

Web Storage

9

Tired of stuffing your client data into that tiny ~~closet~~ cookie?

That was fun in the 90s, but we've got much bigger needs today with web apps. What if we said we could get you five megabytes on every user's browser? You'd probably look at us like we were trying to sell you a bridge in Brooklyn. Well, there's no need to be skeptical—the HTML5 Web storage API does just that! In this chapter we're going to take you through everything you need to store any object locally on your user's device and to make use of it in your web experience.

It's hard to manage my busy life if I can't get rid of these stickies after I'm done with them. Can you add a delete function?

putting javascript to work

Web Workers

10

Slow script—do you want to continue running it? If you've spent enough time with JavaScript or browsing the web you've probably seen the "slow script" message. And, with all those multicore processors sitting in your new machine how could a script be running *too slow*? It's because JavaScript can only do one thing at a time. But, with HTML5 and Web Workers, *all that changes*. You've now got the ability to spawn *your own* JavaScript workers to get more work done. Whether you're just trying to design a more responsive app, or you just want to max out your machine's CPU, Web Workers are here to help. Put your JavaScript manager's hat on, let's get some workers cracking!

JavaScript Thread

Running an init function

Handling a user click

A timer just went off

Handling a submit

chug

whirrr

chug

chug

Process an array of data

chug

whirrr

whirrr

chug

Handling another user click

Updating the DOM

Fetching form data

Validating user input

appendix: leftovers

We covered a lot of ground, and you're almost finished with this book.

We'll miss you, but before we let you go, we wouldn't feel right about sending you out into the world without a little more preparation. We can't possibly fit everything you'll need to know into this relatively small chapter. Actually, we *did* originally include everything you need to know about HTML5 (not already covered by the other chapters), by reducing the type point size to .00004. It all fit, but nobody could read it. So, we threw most of it away, and kept the best bits for this Top Ten appendix.

Index

how to use this book

Intro

In this section, we answer the burning question:
"So why <u>DID</u> they put that in an HTML5 book?"

Who is this book for?

If you can answer "yes" to all of these:

 Do you have a computer with a **web browser** and a **test editor**?

 Do you want to **learn**, **understand**, **remember**, and **create** web applications using the best techniques and most recent standards?

 Do you prefer **stimulating dinner party conversation** to **dry**, **dull**, **academic lectures**?

this book is for you.

Who should probably back away from this book?

If you can answer "yes" to any of these:

 Are you **completely new** to writing web pages?

 Are you already developing web apps and looking for a *reference* **book** on HTML5?

 Are you **afraid to try something different**? Would you rather have a root canal than mix stripes with plaid? Do you believe that a technical book can't be serious if cheesy 50's educational films and anthropomorphized JavaScript APIs are in it?

Check out Head First HTML with CSS and XHTML for an excellent introduction to web development, and then come back and join us.

this book is not for you.

[Note from marketing: this book is for anyone with a credit card. Cash is nice, too — Ed]

We know what you're thinking.

"How can *this* be a serious HTML5 programming book?"

"What's with all the graphics?"

"Can I actually *learn* it this way?"

And we know what your *brain* is thinking.

Your brain craves novelty. It's always searching, scanning, *waiting* for something unusual. It was built that way, and it helps you stay alive.

Your brain thinks THIS is important.

So what does your brain do with all the routine, ordinary, normal things you encounter? Everything it *can* to stop them from interfering with the brain's *real* job—recording things that *matter*. It doesn't bother saving the boring things; they never make it past the "this is obviously not important" filter.

How does your brain *know* what's important? Suppose you're out for a day hike and a tiger jumps in front of you. What happens inside your head and body?

Neurons fire. Emotions crank up. *Chemicals surge*.

And that's how your brain knows...

This must be important! Don't forget it!

But imagine you're at home, or in a library. It's a safe, warm, tiger-free zone. You're studying. Getting ready for an exam. Or trying to learn some tough technical topic your boss thinks will take a week, ten days at the most.

Your brain thinks THIS isn't worth saving.

Great. Only 640 more dull, dry, boring pages.

Just one problem. Your brain's trying to do you a big favor. It's trying to make sure that this *obviously* non-important content doesn't clutter up scarce resources. Resources that are better spent storing the really *big* things. Like tigers. Like the danger of fire. Like how you should never again snowboard in shorts.

And there's no simple way to tell your brain, "Hey brain, thank you very much, but no matter how dull this book is, and how little I'm registering on the emotional Richter scale right now, I really *do* want you to keep this stuff around."

We think of a "Head First" reader as a learner.

So what does it take to *learn* something? First, you have to *get* it, then make sure you don't *forget* it. It's not about pushing facts into your head. Based on the latest research in cognitive science, neurobiology, and educational psychology, *learning* takes a lot more than text on a page. We know what turns your brain on.

Some of the Head First learning principles:

Make it visual. Images are far more memorable than words alone, and make learning much more effective (up to 89% improvement in recall and transfer studies). It also makes things more understandable. **Put the words within or near the graphics** they relate to, rather than on the bottom or on another page, and learners will be up to *twice* as likely to solve problems related to the content.

Use a conversational and personalized style. In recent studies, students performed up to 40% better on post-learning tests if the content spoke directly to the reader, using a first-person, conversational style rather than taking a formal tone. Tell stories instead of lecturing. Use casual language. Don't take yourself too seriously. Which would *you* pay more attention to: a stimulating dinner party companion, or a lecture?

Get the learner to think more deeply. In other words, unless you actively flex your neurons, nothing much happens in your head. A reader has to be motivated, engaged, curious, and inspired to solve problems, draw conclusions, and generate new knowledge. And for that, you need challenges, exercises, and thought-provoking questions, and activities that involve both sides of the brain and multiple senses.

Get—and keep—the reader's attention. We've all had the "I really want to learn this but I can't stay awake past page one" experience. Your brain pays attention to things that are out of the ordinary, interesting, strange, eye-catching, unexpected. Learning a new, tough, technical topic doesn't have to be boring. Your brain will learn much more quickly if it's not.

Touch their emotions. We now know that your ability to remember something is largely dependent on its emotional content. You remember what you care about. You remember when you *feel* something. No, we're not talking heart-wrenching stories about a boy and his dog. We're talking emotions like surprise, curiosity, fun, "what the...?" , and the feeling of "I Rule!" that comes when you solve a puzzle, learn something everybody else thinks is hard, or realize you know something that "I'm more technical than thou" Bob from engineering *doesn't.*

Metacognition: thinking about thinking

If you really want to learn, and you want to learn more quickly and more deeply, pay attention to how you pay attention. Think about how you think. Learn how you learn.

Most of us did not take courses on metacognition or learning theory when we were growing up. We were *expected* to learn, but rarely *taught* to learn.

I wonder how I can trick my brain into remembering this stuff...

But we assume that if you're holding this book, you really want to learn about iPhone development. And you probably don't want to spend a lot of time. And since you're going to build more apps in the future, you need to *remember* what you read. And for that, you've got to *understand* it. To get the most from this book, or *any* book or learning experience, take responsibility for your brain. Your brain on *this* content.

The trick is to get your brain to see the new material you're learning as Really Important. Crucial to your well-being. As important as a tiger. Otherwise, you're in for a constant battle, with your brain doing its best to keep the new content from sticking.

So just how *DO* you get your brain to think that HTML5 (and JavaScript) is a hungry tiger?

There's the slow, tedious way, or the faster, more effective way. The slow way is about sheer repetition. You obviously know that you *are* able to learn and remember even the dullest of topics if you keep pounding the same thing into your brain. With enough repetition, your brain says, "This doesn't *feel* important to him, but he keeps looking at the same thing *over* and *over* and *over*, so I suppose it must be."

The faster way is to do **anything that increases brain activity,** especially different *types* of brain activity. The things on the previous page are a big part of the solution, and they're all things that have been proven to help your brain work in your favor. For example, studies show that putting words *within* the pictures they describe (as opposed to somewhere else in the page, like a caption or in the body text) causes your brain to try to makes sense of how the words and picture relate, and this causes more neurons to fire. More neurons firing = more chances for your brain to *get* that this is something worth paying attention to, and possibly recording.

A conversational style helps because people tend to pay more attention when they perceive that they're in a conversation, since they're expected to follow along and hold up their end. The amazing thing is, your brain doesn't necessarily *care* that the "conversation" is between you and a book! On the other hand, if the writing style is formal and dry, your brain perceives it the same way you experience being lectured to while sitting in a roomful of passive attendees. No need to stay awake.

But pictures and conversational style are just the beginning.

Here's what WE did:

We used *pictures*, because your brain is tuned for visuals, not text. As far as your brain's concerned, a picture really *is* worth a thousand words. And when text and pictures work together, we embedded the text *in* the pictures because your brain works more effectively when the text is *within* the thing the text refers to, as opposed to in a caption or buried in the text somewhere.

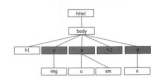

We used *redundancy*, saying the same thing in *different* ways and with different media types, and *multiple senses*, to increase the chance that the content gets coded into more than one area of your brain.

We used concepts and pictures in ***unexpected*** ways because your brain is tuned for novelty, and we used pictures and ideas with at least *some* ***emotional*** *content*, because your brain is tuned to pay attention to the biochemistry of emotions. That which causes you to *feel* something is more likely to be remembered, even if that feeling is nothing more than a little *humor*, *surprise*, or *interest.*

We used a personalized, ***conversational style***, because your brain is tuned to pay more attention when it believes you're in a conversation than if it thinks you're passively listening to a presentation. Your brain does this even when you're *reading*.

BE the Browser

We included loads of ***activities***, because your brain is tuned to learn and remember more when you ***do*** things than when you *read* about things. And we made the exercises challenging-yet-do-able, because that's what most people prefer.

BULLET POINTS

We used ***multiple learning styles***, because *you* might prefer step-by-step procedures, while someone else wants to understand the big picture first, and someone else just wants to see an example. But regardless of your own learning preference, *everyone* benefits from seeing the same content represented in multiple ways.

Puzzles

We include content for ***both sides of your brain***, because the more of your brain you engage, the more likely you are to learn and remember, and the longer you can stay focused. Since working one side of the brain often means giving the other side a chance to rest, you can be more productive at learning for a longer period of time.

And we included ***stories*** and exercises that present ***more than one point of view,*** because your brain is tuned to learn more deeply when it's forced to make evaluations and judgments.

We included ***challenges***, with exercises, and by asking ***questions*** that don't always have a straight answer, because your brain is tuned to learn and remember when it has to *work* at something. Think about it—you can't get your *body* in shape just by *watching* people at the gym. But we did our best to make sure that when you're working hard, it's on the *right* things. That ***you're not spending one extra dendrite*** processing a hard-to-understand example, or parsing difficult, jargon-laden, or overly terse text.

We used ***people***. In stories, examples, pictures, etc., because, well, because *you're* a person. And your brain pays more attention to *people* than it does to *things*.

Here's what YOU can do to bend your brain into submission

So, we did our part. The rest is up to you. These tips are a starting point; listen to your brain and figure out what works for you and what doesn't. Try new things.

Cut this out and stick it on your refrigerator.

---

(1) Slow down. The more you understand, the less you have to memorize.

Don't just *read*. Stop and think. When the book asks you a question, don't just skip to the answer. Imagine that someone really *is* asking the question. The more deeply you force your brain to think, the better chance you have of learning and remembering.

(2) Do the exercises. Write your own notes.

We put them in, but if we did them for you, that would be like having someone else do your workouts for you. And don't just *look* at the exercises. **Use a pencil.** There's plenty of evidence that physical activity *while* learning can increase the learning.

(3) Read the "There are No Dumb Questions"

That means all of them. They're not optional sidebars—*they're part of the core content!* Don't skip them.

(4) Make this the last thing you read before bed. Or at least the last challenging thing.

Part of the learning (especially the transfer to long-term memory) happens *after* you put the book down. Your brain needs time on its own, to do more processing. If you put in something new during that processing time, some of what you just learned will be lost.

(5) Drink water. Lots of it.

Your brain works best in a nice bath of fluid. Dehydration (which can happen before you ever feel thirsty) decreases cognitive function.

(6) Talk about it. Out loud.

Speaking activates a different part of the brain. If you're trying to understand something, or increase your chance of remembering it later, say it out loud. Better still, try to explain it out loud to someone else. You'll learn more quickly, and you might uncover ideas you hadn't known were there when you were reading about it.

(7) Listen to your brain.

Pay attention to whether your brain is getting overloaded. If you find yourself starting to skim the surface or forget what you just read, it's time for a break. Once you go past a certain point, you won't learn faster by trying to shove more in, and you might even hurt the process.

(8) Feel something!

Your brain needs to know that this *matters*. Get involved with the stories. Make up your own captions for the photos. Groaning over a bad joke is *still* better than feeling nothing at all.

(9) Create something!

Apply this to your daily work; use what you are learning to make decisions on your projects. Just do something to get some experience beyond the exercises and activities in this book. All you need is a pencil and a problem to solve… a problem that might benefit from using the tools and techniques you're studying for the exam.

Read me

This is a learning experience, not a reference book. We deliberately stripped out everything that might get in the way of learning whatever it is we're working on at that point in the book. And the first time through, you need to begin at the beginning, because the book makes assumptions about what you've already seen and learned.

We expect you to know HTML and CSS.

If you don't know HTML markup (that is, all about HTML documents including elements, attributes, property structure, structure versus presentation), then pick up a copy of *Head First HTML with CSS & XHTML* before starting this book. Otherwise, you should be good to go.

Some experience helps, but we don't expect you to know JavaScript.

If you've got any programming or scripting in your background (even if it isn't JavaScript), it's going to help you. But, we don't expect you to know JavaScript going into this book; in fact, this book is designed to follow *Head First HTML with CSS & XHTML*, which has no scripting in it.

We encourage you to use more than one browser with this book.

We encourage you to test the pages and web applications in this book with several browsers. This will give you experience in seeing the differences among browsers and in creating pages that work well in a variety of browsers. We most highly recommend Google Chrome and Apple Safari for use with this book as they are, in general, the most up-to-date with the current standards. But we do recommend you also try the most recent versions of the other major browsers including Internet Explorer, Firefox and Opera, as well as mobile browsers on devices with iOS and Android.

The activities are NOT optional.

The exercises and activities are not add-ons; they're part of the core content of the book. Some of them are to help with memory, some are for understanding, and some will help you apply what you've learned. ***Don't skip the exercises.*** Even crossword puzzles are important—they'll help get concepts into your brain. But more importantly, they're good for giving your brain a chance to think about the words and terms you've been learning in a different context.

The redundancy is intentional and important.

One distinct difference in a Head First book is that we want you to *really* get it. And we want you to finish the book remembering what you've learned. Most reference books don't have retention and recall as a goal, but this book is about *learning*, so you'll see some of the same concepts come up more than once.

The Brain Power exercises don't have answers.

For some of them, there is no right answer, and for others, part of the learning experience of the Brain Power activities is for you to decide if and when your answers are right. In some of the Brain Power exercises, you will find hints to point you in the right direction.

Software requirements

To write HTML5 and JavaScript code, you need a text editor, a browser, and, sometimes, a web server (it can be locally hosted on your personal desktop).

The text editors we recommend for Windows are PSPad, TextPad or EditPlus (but you can use Notepad if you have to). The text editors we recommend for Mac are TextWrangler, TextMate or TextEdit. If you're on a Linux system, you've got plenty of text editors built in, and we trust you don't need us to tell you about them.

We hope you've got the browser bit covered and have installed at least two browsers (see the previous page). If not, do it now. It's also worth your time to learn how to use the browser developer tools; each of the major browsers has built-in tools you can use to inspect the JavaScript console (you can see errors as well as output you display using `console.log`, a handy alternative to `alert`), web storage usage, the DOM, CSS style that's been applied to elements, and much much more. Some browsers even have plug-ins for additional developer tools. You don't need the developer tools to get through the book, but if you're willing to spend the time to investigate how to use these, it will make development easier.

Some HTML5 features and JavaScript APIs require that you serve files from a real web server rather than by loading a file (i.e., your URL will start with `http://` rather than `file://`). We've identified which examples you'll need a server for in the appropriate places in the book, but if you're motivated, we recommend you go ahead and install a server on your computer now. For Mac and Linux, Apache comes built-in, so you'll just need to make sure you know how to access it and where to put your files so you can serve them using your local server. For Windows, you'll need to install Apache or IIS; if you go the Apache route, there are plenty of open source tools like WAMP and XAMPP that are fairly easy to install.

That's it! Have fun...

The technical review team

Paul Barry

David Powers

Bert Bates

Not just a reviewer, Paul's an experienced Head First author having written Head First Python and Head First Programming!

Our Master Technical Reviewer.

No simple reviewer here, he's also the series creator! Man, talk about pressure...

Lou Barr

Rebeca Duhn-Kahn

Trevor Farlow

We tried to tell her she only needed to help us with graphics, but she couldn't help herself and was also a stellar tech reviewer.

Rebeca acted as our second pair of eyes; she saved our butts on code details no else saw (including us!).

Our 110% effort reviewer. He even ran around in the middle of the night in his PJs testing our geo code.

Our reviewers:

We're extremely grateful for our technical review team. The whole team proved how much we needed their technical expertise and attention to detail. **David Powers**, **Rebeca Dunn-Krahn**, **Trevor Farlow**, **Paul Barry**, **Louise Barr**, and **Bert Bates** left no stone unturned in their review and the book is a much much better book for it. You guys rock!

Acknowledgments

Even more technical review:

This is becoming a recurring theme in our books, but we wanted to give another shout out to **David Powers**, our esteemed technical reviewer, and author of many books including *PHP Solutions: Dynamic Web Development Made Easy*. David's comments always result in signficant improvements to the text, and we sleep better at night knowing that if it's been through David, then we've hit the technical mark. Thanks again, David.

← Note to Editor: can we see if we can lock this guy in for our next three books? And see if we can make it an exclusive!

At O'Reilly:

Courtney Nash was given the difficult task managing not only the book *Head First HTML5 Programming*, but also managing, well, *us*. Courtney not only cleared all paths for us, but also applied the delicate pressure every editor needs to, to get a book out the door. Most of all, though, Courtney provided extremely valuable feedback on the book and its content, which resulted in a few significant reworks of the book. This is a much better book because of Courtney's efforts. Thank you.

Courtney Nash ↗

↑ Lou Barr, again! (And Toby).

Lou Barr was also an integral part of this book and contributed in many ways—from reviewer, graphic designer, production designer, web designer, to Photoshop wrangler. Thank you Lou, we could not have done it without you!

And thanks to a few other folks that helped make this happen:

From there we'd like to thank the rest of the O'Reilly crew for support in a hundred different ways. That team includes **Mike Hendrickson**, **Mike Loukides**, **Laurel Ruma**, **Karen Shaner**, **Sanders Kleinfeld**, **Kristen Borg**, **Karen Montgomery**, **Rachel Monaghan**, **Julie Hawks** and **Nancy Reinhardt**.

acknowledgments

Even more Acknowledgments!*

And thanks to a bunch of other folks:

James Henstridge wrote the original code that became the fractal viewer in Chapter 10, which we shaped to our purposes for use in the book. Apologies for any code we introduced that may not have been as elegant as his original version. Actor and artist **Laurence Zankowski,** forever type-cast as the Starbuzz CEO, generously reappeared in this book and helped to test the video application in Chapter 8 (a must see). The **Bainbridge Island Downtown Association** kindly allowed us to use their excellent logo, designed by Denise Harris, for the WickedlySmart Headquarters. Thank you to **Anthony Vizzari** and A&A Studios for allowing us to use a photo of their fabulous photo booth. Our TweetShirt startup example uses some fine looking icons from **ChethStudios.Net**. We appreciate the dedicated work of the **Internet Archive**, home of the films we used for Webville TV. And thank you to **Daniel Steinberg** for always being there to bounce things off.

He's baaaaack!

And finally, thanks to Kathy and Bert

Last, and anything but least, to **Kathy Sierra** and **Bert Bates,** our partners in crime and the BRAINS who created the series. We hope, once again, we've done the series justice.

Bert Bates

Kathy Sierra

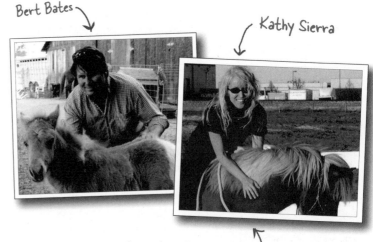

Hard at work researching Head First Parelli.

*The large number of acknowledgments is because we're testing the theory that everyone mentioned in a book acknowledgment will buy at least one copy, probably more, what with relatives and everything. If you'd like to be in the acknowledgment of our *next* book, and you have a large family, write to us.

Safari® Books Online

Safari® Books Online is an on-demand digital library that lets you easily search over 7,500 technology and creative reference books and videos to find the answers you need quickly.

With a subscription, you can read any page and watch any video from our library online. Read books on your cell phone and mobile devices. Access new titles before they are available for print, and get exclusive access to manuscripts in development and post feedback for the authors. Copy and paste code samples, organize your favorites, download chapters, bookmark key sections, create notes, print out pages, and benefit from tons of other time-saving features.

O'Reilly Media has uploaded this book to the Safari Books Online service. To have full digital access to this book and others on similar topics from O'Reilly and other publishers, sign up for free at *http://my.safaribooksonline.com*.

1 getting to know html5

Welcome to Webville

We're going to Webville! There's so much great HTML5 construction going on, we'd be crazy to live anywhere else. Come on, follow us, and we'll point out all the new sights on the way.

HTML has been on a wild ride. Sure, HTML started as a mere markup language, but more recently HTML's put on some major muscle. Now we've got a language tuned for building true web applications with local storage, 2D drawing, offline support, sockets and threads, and more. The story of HTML wasn't always pretty, and it's full of drama (we'll get to all that), but in this chapter, we're first going to go on a quick joyride through Webville to get sense for everything that goes into "HTML5." Come on, hop in, we're headed to Webville, and we're going to start by going from zero to HTML5 in 3.8 pages (flat).

Heads up: XHTML received a "Dear John" letter in 2009 and we'll be visiting XHTML later in the "Where are they now" segment.

Step right up! For a limited time we'll take that grungy old HTML page of yours and in **JUST THREE EASY STEPS** upgrade it to HTML5.

Could it really be that easy?
You betcha; in fact we've got a demonstration already prepared for you.

Check out this tired, worn out, seen-better-days HTML;
we're going to turn it into HTML5 right before your very eyes:

```
<!DOCTYPE html PUBLIC "-//W3C//DTD HTML 4.01//EN"
    "http://www.w3.org/TR/html4/strict.dtd">
<html>
  <head>
    <meta http-equiv="content-type" content="text/html; charset=UTF-8">
    <title>Head First Lounge</title>
    <link type="text/css" rel="stylesheet" href="lounge.css">
    <script type="text/javascript" src="lounge.js"></script>
  </head>
  <body>
    <h1>Welcome to Head First Lounge</h1>
    <p>
      <img src="drinks.gif" alt="Drinks">
    </p>
    <p>
      Join us any evening for refreshing <a href="elixirs.html">elixirs</a>,
      conversation and maybe a game or two of Tap Tap Revolution.
      Wireless access is always provided; BYOWS (Bring Your Own Web Server).
    </p>
  </body>
</html>
```

← This is all just normal HTML 4.01 from the Head First Lounge, which you might remember from Head First HTML (and if not, don't worry, you don't need to).

⚛ BRAIN POWER   **Look how easy it is to write HTML5**

Get your feet wet by reviewing this HTML, which is written in HTML 4.01 (the previous version), not HTML5. Carefully look at each line and refresh your memory of what each part does. Feel free to make notes right on the page. We'll look at how to transition this to HTML5 over the next few pages.

Sharpen your pencil

After taking a careful look at the HTML on the page 2, can you see any markup that might change with HTML5? Or that you'd want to change? We'll point out one for you: the **doctype** definition:

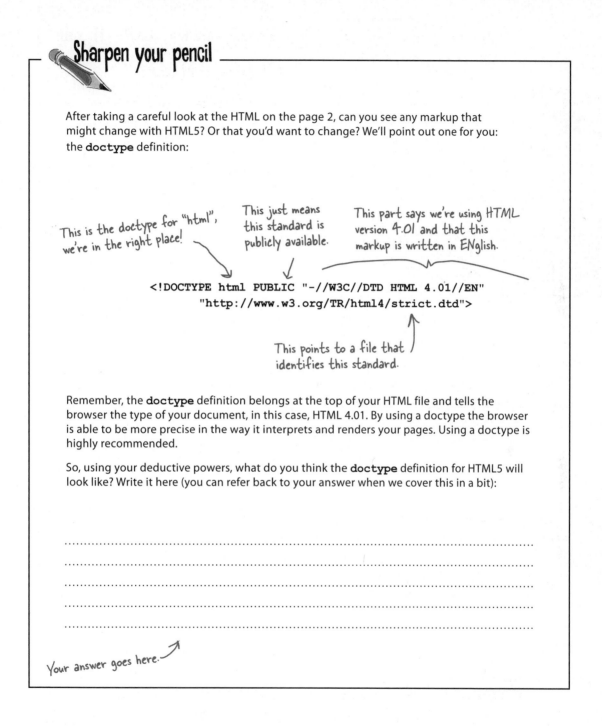

This is the doctype for "html", we're in the right place!

This just means this standard is publicly available.

This part says we're using HTML version 4.01 and that this markup is written in ENglish.

```
<!DOCTYPE html PUBLIC "-//W3C//DTD HTML 4.01//EN"
        "http://www.w3.org/TR/html4/strict.dtd">
```

This points to a file that identifies this standard.

Remember, the **doctype** definition belongs at the top of your HTML file and tells the browser the type of your document, in this case, HTML 4.01. By using a doctype the browser is able to be more precise in the way it interprets and renders your pages. Using a doctype is highly recommended.

So, using your deductive powers, what do you think the **doctype** definition for HTML5 will look like? Write it here (you can refer back to your answer when we cover this in a bit):

....

....

....

....

....

Your answer goes here.

Introducing the **HTML5-o-Matic,** update your HTML now!

Step 1 is going to amaze you: follow along, we're going to start at the top of the Head First Lounge HTML and update the doctype to give it that new HTML5 shine.

Here's the old HTML 4.01 version of the doctype:

```
<!DOCTYPE html PUBLIC "-//W3C//DTD HTML 4.01//EN"
        "http://www.w3.org/TR/html4/strict.dtd">
```

Now you might have guessed that we're going to replace every mention of "4" with "5" in the doctype, right? Oh, no. Here's the amazing part: the new doctype for HTML5 is simply:

```
<!doctype html>
```

Apologies to the crew that got the 4.01 doctype tattoo to remember it.

No more Googling to remember what the doctype looks like, or copying and pasting from another file, this doctype is so simple you can just remember it.

But, wait, there's more...

Not only is this the doctype for HTML5, it's the doctype for *every future version* of HTML. In other words, it's never going to change again. Not only that, it will work in your older browsers too.

The W3C HTML Standards guys have promised us they really mean it this time. ☺

If you're a fan of the *Extreme Makeovers* or *The Biggest Loser* television shows, you're going to love Step 2. In this step we have the content meta tag... here, check out the before/after pictures:

```
<meta http-equiv="content-type" content="text/html; charset=UTF-8">
```

BEFORE (HTML 4)

```
<meta charset="utf-8">
```

AFTER (HTML5)

Yes, the new meta tag ~~has lost a lot of weight~~ is much simpler. When you specify the meta tag in HTML5, just supply the tag along with a character encoding. Believe it or not, all browsers (old and new) already understand this meta description, so you can use it on any page and it *just works.*

And now for Step 3, the step that brings it all home. Here we're also going to focus on the <head> element and upgrade the link tag. Here's what we have now: a link of type text/css that points to a stylesheet:

```
<link type="text/css" rel="stylesheet" href="lounge.css">
```

Old skool

To upgrade this for HTML5, we just need to remove the type attribute. Why? Because CSS has been declared the standard, and default, style for HTML5. So, after we remove the type attribute, the new link looks like this:

```
<link rel="stylesheet" href="lounge.css">
```

HTML5

And, because you acted fast, we've got a special bonus for you. We're going to make your life even easier by simplifying the script tag. With HTML5, JavaScript is now the standard and default scripting language, so you can remove the type attribute from your script tags too. Here's what the new script tag looks like without the type attribute:

```
<script src="lounge.js"></script>
```

Don't worry if you don't know a lot about the script tag yet, we'll get there...

Or if you have some inline code, you can just write your script like this:

```
<script>

    var youRock = true;

</script>
```

All your JavaScript goes here.

We'll talk more about JavaScript in a bit.

Congratulations, you're now certified to upgrade any HTML to HTML5!

As a trained HTML5-o-Matic user, you've got the tools you need to take any valid HTML page and to update it to HTML5. Now it's time to put your certification into practice!

Wait a sec, all this fuss about HTML5 and this is all I needed to do? What is the rest of this book about?

Okay, okay, you got us. So far, we've been talking about updating your older HTML pages so that they're ready to take advantage of everything HTML5 has to offer. And as you can see, if you're familiar with HTML 4.01, then you're in great shape because HTML5 is a superset of HTML 4.01 (meaning practically everything in it is still supported in HTML5) and all you need to do is know how to specify your doctype and the rest of the tags in the <head> element to get started with HTML5.

But, you're right, we were being silly, of course there is more to HTML5 than just updating a few elements. In fact, what everyone is excited about is the ability to build rich, interactive pages (or even sophisticated web applications), and to support that HTML5 provides a whole family of technologies that works hand in hand with the HTML5 markup language.

But hang on; before we get there we've got just a bit more work to do to make sure we're ready with our markup.

Sharpen your pencil

You're closer to HTML5 markup than you think!

Here's some old skool HTML that needs updating. Work through the HTML5-o-Matic process and update this HTML to HTML5. Go ahead and scribble in the book, scratch out the existing markup code, and add any new markup code you need to. We've helped a little by highlighting the areas that need to change.

When you're done, type it in (or grab the exercise files and make your changes if you prefer), load this in your browser, sit back and enjoy your first HTML5. Oh, and you'll find our answers on the next page.

To download all the code and sample files for this book, please visit http://wickedlysmart.com/hfhtml5.

```
<!DOCTYPE html PUBLIC "-//W3C//DTD HTML 4.01//EN"
    "http://www.w3.org/TR/html4/strict.dtd">
<html>
  <head>
    <title>Head First Lounge</title>
    <meta http-equiv="content-type" content="text/html; charset=UTF-8">
    <link type="text/css" rel="stylesheet" href="lounge.css">
    <script type="text/javascript" src="lounge.js"></script>
  </head>
  <body>
    <h1>Welcome to Head First Lounge</h1>
    <p>
      <img src="drinks.gif" alt="Drinks">
    </p>
    <p>
      Join us any evening for refreshing <a href="elixirs.html">elixirs</a>,
      conversation and maybe a game or two of Tap Tap Revolution.
      Wireless access is always provided;  BYOWS (Bring Your Own Web Server).
    </p>
  </body>
</html>
```

Sharpen your pencil
Solution

You're closer to HTML5 markup than you think!

Here's some old skool HTML that needs updating. Work through the HTML5-o-Matic process and update this HTML to HTML5. Go ahead and scribble in the book, scratch out the existing markup code, and add any new markup code you need to. We've helped a little by highlighting the areas that need to change.

Here's our solution.

Here's the updated code:

Here are the four lines we changed to make our Head First Lounge web page officially HTML5.

```
<!doctype html>        ← The doctype...
<html>
  <head>
    <title>Head First Lounge</title>

    <meta charset="utf-8">         ← ... the meta tag...
    <link rel="stylesheet" href="lounge.css">      ← ... the link tag...
    <script src="lounge.js"></script>       ← ... and the script tag.

  </head>
  <body>
    <h1>Welcome to Head First Lounge</h1>
    <p>
      <img src="drinks.gif" alt="Drinks">
    </p>
    <p>
      Join us any evening for refreshing <a href="elixirs.html">elixirs</a>,
      conversation and maybe a game or two of Tap Tap Revolution.
      Wireless access is always provided;  BYOWS (Bring Your Own Web Server).
    </p>
  </body>
</html>
```

Don't believe us? Try http://validator.w3.org/ and you'll see – it validates as HTML5. For real!

there are no Dumb Questions

Q: How does this work on the old browsers? Like the new doctype, meta, and so on... somehow the older browsers work with this new syntax?

A: Yes, through a bit of cleverness and luck. Take the type attributes on the link and script tags; now, it makes sense to get rid of this attribute with HTML5 because CSS and JavaScript are now the standards (and certainly are the default technologies for style and scripting). But as it turns out, the browsers already assumed the defaults of CSS and JavaScript. So the stars aligned and the new markup standard just happens to have been supported in the browser for years. The same is true of the doctype and the meta tag.

Q: What about the new doctype, it seems too simple now; it doesn't even have a version or DTD.

A: Yes, it does seem a little magical that after years of using complex doctypes we can now just simplify it to "we're using HTML." Here's what happened: HTML used to be based on a standard called SGML, and that standard required both the complex form of the doctype and the DTD. The new standard has moved away from SGML as a way to simplify HTML language and make it more flexible. So, we don't need the complex form anymore. Further, as we said above, there is some luck here in that almost all browsers just look for HTML in the doctype to ensure they are parsing an HTML document.

Q: Were you joking about it never changing again? I thought the versioning was really important for browsers. Why not use `<!doctype html5>`? It's not like there isn't going to be an HTML6 too. Right?

A: The use of the doctype evolved with browser makers using the doctype to tell their browsers to render things in their own "standards mode." Now that we have much more of a true standard, the HTML5 doctype tells any browser that this document is standard HTML, be that version 5, 6 or whatever.

Q: Well, I assume different browsers are going to have different capabilities at any one time. How do I handle that?

A: True, especially until HTML5 is 100 percent supported. We'll cover both of these points in the chapter and throughout the book.

Q: Why does this even matter? I just typed a page in without a doctype and meta tag and it worked just fine. Why do I need to worry if this stuff is totally correct?

A: Yes, browsers are great at overlooking small errors in HTML files. But by including the correct doctype and meta tags, you'll make sure browsers know exactly what you want, rather than having to guess. Plus, for people using older browsers, the new doctype means they'll use standards mode, which is what you want. Remember, standards mode is a mode where the browser assumes you're writing HTML that conforms to a standard, so it uses those rules to interpret your page. If you don't specify a doctype, some browsers may go into "quirks mode" and assume your web page is written for older browsers, when the standard wasn't quite up to snuff, and may interpret your page incorrectly (or assume it's just written incorrectly).

Q: Whatever happened to XHTML? It seems like a few years ago that was the future.

A: Yeah it was. Then flexibility won out over strict syntax, and in the process XHTML (XHTML 2, to be precise) died and HTML5 was born to be more accepting of the way people write web pages (and the way browsers render them). That said, don't worry, because knowing about XHTML is only going to make you a stronger author of HTML5 content (and you're going to appreciate HTML5 a whole lot more). And by the way, if you really love XML, there's still a way to write your HTML5 in strict form. More on that later...

Q: What is UTF-8?

A: UTF-8 is a character coding that has support for many alphabets, including non-western ones. You've probably seen other character sets used in the past, but UTF-8 is being promoted as the new standard. And it's way shorter and easier to remember than previous character encodings.

Relax

We don't expect you to know HTML5, yet.

If you've never had exposure to HTML5 before, that's okay, but you should have worked with HTML, and there are some basics you should know about like elements, tags, attributes, nesting, the difference between semantic markup and adding style, and so on.

If you aren't familiar with all these, we're going to make a small suggestion (and a shameless plug): there's another book that proceeds this one, *Head First HTML with CSS & XHTML*, and you should read it. And if you're somewhat familar with markup languages, you might want to skim it or use it as a reference while reading this book.

We've also put a small guide to HTML5 markup & CSS3 in the appendix. If you just want a quick overview of the new additions, have a quick read over them at the end of the book.

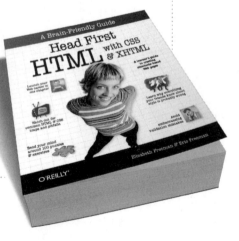

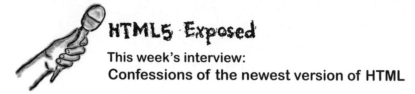

HTML5 Exposed

This week's interview:
Confessions of the newest version of HTML

Head First: Welcome, HTML5. All the Web is buzzing about you. To us, you look a lot like HTML 4. Why is everyone so excited?

HTML5: Everyone's excited because I'm enabling a whole new generation of web applications and experiences.

Head First: Right, but again, why didn't HTML 4 or even the promise of "XHTML" do that?

HTML5: XHTML 2 was a dead-end. Everyone who wrote real web pages hated it. XHTML reinvented the way we write markup for a web page, and would have made all the pages already out there obsolete. I said, "Hey, wait a sec, I can do new things and embrace everything that is already out there." I mean, if something works, why reinvent the wheel? That's my philosophy.

Head First: It seems to be working. But you know, some of the standards guys are still saying that the Web would be better off following their "pure" standards.

HTML5: You know, I don't really care. I listen to the people out there writing real web pages—how are they using me, and how can I help? Second on my list are the developers creating the web browsers. And last on my list are the standards guys. I'll listen to them, but not if it disagrees with what real users are doing.

Head First: Why not?

HTML5: Because if the users and the browser-makers disagree with the standards guys, it is a moot point. Luckily the people working on the HTML5 spec totally agree with me, and that's our philosophy.

Head First: Back to the previous version of HTML, you've said you are a superset of HTML 4.01. That means you're backward-compatible, right? Does that mean you're going to have to keep handling all the bad designs of the past?

HTML5: I promise I'll do my best to handle anything from the past that is thrown at me. That said, it doesn't mean that is the way to treat me. I do want web page authors to be educated on the latest standard and use me in the best way possible. That way, they can really push me to my limits. But again, I won't totally fail, and I will display an old page to the best of my ability if it's not updated.

Head First: My next question is ...

HTML5: Hold on, hold on!!! All these questions about the past. We aren't talking about what is important here. As far as my markup is concerned, my personal mission is to embrace the Web as it is, add some new structured elements that make web author's lives easier, and to help all browser implementors support consistent semantics around my markup. But I'm really here to pitch my new purpose: web applica...

Head First: ...So sorry HTML5, that's all we have time for. Thanks, and we'll be sure to talk about anything you want in an upcoming interview.

HTML5: Argh, I hate when that happens!!!

Would the REAL HTML5 please stand up...

Okay, you've patiently humored us by sitting through our "HTML5-o-Matic" skit, and we're sure you've already guessed there's a lot more to HTML5 than that. The word on the street is that HTML5 removes the need for plug-ins, can be used for everything from simple pages to Quake-style games and is a whipped topping for desserts. HTML5 seems to be something different to everyone...

HTML5 is all about multimedia, getting rid of plug-ins and using the new native support for audio and video.

No, it's all about more descriptive markup.

Actually, it's about rich Internet clients. Instead of building clients with plug-ins like Flash, now I can use canvas, transforms and JavaScript to make cool interfaces and animations.

The good news is, HTML5 is all these things. When people talk about HTML5 they mean a *family of technologies* that, when combined, gives you a whole new palette for building web pages and applications.

How HTML5 really works...

So we've said HTML5 is made up of a family of technologies, but what does that mean? Well you already know there's the HTML markup itself, which has been expanded to include some new elements; there are also lots of additions to CSS with CSS3 that give you even more power to style your pages. And then there's the turbo charger: *JavaScript*, and a whole new set of JavaScript APIs that are available to you.

Let's take a look behind the scenes and see how this all fits together:

 You'll find a nice Webville guide to the new HTML5 markup & CSS3 properties in the appendix.

1 The **browser** loads a document, which includes markup written in HTML and style written in CSS.

2 As the browser loads your page, it also creates an internal **model of your document** that contains all the elements of your HTML markup.

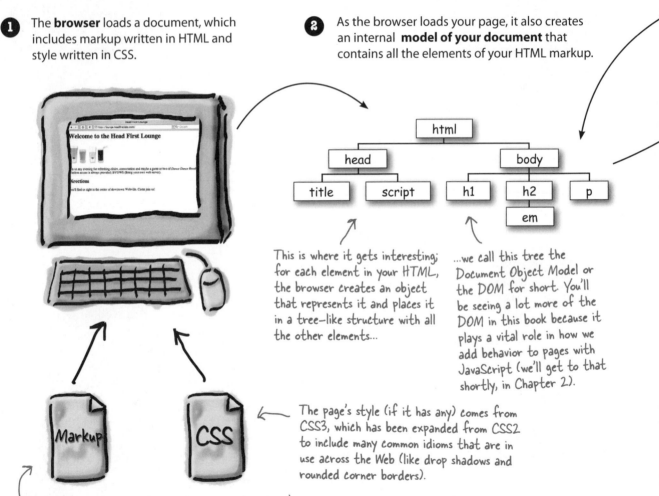

This is where it gets interesting; for each element in your HTML, the browser creates an object that represents it and places it in a tree-like structure with all the other elements...

...we call this tree the Document Object Model or the DOM for short. You'll be seeing a lot more of the DOM in this book because it plays a vital role in how we add behavior to pages with JavaScript (we'll get to that shortly, in Chapter 2).

The page's style (if it has any) comes from CSS3, which has been expanded from CSS2 to include many common idioms that are in use across the Web (like drop shadows and rounded corner borders).

With HTML5 the markup has some improvements, as you've seen with the tags in the <head> element, and there are some additional elements you can use (we'll see a few in this book).

Behind
the Scenes

3 While the browser is loading your page it's also loading your **JavaScript code,** which typically begins executing just after the page loads.

Using JavaScript, you can interact with your page by manipulating the DOM, react to user or browser-generated events, or make use of all the new APIs.

JS

JavaScript interacts with your page through the DOM.

4 The **APIs** give you access to audio, video, 2D drawing with the canvas, local storage and a bunch of other great technologies needed to build apps. And remember, to make use of all these APIs, we need JavaScript.

APIs, otherwise known as Application Programming Interfaces, expose a set of objects, methods, and properties that we can use to access all the functionality of these technologies. We'll be covering many of these APIs in this book.

Meet the JavaScript APIs

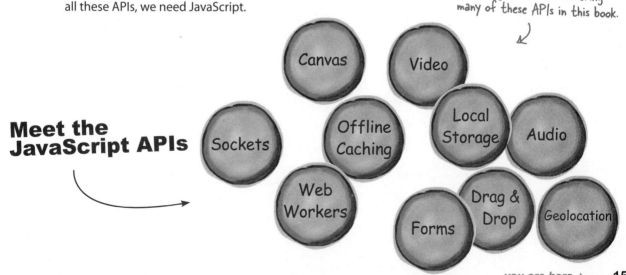

Canvas Video

Sockets Offline Caching Local Storage Audio

Web Workers Forms Drag & Drop Geolocation

WHO DOES WHAT?

We've already talked about the "family of technologies" so much we feel like they're, well, family. But then again we really haven't gotten to know them yet, so isn't it about time? You'll find most of the family below, so go ahead mingle, see if you can figure out who is who. We've gone ahead and figured one out for you. *And don't worry, we know this is your first time meeting the HTML5 family members, so the answers are at the end of the chapter.*

CSS3

Web Workers

Forms

Offline Web Apps

Audio & Video

New Markup

Local Storage

Canvas

Geolocation

Using me, you can draw right on your web page. With me, you can draw text, images, lines, circles, rectangles, patterns and gradients. I'll bring out your inner artist.

You might have used me in HTML 4 to enter information, but I'm even better in HTML5. I can require that you fill out fields, and I can more easily verify that you've typed an email, URL or phone number where you're supposed to.

You used to need a plug-in for us, but now we're first class members of the HTML family of elements. Wanna watch or listen to something? You need us.

We're here to help with the structure and semantic meaning of your page, including new ways of making sections, headers, footers and navigation in your pages.

I'm the most stylish one in the family. You've probably used me before, but did you know I can now animate your elements, give them great rounded corners and even drop shadows?

Use me as a bit of local storage in every user's browser. Need to store a few preferences, some shopping cart items, or maybe even stash a huge cache for efficiency? I'm your API.

Need applications that work even when you aren't connected to the network? I can help.

I'm the API that can tell you where you are, and I play nice with Google maps.

You'll want me whenever you need several scripts running concurrently and in the background, so your user interface remains responsive.

YOUR MISSION...

...should you choose to accept it, is to do some reconnaissance on all the HTML browsers. We're sure you've heard some browsers are ready for HTML5, and some aren't. We need for you to get in close, because the truth is out there...

CASE FILE: HTML5

YOUR FIRST MISSION: **TOP SECRET**
BROWSER RECONNAISSANCE

GO OUT AND DETERMINE ▓▓▓▓▓▓ THE CURRENT LEVEL OF SUPPORT FOR EACH BROWSER BELOW
▓▓▓▓▓▓ (HINT, GO HERE TO FIND SOME RESOURCES THAT KEEP UP WITH SUCH THINGS:
HTTP://WWW.WICKEDLYSMART.COM/HFHTML5/BROWSERSUPPORT.HTML, ▓▓▓▓▓▓
▓▓▓▓▓▓. ASSUME THE LATEST VERSION OF THE BROWSER. FOR EACH BROWSER/
FEATURE PUT A CHECKMARK IF IT IS SUPPORTED, AND THEN GIVE THE BROWSER
YOUR OWN SUBJECTIVE SCORE OF HOW MUCH IT SUPPORTS HTML5
UPON YOUR RETURN, REPORT BACK FOR YOUR NEXT ASSIGNMENT!

Browser \ Feature	Video	Audio	Canvas	Web Storage	Geolocatoin	Web Workers	Offline Web Apps
Firefox							
Safari							
Chrome							
Mobile WebKit							
Opera							
IE 6, 7							
IE 8							
IE 9							

iOS and Android devices (among others) →

YOUR FIRST MISSION: BROWSER RECONNAISSANCE SOLUTION

TOP SECRET

CASE FILE: HTML5

We've cheated on our answers and filled them in for 2015. Yours should reflect the time you're reading the book. But we thought you'd like to look into the future.

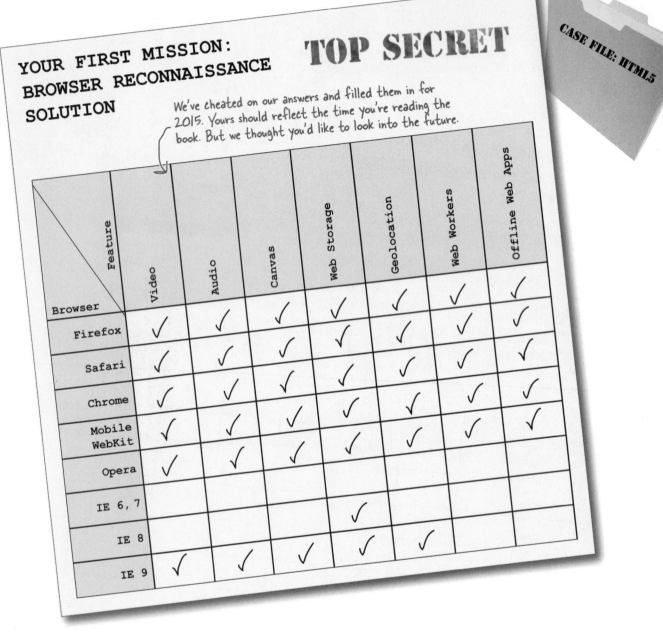

Browser \ Feature	Video	Audio	Canvas	Web Storage	Geolocation	Web Workers	Offline Web Apps
Firefox	✓	✓	✓	✓	✓	✓	✓
Safari	✓	✓	✓	✓	✓	✓	✓
Chrome	✓	✓	✓	✓	✓	✓	✓
Mobile WebKit	✓	✓	✓	✓	✓	✓	✓
Opera	✓	✓	✓	✓	✓		
IE 6, 7				✓			
IE 8				✓	✓	✓	
IE 9	✓	✓	✓	✓			

Even though it will be a while before the standard gets signed, sealed and delivered, you'll be using browsers that fully support HTML5 long before then. In fact, on modern browsers many features are already supported across the board. That's why it's a great idea to get started using HTML5 now. Plus if you start now, you'll be able to impress your friends and coworkers with all your cutting edge knowledge.

And get that raise sooner!

> Wait a sec, if I start using HTML5 now, aren't all those users of old browsers going to be alienated? Or, am I going to have to write two versions of my web page, one for browsers that support HTML5 and one for older browsers?

Hold on, take a deep breath.

First of all HTML5 is a superset of HTML, and so your goal should be to write *only one* HTML page. You're right in that the features supported by any one browser may differ, depending on how current the browser is, and how aggressive your users are in upgrading. So, we need to keep in mind that some of the newer features of HTML5 might not be supported, which leads back to your question of how to handle that.

Now, one of the design principles behind HTML5 is to allow your pages to degrade gracefully—that means if your user's browser doesn't provide a new feature, then you should provide a meaningful alternative. In this book we're going to show you how to write your pages to do that.

But the good news is that all browsers are moving towards the HTML5 standard and related technologies (even the mobile browsers) and so over time graceful degradation will be more the exception than the rule (although you'll always want to do what you can to give your users a meaningful experience no matter what browser they're on).

there are no Dumb Questions

Q: I heard that the HTML5 Standard isn't going to be a final recommendation until 2022! Is that true? And, if so, why are we bothering?

A: The W3C is the standards body that formally recommends the HTML5 standard, and what you need to know about the W3C is that they are a conservative bunch, so conservative that they'd prefer to wait until a few generations of HTML5 browsers have come and gone before they give their signoff. That's okay; the standard should be wrapped up in the next couple years and the browser makers are well on to their way to implementing it. So, yes, it may be quite a while before HTML5 is a "final recommendation," but it's expected to be a stable standard by 2014, and for all practical purposes you should get going now on HTML5.

Q: What happens after HTML5 is final?

A: HTML6? We have no idea, but maybe whatever it is it will come with flying cars, rocket suits and dinner in a pill. Remember that even if we do adopt HTML6, the doctype won't change. Assuming the W3C keeps their promise and future versions of HTML remain backward-compatible, we'll be in good shape to take whatever comes next.

Q: Chrome, Safari, Firefox, a zillion mobile browsers...isn't the world just getting worse? How will we ever make sure our pages work on all these browsers?

A: While there is plenty of healthy competition in the marketplace for browsers (desktop and mobile), in reality many of these browsers are based on a few common HTML engines. For instance Chrome, Safari and the mobile browsers in the Android and iPhone are all based on WebKit, an open source browser engine. So, for the most part, your pages will work out of the gate on multiple browsers without a lot of effort on your part.

Q: Why not just use Flash to solve cross-browser issues?

A: Flash is a great tool for many applications and certainly on the desktop it is pervasive across operating systems and browsers. HTML5 and its family of technologies is trying to allow you to do with open standards many of the same things that Flash can do. So which way should you go? One thing to think about is the amount of investment going into HTML5 technologies within Google, Apple, Microsoft, and others. Over the long term, HTML5 is going to be a huge player, and in the mobile space it already is. So, while the choice is yours, and we're sure both are going to be around for a long time, the industry is heading towards open standards.

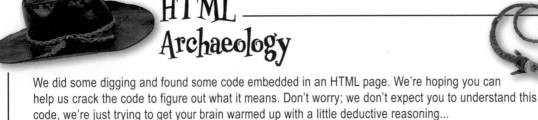

HTML Archaeology

We did some digging and found some code embedded in an HTML page. We're hoping you can help us crack the code to figure out what it means. Don't worry; we don't expect you to understand this code, we're just trying to get your brain warmed up with a little deductive reasoning...

```
<script>
    var walksLike = "duck";
    var soundsLike = document.getElementById("soundslike");
    if (walksLike == "dog") {
        soundsLike.innerHTML = "Woof! Woof!";
    } else if (walksLike == "duck") {
        soundsLike.innerHTML = "Quack, Quack";
    } else {
        soundsLike.innerHTML = "Crickets...";
    }
</script>
```

A hint: document represents the entire HTML page, and getElementById probably has something to do with HTML elements and ids.

I'm just sayin', if you're going to get serious about building web apps and using HTML5, you've got to have JavaScript chops.

We've gotta talk.

If you've been with us since *Head First HTML & CSS* (or, you've read this far into the book without repurposing it as firewood) we know you probably have a good understanding of using markup languages and stylesheets to create great looking web pages. Knowing those two technologies can you get a long way...

But, with HTML5 things are changing: web pages are becoming rich experiences (and full blown applications) that have behavior, are updated on the fly, and interact with the user. Building these kinds of pages requires a fair bit of programming and if you're going to write code for the browser, there's only one game in town: *JavaScript*.

Now, if you've programmed or written simple scripts before, you're going to be in good shape: JavaScript (despite some rumors) is a fantastic language and we'll take you through everything you need to know to write the applications in this book. If you haven't programmed before, we're going to do everything we can to take you along for the ride. In either case, one of the huge benefits of JavaScript is how accessible it is to new programmers.

We can't think of a better or more fun way to learn to program!

So, what now? Let's just briefly get introduced to a little JavaScript and then we'll really dive in deep in Chapter 2. In fact, for now, don't worry too much about getting every detail over the next few pages—we just want you to get a *feel for JavaScript.*

What can you do with JavaScript?

JavaScript opens up a whole new universe of expression and functionality to your web pages. Let's look at just a few things you might do with JavaScript and HTML5...

Interact with your pages in new ways that work for the desktop and mobile devices.

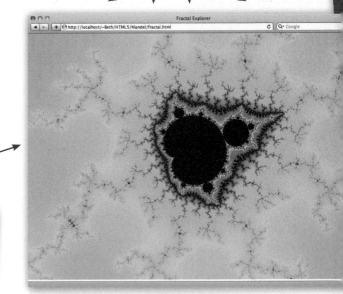

With HTML5 & JavaScript you can create a 2D drawable surface right in your page, no plug-ins required.

Make your pages location aware to know where your users are, show them what's nearby, take them on a scavenger hunt, give them directions, or to bring people with common interests together in the same area.

Use web workers to turbo-charge your JavaScript code and do some serious computation or make your app more responsive. You can even make better use of your user's multicore processor!

Access any web service and bring that data back to your app, in near real time.

Cache data locally using browser storage to speed up mobile apps.

No need for special plug-ins to play video.

Create your own video playback controls using HTML and JavaScript.

Integrate your pages with Google Maps and even let your users track their movement in real time.

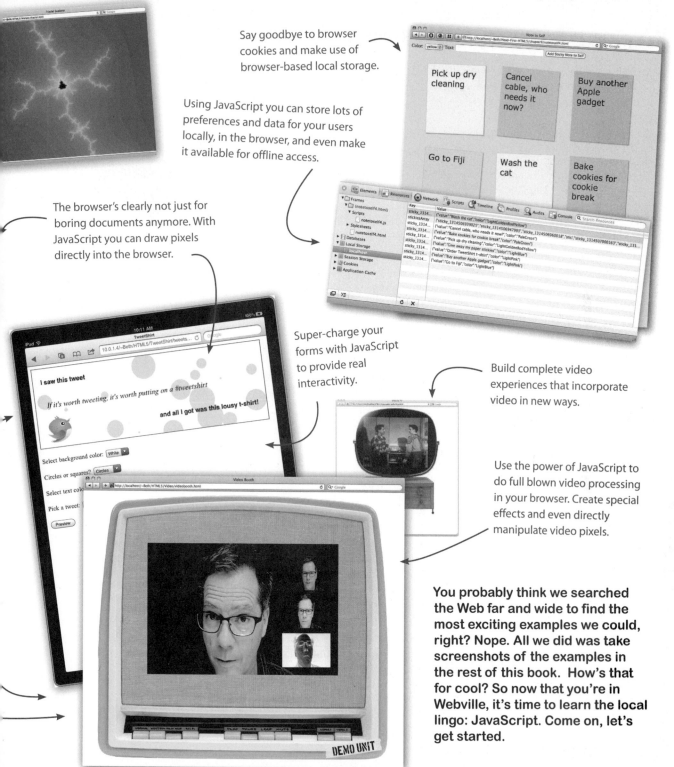

Say goodbye to browser cookies and make use of browser-based local storage.

Using JavaScript you can store lots of preferences and data for your users locally, in the browser, and even make it available for offline access.

The browser's clearly not just for boring documents anymore. With JavaScript you can draw pixels directly into the browser.

Super-charge your forms with JavaScript to provide real interactivity.

Build complete video experiences that incorporate video in new ways.

Use the power of JavaScript to do full blown video processing in your browser. Create special effects and even directly manipulate video pixels.

You probably think we searched the Web far and wide to find the most exciting examples we could, right? Nope. All we did was take screenshots of the examples in the rest of this book. How's that for cool? So now that you're in Webville, it's time to learn the local lingo: JavaScript. Come on, let's get started.

 **JavaScript Exposed**

This week's interview:
Confessions of a Scripting Language

Head First: Welcome, JavaScript. We're glad you could work us into your busy schedule. Let me just put it out there: HTML5 is becoming quite a celebrity—what's your take on this?

JavaScript: I'm not someone who seeks the limelight, I'm a behind the scenes kinda guy. That said, a lot of the credit going to HTML5 should be going to me.

Head First: Why do you say that?

JavaScript: There's a whole family of technologies that makes "HTML5" work, like the 2D canvas, local storage, web workers, that kind of thing. And the truth is, it takes me, JavaScript, to really make use of them. Sure, HTML5 gives you a place to hold the whole experience together and present it, but without me, you wouldn't have an interesting experience at all. That's okay, more power to HTML5; I'm just going to keep on doing my job.

Head First: What's your advice for new HTML5 authors?

JavaScript: That's easy. If you want to really master HTML5, spend your time on JavaScript and all the libraries that work with HTML5.

Head First: You know, you haven't always had the best reputation. I'll quote a review from 1998: "JavaScript is at best a half-baked, wimpy scripting language."

JavaScript: That hurts. I may not have started life in the clean, academic environment of many programming languages, but I've become one of the most widely used programming languages of all time, so I wouldn't discount me so quickly. Not only that, but enormous resources have been poured into making me robust and extremely fast. I'm at least 100 times faster than I was a decade ago.

Head First: That's impressive.

JavaScript: Oh, and if you haven't heard, the standards guys also just told me I'm now the default scripting language for HTML5. So, I'm here to stay. In fact, you don't even have to say "JavaScript" in your `<script>` tag anymore. So they may have called me wimpy in '98, but where are JScript, VBScript, Java Applets and all those failed attempts at browser languages now?

Head First: Well it certainly sounds like you are the key to creating great HTML5 experiences. You do have a reputation for being a confusing language.

JavaScript: I'm a very powerful language, despite some rumors, so you should really spend some time learning to use me well. On the other hand, I'm popular because I'm so easy to get up and running with. The best of both worlds, don't you think?

Head First: It sounds that way! Thanks, JavaScript, for joining us.

JavaScript: My pleasure, anytime.

Writing Serious JavaScript

With all this talk about JavaScript, we bet you're ready to jump in and see what it's all about. They don't call this *Head First* for nothing, we've got a super serious business application below that we're going to throw at you. For now, get started by going through the code to get a feel for it. Write down what you think each line does. Don't worry, we don't expect you to understand everything yet, but we bet you can make some really good guesses about what this code does. And, when you're done, turn the page and see how close you were...

Write your answers here.

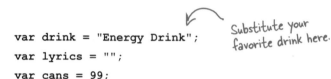

Substitute your favorite drink here.

```
var drink = "Energy Drink";
var lyrics = "";
var cans = 99;

while (cans > 0) {
    lyrics = lyrics + cans + " cans of "
            + drink + " on the wall <br>";
    lyrics = lyrics + cans + " cans of "
            + drink + "<br>";
    lyrics = lyrics + "Take one down, pass it around,<br>";

    if (cans > 1) {
        lyrics = lyrics + (cans-1) + " cans of "
            + drink + " on the wall <br>";
    }

    else {
        lyrics = lyrics +  "No more cans of "
            + drink + " on the wall <br>";
    }
    cans = cans - 1;
}
document.write(lyrics);
```

Writing Serious JavaScript Revisited...

Walk through the code again and see if you were on the mark. At this point you just want to get a feel for the code; we'll be stepping through everything in detail soon enough.

```javascript
var drink = "Energy Drink";

var lyrics = "";

var cans = 99;


while (cans > 0) {


    lyrics = lyrics + cans + " cans of "

            + drink + " on the wall <br>";

    lyrics = lyrics + cans + " cans of "

            + drink + "<br>";

    lyrics = lyrics + "Take one down, pass it around,<br>";

    if (cans > 1) {

        lyrics = lyrics + (cans-1) + " cans of "

                    + drink + " on the wall <br>";

    }
    else {

        lyrics = lyrics +  "No more cans of "

                    + drink + " on the wall <br>";

    }
    cans = cans - 1;

}


document.write(lyrics);
```

Declare a variable, and assign it a value of "Energy Drink".
Declare another variable and assign it empty string value.
Declare another variable and assign it a number value, 99.
This is a while loop. It says, while the number of cans is greater than 0, do everything between the curly brackets. Stop when there are no cans left.
Add the next line of the song to the variable lyrics, using the string concatenation operator "+".
End the line with a HTML line break.
Do it again—after all that's how the song goes, right?
Add the next verse, again using concatentation.
If there's still a can left (that is, the value of cans is greater than 1)...
... add the last line.
otherwise, there are no cans left...
... so add "No more cans" to the end of lyrics.
Reduce the number of cans left by 1
We've stored all the lines to the song in the variable lyrics, so now we tell the web page to write it, which just means the string is added to the page so you can see the song.

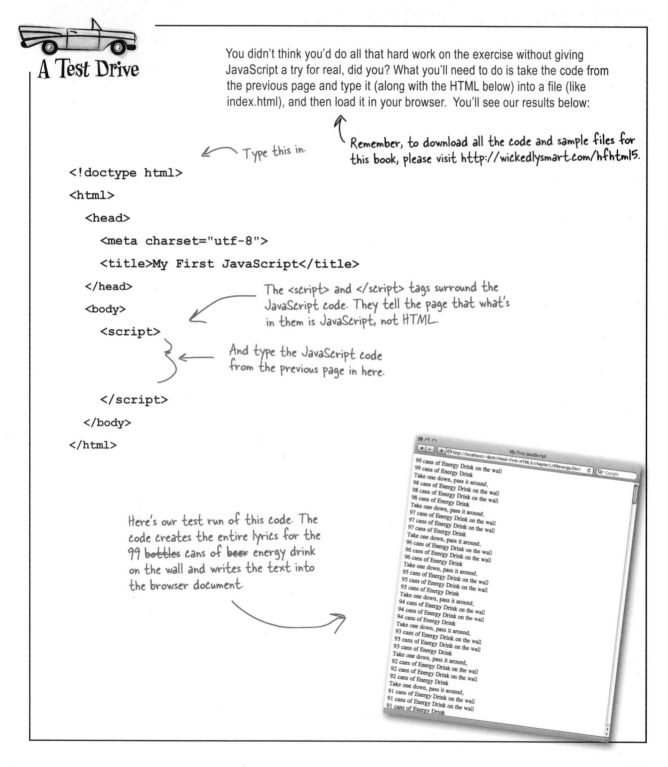

A Test Drive

You didn't think you'd do all that hard work on the exercise without giving JavaScript a try for real, did you? What you'll need to do is take the code from the previous page and type it (along with the HTML below) into a file (like index.html), and then load it in your browser. You'll see our results below:

← Type this in.

Remember, to download all the code and sample files for this book, please visit http://wickedlysmart.com/hfhtml5.

```html
<!doctype html>
<html>
  <head>
    <meta charset="utf-8">
    <title>My First JavaScript</title>
  </head>
  <body>
    <script>



    </script>
  </body>
</html>
```

The <script> and </script> tags surround the JavaScript code. They tell the page that what's in them is JavaScript, not HTML.

And type the JavaScript code from the previous page in here.

Here's our test run of this code. The code creates the entire lyrics for the 99 ~~bottles~~ cans of ~~beer~~ energy drink on the wall and writes the text into the browser document.

```
99 cans of Energy Drink on the wall
99 cans of Energy Drink
Take one down, pass it around,
98 cans of Energy Drink on the wall
98 cans of Energy Drink on the wall
98 cans of Energy Drink
Take one down, pass it around,
97 cans of Energy Drink on the wall
97 cans of Energy Drink on the wall
97 cans of Energy Drink
Take one down, pass it around,
96 cans of Energy Drink on the wall
96 cans of Energy Drink on the wall
96 cans of Energy Drink
Take one down, pass it around,
95 cans of Energy Drink on the wall
95 cans of Energy Drink on the wall
95 cans of Energy Drink
Take one down, pass it around,
94 cans of Energy Drink on the wall
94 cans of Energy Drink on the wall
94 cans of Energy Drink
Take one down, pass it around,
93 cans of Energy Drink on the wall
93 cans of Energy Drink on the wall
93 cans of Energy Drink
Take one down, pass it around,
92 cans of Energy Drink on the wall
92 cans of Energy Drink on the wall
92 cans of Energy Drink
Take one down, pass it around,
91 cans of Energy Drink on the wall
91 cans of Energy Drink on the wall
91 cans of Energy Drink
```

there are no
Dumb Questions

Q: Why was there nothing in the body of that HTML except the script?

A: We chose to start with an empty body because we created all the content for this page using JavaScript code. Now, sure, we could have just typed the song lyrics directly into the body element (and that would have taken a lot of typing), or we can have code do all the hard work for us (which we did), and then just have the code insert the lyrics into the page with document.write.

Keep in mind we're just getting our feet wet here; we're going to spend a lot more time in this book seeing how we can take a page and dynamically fill in its content with code.

Q: I get that we built up the entire lyrics to the song, but what exactly did the document.write do and how did the text get in the document?

A: Well, document.write takes a string of text and inserts it into the document; in fact, it outputs the string precisely where the script tag is located. So, in this case document.write outputs the string right into the body of the page.

You're soon going to see more sophisticated ways to alter the text of a live document with JavaScript, but this example should give you a flavor of how code can dynamically change a page.

Q: You've been using the terms web page and web application; are they two different things? What makes something a web application?

A: That's a great question because we're using the terms loosely. There's no technical difference between the two; in other words, there's nothing special you do to turn a page written with HTML, JavaScript and/or CSS into a web application. The distinction is more one of perspective.

When we have a page that is acting more like an application than just a static document, then we start thinking of it as a web application and less as a web page. We think of applications as having a number of qualities such as holding lots of state, managing more complex interactions with the user, displaying dynamic and constantly updated data without a page refresh, or even doing more complex tasks or calculations.

Q: Hey, all this JavaScript is great, but what about CSS? I'm really itching to take advantage of some of the new CSS3 stuff I've been hearing about to make my pages look better.

A: Yes, CSS has come a long way and we're thrilled it works so well with HTML5. Now, while this book isn't about CSS3, you can be sure we're going to take full advantage of some of its new capabilities. As you might know, many of the tricks we used to do to add rounded corners and shadows with images in HTML, and simple animation with JavaScript, can now be easily done with CSS3.

So, yes, we're going to make use of the power of CSS3 in this book, and we'll point out when we're doing so.

We've talked about a bunch of things including HTML markup, JavaScript APIs, a "family of technologies" and CSS3. What exactly is HTML5? It can't just be the markup everyone is so excited about...

We'll give you our unofficial answer:

HTML5

Markup + JavaScript APIs + CSS = ~~Crazy Delicious~~

You see, when most people are talking about the promise of HTML5, what they mean is all of these technologies combined. That is, we have markup to build the core structure of our pages, we have JavaScript along with all its APIs to add behavior and new functionality, and we have CSS to style our pages—and together, these are the technologies we're all going to use to build tomorrow's web apps.

Now, why did we say unofficial? Well, there are people who like to make hard distinctions among these technologies and which standard each belongs to. And that is fine and has its place. But, what we care about is this: what technologies are available in the browser, and are they ready for us to use to craft our pages and applications? So, we say HTML5 is markup + JavaScript APIs + CSS, and we think that is what people generally mean when talking about HTML5 as a technology.

If you're really interested in how these technologies fit together as a set of standards (and we all should be) then we encourage you to visit w3.org for more information.

Congratulations, you've finished Chapter 1 and written your first HTML5!

← And your first JavaSript code!

Before you run off to the next chapter, we've got one more task for you to drive it all home. Use the magnets below to fill in the formula that solves the equation of "what is HTML5?" Careful now, there are some distractions thrown in with that pile of magnets. Once you've solved it, get some rest and refresh yourself before moving on to Chapter 2.

.... + ... + ... = ...

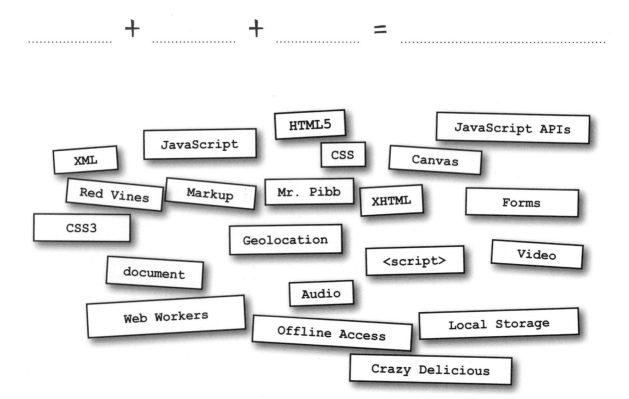

BULLET POINTS

- HTML5 is the newest version of HTML. It introduces simplified tags, new semantic and media elements, and relies on a set of JavaScript libraries that enable web applications.

- XHTML is no longer the standard for web pages. Developers and the W3C decided to keep extending and improving HTML instead.

- The new, simpler HTML5 doctype is supported by older browsers—they use standards mode when they see this doctype.

- The type attribute is no longer needed in the <script> tag or in a stylesheet link to CSS. JavaScript and CSS are now the defaults.

- The <meta> tag used for specifying the character set has been simplified to include only the character encoding.

- UTF-8 is now the standard charset in use on the Web.

- Making changes to the doctype and <meta> tag won't break your pages in older browsers.

- HTML5's new elements are a superset of HTML 4 elements, which means older pages will continue to work in modern browsers.

- The HTML5 standard won't be officially complete until 2014, but most modern browsers will support it long before then (many support it now!).

- HTML5 introduces elements that add new semantics to your pages, giving you more options for creating web page structure than we had with HTML 4.01. We aren't covering these in this book, but we have a small guide to them in the appendix.

- Many of the new features in HTML5 require JavaScript to make the most of them.

- Using JavaScript, you can interact with the DOM—the Document Object Model.

- The DOM is the browser's internal representation of a web page. Using JavaScript, you can access elements, change elements, and add new elements to the DOM.

- A JavaScript API is an "Application Programming Interface." APIs make it possible to control all aspects of HTML5, like 2D drawing, video playback, and more.

- JavaScript is one of the most popular languages in the world. JavaScript implementations have improved dramatically in recent years.

- You'll be able to detect whether a new feature is supported in a browser and gracefully degrade the experience if not.

- CSS is the style standard for HTML5; many people include CSS when they use the term "HTML5" to describe the family of technologies used to create web applications.

HTML5cross

It's time to give the right side of your brain a break
and put that left side to work. All these words are
HTML-related and from this chapter.

Across

2. _____ plug could also be called spam.
8. Product that cleans up your HTML5 in three steps.
11. Your mission was browser _____.
13. The real power of HTML5 is the JavaScript ____.
14. JavaScript is _____ times faster than a decade ago.
15. Use a _____ loop to print verses of a song.
16. Got the Dear John letter.

Down

1. The _____ is an internal representation of a web page.
3. The version of HTML before HTML5.
4. The <_____> tag tells the browser what follows is JavaScript, not HTML.
5. We want our web experiences to degrade _____.
6. Much simpler than the HTML 4.01 version.
7. The standard scripting language of HTML5.
9. This attribute of the link and script tags is no longer needed in HTML5.
10. The official style standard for HTML5.
12. New _____ in HTML add semantics and structure.

WHO DOES WHAT?
SOLUTION

We've already talked about the "family of technologies" so much we feel like they're, well, family. But then again we really haven't gotten to know them yet, so isn't it about time? You'll find the whole family below. Go ahead, mingle, see if you can figure out who is who. We've gone ahead and figured one out for you. And don't worry, we know this is your first time meeting the HTML5 family members, so here is the solution.

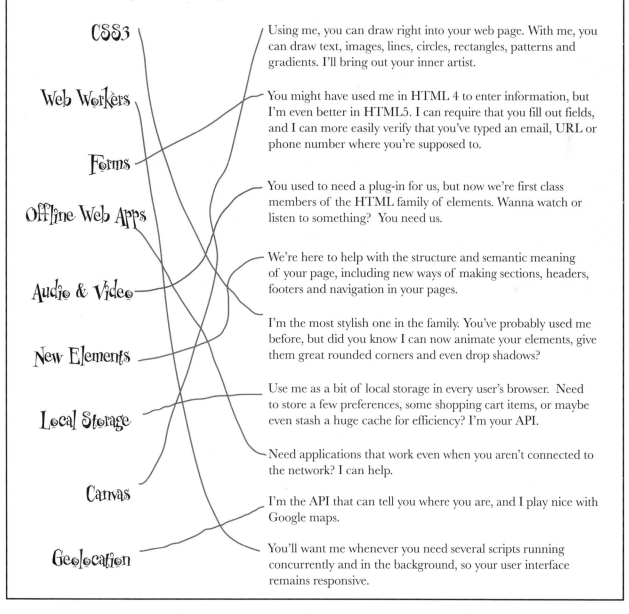

CSS3

Web Workers

Forms

Offline Web Apps

Audio & Video

New Elements

Local Storage

Canvas

Geolocation

Using me, you can draw right into your web page. With me, you can draw text, images, lines, circles, rectangles, patterns and gradients. I'll bring out your inner artist.

You might have used me in HTML 4 to enter information, but I'm even better in HTML5. I can require that you fill out fields, and I can more easily verify that you've typed an email, URL or phone number where you're supposed to.

You used to need a plug-in for us, but now we're first class members of the HTML family of elements. Wanna watch or listen to something? You need us.

We're here to help with the structure and semantic meaning of your page, including new ways of making sections, headers, footers and navigation in your pages.

I'm the most stylish one in the family. You've probably used me before, but did you know I can now animate your elements, give them great rounded corners and even drop shadows?

Use me as a bit of local storage in every user's browser. Need to store a few preferences, some shopping cart items, or maybe even stash a huge cache for efficiency? I'm your API.

Need applications that work even when you aren't connected to the network? I can help.

I'm the API that can tell you where you are, and I play nice with Google maps.

You'll want me whenever you need several scripts running concurrently and in the background, so your user interface remains responsive.

HTML5cross Solution

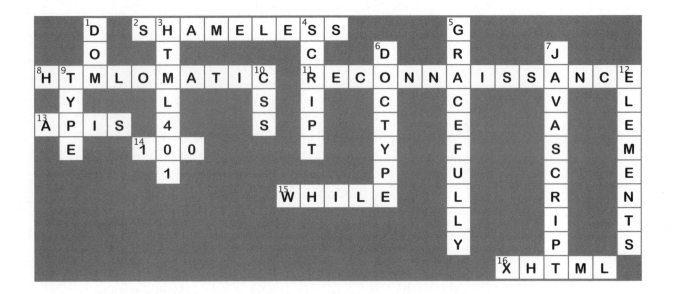

2 Introducing JavaScript and the DOM

A Little Code

```
var pet = "dog";
var sound = "bark";
```

JavaScript is going to take you to new places. You already know all about HTML markup (otherwise known as *structure*) and you know all about CSS style (otherwise known as *presentation*), but what you've been missing is JavaScript (otherwise known as *behavior*). If all you know about are structure and presentation, sure, you can create some great-looking pages, but they're still *just pages*. When you add behavior with JavaScript, you can create an interactive experience; or, even better, you can create full blown web applications. Get ready to add the most interesting and versatile skill in your web toolkit: JavaScript and programming!

And if you need more motivation, the most lucrative!

The Way JavaScript Works

Our goal is to write JavaScript code that runs in the browser when your web page is loaded—that code might respond to user actions, update or change the page, communicate with web services, and in general make your page feel more like an application than a document. Let's look at how all that works:

```
<html>
<head>
<script>
 var x = 49;
</script>
<body>
<h1>My first JavaScript</h1>
<p></p>
<script>
 x = x + 2;
</script>
</body>
</html>
```

Browser

Writing
1

You create your HTML markup and your JavaScript code and put them in files, say index.html and index.js (or they both can go in the HTML file).

Loading
2

The browser retrieves and loads your page, parsing its contents from top to bottom.

As it encounters JavaScript, the browser parses the code and checks it for correctness, and then executes the code.

The browser also builds an internal model of the HTML page, called the DOM.

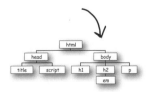

Running
3

JavaScript continues executing, using the DOM to examine the page, change it, receive events from it, or ask the browser to retrieve other data from the web server.

What can you do with JavaScript?

Once you've got a page with a `<script>` element (or a reference to a separate JavaScript file), you're ready to start coding. JavaScript is a full-fledged programming language and you can do pretty much anything with it you can with other languages, and even more because we're programming inside a web page!

You can tell JavaScript to:

❶ make a statement

Create a variable and assign values, add things together, calculate things, use built-in functionality from a JavaScript library.

```javascript
var temp = 98.6;
var beanCounter = 4;
var reallyCool = true;
var motto = "I Rule";
temp = (temp - 32) * 5 / 9;
motto = motto + " and so do you!";
var pos = Math.random();
```

❷ do things more than once, or twice

Perform statements over and over, as many times as you need to.

```javascript
while (beanCounter > 0) {
    processBeans();
    beanCounter = beanCounter - 1;
}
```

❸ make decisions

Write code that is conditional, depending on the state of your app.

```javascript
if (isReallyCool) {
    invite = "You're invited!";
} else {
    invite = "Sorry, we're at capacity.";
}
```

Declaring a variable

Variables hold things. With JavaScript they can hold lots of different things. Let's declare a few variables that hold things:

```
var winners = 2;       ← Integer numeric values.
var boilingPt = 212.0;   ← Or floating point numeric values.
var name = "Dr. Evil";   ← Or, strings of characters (we
                            call those "strings," for short).
var isEligible = false;
                         ← Or a boolean value,
                           which is true or false.
```

winners

boilingPt

name

isEligible

Three steps of creating a variable

```
var scoops = 10;
```
① ③ ②

① The first step is to declare your variable, in this case `scoops`. Notice that JavaScript, unlike some languages, doesn't need a type for the variable, it just creates a generic container that can hold lots of things:

> I'm a variable all ready to hold something.

scoops

② Next we need a value to put in the variable. We can specify a value in a few ways:

```
var scoops = 10;
var scoops = totalScoops / people;
var scoops = Math.random() * 10;
```

Your value can be a literal value, like a number or a string.

Or, the value can be the result of an expression.

Or use one of JavaScript's internal library functions, like a random number generator, to create a value. More on this and your own functions later.

Variables are containers for holding values. JavaScript variables don't have strict types, so any variable can hold a number, a string or a boolean.

3. Finally, we have a variable and we have a value (a literal value, like 10, or the result of evaluating an expression (like `totalScoops / people`)), and all we need to do is assign the value to the variable:

Ahh, I'm no longer undefined, I now have a value of my very own.

10

scoops

Of course, once you have a variable created, you can change its value at any time, or even change it to a value that has a different type. Here are some examples:

```
scoops = 5;
```
We can reset scoops to another integer value.

```
scoops = scoops * 10;
```
Or even use scoops itself in an expression that changes its value. In this case scoops will be 50.

```
scoops = "Tired of being an integer";
```

```
scoops = null;
```
Or, we can change the value and type of scoops, in this case to a string. Careful, this could cause big issues in your code if you're expecting scoops to be a number. More on this in a bit..

Or, there's even a value in JavaScript that means "no value". It's called null. We'll see how this is used later.

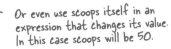

Syntax Fun

- Each statement ends in a semicolon.
  ```
  x = x + 1;
  ```

- A single line comment begins with two forward slashes. Comments are just notes to you or other developers about the code. They aren't evaluated.
  ```
  // I'm a comment
  ```

- White space doesn't matter (almost everywhere).
  ```
  x        =        2233;
  ```

- Surround strings of characters with double quotes.
  ```
  "You rule!"
  ```

- Variables are declared using var and a name. No types are required, unlike some other languages.
  ```
  var width;
  ```

- Don't use quotes around the boolean values true and false.
  ```
  rockin = true;
  ```

- Variables don't have to be given a value when they are declared:
  ```
  var width;
  ```

there are no
Dumb Questions

Q: What is the value of my variable when I just write:

```
var winner;
```

A: After this statement is executed, the variable `winner` will be assigned the value `undefined`, which is another JavaScript value and type. We'll see where and how to use this later in the book.

Q: I've seen other programming languages where variables are declared with a type. Like `int x` or `String y`. **Does JavaScript not have types?**

A: JavaScript does have types, but unlike languages you might have used before, JavaScript has dynamic typing, which means that you don't have to specify a type, and the JavaScript interpreter will figure out what type to use as your code is running.

How to name your variables

You might be wondering how you pick names for your variables? If you're used to naming ids in your HTML elements, you'll find variables very similar. There are only a few rules for creating names:

Rule#1: Start your variables with a letter, an underscore or a dollar sign.

You want to get off to a good start with naming your variables, not just by making them meaningful, but also by using a letter (small or uppercase), an underscore character or a dollar sign. Here are some examples:

```
var thisIsNotAJoke;
var _myVariable;
var $importantVar;
```

Do this...

Begins with number, not good. → `var 3zip;`

Begin with symbols (% and ~) that aren't allowed. → `var %entage;`
→ `var ~approx;`

...not this.

> ### Serious Coding
>
> Numbers, strings and booleans are all known as *primitive types* in JavaScript. There is one other thing you can store in a variable, an *object*. We'll be talking about objects soon enough, but for now you can think of an object as a collection of things, whereas a primitive is just one thing that can't be broken up into anything else.

Rule #2: Then you can use any number of letters, numeric digits, underscores or dollar signs.

Keep using letters, dollar signs, and underscores to create your variable name. After the first character you can also thrown in numbers if you like:

```
var my3sons;
var cost$;
var vitaminB12;
```

Do this...

Got a space, not allowed → `var zip code;`

Got -, + signs. Not allowed and will seriously confuse JavaScript. → `var first-name;`
→ `var to+do;`

...not this.

Rule #3: Make sure you avoid all of JavaScript's reserved words.

JavaScript contains a number of words that are reserved, such as if, else, while, and for (to name just a few), and JavaScript doesn't take too kindly to you trying to use those reserved words for your variable names. Here's a list of JavaScript's reserved words. Now, you don't need to memorize them, and you'll develop a sense of what they are as you learn JavaScript, but if you're ever perplexed by JavaScript complaining about how you've declared your variables, think, "Hmm, is that a reserved word I'm trying to use?"

abstract	delete	goto	null	throws
as	do	if	package	transient
boolean	double	implements	private	true
break	else	import	protected	try
byte	enum	in	public	typeof
case	export	instanceof	return	use
catch	extends	int	short	var
char	false	interface	static	void
class	final	is	super	volatile
continue	finally	long	switch	while
const	float	namespace	synchronized	with
debugger	for	native	this	
default	function	new	throw	

Avoid these as variable names!

there are no Dumb Questions

Q: What if I used a reserved word as part of my variable name? Like, can I have a variable named ifOnly (that is, a variable that contains the reserved word if)?

A: You sure can, just don't match the reserved word exactly. It's also good to write clear code, so you wouldn't in general want to use something like `elze`, which might be confused with `else`.

Q: Is JavaScript case sensitive? In other words are myvariable and MyVariable the same thing?

A: If you're used to HTML markup you may be used to case insentitive languages, after all <head> and <HEAD> are treated the same by the browser. With JavaScript however, case matters and myvariable and MyVariable are two different variables.

Q: I get that JavaScript can assign a value at any time (number, string, and so on) to a variable. But what happens when I add two variables together and one is a number and the other is a string of characters?

A: JavaScript tries to be smart about converting types for you as needed. For instance if you add a string and a number, it usually tries to convert the number to a string and concatenate the two together. Now in some cases that is great, and in some cases it isn't what you wanted. Hang on to that thought and we'll come back to it in just a sec.

Webville Guide to Better Naming

You've got a lot of flexibility in choosing your variable names, so we wanted to give you a few tips to make your naming easier:

Choose names that mean something.

Variable names like _m, r and foo might mean something to you but they are generally frowned upon in Webville. Not only are you likely to forget them over time, your code will be much more readable with names like angle, currentPressure and passed.

Use "camel case" when creating multiword variable names.

At some point you're going to have to decide how you name a variable that represents, say, a two-headed dragon with fire. How? Just use camel case, in which you capitalize the first letter of each word (other than the first): twoHeadedDragonWithFire. Camel case is easy to form, widely spoken in Webville and gives you enough flexibility to create as specific a variable name as you need. There are other schemes too, but this is one of the more commonly used (even beyond JavaScript).

Use variables that begin with _ and $ only with very good reason.

Variables that begin with $ are usually reserved for JavaScript libraries and while some authors use variables beginning with _ for various conventions, they aren't widely used and we recommend you stay away from both unless you have very good reason (you'll know if you do).

Be safe.

Be safe in your variable naming; we'll cover a few more tips for staying safe later in the book, but for now be clear in your naming, avoid reserved words, and always use var when declaring a variable.

Getting Expressive

We've already seen some JavaScript statements that look like:

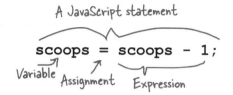

A JavaScript statement

```
scoops = scoops - 1;
```

Variable   Assignment   Expression

But let's take a closer look at expressions, like the one in this statement. It turns out expressions are everywhere in JavaScript, so it's important to know the kinds of things you can express. Here are a few...

You can write expressions that result in numbers...

Numeric expressions

```
(9 / 5) * tempC + 32

x - 1

Math.random() * 10

2.123 + 3.2
```

You can write expressions that result in the boolean values true or false (these are, obviously, boolean expressions).

Boolean expressions

```
2 > 3                startTime > now

tempF < 75

pet == "Duck"        level == 4
```

...and you can write expressions that result in strings.

String expressions

```
"super" + "cali" + youKnowTheRest

"March" + "21" + "st"        P.innerHTML

phoneNumber.substring(0, 3)
```

There are other types of expressions too; we'll be getting to these later.

Other expressions

```
function () {...}

document.getElementById("pink")

new Array(10)
```

Keep an eye on expressions over the next few pages (not to mention the rest of the book), and you're going to see how they are used to compute things, do things multiple times and to make decisions in your code.

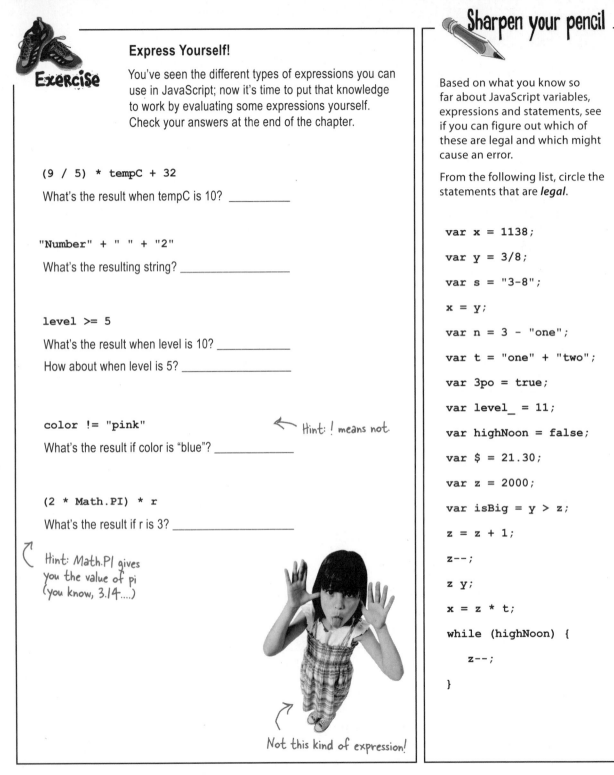

Exercise

Express Yourself!

You've seen the different types of expressions you can use in JavaScript; now it's time to put that knowledge to work by evaluating some expressions yourself. Check your answers at the end of the chapter.

```
(9 / 5) * tempC + 32
```

What's the result when tempC is 10? _____

```
"Number" + " " + "2"
```

What's the resulting string? _____

```
level >= 5
```

What's the result when level is 10? _____
How about when level is 5? _____

```
color != "pink"
```

← Hint: ! means not.

What's the result if color is "blue"? _____

```
(2 * Math.PI) * r
```

What's the result if r is 3? _____

Hint: Math.PI gives you the value of pi (you know, 3.14....)

↗ Not this kind of expression!

Sharpen your pencil

Based on what you know so far about JavaScript variables, expressions and statements, see if you can figure out which of these are legal and which might cause an error.

From the following list, circle the statements that are *legal*.

```
var x = 1138;

var y = 3/8;

var s = "3-8";

x = y;

var n = 3 - "one";

var t = "one" + "two";

var 3po = true;

var level_ = 11;

var highNoon = false;

var $ = 21.30;

var z = 2000;

var isBig = y > z;

z = z + 1;

z--;

z y;

x = z * t;

while (highNoon) {

    z--;

}
```

Everything seems to work well if I add numbers to numbers or strings to strings, but what if I add a number to a string? Or an integer to a floating point number?

Remember when we said JavaScript makes programming easy to get into? One of the ways it does that is by taking care of converting types to other types as needed to make expressions make sense.

As an example, say you have the expression:

```
message = 2 + " if by sea";
```

Now, we know that + could be for adding numbers together, and it's also the operator used to concatenate strings together. So which is it? Well, JavaScript knows that the string " if by sea" is never going to look like a number, so it decides this is a string expression, converts the 2 to a string "2", and the variable message is assigned to "2 if by sea".

Or, if we have the statement:

```
value = 2 * 3.1;
```

JavaScript converts the integer 2 into a floating point number and the result is 6.2.

As you might guess, however, JavaScript doesn't always do what you want, and in some cases it needs a little help in conversions. We'll be coming back to that topic a little later.

BRAIN POWER

What does JavaScript evaluate the following statements to?

```
numORString1 = "3" + "4"

numORString2 = "3" * "4"
```

And why?

```
while (juggling) {
    keepBallsInAir();
}
```

Doing things over and over...

If we did everything just once in a JavaScript program it would probably be a pretty boring program. You do a lot of things multiple times—you rinse, lather, repeat, until hair is clean, or, keep driving until you reach your destination, or keep scooping your ice cream until it's all gone—and to handle these situations, JavaScript gives you a few ways to loop over blocks of code.

You can use JavaScript's `while` loop to do something until a condition is met:

We've got a tub of ice cream, and its got ten scoops left in it. Here's a variable declared and initalized to ten.

```
var scoops = 10;
```

While uses a boolean expression that evaluates to true or false. If true, the code after it is executed.

While there are more than zero scoops left, we're going to keep doing everything in this code block.

```
while (scoops > 0) {
    alert("More icecream!");
    scoops = scoops - 1;
}
```

Each time through the while loop, we alert the user there is more ice cream, and then we take one scoop away by subtracting one from the number of scoops.

```
alert("life without ice cream isn't the same");
```

When the condition (scoops > 0) is false, the loop is done, and the code execution continues here, with whatever the next line of your program is.

So if you think about the while loop, we're *initializing* some values, say, the number of ice cream scoops left, which the while loop *tests*, and if true, we *execute* a block of code. And, the block of code does some work that at some point *updates* the value involved in the conditional test so that the *condition fails* and the loop ends.

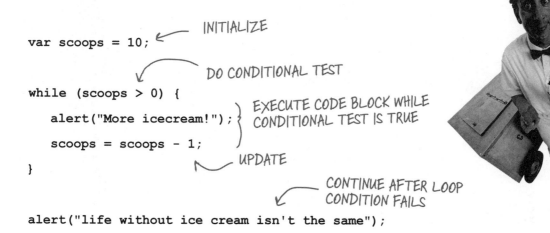

```
var scoops = 10;     ← INITIALIZE

                     DO CONDITIONAL TEST
while (scoops > 0) {
    alert("More icecream!");  }  EXECUTE CODE BLOCK WHILE
                                 CONDITIONAL TEST IS TRUE
    scoops = scoops - 1;
                         UPDATE
}
                            CONTINUE AFTER LOOP
                            CONDITION FAILS
alert("life without ice cream isn't the same");
```

JavaScript also provides a for loop, which formalizes this structure a little more. Here's our ice cream code written with a for loop instead:

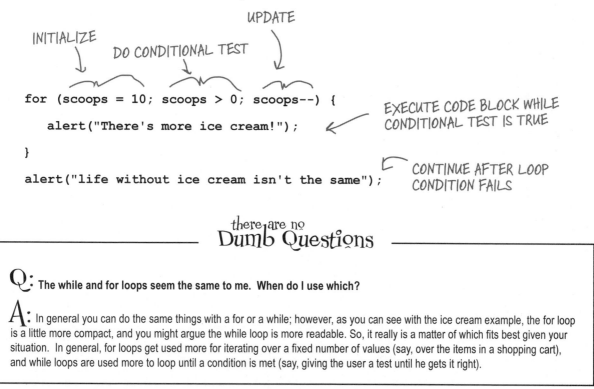

```
                                    UPDATE
    INITIALIZE    DO CONDITIONAL TEST
for (scoops = 10; scoops > 0; scoops--) {
                                            EXECUTE CODE BLOCK WHILE
    alert("There's more ice cream!");   ←  CONDITIONAL TEST IS TRUE

}
                                            CONTINUE AFTER LOOP
alert("life without ice cream isn't the same");   CONDITION FAILS
```

there are no Dumb Questions

Q: The while and for loops seem the same to me. When do I use which?

A: In general you can do the same things with a for or a while; however, as you can see with the ice cream example, the for loop is a little more compact, and you might argue the while loop is more readable. So, it really is a matter of which fits best given your situation. In general, for loops get used more for iterating over a fixed number of values (say, over the items in a shopping cart), and while loops are used more to loop until a condition is met (say, giving the user a test until he gets it right).

BE the Browser

Each of the JavaScript snippets on this page is a separate piece of code. Your job is to play browser, and evaluate each snippet of code and answer a question about the result. Write your answer to the question below the code.

Check your answers at the end of the chapter.

Snippet 1

```
var count = 0;
for (var i = 0; i < 5; i++) {
    count = count + i;
}
alert("count is " + count);
```

What count does the alert show?

_____

Snippet 2

```
var tops = 5;
while (tops > 0) {
    for (var spins = 0; spins < 3; spins++) {
        alert("Top is spinning!");
    }
    tops = tops - 1;
}
```

_____

How many times do you see the alert, "Top is spinning!"?

Snippet 3

```
for (var berries = 5; berries > 0; berries--) {
    alert("Eating a berry");
}
```

How many berries did you eat? _____

Snippet 4

```
for (scoops = 0; scoops < 10; scoop++) {
    alert("There's more ice cream!");
}
alert("life without ice cream isn't the same");
```

How many scoops of ice cream did you eat? _____

```
if (cashInWallet > 5) {
    order = "I'll take the works: cheeseburger, fries and a coke";
} else {
    order = "I'll just have a glass of water";
}
```

Make decisions with JavaScript

We've been using boolean expressions in `for` and `while` statements as a conditional test to decide whether to continue looping. You can also use them to make decisions in JavaScript. Here's an example:

Here's our boolean expression, testing to see how many scoops are left.

If there are < 3 scoops left we then execute the code block.

```
if (scoops < 3) {

    alert("Ice cream is running low!");

}
```

We can string together more than one test too:

```
if (scoops < 3) {

    alert("Ice cream is running low!");

} else if (scoops > 9) {

    alert("Eat faster, the ice cream is going to melt!");

}
```

Add as many tests with "else if" as you need, each with its own associated code block that will be executed when the condition is true.

Making more decisions... and, adding a catchall

You can provide a catchall for your `if` statements as well—a final `else` that is run if all the other conditions fail. Let's add a few more if/elses and also a catchall:

← Notice we changed this to only happen when scoops is precisely 3.

```javascript
if (scoops == 3) {
    alert("Ice cream is running low!");
} else if (scoops > 9) {
    alert("Eat faster, the ice cream is going to melt!");
} else if (scoops == 2) {
    alert("Going once!");
} else if (scoops == 1) {
    alert("Going twice!");
} else if (scoops == 0) {
    alert("Gone!");
} else {
    alert("Still lots of ice cream left, come and get it.");
}
```

We've added additional conditions to have a countdown to zero scoops.

Here's our catchall; if none of the conditions above are true, then this block is guaranteed to execute.

Exercise

Take the code above and insert it into the while loop below. Walk through the while loop and write down the alerts in the sequence they occur. Check your answer at the end of the chapter.

```javascript
var scoops = 10;

while (scoops >= 0) {

    Insert the code above here...

    scoops = scoops - 1;

}

alert("life without ice cream isn't the same");
```

Write the output here. ↗

Code Magnets

This code prints out a well-known palindrome in an alert. The problem is that some of the code was on fridge magnets and fell on the floor. It's your job to put the code back together again to make the palindrome work. Watch out; there were a few magnets already on the floor that don't belong here, and you'll have to use some of the magnets more than once! Check your answer at the end of the chapter before you go on.

```
var word1 = "a";
var word2 = "nam";
var word3 = "nal p";
var word4 = "lan a c";
var word5 = "a man a p";

var phrase = "";

for (var i = 0; _____; ____) {
    if (i == 0) {
        phrase = _____;
    }
    else if (i == 1) {
        phrase = _____ + word4;
    }
    _____ (i == 2) {
        _____ = phrase + word1 + word3;
    }
    _____ (_____) {
        phrase = phrase + _____ + word2 + word1;
    }
}
alert(phrase);
```

http://localhost
a man a plan a canal panama
OK

A palindrome is a sentence that can be read the same way backwards and forwards! Here's the palindrome you should see if the magnets are all in the right places.

else if (i == 0)   word5   i == 3   i++   else if   phrase   i == 4   word2   word4   i < 3   word1   i < 4   else   word0   i = 0   +   i--   i = 3   word3

I was told we'd be putting JavaScript in *our web pages*. When are we going to get there, or are we just going to keep playing around with JavaScript?

Yes, that is the point. First, you needed to know a few basics. Here's what we've done so far: you know how to declare and use JavaScript variables, and you know how to build basic statements and expressions. You also know how to use all those together to write conditional code with `if/else` statements, not to mention do things iteratively with `while` and `for` statements.

With that under your belt, now we're going to see how to place JavaScript in your page, and more importantly, how JavaScript interacts with your page. That is, how you determine what's in your page, how you change your page, and, a bit more down the road, how you write code to react to things happening in your pages.

So, while we're not done with JavaScript yet, your wait is over; it's time to see how markup and behavior work together...

How and where to add JavaScript to your pages

To use JavaScript you've got to add it to a web page. But where and how? You already know there is a `<script>` element, so let's see where we can use it and how that affects the way JavaScript executes within your pages. Here are three different ways you might add code to your page:

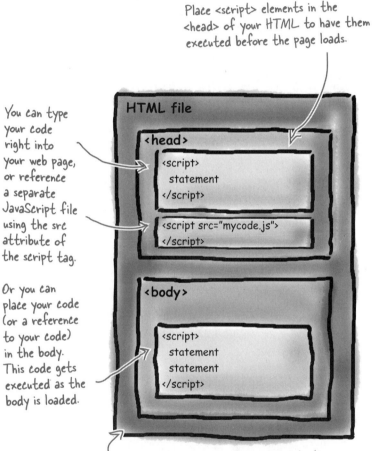

Place `<script>` elements in the `<head>` of your HTML to have them executed before the page loads.

You can type your code right into your web page, or reference a separate JavaScript file using the src attribute of the script tag.

Or you can place your code (or a reference to your code) in the body. This code gets executed as the body is loaded.

Most of the time code is added to the head of the page. There are some slight performance advantages to adding your code at the end of body, but only if you really need to super-optimize your page's performance.

Place your script inline, in the <head> element.

The most common way to add code to your pages is to put a `<script>` element in the head of your page. When you add JavaScript in the `<head>` element, it is executed as soon as the browser parses the head (which it does first!), before it has parsed the rest of the page.

Add your script by referencing a separate JavaScript file.

You can also link to a separate file containing JavaScript code. Put the URL of the file in the src attribute of the opening `<script>` tag and make sure you close the script element with `</script>`. If you're linking to a file in the same directory, you can just use the name of the file.

Add your code in the body of the document, either inline or as a link to a separate file.

Or, you can put your code right in the body of your HTML. Again, enclose your JavaScript code in the `<script>` element (or reference a separate file in the src attribute). JavaScript in the body of your page is executed when the browser parses the body (which it does, typically, top down).

How JavaScript interacts with your page

JavaScript and HTML are two different things. HTML is markup and JavaScript is code. So how do you get JavaScript to interact with the markup in your page? You use the Document Object Model.

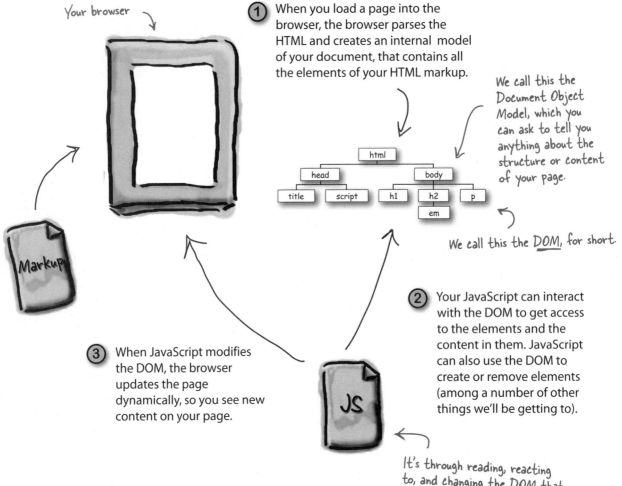

Your browser

① When you load a page into the browser, the browser parses the HTML and creates an internal model of your document, that contains all the elements of your HTML markup.

We call this the Document Object Model, which you can ask to tell you anything about the structure or content of your page.

We call this the DOM, for short.

② Your JavaScript can interact with the DOM to get access to the elements and the content in them. JavaScript can also use the DOM to create or remove elements (among a number of other things we'll be getting to).

③ When JavaScript modifies the DOM, the browser updates the page dynamically, so you see new content on your page.

It's through reading, reacting to, and changing the DOM that JavaScript can be used to write interactive web pages/apps. This book will show you how.

How to bake your very own DOM

Let's take some markup and create a DOM for it. Here's a simple recipe for doing that:

Ingredients

One well-formed HTML5 page

One or more web browsers

Instructions

1. Start by creating a document node at the top.

2. Next, take the top level element of your HTML page, in our case the <html> element, call it the current element and add it as a child of the document.

document
|
html

3. For each element nested in the current element, add that element as a child of the current element in the DOM.

document
|
html
/   \
head   body

4. Return to (3) for each element you just added, and repeat until you are out of elements.

```html
<!doctype html>
<html lang="en">
<head>
  <title>My blog</title>
  <meta charset="utf-8">
  <script src="blog.js"></script>
</head>
<body>
  <h1>My blog</h1>
  <div id="entry1">
    <h2>Great day bird watching</h2>
    <p>
      Today I saw three ducks!
      I named them
      Huey, Louie, and Dewey.
    </p>
    <p>
      I took a couple of photos...
    </p>
  </div>
</body>
</html>
```

We've already fully baked this DOM for you. Turn the page to see the finished DOM.

A first taste of the DOM

The beauty of the Document Object Model is that it gives us a consistent way, across all browsers, to gain access to the structure and content of the HTML from code. That's huge. And we're going to see how all that works in a sec...

Back to our example; if you follow the recipe for creating a DOM you'll end up with a structure like the one below. Every DOM has a document object at the top and then a tree complete with branches and leaf nodes for each of the elements in the HTML markup. Let's take a closer look.

We compare this structure to a tree because a "tree" is a data structure that comes from computer science.

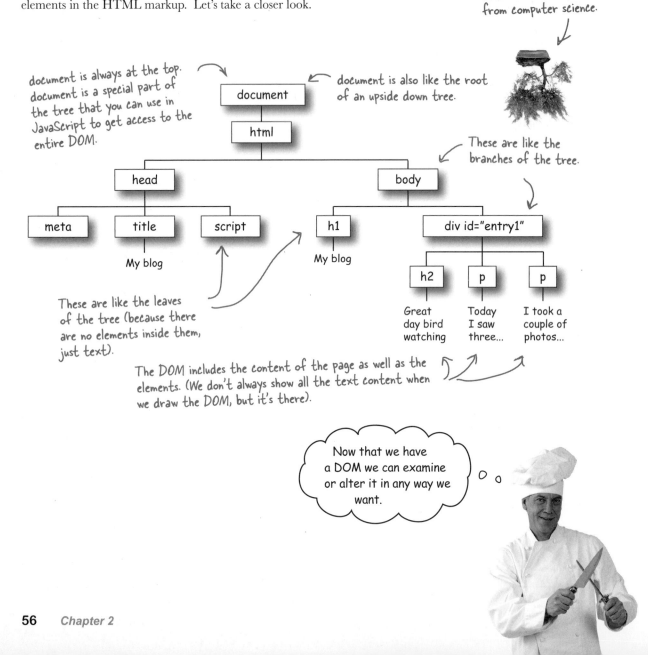

document is always at the top. document is a special part of the tree that you can use in JavaScript to get access to the entire DOM.

document is also like the root of an upside down tree.

These are like the branches of the tree.

These are like the leaves of the tree (because there are no elements inside them, just text).

The DOM includes the content of the page as well as the elements. (We don't always show all the text content when we draw the DOM, but it's there).

Now that we have a DOM we can examine or alter it in any way we want.

BE the Browser

Your job is the act like you're the browser. You need to parse the HTML and build your very own DOM from it. Go ahead and parse the HTML to the right, and draw your DOM below. We've already started it for you.

Check your answer with our solution at the end of the chapter before you go on.

Movie Showtimes

Plan 9 from Outer Space

Playing at 3:00pm, 7:00pm. Special showing tonight at *midnight*!

Forbidden Planet

Playing at 5:00pm, 9:00pm.

```html
<!doctype html>
<html lang="en">
  <head>
    <title>Movies</title>
  </head>
  <body>
    <h1>Movie Showtimes</h1>
    <h2 id="movie1" >Plan 9 from Outer Space</h2>
    <p>Playing at 3:00pm, 7:00pm.
      <span>
        Special showing tonight at <em>midnight</em>!
      </span>
    </p>
    <h2 id="movie2">Forbidden Planet</h2>
    <p>Playing at 5:00pm, 9:00pm.</p>
  </body>
</html>
```

document

Draw your DOM here.

html

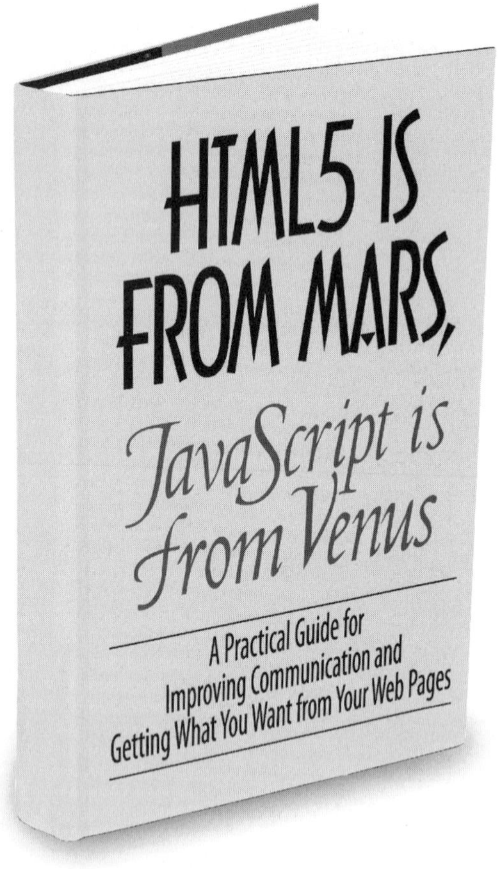

HTML5 IS FROM MARS,

JavaScript is from Venus

A Practical Guide for
Improving Communication and
Getting What You Want from Your Web Pages

Or, how two totally different technologies hooked up.

HTML and JavaScript are from different planets for sure. The proof? HTML's DNA is made of declarative markup that allows you to describe a set of nested elements that make up your pages. JavaScript, on the other hand, is made of pure algorithmic genetic material, meant for describing computations.

Are they so far apart they can't even communicate? Of course not, because they have something in common: the DOM. Through the DOM, JavaScript can communicate with your page, and vice versa. There are a few ways to make this happen, but for now lets concentrate on one—it's a little wormhole of sorts that allows JavaScript to get access to any element, and it's called getElementById.

Let's see how it works...

Let's start with a DOM. Here's a simple DOM; it's got a few HTML paragraphs, each with an `id` identifying it as the green, red or blue planet. Each paragraph has some text as well. Of course there's a <head> element too, but we've left the details out to keep things simpler.

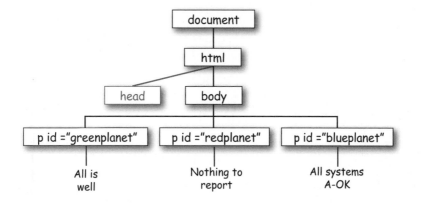

Now let's use JavaScript to make things more interesting. Let's say we want to change the greenplanet's text from "All is well" to "Red Alert: hit by phaser fire!' Down the road you might want to do something like this based on a user's actions or even based on data from a web service. But we'll get to all that; for now let's just get the greenplanet text updated. To do that we need the element with an `id` of greenplanet. Here's some code that does that:

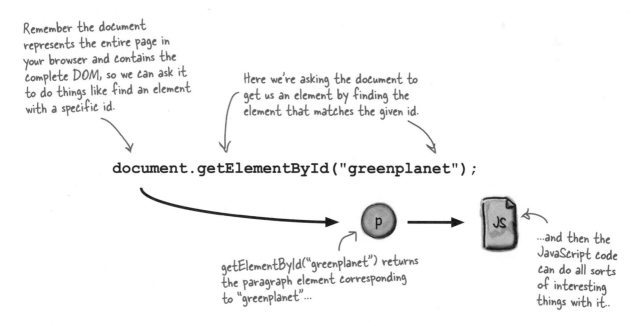

Remember the document represents the entire page in your browser and contains the complete DOM, so we can ask it to do things like find an element with a specific id.

Here we're asking the document to get us an element by finding the element that matches the given id.

```
document.getElementById("greenplanet");
```

getElementById("greenplanet") returns the paragraph element corresponding to "greenplanet"...

...and then the JavaScript code can do all sorts of interesting things with it.

Once getElementById gives you an element, you're ready do something with it

(like change its text to "Red Alert: hit by phaser fire!"). To do that, we typically assign the element to a variable so we can refer to the element thoughout our code; let's do that and then change the text:

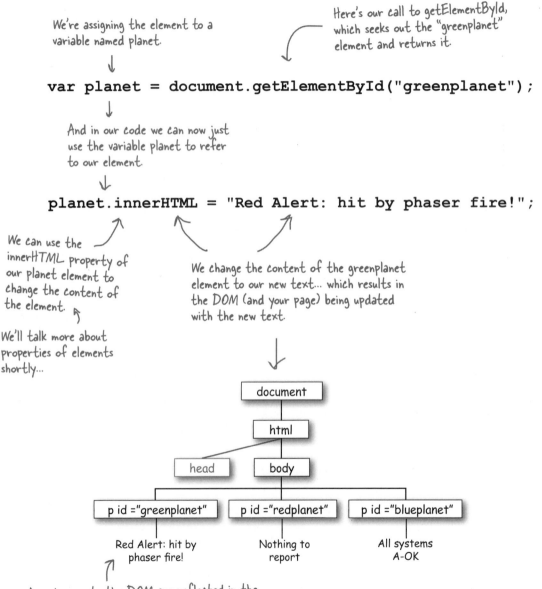

We're assigning the element to a variable named planet.

Here's our call to getElementById, which seeks out the "greenplanet" element and returns it.

```
var planet = document.getElementById("greenplanet");
```

And in our code we can now just use the variable planet to refer to our element.

```
planet.innerHTML = "Red Alert: hit by phaser fire!";
```

We can use the innerHTML property of our planet element to change the content of the element.

We'll talk more about properties of elements shortly...

We change the content of the greenplanet element to our new text... which results in the DOM (and your page) being updated with the new text.

document

html

head

body

p id ="greenplanet"

p id ="redplanet"

p id ="blueplanet"

Red Alert: hit by phaser fire!

Nothing to report

All systems A-OK

Any changes to the DOM are reflected in the browser's rendering of the page, so you'll see the paragraph change to contain the new content!

Sharpen your pencil

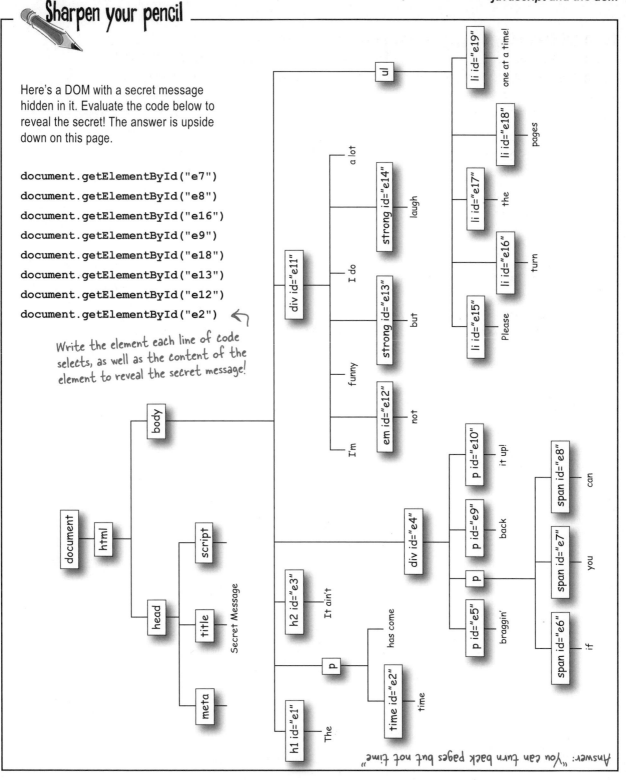

Here's a DOM with a secret message hidden in it. Evaluate the code below to reveal the secret! The answer is upside down on this page.

```
document.getElementById("e7")
document.getElementById("e8")
document.getElementById("e16")
document.getElementById("e9")
document.getElementById("e18")
document.getElementById("e13")
document.getElementById("e12")
document.getElementById("e2")
```

Write the element each line of code selects, as well as the content of the element to reveal the secret message!

Answer: "You can turn back pages but not time"

Test drive the planets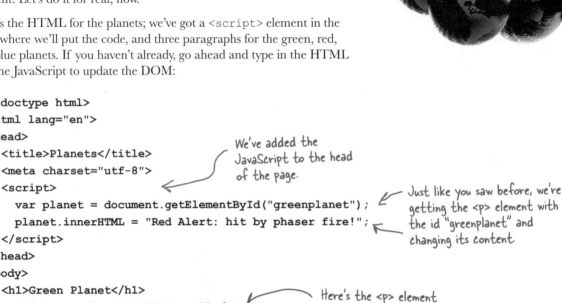

You've seen how to use `document.getElementById` to get access to an element, and how to use `innerHTML` to change the content of that element. Let's do it for real, now.

Here's the HTML for the planets; we've got a `<script>` element in the head where we'll put the code, and three paragraphs for the green, red, and blue planets. If you haven't already, go ahead and type in the HTML and the JavaScript to update the DOM:

```
<!doctype html>
<html lang="en">
<head>
    <title>Planets</title>
    <meta charset="utf-8">
    <script>
        var planet = document.getElementById("greenplanet");
        planet.innerHTML = "Red Alert: hit by phaser fire!";
    </script>
</head>
<body>
    <h1>Green Planet</h1>
    <p id="greenplanet">All is well</p>
    <h1>Red Planet</h1>
    <p id="redplanet">Nothing to report</p>
    <h1>Blue Planet</h1>
    <p id="blueplanet">All systems A-OK</p>
</body>
</html>
```

We've added the JavaScript to the head of the page.

Just like you saw before, we're getting the <p> element with the id "greenplanet" and changing its content.

Here's the <p> element you're going to change with JavaScript.

After you've got it typed in, go ahead and load the page into your browser and see the DOM magic happen on the green planet.

UH OH! Houston, we've got a problem, the green planet still shows "All is well". What's wrong?

Green Planet

All is well

Red Planet

Nothing to report

Blue Planet

All systems A-OK

> I've triple-checked my markup and code, and this just isn't working for me either. I'm not seeing any changes to my page.

Oh yeah, we forgot to mention one thing.

Most of the time it makes sense to start executing your JavaScript code *after* the page is fully loaded. The reason? Well, if you don't wait until the page has loaded, then the DOM won't be fully created when your code executes. In our case, the JavaScript is executing when the browser first loads the head of the page, and before the rest of the page has loaded, and so the DOM hasn't been fully created yet. And, if the DOM isn't created, then the `<p id="greenplanet">` element doesn't exist yet!

So what happens? The call to get the element with an id of `greenplanet` isn't going to return anything because there is no matching element, and so the browser just keeps moving on and renders the page anyway after your code has run. So you'll see the page rendered, but the text in the green planet won't be altered by the code.

What we need is a way to tell the browser "run my code after you've fully loaded in the page and created the DOM." Let's see how to do that next.

You can't mess with the DOM until the page has fully loaded.

But how do you tell the browser to execute your code only *after* it's loaded?

To tell the browser to wait before executing code we're going to use two parts of JavaScript you haven't seen much of yet: the `window` object, and a function. We'll get to the details of both these later; for now, just go with it so you can get the code to work.

Update your JavaScript code like this:

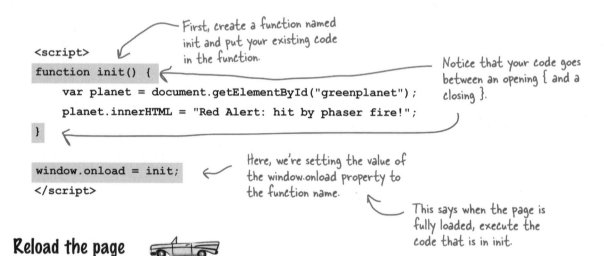

First, create a function named init and put your existing code in the function.

```
<script>
function init() {
    var planet = document.getElementById("greenplanet");
    planet.innerHTML = "Red Alert: hit by phaser fire!";
}

window.onload = init;
</script>
```

Notice that your code goes between an opening { and a closing }.

Here, we're setting the value of the window.onload property to the function name.

This says when the page is fully loaded, execute the code that is in init.

Reload the page

Go ahead and reload the page and see if you have the answer:

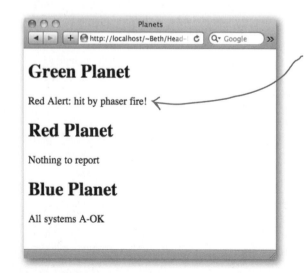

Green Planet

Red Alert: hit by phaser fire!

Red Planet

Nothing to report

Blue Planet

All systems A-OK

Yes! Now we see the new content in the green planet <p> element. Isn't it great?

Well, what IS great is that now you know how to tell the browser to wait until the DOM has completely loaded before running code that accesses elements.

Sharpen your pencil

Here's some HTML for a playlist of songs, except that the list is empty. It's your job to complete the JavaScript below to add the songs to the list. Fill in the blank with the JavaScript that will do the job. Check your answer with our solution and the end of the chapter before you go on.

Here's the HTML for the page.

```
<!doctype html>
<html lang="en">
<head>
  <title>My Playlist</title>
  <meta charset="utf-8">
```

Here's our script. This code should fill in the list of songs below, in the <ul>.

```
  <script>
  _____ addSongs() {
    var song1 = document._____("_____");
    var _____ = _____("_____");
    var _____ = _____.getElementById("_____");

    _____.innerHTML = "Blue Suede Strings, by Elvis Pagely";
    _____ = "Great Objects on Fire, by Jerry JSON Lewis";
    song3._____ = "I Code the Line, by Johnny JavaScript";
  }
  window._____ = _____;
  </script>
</head>
<body>
  <h1>My awesome playlist</h1>
  <ul id="playlist">
    <li id="song1"></li>
    <li id="song2"></li>
    <li id="song3"></li>
  </ul>
</body>
</html>
```

Fill in the blanks with the missing code to get the playlist filled out.

Here's the empty list of songs. The code above should add content to each <li> in the playlist.

When you get the JavaScript working, this is what the web page will look like after you load the page.

My awesome playlist
- Blue Suede Strings, by Elvis Pagely
- Great Objects on Fire, by Jerry JSON Lewis
- I Code the Line, by Johnny JavaScript

So, what else is a DOM good for anyway?

The DOM can do a fair bit more than we've seen so far and we'll be using a lot of its other functionality as we move forward in the book, but for now let's just take a quick look so you've got it in the back of your mind:

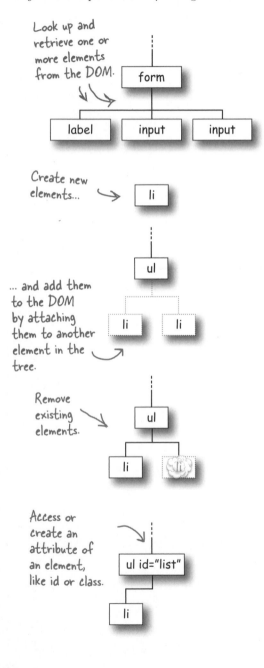

Look up and retrieve one or more elements from the DOM.

Create new elements...

... and add them to the DOM by attaching them to another element in the tree.

Remove existing elements.

Access or create an attribute of an element, like id or class.

Get elements from the DOM.

Of course you already know this because we've been using document.getElementById, but there are other ways to get elements as well; in fact, you can use tag names, class names and attributes to retrieve not just one element, but a whole set of elements (say all elements in the class "on_sale"). And you can get form values the user has typed in, like the text of an input element.

Create or add elements to the DOM.

You can create new elements and you can also add those elements to the DOM. Of course, any changes you make to the DOM will show up immediately as the DOM is rendered by the browser (which is a good thing!).

Remove elements from the DOM.

You can also remove elements from the DOM by taking a parent element and removing any of its children. Again, you'll see the element removed in your browser window as soon as it is deleted from the DOM.

Get and set the attributes of elements.

So far you've accessed only the text content of an element, but you can access attributes as well. For instance, you might want to know what an element's class is, and then change the class it belongs to on the fly.

Can we talk about JavaScript again? Or, how to store multiple values in JavaScript

You've been hanging right in there with JavaScript and the DOM, and before we let you get some rest and relaxation, we wanted to tell you about one more JavaScript type that you'll use all the time—the Array. Let's say you wanted to store the names of thirty-two ice cream flavors or the item numbers of all the items in your user's shopping cart or maybe the outside temperature by the hour. To do that with variables would get awkward fast, especially if we need to store tens, hundreds or thousands of values. Luckily, we've got the Array to help out.

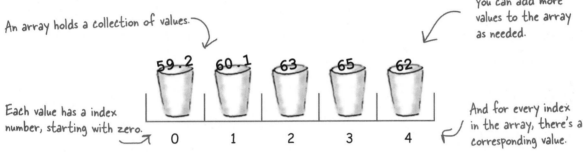

An array holds a collection of values.

You can add more values to the array as needed.

Each value has a index number, starting with zero.

And for every index in the array, there's a corresponding value.

How to create an array

We need to create an array before we use it, and we need to assign the array itself to a variable so we have something to refer to it by in our code. Let's create the array above with hourly temperatures:

Here's our variable for the array...

...and here's how we actually create a new empty array.

```
var tempByHour = new Array();
tempByHour[0] = 59.2;
tempByHour[1] = 60.1;
tempByHour[2] = 63;
tempByHour[3] = 65;
tempByHour[4] = 62;
```

The index.

We'll come back to this syntax in Chapter 4, but for now, just know that it creates a new array.

To add new values to the array, we just reference the index number of the array item, and give it a value.

Just like a variable in JavaScript you can assign any value (or type of value) to an array index.

Or, if you're really in a hurry, JavaScript gives you a shortcut to type in an array (what we call a "literal array") to create and intialize it with values:

```
var tempByHour = [59.2, 60.1, 63, 65, 62];
```

This creates the same array as above, just with a lot less code.

Adding another item to the array

At any time you can keep adding new items to your array simply by using
the next, unused index, like this:

```
tempByHour[5] = 61;
```

By using a new index, we get
a new item in the array.

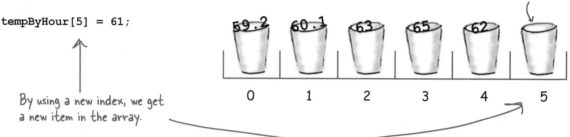

Using your array items

You can get the value of an array item just by referencing the array
variable with an index, like this:

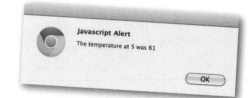

```
var message = "The temperature at 5 was " + tempByHour[5];
alert(message);
```

To access the value of the
temperature at index 5, we just
reference the array at index 5.

Know the size of your array, or else

You can easily get the size of your array by referring to a property of the
array called length:

```
var numItems = tempByHour.length;
```

We'll talk more about properties in the
next chapter; for now, just know that
every array has this length property that
tells you the number of items in the array.

And now that we know how to get length of an array, let's see if we
can combine what you know about loops with arrays...

Sharpen your pencil

Below you'll find a web page with a list of empty items ready for your JavaScript to fill in with temperatures. We've given you most of the code; it's your job to finish it up so that it sets the content of each list item to the corresponding temperature from the array (e.g., the list item with id = "temp0" will get the temperature at index 0 in the array, and so on). So, list item with id = "temp3" will read, "The temperature at 3 was 65". For extra credit, see if you can figure out how to get the temperature at 0 to read "noon" instead of 0.

```html
<!doctype html>
<html lang="en">
<head>                              ← Here's the HTML.
<title>Temperatures</title>
<meta charset="utf-8">
<script>
function showTemps() {
    var tempByHour = new _____;
    tempByHour[0] = 59.2;
    tempByHour[1] = 60.1;
    tempByHour[2] = 63;
    tempByHour[3] = 65;
    tempByHour[4] = 62;
    for (var i = 0; i < _____; _____) {
        var theTemp = _____[i];
        var id = "_____" + i;
        var li = document._____(id);
        if (i == _____) {
            li._____ = "The temperature at noon was " + theTemp;
        } else {
            li.innerHTML = "The temperature at " + _____ + " was " + _____;
        }
    }
}
window.onload = showTemps;
</script>
</head>
<body>
<h1>Temperatures</h1>
<ul>
    <li id="temp0"></li>
    <li id="temp1"></li>
    <li id="temp2"></li>
    <li id="temp3"></li>
    <li id="temp4"></li>
</ul>
</body>
</html>
```

Here's where we're combining loops and arrays. Can you see how we're accessing each item in the array using a variable index? ←

The code above will fill in each list item with a phrase with the temperature.

Temperatures

http://localhost/~Beth/Head-Fir

Temperatures

- The temperature at noon was 59.2
- The temperature at 1 was 60.1
- The temperature at 2 was 63
- The temperature at 3 was 65
- The temperature at 4 was 62

Check out this code for the
hot new Phrase-o-Matic app
and see if you can figure out
what it does before you go on...

Try my new
Phrase-o-Matic and
you'll be a slick talker
just like the boss or those
guys in marketing.

You didn't think our serious business
application from Chapter 1 was serious
enough? Fine. Try this one, if you need
something to show the boss.

```html
<!doctype html>
<html lang="en">
<head>
    <title>Phrase-o-matic</title>
<meta charset="utf-8">
<style>
body {
    font-family: Verdana, Helvetica, sans-serif;
}
</style>
<script>
function makePhrases() {
    var words1 = ["24/7", "multi-Tier", "30,000 foot", "B-to-B", "win-win"];
    var words2 = ["empowered", "value-added", "oriented", "focused", "aligned"];
    var words3 = ["process", "solution", "tipping-point", "strategy", "vision"];

    var rand1 = Math.floor(Math.random() * words1.length);
    var rand2 = Math.floor(Math.random() * words2.length);
    var rand3 = Math.floor(Math.random() * words3.length);

    var phrase = words1[rand1] + " " + words2[rand2] + " " + words3[rand3];
    var phraseElement = document.getElementById("phrase");
    phraseElement.innerHTML = phrase;
}
window.onload = makePhrases;
</script>
</head>
<body>
    <h1>Phrase-o-Matic says:</h1>
    <p id="phrase"></p>
</body>
</html>
```

The Phrase-O-Matic

We hope you figured out this code is the perfect tool
for creating your next start-up marketing slogan. It has
created winners like "Win-win value-added solution"
and "24/7 empowered process" in the past and we have
high hopes for more winners in the future. Let's see how
this thing really works:

 First, we define the makePhrases function, which we run after the page has fully
loaded so we know we can safely access the DOM:

*We're defining a function named
makePhrases, that we can call later.*

```
function makePhrases() {

        All the code for makePhrases goes here, we'll get to it in a sec...

}
window.onload = makePhrases;
```

*We run makePhrases as soon
as the page is done loading.*

② With that out of the way we can write the code for the makePhrases function. Let's start
by setting up three arrays. Each will hold words that we'll use to create the phrases. We'll
use the short cut for creating these arrays:

*We create a variable named words1, that we
can use to reference the first array.*

```
var words1 = ["24/7", "multi-Tier", "30,000 foot", "B-to-B", "win-win"];
```

*We're putting five strings in the array. Feel free to
change these to the latest buzzwords out there.*

```
var words2 = ["empowered", "value-added", "oriented", "focused", "aligned"];
var words3 = ["process", "solution", "tipping-point", "strategy", "vision"];
```

*And here are two more arrays of words, assigned
to two new variables, words2 and words3.*

3 Okay, we've got three new arrays of nice buzzwords; now, what we're going to do is randomly choose one word from each, and then put them together to create a phrase.

Here's how we choose one word from each array:

We create one random number for each array and assign it to a new variable (rand1, rand2, and rand3 respectively).

```
var rand1 = Math.floor(Math.random() * words1.length);
var rand2 = Math.floor(Math.random() * words2.length);
var rand3 = Math.floor(Math.random() * words3.length);
```

This code generates a random number based on the number of items in each array (in our case five, but feel free to add more to any array, it will still work).

4 Now we create the slick marketing phrase by taking each randomly choosen word and concatenating them all together, with a nice space in between for readability:

We use each random number to index into the word arrays...

We define another variable to hold the phrase.

```
var phrase = words1[rand1] + " " + words2[rand2] + " " + words3[rand3];
```

5 We're almost done, we have the phrase, now we just have to display it. By now you already know the drill: we're going to use `getElementById` to locate our paragraph element and then use its `innerHTML` to put the new phrase there.

We get the <p> element with the id "phrase".

```
var phraseElement = document.getElementById("phrase");
phraseElement.innerHTML = phrase;
```

Then we set the content of the <p> element to the phrase.

Okay, finish that last line of code, have one more look over it all and feel that sense of accomplishment before you load it into your browser. Give it a test drive and enjoy the phrases.

Here's what ours looks like!

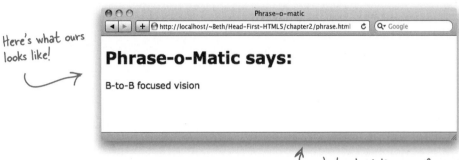

Just reload the page for endless start–up possibilities (okay, not endless, but work with us here, we're trying to make this simple code exciting!).

there are no Dumb Questions

Q: What exactly is Math, and what do Math.random and Math.floor do?

A: Math is a built-in JavaScript library that has a bunch of math-related functions in it. Math.random generates a random number between 0 and 1. We multiply that by the number of items in the array (which we get using the length property of the array) to get a number between 0 and the length of the array. The result is likely to be a floating point number, like 3.2, so we use Math.floor to make sure we get an integer number that we can use as an index into the array to pick the random word. All Math.floor does is drop the numbers after the decimal point in a floating point number. For example, Math.floor(3.2) is 3.

Q: Where can I find documentation on things like Math?

A: A great reference for JavaScript is *JavaScript: The Definitive Guide* by David Flanagan (O'Reilly).

Q: Earlier you said that you can store primitives (like number, string and boolean) in variables or objects. But we're storing arrays in variables. So what is an array, a primitive or an object?

A: Good catch! An array is a special kind of object that's built into JavaScript. It's special because you can use numerical indexes to access the values stored in the array, something you can't do with other (non-array) objects, or objects that you create yourself. You'll learn how to create your own objects in Chapter 4.

Q: What happens if I try to access an array index that doesn't exist? Like if I have 5 words stored in myWords and I tried to access myWords[10].

A: You get undefined, which, if you recall, is the value of a variable that hasn't been assigned a value yet.

Q: Can I remove an item from an Array? If so, what happens to the index of the other elements?

A: You can remove an item from an Array, and you can do it a couple of different ways. You could set the value of the array at the index to null; for example, myArray[2] = null. But that would mean the length of the Array stays the same. Or you can remove the item altogether (using the function splice). In that case, the indexes of the items that come after the one you remove will all shift down by 1. So if myArray[2] = "dog" and myArray[3] = "cat", and you remove "dog", then myArray[2] = "cat" and the length of your array is 1 shorter than it was.

Learning a language is hard work and it requires you not only work your brain, but that you also <u>rest</u> your brain. So after this chapter take some well needed downtime, have a treat on us, but before you go, check out the bullet points and do the crossword to make things really stick.

We haven't figured out the digital to analog conversion yet, so you'll need to supply your own real treats.

BULLET POINTS

- Declare a JavaScript variable using var.

- Number, boolean and string are primitive types.

- Boolean values are true and false.

- Numbers can be integers or floating point numbers.

- An unassigned variable has the value undefined.

- Undefined and null are two different values. Undefined means a variable hasn't been assigned a value; null means the variable has the no value.

- Numerical, boolean and string expressions result in a number, a boolean, or a string value respectively.

- To repeat blocks of code, use a for or a while loop.

- For loops and while loops can do the same thing; use whichever one works best for the situation.

- To end a for or while loop, the conditional test must be false at some point.

- Use if/else statements to make a decision based on a conditional test.

- Conditional tests are boolean expressions.

- You can add JavaScript to the head or body of your web page, or put it in a separate file and link to it from your web page.

- Enclose your JavaScript (or link to it) using the <script> element.

- When the browser loads a web page, it creates a Document Object Model (DOM), which is an internal representation of the web page.

- You make your web pages interactive by examining and changing the DOM using JavaScript.

- Get access to an element in your web page using document.getElementById.

- document.getElementById uses the id of an element to find the element in the DOM.

- Use the innerHTML property of an element to change the element's content.

- If you try to access or change elements before the web page has completely loaded, you'll get a JavaScript error and your code won't work.

- Assign a function to the window.onload property to run the code in that function after the browser has finished loading the web page.

- Use an array to store more than one value.

- To access a value in an array, use an index. An index is an integer number that is the position of the item in the array (starting at 0).

- The length property of an array tells you how many items are in the array.

- By combining loops and arrays, you can access each item of an array sequentially.

- Math is a JavaScript library with several math-related functions in it.

- Math.random returns a floating point number between 0 and 1 (but never 1 precisely).

- Math.floor converts a floating point number to an integer by dropping all the digits after the decimal point.

HTML5Cross

Time to work a different part of your brain with a
crossword. Have fun!

Across

2. 5 < 10 is a _____ expression.
7. You can add your JavaScript to the _____ or body of
   your HTML.
8. _____ is the root of the DOM tree.
9. Variables start with a _____ , $ or _.
10. The DOM is an internal representation of _____.
11. Use an _____ to get a value from an array.
12. Pick good names and use _____ case for long names.
13. If you write 3 + "Stooges", JavaScript will _____ 3
    into a string.
15. Store all your ice cream flavors together in one _____.
16. Do things again and again with a _____ loop.
17. You know how many items are in an array if you check
    the _____.
18. document._____ is how you get an element
    from the DOM in JavaScript.

Down

1. While and for loops use a _____ expression as a
   conditional test.
3. The browser builds a Document _____ _____ when it
   loads a page.
4. The id of the planet hit by phaser fire.
5. Add this to make your web pages interactive.
6. Enclose your JavaScript with a <_____> tag if it's in
   an HTML page.
14. If you're almost done, drink tea, _____ not even
    close, keep working!
19. Don't mess with the _____ until the page has fully
    loaded.

Exercise Solution

Express Yourself!

You've seen the different types of expressions you can use in JavaScript, now it's time to put that knowledge to work by evaluating some expressions yourself. Here's our solution.

`(9 / 5) * tempC + 32`

What's the result when tempC is 10? _____50_____

`"Number" + " " + "2"`

What's the resulting string? _____Number 2_____

`level >= 5`

What's the result when level is 10? _____true_____   >= is "greater
How about when level is 5? _____true_____   than or equal to"

`color != "pink"`

What's the result if color is "blue"? _____true_____   color "is not
                                                          equal" to pink

`(2 * Math.PI) * r`

What's the result if r is 3? _____18.84_____   approximately!

Math.PI gives you the value
of pi (you know, 3.14....)

Not this kind of expression!

Sharpen your pencil Solution

Based on what you know so far about JavaScript variables, expressions and statements, see if you can figure out which of these are legal and which might cause an error.

From the following list, circle the statements that are *legal*.

`var x = 1138;`

`var y = 3/8;`

`var s = "3-8";`

`x = y;`

`var n = 3 - "one";`

Technically, this one is legal,
but results in a value you
can't use.

`var t = "one" + "two";`

`var 3po = true;`   illegal!

`var level_ = 11;`

`var highNoon = false;`

`var $ = 21.30;`

`var z = 2000;`

`var isBig = y > z;`

`z = z + 1;`

`z--;`

`z y;`   illegal!

`x = z * t;`

```
while (highNoon) {

    z--;

}
```

BE the Browser Solution

Each of the JavaScript snippets on this page is a separate piece of code. Your job is to play browser, and evaluate each snippet of code and answer a question about the result. Write your answer to the question below the code.

Snippet 1

```
var count = 0;
for (var i = 0; i < 5; i++) {
    count = count + i;
}
alert("count is " + count);
```

What count does the alert show?

↳ __10__

Each time through the loop, we're adding the value of i to count, and i is increasing, so we're not just adding 1 to count each time through, but 0, 1, 2, 3, and 4.

Snippet 2

```
var tops = 5;
while (tops > 0) {
    for (var spins = 0; spins < 3; spins++) {
        alert("Top is spinning!");
    }
    tops = tops - 1;
}
```

__15__

How many times do you see the alert, "Top is spinning!"?

The outer while loop runs 5 times, and the inner for loop runs 3 times each time through the outer loop, so the total is 5 * 3, or 15!

Snippet 3

Here, we're starting at 5 and looping until berries is 0, counting down each time (instead of up).

```
for (var berries = 5; berries > 0; berries--) {
    alert("Eating a berry");
}
```

How many berries did you eat? → __5__

Snippet 4

```
for (scoops = 0; scoops < 10; scoop++) {
    alert("There's more ice cream!");
}
alert("life without ice cream isn't the same");
```

An easy one; we just loop 10 times so we eat 10 scoops!

__10__ ↞ How many scoops of icecream did you eat?

Exercise Solution

Take the code above and insert it into the code below. Walk through the while loop and write down the alerts in the sequence they occur. Here's our solution.

```javascript
var scoops = 10;

while (scoops >= 0) {
    if (scoops == 3) {                          ← Inserted code
        alert("Ice cream is running low!");      ← This happens once, when scoops is 3.
    } else if (scoops > 9) {
        alert("Eat faster, the ice cream is going to melt!");   ← This also happens once, when scoops is 10.
    } else if (scoops == 2) {
        alert("Going once!");           ← Each of these happen once,
    } else if (scoops == 1) {               when scoops is 2, 1, and 0.
        alert("Going twice!");
    } else if (scoops == 0) {
        alert("Gone!");                 And this happens whenever none of the other conditions
    } else {                            is true, that is, when scoops is 9, 8, 7, 6, 5, and 4.
        alert("Still lots of ice cream left, come and get it.");  ←

    }
    scoops = scoops - 1;        ←  We subtract 1 scoop each time through the loop.

}
alert("Life without ice cream isn't the same.");    ←  This is run after the loop is done.
```

The alerts: →
```
Eat faster, the ice cream is going to melt!
Still lots of ice cream left, come and get it.
Still lots of ice cream left, come and get it.
Still lots of ice cream left, come and get it.
Still lots of ice cream left, come and get it.
Still lots of ice cream left, come and get it.
Still lots of ice cream left, come and get it.
Ice cream is running low!
Going once!
Going twice!
Gone!
Life without ice cream isn't the same.
```

Code Magnets Solution

This code prints out a well-known palindrome in an alert. The problem is that some of the code was on fridge magnets and fell on the floor. It's your job to put the code back together again to make the palindrome work. Watch out; we put a few extra in, and you'll have to use some of the magnets more than once! Here's our solution.

```javascript
var word1 = "a";
var word2 = "nam";
var word3 = "nal p";
var word4 = "lan a c";
var word5 = "a man a p";

var phrase = "";

for (var i = 0; i < 4 ; i++ ) {
    if (i == 0) {
        phrase = word5 ;
    }
    else if (i == 1) {
        phrase = phrase + word4;
    }
    else if (i == 2) {
        phrase = phrase + word1 + word3;
    }
    else if ( i == 3 ) {
        phrase = phrase + word1 + word2 + word1;
    }
}
alert(phrase);
```

http://localhost
a man a plan a canal panama
OK

A palindrome is a sentence that can be read the same way backwards and forwards! Here's the palindrome you should see if the magnets are all in the right places.

Leftover magnets.

else if (i == 0)

i == 4   word2   word4   i < 3

else   word0   i = 0   +   i--   i = 3   word3

BE the Browser Solution

Your job is the act like you're the browser. You need to parse the HTML and build your very own DOM from it. Go ahead and parse the HTML to the right, and draw your DOM below. We've already started it for you.

```html
<!doctype html>
<html lang="en">
  <head>
    <title>Movies</title>
  </head>
  <body>
    <h1>Movie Showtimes</h1>
    <h2 id="movie1" >Plan 9 from Outer Space</h2>
    <p>Playing at 3:00pm, 7:00pm.
      <span>
        Special showing tonight at <em>midnight</em>!
      </span>
    </p>
    <h2 id="movie2">Forbidden Planet</h2>
    <p>Playing at 5:00pm, 9:00pm.</p>
  </body>
</html>
```

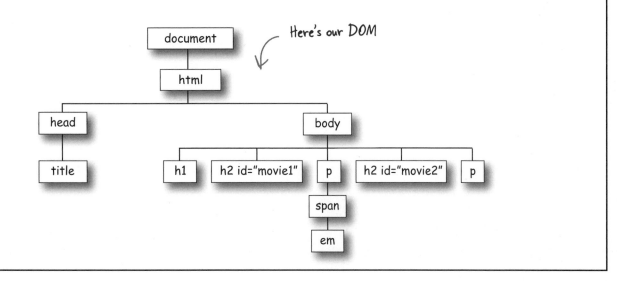

Here's our DOM

Sharpen your pencil
Solution

Here's some HTML for a playlist of songs, except that the list is empty. It was your job to complete the JavaScript below to add the songs to the list. Our solution is below.

[browser window showing:]

My Playlist
http://localhost/~Beth/Head-I

My awesome playlist

- Blue Suede Strings, by Elvis Pagely
- Great Objects on Fire, by Jerry JSON Lewis
- I Code the Line, by Johnny JavaScript

If you get the JavaScript working, this is what the web page will look like after you load the page.

```
<!doctype html>
<html lang="en">
<head>
  <title>My Playlist</title>
  <meta charset="utf-8">
  <script>
    function   addSongs() {
     var song1 = document. getElementById (" song1 ");
     var song2 = document.getElementById (" song2 ");
     var song3 = document .getElementById(" song3 ");


     song1 .innerHTML = "Blue Suede Strings, by Elvis Pagely";
     song2.innerHTML = "Great Objects on Fire, by Jerry JSON Lewis";
     song3. innerHTML = "I Code the Line, by Johnny JavaScript";
    }
    window. onload = addSongs ;
  </script>
</head>
<body>
  <h1>My awesome playlist</h1>
  <ul id="playlist">
    <li id="song1"></li>
    <li id="song2"></li>
    <li id="song3"></li>
  </ul>
</body>
</html>
```

Here's the code that will make the playlist work.

Feel free to substitute your favorite songs!

The code above sets the content of these <li> elements by grabbing each element from the DOM and setting the innerHTML to the song name.

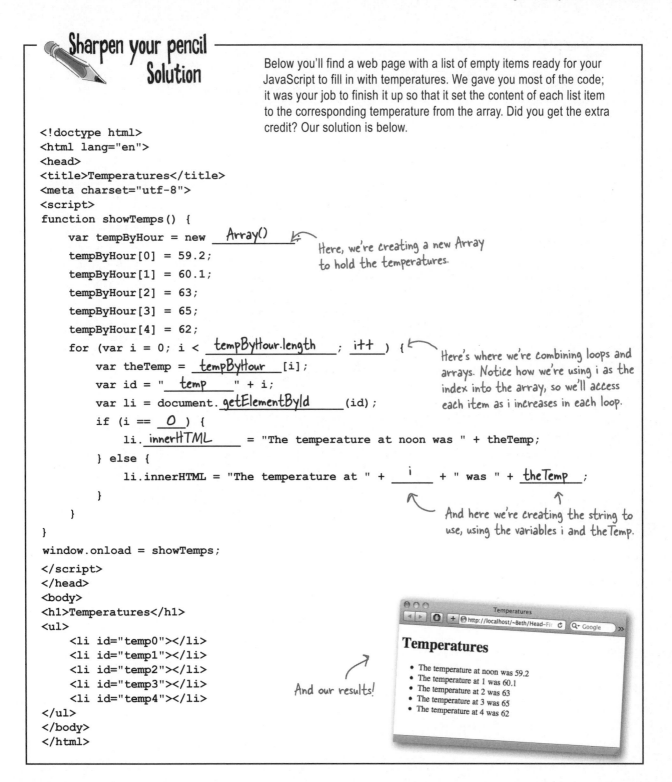

Sharpen your pencil
Solution

Below you'll find a web page with a list of empty items ready for your JavaScript to fill in with temperatures. We gave you most of the code; it was your job to finish it up so that it set the content of each list item to the corresponding temperature from the array. Did you get the extra credit? Our solution is below.

```html
<!doctype html>
<html lang="en">
<head>
<title>Temperatures</title>
<meta charset="utf-8">
<script>
function showTemps() {
    var tempByHour = new ___Array()___
    tempByHour[0] = 59.2;
    tempByHour[1] = 60.1;
    tempByHour[2] = 63;
    tempByHour[3] = 65;
    tempByHour[4] = 62;
    for (var i = 0; i < __tempByHour.length__ ; __i++__ ) {
        var theTemp = __tempByHour__ [i];
        var id = "__temp__" + i;
        var li = document.__getElementById__ (id);
        if (i == __0__) {
            li.__innerHTML__ = "The temperature at noon was " + theTemp;
        } else {
            li.innerHTML = "The temperature at " + __i__ + " was " + __theTemp__ ;
        }
    }
}
window.onload = showTemps;
</script>
</head>
<body>
<h1>Temperatures</h1>
<ul>
    <li id="temp0"></li>
    <li id="temp1"></li>
    <li id="temp2"></li>
    <li id="temp3"></li>
    <li id="temp4"></li>
</ul>
</body>
</html>
```

Here, we're creating a new Array to hold the temperatures.

Here's where we're combining loops and arrays. Notice how we're using i as the index into the array, so we'll access each item as i increases in each loop.

And here we're creating the string to use, using the variables i and theTemp.

And our results!

Temperatures

- The temperature at noon was 59.2
- The temperature at 1 was 60.1
- The temperature at 2 was 63
- The temperature at 3 was 65
- The temperature at 4 was 62

HTML5Cross Solution

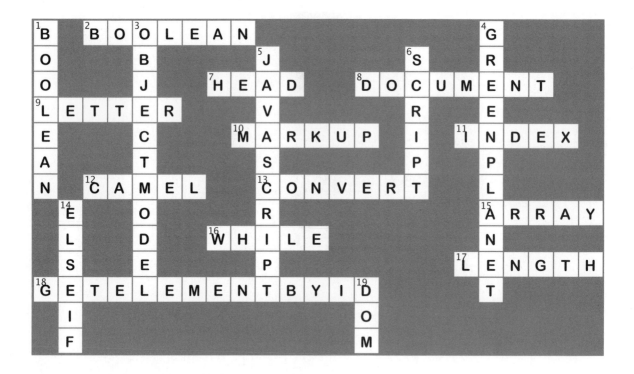

3 events, handlers and all that jazz

A Little Interaction

Sure, he looks great, but this relationship would be so much more fun if he'd actually *do* something now and then.

Man or mannequin? You decide. ⟶

You still haven't reached out to touch your user.

You've learned the basics of JavaScript but can you get interactive with your users? When pages respond to user input, they aren't just documents anymore, they're living, reacting applications. In this chapter you're going to learn how to handle one form of user input (excuse the pun), and wire up an old-fashioned HTML <form> element to actual code. It might sound dangerous, but it's also powerful. Strap yourself in, this is a fast moving to-the-point-chapter where we go from zero to interactive app in no time.

Get ready for Webville Tunes

Okay, we've dragged you through a lot of JavaScript fundamentals so far in this book, and while we've talked a good game on building web apps, we don't have a lot to show for it, yet. So, now we're going to get serious (no really! we mean it this time!) and build something real world.

How about a playlist manager. We'll call it something original, like... hmm, say Webville Tunes.

Add new songs anytime.

Displays all your favorite Webville tunes, right in the browser.

What we're going to build.

Completely browser-based. No server-side code needed or required.

Given what you know about this code:

```
window.onload = init;
```

Can you guess what this code might do?

```
button.onclick = handleButtonClick;
```

Getting started...

We don't need to create a big, complex web page to get this started. In fact we can start very simply. Let's just create an HTML5 document with a form and a list element to hold the playlist:

Just your standard HTML5 head and body.

```
<!doctype html>
<html lang="en">
<head>
    <title>Webville Tunes</title>
    <meta charset="utf-8">
    <script src="playlist.js"></script>
    <link rel="stylesheet" href="playlist.css">
</head>
<body>
    <form>
        <input type="text" id="songTextInput" size="40" placeholder="Song name">
        <input type="button" id="addButton" value="Add Song">
    </form>
    <ul id="playlist">

    </ul>
</body>
</html>
```

We're going to be putting all our JavaScript in the playlist.js file.

We've included a stylesheet to give our playlist app a nice look & feel.*

All we need is a simple form. Here it is with a text field to type in your songs. We're using the HTML5 placeholder attribute that shows an example of what to type in the input field.

And we've got a button with an id of "addButton" to submit your new additions to the playlist.

We're going to use a list for the songs. For now it's empty, but we'll change that with JavaScript code in a sec...

Give it a test drive

Go ahead and type in the code above, load it into your favorite browser and give it a spin before moving on to the next page.

Here's what you should see.

```
⬤⬤⬤                Webville Tunes
◀ ▶  +  🌐 http://localhost/~Beth/HTML5/JavaScri  ⟳  Q▾ Google
Song name                                        ( Add Song )


```

* Remember you can download the stylesheet (and all the code) from http://wickedlysmart.com/hfhtml5

But nothing happens when I click "Add Song"

Well, yes and no. Nothing *appears* to happen, but your browser knows you clicked on the button (depending on your browser, you will also see the button depress).

The real question is how do we get the button to do something when you click on it? And what that question really means is, how do we get some JavaScript code invoked when you click on a button?

We need two things:

 We need a bit of JavaScript code that will get evaluated when the user clicks on the "Add Song" button. This code will (once we've written it) add a song to your playlist.

 We need a way to hook up that bit of code so that when the button is clicked, JavaScript knows to run your "add song" code.

When the user clicks (or touches on a gesture-based device) a button, we want to know about it. We're interested in the "button was just clicked event".

Hey, I'm really interested in you, button... could you let me know if anyone clicks on you?

Great, you'll be the first to know in the event that happens.

Add Song

↖ Your button.

↑

Your code.

Handling Events

You're going to see that many things are happening in the browser while your page is being displayed—buttons are being clicked, additional data your code requested from the network may be arriving, timers may be going off (we'll get to all that). All these things cause events to happen, a button click event, a data available event, a time expired event, and so on (there are many more).

Whenever there is an event, there is an opportunity for your code to *handle it*; that is, to supply some code that will be invoked when the event occurs. Now, you're not required to handle any of these events, but you'll need to handle them if you want interesting things to happen when they occur—like, say, when the button click event happens, you might want to add a new song to the playlist; when new data arrives you might want to process it and display it on your page; when a timer fires you might want to tell the user their hold on front row tickets is going to expire, and so on.

So, we know we want to handle the button click event, let's see how we do that.

Making a Plan...

Let's step back for a second before we lose ourselves in handlers and events.
The goal here is to click on "Add Song" and have a song added to a playlist on
the page. Let's attack the task like this:

> 1. Set up a handler to handle the user's click on the "Add Song" button.
> 2. Write the handler to get the song name the user typed in, and then...
> 3. Create a new element to hold the new song, and...
> 4. Add the element to the page's DOM.

If these steps aren't clear to you, don't worry, we'll explain it as we go... for now,
just get a feel for the steps and follow along as we get that handler written. Go
ahead an open up a new file, `playlist.js` for all your JavaScript code.

Getting access to the "Add Song" button

To ask the button to let us know when a click event occurs, we first need to get
access to the button. Luckily we created the button using HTML markup and
that means...you guessed it, it is represented in the DOM, and you already
know how to get elements in the DOM. If you look back at the HTML you'll
see we gave the button an id of `addButton`. So, we'll use `getElementById`
to get a reference to the button:

```
var button = document.getElementById("addButton");
```

Now we just need to give the button some code to call when a click occurs.
To do that we're going to create a function, named `handleButtonClick`,
that will handle the event. We'll get into functions in a bit; for now, here's the
function:

> The function is named
> handleButtonClick; we'll
> get to the specifics of
> the syntax in a bit.

> A function gives you a way to
> package up code into a chunk. You
> can give it a name, and reuse the
> chunk of code wherever you want.

```
function handleButtonClick() {
    alert("Button was clicked!");
}
```

> Right now we're just going
> to display an alert when this
> function is called.

> We put all the code we want
> to execute when the function
> is called within the braces.

Giving the button a click handler

1. Set up a handler to handle the user's click
2. Write the handler to get the song name
3. Create a new element to hold the new song
4. Add the element to the page's DOM

Okay, we've got a button and we've got a function that will act as a handler, `handleButtonClick`, so let's put them together. To do that we're going to use a property of the button, `onclick`. We set the `onclick` property like this:

```
var button = document.getElementById("addButton");
button.onclick = handleButtonClick;
```

With a button in hand, after calling getElementById, we set the onclick property to the function we want called when a click event occurs.

You might remember that we did something similar when we used the `window.onload` property to call a function after the window was loaded. In this case though, we'll call the function when the button is clicked. Now let's put all of this together:

Just like we did in the last chapter, we're using an init function that won't be called and executed until the page is fully loaded.

```
window.onload = init;
function init() {
    var button = document.getElementById("addButton");
    button.onclick = handleButtonClick;
}
function handleButtonClick() {
    alert("Button was clicked!");
}
```

After the page loads we'll grab the button and set up its onclick handler.

And the click handler will display an alert when we click on the button.

Putting it to a test...

Go ahead and type in the code above (in your `playlist.js` file), load the page, click on that button as much as you want and you'll see an alert each time.

After you're finished testing your new button click handler, sit back and study the code and think through how all this works.

When you think you've got it in your head, turn the page and we'll step through the details to make sure it really sticks.

http://localhost

Button was clicked!

OK

A closer look at what just happened...

We just introduced a lot of new ideas over the last few pages, let's step through the code again and make sure we've got it clear in our heads. Here we go:

1 The first thing you did was throw a button in your HTML form. And with that in place, you needed a way to capture a user's click on that button so that you could have some code executed. To do that we created a handler and assigned it to the onclick property of our button.

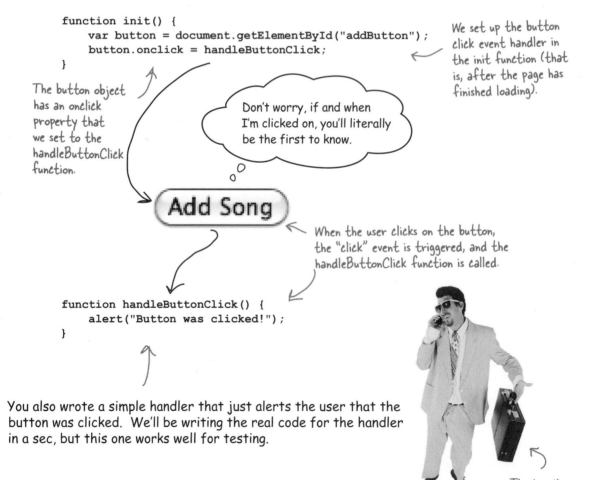

```
function init() {
    var button = document.getElementById("addButton");
    button.onclick = handleButtonClick;
}
```

We set up the button click event handler in the init function (that is, after the page has finished loading).

The button object has an onclick property that we set to the handleButtonClick function.

Don't worry, if and when I'm clicked on, you'll literally be the first to know.

Add Song

When the user clicks on the button, the "click" event is triggered, and the handleButtonClick function is called.

```
function handleButtonClick() {
    alert("Button was clicked!");
}
```

2 You also wrote a simple handler that just alerts the user that the button was clicked. We'll be writing the real code for the handler in a sec, but this one works well for testing.

The handler with your code

3 With the code written, the page is loaded and displayed by the browser, the handler is installed...it's all up to the user now...

> Come on... click the button... just do it...

4 Finally, the user clicks on your button, the button springs into action, notices it has a handler, and calls it...

> Time to wake up, there's a click from the user.

> I see I have a handler for this, better let him know.

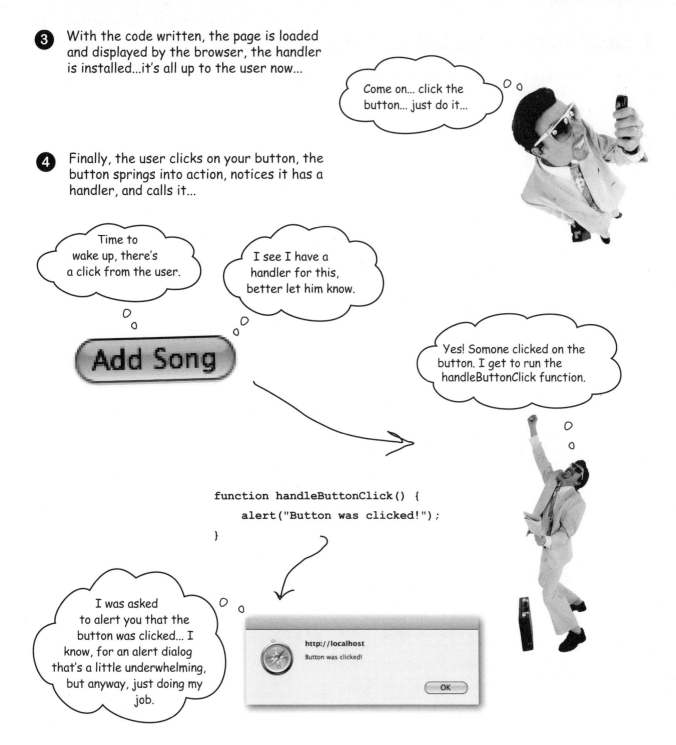

> Yes! Somone clicked on the button. I get to run the handleButtonClick function.

```
function handleButtonClick() {
    alert("Button was clicked!");
}
```

> I was asked to alert you that the button was clicked... I know, for an alert dialog that's a little underwhelming, but anyway, just doing my job.

http://localhost
Button was clicked!
OK

1. Set up a handler to handle the user's click
2. Write the handler to get the song name
3. Create a new element to hold the new song
4. Add the element to the page's DOM

Getting the song name

We're ready to move on to the second step of our task: getting the song name that the user has typed in. Once we have that, we can think about how we're going to display the playlist in the browser.

But how are we going to get the song name? That's something the user has typed in, right? Ah, but anything that happens in the web page gets reflected in the DOM, so the text the user typed must be there too.

To get the text from a form text input element, you first have to get the input element from the DOM, and you know how to do that: getElementById. And, once you've done that you can use the value property of the text input element to access the text the user types into the form field, here's how:

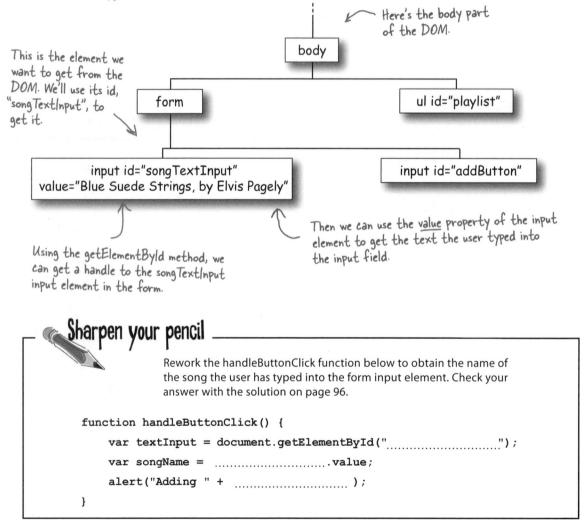

Here's the body part of the DOM.

body

This is the element we want to get from the DOM. We'll use its id, "songTextInput", to get it.

form

ul id="playlist"

input id="songTextInput" value="Blue Suede Strings, by Elvis Pagely"

input id="addButton"

Using the getElementById method, we can get a handle to the songTextInput input element in the form.

Then we can use the value property of the input element to get the text the user typed into the input field.

Sharpen your pencil

Rework the handleButtonClick function below to obtain the name of the song the user has typed into the form input element. Check your answer with the solution on page 96.

```
function handleButtonClick() {
    var textInput = document.getElementById("...........................");
    var songName = ...........................value;
    alert("Adding " + ........................... );
}
```

Sharpen your pencil ——————————————— BONUS

What if you wanted to test to make sure the user actually entered some text before clicking the button? How might you do that? (Again, find the solution on page 96.)

....

....

there are no Dumb Questions

Q: What is the value of the value property of the text input if the user didn't type anything? Is the value null? Or does the "Add Song" button not invoke the handler if the user hasn't entered anything?

A: The "Add Song" button isn't that smart. If you want to determine if the user typed something, that's up to your code. And, to know if the text input is empty (that is, the user didn't type anything), you can check to see if its value is equal to a string with nothing in it, otherwise known as the empty string, which is written as "", or two double quotes with nothing in between. We see why you'd think it might be null, because we said that is the value of a variable that has no value, but from the text input field's perspective, it isn't holding nothing, it's holding on to a string with nothing in it yet. Go figure. ;-)

Q: I thought that the text input "value" was an attribute. You're calling it a property, why?

A: You're right, value *is* an attribute of the HTML text input element. You can initialize the value of a text input element using the value attribute. But in JavaScript, to access the value that a user has typed in, you need to use the value *property* of the input element we get from the DOM.

Q: What other kinds of events can I handle in JavaScript other than button clicks?

A: There are a whole slew of other mouse events you can handle. For instance, you can detect and handle a key press, a mouse moving over or out of an element, the mouse dragging, even a mouse press and hold (different from a mouse click). And then there are many other types of events we've mentioned in passing, like events when new data is available, timer events, events related to the browser window, and so on. You'll see quite a few other kinds of event handling in the rest of the book; once you know how to do one, you can pretty much do them all!

Q: What is JavaScript doing while it's waiting for events?

A: Unless you've programmed your JavaScript to do something, it sits idle until something happens (the user interacts with the interface, data comes in from the Web, a timer goes off, and so on). This is a good thing; it means the processing power of your computer is going to other things, like making your browser responsive. Later in the book, you'll learn how to create tasks that run in the background so your browser can run the task code and respond to events at the same time.

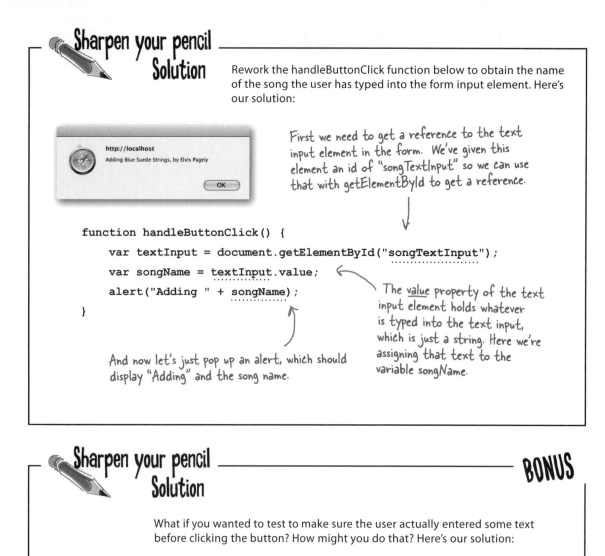

Sharpen your pencil Solution

Rework the handleButtonClick function below to obtain the name of the song the user has typed into the form input element. Here's our solution:

> First we need to get a reference to the text input element in the form. We've given this element an id of "songTextInput" so we can use that with getElementById to get a reference.

```
function handleButtonClick() {
    var textInput = document.getElementById("songTextInput");
    var songName = textInput.value;
    alert("Adding " + songName);
}
```

> The value property of the text input element holds whatever is typed into the text input, which is just a string. Here we're assigning that text to the variable songName.

> And now let's just pop up an alert, which should display "Adding" and the song name.

Sharpen your pencil Solution ──────────────── **BONUS**

What if you wanted to test to make sure the user actually entered some text before clicking the button? How might you do that? Here's our solution:

```
function handleButtonClick() {
    var textInput = document.getElementById("songTextInput");
    var songName = textInput.value;
    if (songName == "") {
        alert("Please enter a song");
    } else {
        alert("Adding " + songName);
    }
}
```

> We can use an if statement and compare the songName string to an empty string to make sure the user typed something. If they didn't type anything we'll alert them and ask them to enter a song.

How do we add a song to the page?

1. Set up a handler to handle the user's click
2. Write the handler to get the song name
3. **Create a new element to hold the new song**
4. Add the element to the page's DOM

We've already got a lot working! You can type a song name into a form, click the Add Song button and get the text you typed into the form, *all within your code*. Now we're going to display the playlist on the page itself. Here's what it's going to look like:

When you click "Add Song", your JavaScript will add the song to a list of songs on the page.

Here's what we need to do:

① You might have noticed that we already put an empty list in the HTML markup (an empty <ul> element to be exact) back when we first typed it in. Given that, here's what the DOM looks like right now.

② Every time we enter a new song, we want to add a new item to the unordered list. To do that, we'll create a new <li> element that will hold the song name. Then we'll take the new <li> element and add it to the <ul> in the DOM. Once we do that, the browser will do its thing and you'll see the page update, just like the <li> was there all along. And of course, we'll do all this in code. Check out the DOM one more time and make sure you understand what we need to do.

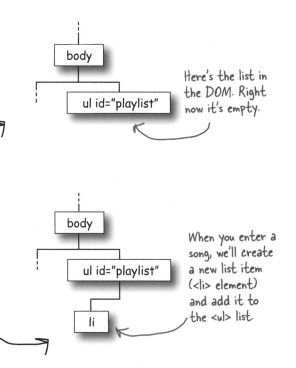

Here's the list in the DOM. Right now it's empty.

When you enter a song, we'll create a new list item (<li> element) and add it to the <ul> list.

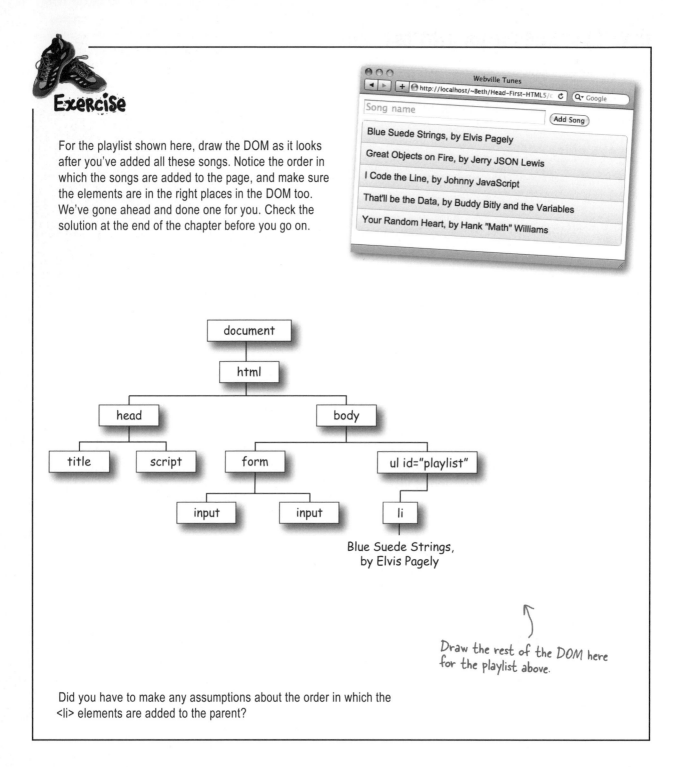

Exercise

For the playlist shown here, draw the DOM as it looks after you've added all these songs. Notice the order in which the songs are added to the page, and make sure the elements are in the right places in the DOM too. We've gone ahead and done one for you. Check the solution at the end of the chapter before you go on.

Webville Tunes

http://localhost/~Beth/Head-First-HTML5/c

Song name   Add Song

Blue Suede Strings, by Elvis Pagely

Great Objects on Fire, by Jerry JSON Lewis

I Code the Line, by Johnny JavaScript

That'll be the Data, by Buddy Bitly and the Variables

Your Random Heart, by Hank "Math" Williams

document
└ html
   ├ head
   │ ├ title
   │ └ script
   └ body
      ├ form
      │ ├ input
      │ └ input
      └ ul id="playlist"
         └ li
            Blue Suede Strings,
            by Elvis Pagely

↖ Draw the rest of the DOM here for the playlist above.

Did you have to make any assumptions about the order in which the
<li> elements are added to the parent?

How to create a new element

You've already seen how to get access to *existing elements* through the DOM. But you can also use the DOM to create *new elements* (and then as a second step, *add them to* the DOM, which we'll get to in a sec).

Let's say we want to create a `<li>` element. Here's how we do that:

Use document.createElement to create new elements. A reference to the new element is returned.

> We better get to work building these elements, Betty. They're updating the DOM again.

```
var li = document.createElement("li");
```

Here we're assigning the new element to the variable li.

Pass the kind of element you want to create as a string to createElement.

li

createElement creates a brand new element. Note that it isn't inserted into the DOM just yet. Right now it is just a free-floating element in need of a place in the DOM.

So now we have a new `<li>` element with nothing in it. You already know one way to get text into an element:

```
li.innerHTML = songName;
```

Our li variable.

This sets the content of the `<li>` to the song title.

li

Blue Suede Strings, by Elvis Pagely

Here's our new li element object ready to go. But it's not part of the DOM yet!

Adding an element to the DOM

1. Set up a handler to handle the user's click
2. Write the handler to get the song name
3. Create a new element to hold the new song
4. Add the element to the page's DOM

To add a new element to the DOM you have to know where you want to put it. Well, we do know where to put it: we're going to put the `<li>` element in the `<ul>` element. But how do we do that? Let's take another look at the DOM. Remember how we said it was like a tree? Think *family tree*:

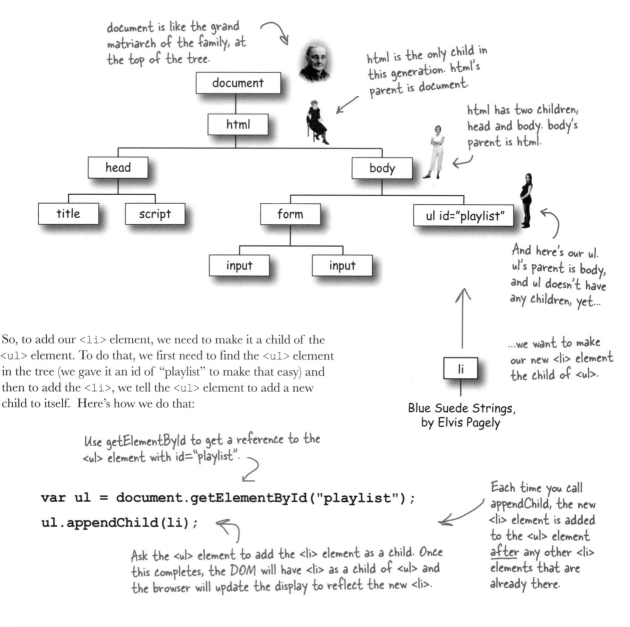

document is like the grand matriarch of the family, at the top of the tree.

html is the only child in this generation. html's parent is document.

html has two children, head and body. body's parent is html.

And here's our ul. ul's parent is body, and ul doesn't have any children, yet...

...we want to make our new `<li>` element the child of `<ul>`.

Blue Suede Strings, by Elvis Pagely

So, to add our `<li>` element, we need to make it a child of the `<ul>` element. To do that, we first need to find the `<ul>` element in the tree (we gave it an id of "playlist" to make that easy) and then to add the `<li>`, we tell the `<ul>` element to add a new child to itself. Here's how we do that:

Use getElementById to get a reference to the `<ul>` element with id="playlist".

```
var ul = document.getElementById("playlist");
ul.appendChild(li);
```

Ask the `<ul>` element to add the `<li>` element as a child. Once this completes, the DOM will have `<li>` as a child of `<ul>` and the browser will update the display to reflect the new `<li>`.

Each time you call appendChild, the new `<li>` element is added to the `<ul>` element *after* any other `<li>` elements that are already there.

Put it all together...

Let's put all that code together and add it to the `handleButtonClick`
function. Go ahead and type it in if you haven't already so you can test it.

```
function handleButtonClick() {

    var textInput = document.getElementById("songTextInput");

    var songName = textInput.value;

    var li = document.createElement("li");

    li.innerHTML = songName;

    var ul = document.getElementById("playlist");

    ul.appendChild(li);

}
```

First, create the new <li> element where
the song name is going to go.

Then, set the content of that element to
the song name.

The <ul> with the id "playlist" is the
parent element for our new <li>. So we
get that next.

Then we add the li object to the
ul using appendChild.

Notice that we ask the <u>parent</u> element, ul,
to add li as a new <u>child</u>.

... and take it for a test drive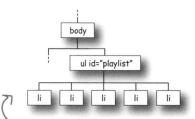

Put Webville Tunes through its paces, add a few songs.
Here are our results.

And here's how the DOM looks now that
we've added all those new <li> elements.

Now when we type in a song name and
click add, the song is added to the
DOM, so we see the page change and
the new song in the list.

Review—what we just did

You did a lot in this chapter (and in a short amount of time!). You built a playlist app that you can use to enter a song, click a button and add that song to a list on the page, all using JavaScript code.

1 The first thing you did was set up an event handler to handle the user's click on the "Add Song" button. You created a function, handleButtonClick, and set the onclick property of the "Add Song" button to this function.

> When the user clicks the "Add Song" button, your handleButtonClick handler will be called.

2 Next, you wrote code for the button click handler to get the song name from the input text field. You used the input.value property to get the text, and you even added a check to make sure the user had typed in a song. If they didn't, you alerted them.

> In handleButtonClick, you're getting the song name the user typed in, by using the input.value property to get the text from the DOM.

3 To add the song to the playlist, you then created a <li> element using document.createElement, and set the content of the element to the song name using innerHTML.

> You create a new <li> element and set the content of the <li> element to the song name.

4 Finally, you added the new <li> element to the DOM by adding it as a child of the parent <ul> element. You did this using appendChild, telling the <ul> element to "append the <li> element as a child", which added it to the DOM. When the element is added to the DOM, the browser updates the page the user sees, and the playlist contains the song.

> Adding a new child to the DOM updates the page. →

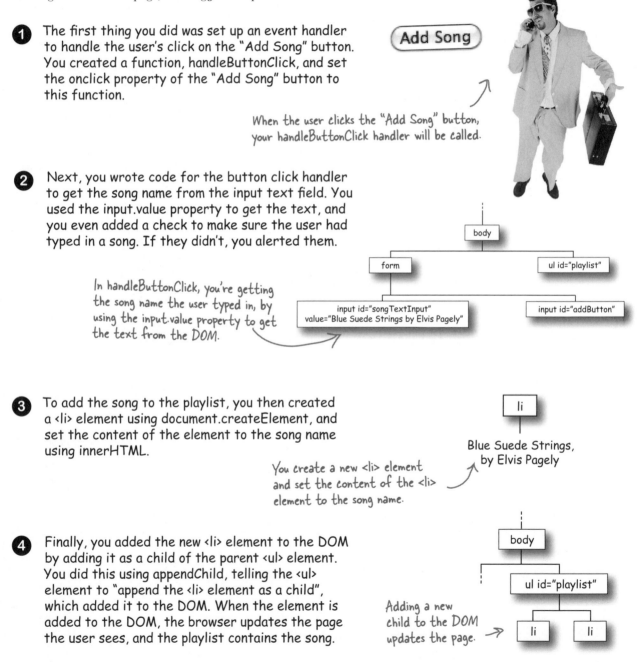

Wait a sec, I get we're interacting with the DOM and all, but how is this a real web App? If I close my browser, all my songs are gone. Shouldn't my playlist items stick around if this is really an application?

We agree, the playlist should be persistent;

after all, what's the point of entering all those songs if they don't stick around? And there's a lot of other functionality you might want to add as well. You might, for instance, want to add an audio interface using the audio/video API so you can actually listen to the songs, share songs out to friends using a web service (like Facebook and Twitter), find other people in the local area that like the same artists (using the geolocation APIs), and we're sure you can come up with more.

But back to the playlist...we wanted to get you up and running by building a small interactive app, and the playlist does a good job of that. Plus, storing the songs requires the HTML5 Web Storage API, which is a few chapters away.

Hmm, on the other hand we really don't want to under-deliver here...

Turn page

Ready Bake Code

We pre-baked some code so you don't have to make it yourself.

We've gone ahead and baked a little code for you to save your playlists. For now you just need to type it in and make two tiny changes to your existing code and you'll have an HTML5-stored playlist.

We'll be covering all the specifics of storing things locally in your browser in the Web Storage chapter, but for now you can get your playlist up and running.

Of course, it never hurts to look over the Ready Bake code. You might be surprised how much you already know, not to mention how much of it you can figure out if you don't know it.

Watch it!

The Ready Bake Code won't work in IE 6 or 7.

IE versions 6 and 7 don't support localStorage. So if you're using IE, make sure you're using version 8 or above.

Watch it!

The Ready Bake Code won't work in some browsers if you're serving your pages from file:// instead of a server like localhost:// or an online hosted server.

We'll deal with this situation more in future chapters (it pops up fairly often with new HTML5 features). For now, if you don't want to run a server or copy the files to a hosted server online, try using Safari or Chrome.

How to add the Ready Bake Code...

Here's the Ready Bake code for you to add to your Webville Tunes app so you can save that fabulous playlist you've created. All you have to do is make a new file, `playlist_store.js`, type in the code below, and then make a couple of changes to your existing code (on the next page).

Ready Bake Code

```javascript
function save(item) {
    var playlistArray = getStoreArray("playlist");
    playlistArray.push(item);
    localStorage.setItem("playlist", JSON.stringify(playlistArray));
}

function loadPlaylist() {
    var playlistArray = getSavedSongs();
    var ul = document.getElementById("playlist");
    if (playlistArray != null) {
        for (var i = 0; i < playlistArray.length; i++) {
            var li = document.createElement("li");
            li.innerHTML = playlistArray[i];
            ul.appendChild(li);
        }
    }
}

function getSavedSongs() {
    return getStoreArray("playlist");
}

function getStoreArray(key) {
    var playlistArray = localStorage.getItem(key);
    if (playlistArray == null || playlistArray == "") {
        playlistArray = new Array();
    }
    else {
        playlistArray = JSON.parse(playlistArray);
    }
    return playlistArray;
}
```

Type this into "playlist_store.js".

Integrating your Ready Bake Code

Ready Bake Code

We need to make a few little tweaks to integrate the storage code. First, add a reference to `playlist_store.js` in your `<head>` element in `playlist.html`:

```
<script src="playlist_store.js"></script>
<script src="playlist.js"></script>
```

Add this just above your link to playlist.js. It loads the Ready Bake code.

Now you just need to add two lines to your code, in `playlist.js`, that will load and save the playlist:

```
function init() {
    var button = document.getElementById("addButton");
    button.onclick = handleButtonClick;
    loadPlaylist();
}
```

This loads the saved songs from localStorage when you load your page, so you see your saved songs.

```
function handleButtonClick() {
    var textInput = document.getElementById("songTextInput");
    var songName = textInput.value;
    var li = document.createElement("li");
    li.innerHTML = songName;
    var ul = document.getElementById("list");
    ul.appendChild(li);
    save(songName);
}
```

And this saves your song each time you add one to the playlist.

Test drive the saved songs

Okay, reload the page and type in some songs. Quit the browser. Open the browser and load the page again. You should see all the songs stored safely in your playlist.

Okay, are you tired of your playlist and want to delete it? You'll have to check out the Web Storage chapter!

```
  ⬤ ⬤ ⬤              Webville Tunes
  ◀ ▶  +  http://localhost/~Beth/Head-First-HTML5/c  ↻  Q▾ Google
  Song name                                    (Add Song)
  ┌─────────────────────────────────────────────────────┐
  │ Blue Suede Strings, by Elvis Pagely                  │
  ├─────────────────────────────────────────────────────┤
  │ Great Objects on Fire, by Jerry JSON Lewis           │
  ├─────────────────────────────────────────────────────┤
  │ I Code the Line, by Johnny JavaScript                │
  ├─────────────────────────────────────────────────────┤
  │ That'll be the Data, by Buddy Bitly and the Variables│
  ├─────────────────────────────────────────────────────┤
  │ Your Random Heart, by Hank "Math" Williams           │
  └─────────────────────────────────────────────────────┘
```

We added all these songs, closed the browser, reopened the browser, loaded the page, and there they were.

> This is cool, we're really starting to make the code and the page interact with each other. I'm curious though about functions, objects, and things like element.appendChild(). Do I need to learn more about those things?

Perfect timing.

We really wanted to take you through a complete interactive example of HTML markup and JavaScript working together to build the first part of a web applications. If you think about it, you've already done a lot:

1) Inserted code into your page.

2) Set up a button click event and written the code to capture and handle the button click.

3) Asked the DOM for information.

4) Created and added new elements to the DOM.

Not bad! And now that you have a bit of an intuitive sense of how this all works together, let's take a little detour down JavaScript Avenue to see how things like functions and objects *really work*.

This isn't going to be the regular tour, oh no, we're going to pull up the manhole covers and get a rare look at how Webville functions.

Interested? Come on, join us in Chapter 4...

BULLET POINTS

- There are lots of events happening in your browser all the time. If you want to respond to these events, you need to handle the events with event handlers.

- A button click event is triggered when you click on a button in a web page.

- You handle a button click event by registering a function to handle the event. You do this by writing a function, and setting the button's onclick property to the function name.

- If a button click event handler is registered, that function will be called when you click on the button.

- You write code in the handler function to respond to the button click event. You can alert the user or update the page or something else.

- To get the text a user has typed into a form input text field, you use the input's value property.

- If a user has not entered anything into a form input text field, the value of the field will be the empty string ("").

- You can compare a variable to the empty string using an if test and ==.

- To add a new element to the DOM, you first need to create the element and then add it as a child of an element.

- Use document.createElement to create a new element. Pass the tag name (e.g., "li") into the function call to indicate what element to create.

- To add an element as a child of a parent element in the DOM, get a reference to the parent, and call appendChild on the parent, passing in the child element you're adding.

- If you add multiple children to a parent by using appendChild, each new child is appended after the other children, so they appear after or below the other children in the page (assuming you're not changing the layout with CSS).

- You can use the Web Storage API (localStorage) to store data in a user's browser.

- We used localStorage to save playlist songs, using Ready Bake Code. You'll learn more about localStorage in Chapter 9.

- You'll learn more about the DOM and JavaScript features like functions and objects in the next chapter.

HTML5cross

Give yourself some time to understand the
interactions between HTML and JavaScript. Think
through how it all works together. While you're
doing that mix it up a little by doing this crossword.
All the words are from this chapter.

Across

2. DOM's method for creating new elements.
3. DOM's method for adding new elements.
5. Happens when the user clicks on a button.
6. The DOM is like a family _____.
7. The grand matriarch of the DOM tree.
9. The default value of a form input element if the user
   doesn't type anything is the _____ string.
10. Used in Ready Bake to enable storage.

Down

1. Code that takes care of events.
2. Insert new elements as a _____.
4. Artist used in our example song.
8. What's ahead? Functions and _____.
9. A button click is an _____.

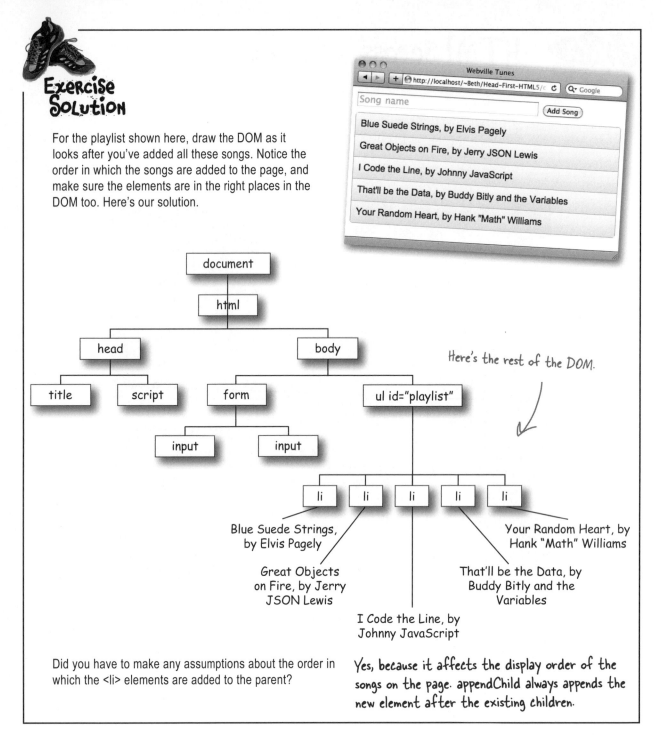

Exercise Solution

For the playlist shown here, draw the DOM as it looks after you've added all these songs. Notice the order in which the songs are added to the page, and make sure the elements are in the right places in the DOM too. Here's our solution.

Here's the rest of the DOM.

Did you have to make any assumptions about the order in which the <li> elements are added to the parent?

Yes, because it affects the display order of the songs on the page. appendChild always appends the new element after the existing children.

HTML5cross Solution

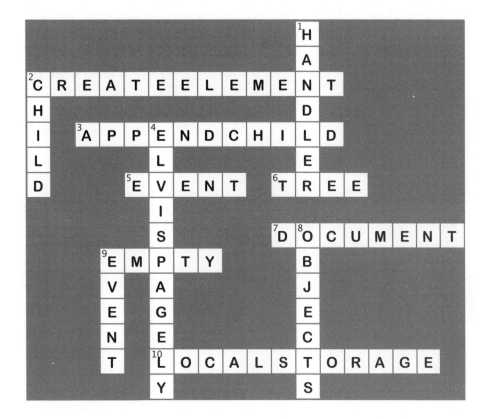

4 javascript functions and objects

Serious JavaScript

Can you call yourself a scripter yet? Probably—you already know your way around a lot of JavaScript. But who wants to be a scripter when you can be a programmer? It's time to get serious and take it up a notch—it's time you learn about **functions** and **objects**. They're the key to writing code that is more powerful, better organized and more maintainable. They're also heavily used across HTML5 JavaScript APIs, so the better you understand them the faster you can jump into a new API and start ruling with it. Strap in, this chapter is going to require your undivided attention...

Expanding your vocabulary

You can already do a lot with JavaScript, let's take a look at some
of the things you know how to do:

> Grab an element from the
> document object model.

```
<script>
  var guessInput = document.getElementById("guess");
  var guess = guessInput.value;
  var answer = null;

  var answers = [ "red",
                  "green",
                  "blue"];

  var index = Math.floor(Math.random() * answers.length);

  if (guess == answers[index]) {
    answer = "You're right! I was thinking of " + answers[index];
  } else {
    answer = "Sorry, I was thinking of " + answers[index];
  }
  alert(answer);
</script>
```

> Get the value of a form
> input text field.

> Create a new array
> filled with strings.

> Use libraries of
> functions.

> Get a property of an
> array, like length.

> Make decisions based
> on conditionals.

> Use the elements
> of an array.

> Use browser
> functions, like alert.

So far, though, a lot of your knowledge is informal—sure, you can get an
element out of the DOM and assign some new HTML to it, but if we asked
you to explain exactly what `document.getElementById` is technically,
well, that might be a little more challenging. No worries; by the time you
leave this chapter you're going to have it down.

Now to get you there, we're not going to start with a deep, technical analysis
of `getElementById`, no no, we're going to do something *a little more
interesting*: We're going to extend JavaScript's vocabulary and make it do
some new things.

How t‹...›

You've bee‹...› .dom, but what if
you wante‹...› ›de like this:

```
var g
var ç
```
```
var
ale›
```

");

↖ We're grabbing the user's
guess just like we were on
the previous page...

the rest of the code on the
‹...›e main code, we'd rather just have a
‹...› we can call that does the same thing.

Crea‹...›

1 ‹...› word and
‹...›ss".

2 Give your function zero or more
parameters. Use parameters to
pass values to your function. We
need just one parameter here:
the user's guess.

```
function checkGuess(guess) {
    var answers = [ "red",
                    "green",
                    "blue"];

    var index = Math.floor(Math.random() * answers.length);

    if (guess == answers[index]) {
        answer = "You're right! I was thinking of " + answers[index];
    } else {
        answer = "Sorry, I was thinking of " + answers[index];
    }
    return answer;
}
```

4 Optionally, return a value
as the result of calling the
function. Here we're returning
a string with a message.

3 Write a body for your function, which
goes between the curly braces. The body
contains all the code that does the work of
the function. For the body here, we'll reuse
our code from the previous page.

How a function works

So how does this all work? What happens when we *actually invoke* a function? Here's the 10,000-foot view:

Okay, first we need a function.

Let's say you've just written your new `bark` function, which has two parameters, `dogName` and `dogWeight`, and also a very impressive bit of code that returns a dog's bark, depending on its weight of course.

Here's our handy bark function.

```
function bark(dogName, dogWeight) {
    if (dogWeight <= 10) {
        return dogName + " says Yip";
    } else {
        return dogName + " says Woof";
    }
}
```

Now let's invoke it!

You know how to call a function already: just use its name and give it any arguments it needs. In this case we need two: a string with the dog's name, and the dog's weight, which is an integer.

Let's make that call and see how this works:

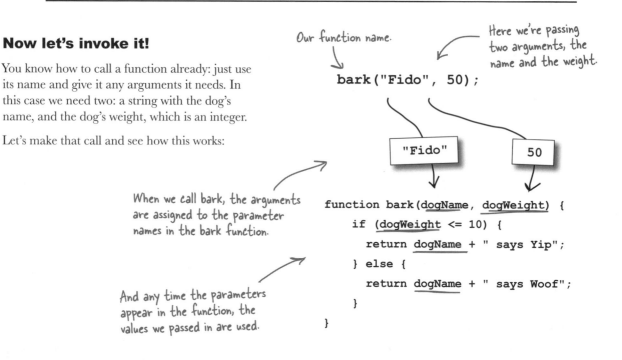

Our function name.

Here we're passing two arguments, the name and the weight.

```
bark("Fido", 50);
```

`"Fido"` `50`

When we call bark, the arguments are assigned to the parameter names in the bark function.

And any time the parameters appear in the function, the values we passed in are used.

```
function bark(dogName, dogWeight) {
    if (dogWeight <= 10) {
        return dogName + " says Yip";
    } else {
        return dogName + " says Woof";
    }
}
```

And, let the body of the function do its work.

After we've assigned the value of each argument to its corresponding parameter in the function—like "Fido" to dogName and the integer 50 to dogWeight—then we're ready to evaluate all the statements in the function body.

Statements are evaluated from top to bottom, just like all the other code you've been writing. What's different is that we're doing it in an environment where the parameter names dogName and dogWeight are assigned to the arguments you passed into the function.

```javascript
function bark(dogName, dogWeight) {
    if (dogWeight <= 10) {
        return dogName + " says Yip";
    } else {
        return dogName + " says Woof";
    }
}
```

Here we evaluate all the code in the body.

Optionally, we can have return statements in the body...

Remember, functions aren't required to return a value. But in this case, the bark function does return a value.

... and that's where we return a value back to the code that makes the call. Let's see how that works:

The string "Fido says Woof" is returned to the calling code (that's the code that invoked the bark function).

And when the string is returned, it is assigned to the variable sound, which is then passed to alert, resulting in the dialog.

Tracing through the function, dogWeight is not less than or equal to 10 so we use the else clause and return "Fido says Woof" as a string value.

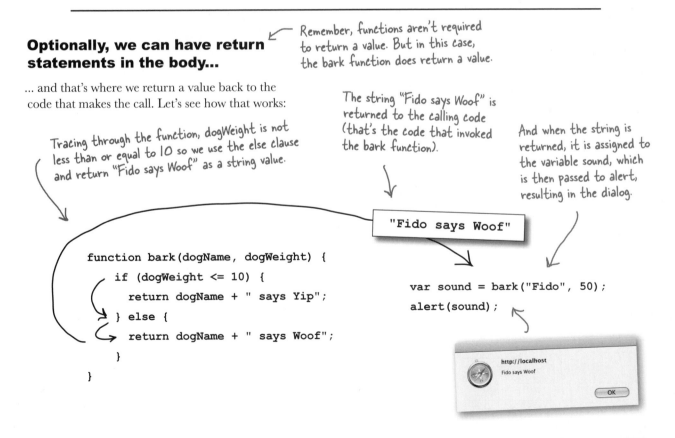

```javascript
function bark(dogName, dogWeight) {
    if (dogWeight <= 10) {
        return dogName + " says Yip";
    } else {
        return dogName + " says Woof";
    }
}
```

`"Fido says Woof"`

```javascript
var sound = bark("Fido", 50);
alert(sound);
```

http://localhost
Fido says Woof

OK

If we could have another moment to talk...

We know, we know, by Chapter 4 you thought you'd be flying in an HTML5 jetpack by now, and we'll get there. But before we do, you really need to understand *the underpinnings* of the HTML5 JavaScript APIs, and we're going to do that in this chapter.

So what are these underpinnings? Think of the HTML5 JavaScript APIs as made up of objects, methods (otherwise known as functions) and properties. And so to really get in and master these APIs, you need to understand those things pretty well. Sure, you could try to get by without knowing them, but you'll always be guessing your way around the APIs while failing to use them fully (not to mention making lots of mistakes and writing buggy code).

So we just wanted to drop you a note before you got too far into this chapter to tell you what we are up to. Here's the great thing: by the end of this chapter you're going to understand objects, functions, methods and a lot of other related things better than about 98% of JavaScript scripters out there. Seriously.

javascript functions and objects

The Function Exposed

This week's interview: a few things you didn't know...

Head First: Welcome Function! We're looking forward to digging in and finding out what you're all about.

Function: Glad to be here.

Head First: Now we've noticed many people who are new to JavaScript don't tend to use you a lot. They just get in and write their code, line by line, top to bottom. Why should they take a look at you?

Function: Yes, and that is unfortunate, because I'm powerful. Think about me like this: I give you a way to take code, write it once, and then reuse it over and over.

Head First: Well, excuse me for saying this, but if you're just giving them the ability to do the same thing, over and over...that's a little boring isn't it?

Function: No no, functions are parameterized— in other words, each time you use the function, you pass it arguments so that you can get back results that vary, depending on what you pass in.

Head First: Err, example?

Function: Let's say you need to tell your users how much the items in their shopping cart are going to cost, so you write a function `computeShoppingCartTotal`. Then you can pass that function different shopping carts belonging to different users and each time you get the appropriate cost of the shopping cart.

...By the way, back to your comment about new coders not using functions; that's simply not true, they use them all the time: `alert`, `document.getElementById`, `Math.random`. They just aren't defining *their own* functions.

Head First: Well, right, `alert`, that makes sense, but the other two don't look quite like functions.

Function: Oh they're functions, you see... hold on just a sec...

...oh, I was just told the readers haven't learned about those kinds of functions yet, but they're getting there in a few pages. Anyway, functions are everywhere.

Head First: So, one thing a function has to do is return a value, right? I mean, what if I don't have a value I want to return?

Function: Many functions return values, but a function doesn't have to. Lots of functions just do something like update the DOM and then return without any value, and that's just fine.

Head First: So in those functions I just don't have a return statement?

Function: You got it.

Head First: Well, what about naming your functions, I've heard you don't have to do that either, if you don't want to.

Function: Okay, let's not freak the audience out too much. How about we come back to that topic after they know a bit more about me?

Head First: As long as you give me an exclusive?

Function: We'll talk...

you are here ▸ 119

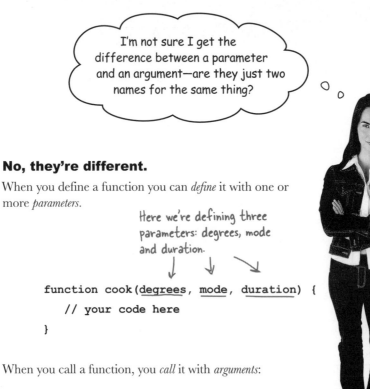

I'm not sure I get the difference between a parameter and an argument—are they just two names for the same thing?

No, they're different.

When you define a function you can *define* it with one or more *parameters*.

Here we're defining three parameters: degrees, mode and duration.

```
function cook(degrees, mode, duration) {
    // your code here
}
```

When you call a function, you *call* it with *arguments*:

```
cook(425.0, "bake", 45);
```

These are arguments. There are three arguments, a floating point number, a string and an integer.

```
cook(350.0, "broil", 10);
```

So you'll only define your parameters once, but you'll probably call your functions with a lot of different arguments.

You'd be amazed how many people get this wrong—even books get it wrong, so if you read it differently elsewhere, now you know better....

You define a function with parameters, you call a function with arguments.

Anatomy of a Function

Now that you know how to define and call a function, let's make sure we've got the syntax down cold. Here are all the parts of a function's anatomy:

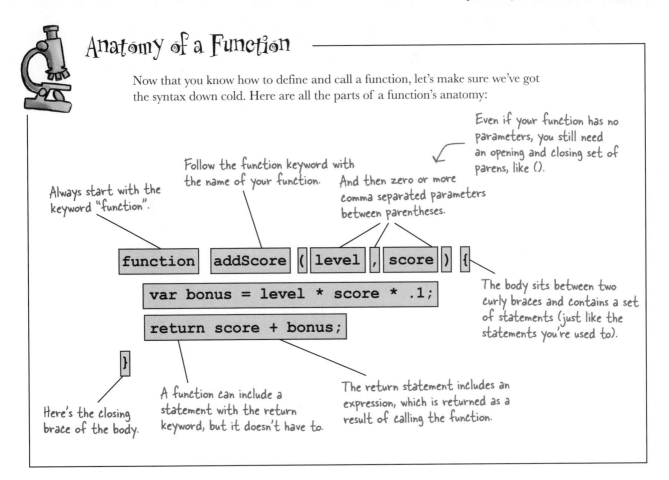

Even if your function has no parameters, you still need an opening and closing set of parens, like ().

Follow the function keyword with the name of your function.

And then zero or more comma separated parameters between parentheses.

Always start with the keyword "function".

```
function addScore ( level , score ) {
    var bonus = level * score * .1;
    return score + bonus;
}
```

The body sits between two curly braces and contains a set of statements (just like the statements you're used to).

Here's the closing brace of the body.

A function can include a statement with the return keyword, but it doesn't have to.

The return statement includes an expression, which is returned as a result of calling the function.

there are no Dumb Questions

Q: Why don't the parameter names have var in front of them? A parameter is a new variable right?

A: Effectively yes. The function does all the work of instantiating the variable for you, so you don't need to supply the var keyword in front of your parameter names.

Q: What are the rules for function names?

A: The rules for naming a function are the same as the rules for naming a variable.

Q: I'm passing a variable to my function—if I change the value of the corresponding parameter in my function does it also change my original variable?

A: No. When you pass a primitive value it is copied into the parameter. We call this "passing by value." So if you change the value of the parameter in your function body it has no affect on our original argument's value. The exception to this is passing an array or object, and we'll get to that in a bit.

Q: So how can I change values in a function?

A: You can only change the values of global variables (those defined outside of functions), or variables you've explicitly defined in your function. We're going to talk about that in a little more detail shortly.

Q: What does a function return if it doesn't have a return statement?

A: A function without a return statement returns undefined.

Sharpen your pencil

Use your knowledge of functions and passing arguments to parameters to evaluate the code below. After you've traced through the code, write the value of each variable below. Check your answers with the solution at the end of the chapter before you go on.

```
function dogsAge(age) {
    return age * 7;
}


var myDogsAge = dogsAge(4);

function rectangleArea(width, height) {
    var area = width * height;
    return area;
}

var rectArea = rectangleArea(3, 4);

function addUp(numArray) {
    var total = 0;
    for (var i = 0; i < numArray.length; i++) {
        total += numArray[i];
    }
    return total;
}

var theTotal = addUp([1, 5, 3, 9]);

function getAvatar(points) {
    var avatar;
    if (points < 100) {
        avatar = "Mouse";
    } else if (points > 100 && points < 1000) {
        avatar = "Cat";
    } else {
        avatar = "Ape";
    }
    return avatar;
}
var myAvatar = getAvatar(335);
```

Write the value of each variable here...

myDogsAge = ...

rectArea = ...

theTotal = ...

myAvatar = ...

We need to talk about your variable usage...

Local and Global Variables
Know the difference or risk humiliation

You already know that you can declare a variable by using the `var` keyword and a name anywhere in your script:

```
var avatar;
var levelThreshold = 1000;
```

These are global variables; they're accessible everywhere in your JavaScript code.

And you've seen that you can also declare variables inside a function:

```
function getScore(points) {
    var score;

    for (var i = 0; i < levelThreshold; i++) {
        //code here
    }

    return score;
}
```

The points, score and i variables are all declared within a function.

We call them local variables because they are only known locally within the function itself.

Even if we use levelThreshold inside the function, it's global because it's <u>declared</u> outside the function.

But what does it matter? Variables are variables, right? Well, *where* you declare your variables determines *how visible* they are to other part of your code, and, later, understanding how these two kinds of variables operate will help you write more maintainable code (not to mention, help you understand the code of others).

> If a variable is declared outside a function, it's GLOBAL. If it's declared inside a function, it's LOCAL.

Knowing the scope of your local and global variables

Where you define your variables determines their *scope*; that is, where they are defined and where they aren't, where they're visible to your code and where they aren't. Let's look at an example of both locally and globally scoped variables—remember, the variables you define outside a function are globally scoped, and the function variables are locally scoped:

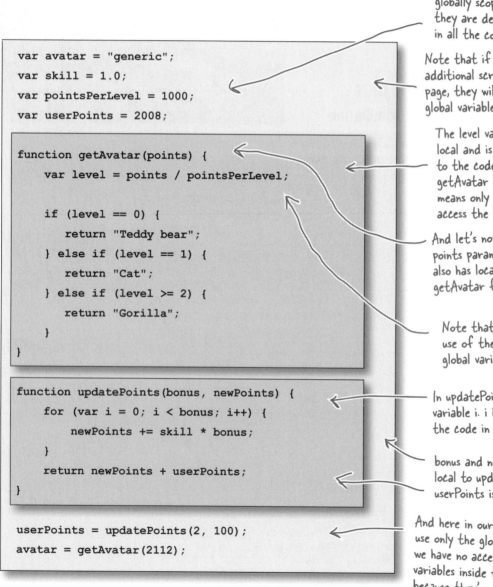

```
var avatar = "generic";
var skill = 1.0;
var pointsPerLevel = 1000;
var userPoints = 2008;

function getAvatar(points) {
    var level = points / pointsPerLevel;

    if (level == 0) {
        return "Teddy bear";
    } else if (level == 1) {
        return "Cat";
    } else if (level >= 2) {
        return "Gorilla";
    }
}

function updatePoints(bonus, newPoints) {
    for (var i = 0; i < bonus; i++) {
        newPoints += skill * bonus;
    }
    return newPoints + userPoints;
}

userPoints = updatePoints(2, 100);
avatar = getAvatar(2112);
```

These four variables are globally scoped. That means they are defined and visible in all the code below.

Note that if you link to additional scripts in your page, they will see these global variables too!

The level variable here is local and is visible only to the code within the getAvatar function. That means only this function can access the level variable.

And let's not forget the points parameter, which also has local scope in the getAvatar function.

Note that getAvatar makes use of the pointsPerLevel global variable too.

In updatePoints we have a local variable i. i is visible to all of the code in updatePoints.

bonus and newPoints are also local to updatePoints, while userPoints is global.

And here in our code we can use only the global variables, we have no access to any variables inside the functions because they're not visible in the global scope.

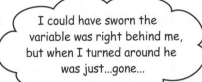

> I could have sworn the variable was right behind me, but when I turned around he was just...gone...

The short lives of variables

When you're a variable, you work hard and life can be short. That is, unless you're a global variable, but even with globals, life has its limits. But what determines the life of a variable? Think about it like this:

Globals live as long as the page. A global variable begins life when its JavaScript is loaded into the page. But, your global variable's life ends when the page goes away. Even if you reload the same page, all your global variables are destroyed and then recreated in the newly loaded page.

Local variables typically disappear when your function ends. Local variables are created when your function is first called and live until the function returns (with a value or not). That said, you can take the values of your local variables and return them from the function before the variables meet their digital maker.

So, there really is NO escape from the page is there? If you're a local variable, your life comes and goes quickly, and if you're lucky enough to be a global, you're good as long as that browser doesn't reload the page.

But there just *has* to be a way to escape the page! We can find a way! Can't we?

We say "typically" because there are some advanced ways to retain locals a little longer, but we're not going to worry about them now.

Join us in the Web Storage chapter where we'll help our data escape the dreaded page refresh!

> What happens when I name a local variable the same thing as an existing global variable?

You "shadow" your global.

Here's what that means: say you have a global variable **beanCounter** and you then declare a function, like this:

```
var beanCounter = 10;


function getNumberOfItems(ordertype) {
    var beanCounter = 0;
    if (ordertype == "order") {
        // do some stuff with beanCounter...
    }
    return beanCounter;
}
```

We've got a global and a local!

When you do this, any references to **beanCounter** within the function refer to the local variable and not the global. So we say the global variable is in the shadow of the local variable (in other words we can't see it because the local version is in our way).

Note that the local and global variables have no effect on each other: if you change one, it has no effect on the other. They are independent variables.

there are no
Dumb Questions

Q: Keeping track of the scope of all these locals and globals is confusing, so why not just stick to globals? That's what I've always done.

A: If you're writing code that is complex or that needs to be maintained over a long period of time, then you really have to watch how you manage your variables. When you're overzealous in creating global variables, it becomes difficult to track where your variables are being used (and where you're making changes to your variables' values), and that can lead to buggy code. All this becomes even more important when you're writing code with coworkers or you're using third-party libraries (although if those libraries are written well, they should be structured to avoid these issues).

So, use globals where it makes sense, but use them in moderation, and whenever possible, make your variables local. As you get more experience with JavaScript, you can investigate additional techniques to structure code so that it's more maintainable.

Q: I have global variables in my page, but I'm loading in other JavaScript files as well. Do those files have separate sets of global variables?

A: There is only one global scope so every file you load sees the same set of variables (and creates globals in the same space). That's why it is so important you be careful with your use of variables to avoid clashes (and reduce or eliminate global variables when you can).

Q: I've seen code where people don't use the var keyword when assigning a value to a new variable name. How does that work?

A: Yes, that can be done; when you assign a value to a variable name that hasn't been previously declared, it is treated as a new, global variable. So be careful, if you do this within a function you are creating a global variable. Note that we don't recommend this coding practice; not only is it potentially confusing when reading code, some

people think this behavior may change some day in the JavaScript implementations (which would probably break your code).

Q: Do I need to define a function before I use it, or can it appear anywhere in my script?

A: Function declarations can appear anywhere in your script. You can declare a function below where you use it if you want. This works because when you first load your page, the browser parses all the JavaScript in the page (or in the external file) and sees the function declaration before it starts executing the code. You can also put your global variable declarations anywhere in your script, although we recommend declaring all your global variables at the top of your files so they're easy to locate.

One thing to keep in mind when using more than one external JavaScript file is that if you have two functions in different files named the same thing, the function that the browser sees last will be the one that is used.

Q: Everyone seems to complain about the overuse of global variables in JavaScript. Why is this? Was the language badly designed or do people not know what they're doing, or what? And what do we do about it?

A: Globals are often overused in JavaScript. Some of this is because the language makes it easy to just jump in and start coding—and that's a good thing—because JavaScript doesn't enforce a lot of structure or overhead on you. The downside is when people write serious code this way and it has to be changed and maintained over the long term (and that pretty much describes all web pages). All that said, JavaScript is a powerful langauge and includes features like objects that you can use to organize your code in a modular way. Many books have been written on that topic alone, and we're going to give you just a taste of objects in the second half of this chapter (which is only a few pages away).

If this were a book on in-depth JavaScript programming we'd take you further into this topic, but given that this is Head First HTML5 Programming, we'll just suggest you explore this topic further to improve the quality of your code!

Oh, did we mention functions are also values?

OK, you've used variables to store numbers, boolean values, strings, arrays, all kinds of things, but did we mention you can also assign a function to a variable? Check this out:

```
function addOne(num) {
    return num + 1;
}
```
Let's define a simple function that adds one to its argument.

```
var plusOne = addOne;
```
Now let's do something new. We'll use the name of the function addOne and assign addOne to a new variable, plusOne.

Notice we're not calling the function with addOne(), we're just using the function name.

```
var result = plusOne(1);
```
plusOne is assigned to a function, so we can call it with an integer argument of 1.

After this call result is equal to 2.

Well, not only did we fail to mention this little detail about functions before now, but we also weren't totally honest when we told you about the anatomy of a function—as it turns out, you don't even have to give your function a name. That's right: your function can be *anonymous*. What the heck does that mean, and why would you want to do such a thing? First let's see how you create a function without a name:

```
function(num) {
    return num + 1;
}
```
Here we're creating a function and not using a name... hmm... but how do we do anything with it?

Let's do it again and this time assign it to a variable.

```
var f = function(num) {
    return num + 1;
}
var result = f(1);
alert(result);
```
And then we can use that variable to call the function.

After this call result is equal to 2.

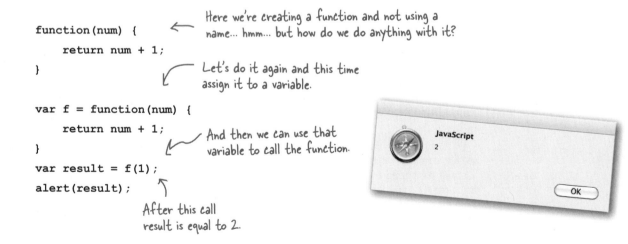

JavaScript

2

OK

BRAIN POWER

Take a look at this code: what do you think is going on?

> This should start to look a little more understandable with what we just covered...

```
var element = document.getElementById("button");
element.onclick = function () {
    alert("clicked!");
}
```

> Don't worry if you're still not getting 100% of it, we'll get there...

What you can do with functions as values?

So what's the big deal? Why is this useful? Well, the important thing isn't so much that we can assign a function to a variable, that's just our way of showing you that a function *actually is a value.* And you know you can store values in variables or arrays, you can pass them as arguments to functions, or as we'll soon see, you can assign them to the properties of objects. But, rather than talking you through how anonymous functions are useful, let's just look at one of the many ways using functions as values starts to get interesting:

> Here's a simple init function.

```
function init() {
    alert("you rule!");
}
window.onload = init;
```

> Here we're assigning the function we defined to the onload handler.

> Hey look, we were already using functions as values!

Or we could get even fancier:

> So here we're creating a function, without an explicit name, and then assigning its value to the window.onload property directly.

```
window.onload = function() {
    alert("you rule!");
}
```

> Don't worry if window.onload is still a little unclear, we're just about to cover all that.

> Wow, isn't that simpler and more readable?

You might be starting to see that functions can do some useful things beyond just packaging up code for reuse; to give you a better idea of how to fully take advantage of functions, we're going to take a look at objects and see how they fit into JavaScript, and then we'll put it all together.

Authors? Hello?
Hello? I'm the girl who bought the HTML5 book, remember me? What does all this have to do with HTML5???

Well we thought we'd covered that already... but if it looks like we've picked you up and have driven you halfway around the city with the meter running (when we could have driven you straight downtown), well, then remember we're about to start diving into the APIs that work with HTML5 *in the next chapter*. And, doing that is going to require that you *really understand* functions, objects and a few other related topics.

So hang in there—in fact you're halfway there! And don't forget, this is the chapter where you're going from scripter to programmer, from an HTML/CSS jockey to someone who is capable of building real apps.

Did we already mention that is probably going to make you a lot more money too?

With objects, the future's so bright we really DO have to wear shades...

Did someone say "Objects"?!

Ah, our favorite topic! Objects are going to take your JavaScript programming skills to the next level—they're the key to managing complex code, to understanding the DOM, to organizing your data, and they're even the fundamental way HTML5 JavaScript APIs are packaged up (and that's just our short list!). That said, objects are a difficult topic, right? Hah! We're going to just jump in head first and you'll be using them in no time.

Here's the secret to JavaScript objects: they're just a collection of properties. Let's take an example, say, a dog. A dog's got properties:

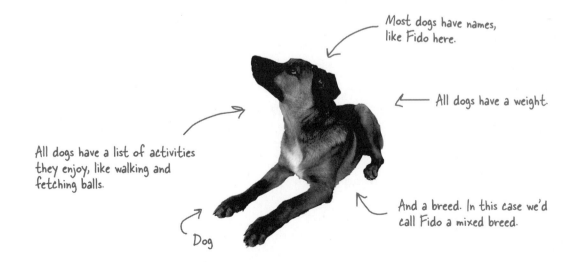

Most dogs have names, like Fido here.

All dogs have a weight.

All dogs have a list of activities they enjoy, like walking and fetching balls.

And a breed. In this case we'd call Fido a mixed breed.

Dog

Thinking about properties...

Of course Fido would be the first to admit there's a lot more to him than just a few properties, but for this example, those are going to be the ones we need to capture in software. Let's think about those properties in terms of JavaScript data types:

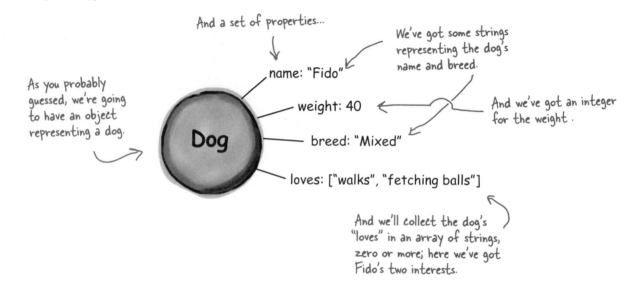

And a set of properties...

We've got some strings representing the dog's name and breed.

name: "Fido"

weight: 40

And we've got an integer for the weight.

As you probably guessed, we're going to have an object representing a dog.

Dog

breed: "Mixed"

loves: ["walks", "fetching balls"]

And we'll collect the dog's "loves" in an array of strings, zero or more; here we've got Fido's two interests.

How to create an object in JavaScript

So we've got a object with some properties; how do we create this using JavaScript? Here's how:

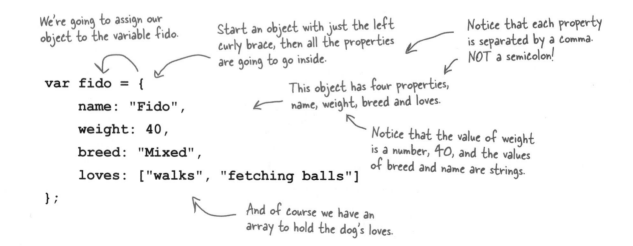

We're going to assign our object to the variable fido.

Start an object with just the left curly brace, then all the properties are going to go inside.

Notice that each property is separated by a comma. NOT a semicolon!

```
var fido = {
    name: "Fido",
    weight: 40,
    breed: "Mixed",
    loves: ["walks", "fetching balls"]
};
```

This object has four properties, name, weight, breed and loves.

Notice that the value of weight is a number, 40, and the values of breed and name are strings.

And of course we have an array to hold the dog's loves.

Some things you can do with objects

1 Access object properties with "dot" notation:

```
if (fido.weight > 25) {
    alert("WOOF");
} else {
    alert("yip");
}
```

Use the object along with a "." and a property name to access the value of that property.

Use a "."

fido.weight

Here's the object...

... and then the property name.

2 Access properties using a string with [] notation:

```
var breed = fido["breed"];
if (breed == "mixed") {
    alert("Best in show");
}
```

Use the object along with the property name wrapped in quotes and in brackets to access the value of that property.

Now we use [ ] around the property name.

fido["weight"]

Here's the object...

... and the property name in quotes.

We find dot notation the more readable of the two.

3 Change a property's value:

We're changing Fido's weight...

```
fido.weight = 27;
fido.breed = "Chawalla/Great Dane mix";
fido.loves.push("chewing bones");
```

... his breed...

... and adding a new item to his loves array.

push simply adds a new item to the end of an array.

4 Enumerate all an object's properties:

To enumerate is to go through all the properties of the object.

```
var prop;
for (prop in fido) {
    alert("Fido has a " + prop + " property ");
    if (prop == "name") {
        alert("This is " + fido[prop]);
    }
}
```

To enumerate the properties we use a for-in loop.

Each time through the loop, the variable prop gets the string value of the next property name.

And we use the [ ] notation to access the value of that property.

Note the order of the properties is arbitrary, so don't count on a particular ordering.

5 Have fun with an object's array:

```
var likes = fido.loves;
var likesString = "Fido likes";

for (var i = 0; i < likes.length; i++) {
    likesString += " " + likes[i];
}
alert(likesString);
```

Here, we're assigning the value of fido's loves array to the variable likes.

We can loop through the likes array and create a likesString of all fido's interests.

And we can alert the string.

6 Pass an object to a function:

```
function bark(dog) {
    if (dog.weight > 25) {
        alert("WOOF");
    } else {
        alert("yip");
    }
}

bark(fido);
```

We can pass an object to a function just like any other variable.

And in the function, we can access the object's properties like normal, using the parameter name for the object, of course.

We're passing fido as our argument to the function bark, which expects a dog object.

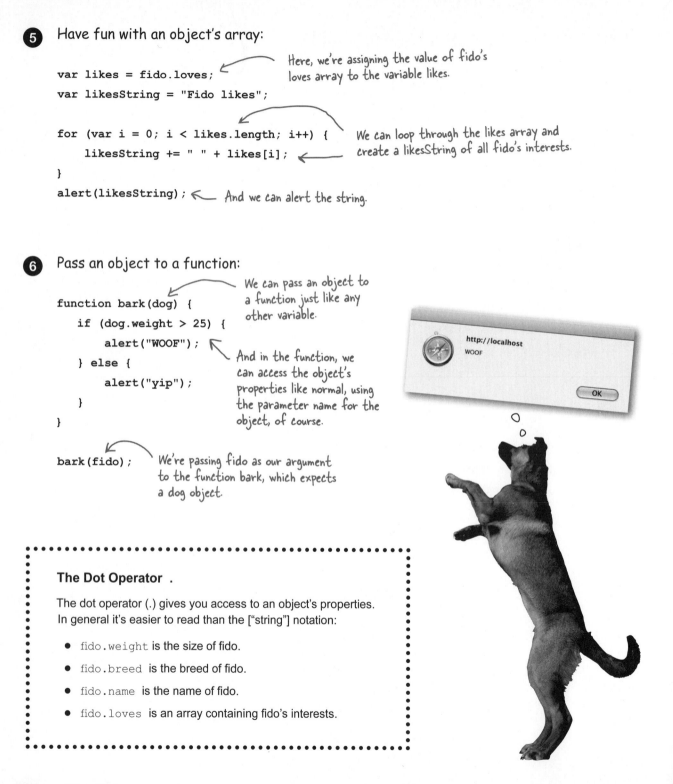

http://localhost
WOOF

OK

The Dot Operator .

The dot operator (.) gives you access to an object's properties. In general it's easier to read than the ["string"] notation:

- `fido.weight` is the size of fido.

- `fido.breed` is the breed of fido.

- `fido.name` is the name of fido.

- `fido.loves` is an array containing fido's interests.

Can we add properties to objects after we've defined them?

Yes, you can add or delete properties at any time.

To add a property to an object you simply assign a new property a value, like this:

```
fido.age = 5;
```

and from that point on `fido` will have a new property: `age`.

Likewise, you can delete any property with the `delete` keyword, like this:

```
delete fido.age;
```

When you delete a property, you're not just deleting the value of the property, you're deleting the property itself. In fact, if you use `fido.age` after deleting it, it will evaluate to `undefined`.

The `delete` expression returns `true` if the property was deleted successfully (or if you delete a property that doesn't exist or if what you're trying to delete isn't a property of an object).

Let's talk about passing objects to functions

We've already talked a bit about how arguments are passed to functions—arguments are passed *by value*, so if we pass an integer, the corresponding function parameter gets a *copy* of the *value* of that integer for its use in the function. The same rules hold true for objects, *however* we've got to look a little more closely at what a variable holds when it is assigned to an object to know what this means.

When an object is assigned to a variable, that variable holds a *reference* to the object, not the object itself. Think of a reference as a pointer to the object.

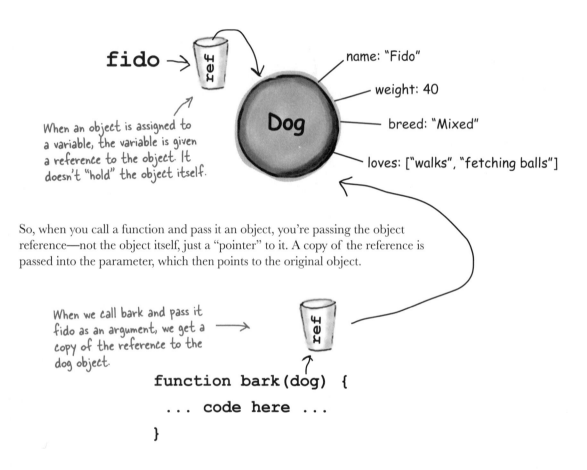

fido →

When an object is assigned to a variable, the variable is given a reference to the object. It doesn't "hold" the object itself.

Dog

name: "Fido"

weight: 40

breed: "Mixed"

loves: ["walks", "fetching balls"]

So, when you call a function and pass it an object, you're passing the object reference—not the object itself, just a "pointer" to it. A copy of the reference is passed into the parameter, which then points to the original object.

When we call bark and pass it fido as an argument, we get a copy of the reference to the dog object.

```
function bark(dog) {
    ... code here ...
}
```

So, what does this all mean? Well, when you change a property of the object, you're changing the property in the *original* object, not a copy, and so, you'll see all the changes you make to an object within and outside of your function. Let's step through an example using a loseWeight function for dogs...

Putting Fido on a diet....

Let's take a look at what's going on when we pass `fido` to `loseWeight`
and change the `dog.weight` property.

1 We've defined an object, fido, and we are passing
that object into a function, loseWeight.

*fido is a reference to an
object, which means the
object doesn't live in the fido
variable, but is pointed to by
the fido variable.*

name: "Fido"

weight: 48

Dog

breed: "Mixed"

loves: ["walks", "fetching balls"]

```
fido.weight = 48;
...
loseWeight(fido);
```

*When we pass fido
to a function, we are
passing the reference
to the object.*

2 The dog parameter of the loseWeight function
gets a copy of the reference to fido. And so, any
changes to the properties of the parameter affect
the object that was passed in.

*When we pass fido into loseWeight, what gets
assigned to the dog parameter is a copy of
the reference, not a copy of the object. So
fido and dog point to the same object.*

*The dog reference
is a copy of the
fido reference.*

ref

http://localhost
Fido now weighs 38

OK

```
function loseWeight(dog) {
    dog.weight = dog.weight - 10;
}

alert(fido.name + " now weighs " + fido.weight);
```

*So, when we subtract 10 pounds
from dog.weight, we're changing
the value of fido.weight.*

NOW SHOWING AT THE WEBVILLE CINEMA

The Webville Cinema has come to us for help with their JavaScript API; let's start simple and design the movie object for them. What we need is a couple of movie objects that each include a title, a genre, a movie rating (1-5 stars) and a set of showtimes. Go ahead and sketch out your movie object design here (you can use our dog object as a model). Here's some sample data you can use to populate your objects:

Plan 9 from Outer Space, which shows at 3:00pm, 7:00pm and 11:00pm; it's in the genre "cult classic"; and has a 2-star rating.

Forbidden Planet, which shows at 5:00pm and 9:00pm; is in the genre "classic sci-fi"; and has a 5-star rating.

The solution's right on the next page, but don't look until you've done the exercise. Really. We mean it.

Feel free to add your own favorites instead.

Design your objects here.

NOW SHOWING AT THE WEBVILLE CINEMA SOLUTION

How did it go creating your movie object?

Here's our solution:

We created two objects, movie1 and movie2 for the two movies.

movie1 has four properties, title, genre, rating and showtimes.

```
var movie1 = {
    title: "Plan 9 from Outer Space",
    genre: "Cult Classic",
    rating: 5,
    showtimes: ["3:00pm", "7:00pm", "11:00pm"]
};
```

title and genre are strings.

rating is a number.

And showtimes is an array containing the show times of the movie as strings.

movie2 also has four properties, title, genre, rating and showtimes.

```
var movie2 = {
    title: "Forbidden Planet",
    genre: "Classic Sci-fi",
    rating: 5,
    showtimes: ["5:00pm", "9:00pm"]
};
```

Remember to separate your properties with commas.

We use the same property names but different property values as movie1.

Our next showing is at....

We've already had a small taste of mixing objects and functions. Let's take this further by writing some code to tell us when the next showing of a movie is. Our function's going to take a movie as an argument, and return a string containing the next time it plays, based on your current time.

Here's our new function, which takes a movie object.

We're grabbing the current time using JavaScript's Date object. We're not going to worry about the details of this one yet, but just know that it returns the current time in milliseconds.

```javascript
function getNextShowing(movie) {
    var now = new Date().getTime();

    for (var i = 0; i < movie.showtimes.length; i++) {
        var showtime = getTimeFromString(movie.showtimes[i]);
        if ((showtime - now) > 0) {
            return "Next showing of " + movie.title + " is " + movie.showtimes[i];
        }
    }
    return null;
}
```

Now use the movie's array, showtimes, and iterate over the showtimes.

For each showtime we get its time in milliseconds and then compare.

If the time hasn't happened yet, then it's the next showing, so return it.

If there are no more shows, we just return null;

```javascript
function getTimeFromString(timeString) {
    var theTime = new Date();
    var time = timeString.match(/(\d+)(?::(\d\d))?\s*(p?)/);
    theTime.setHours( parseInt(time[1]) + (time[3] ? 12 : 0) );
    theTime.setMinutes( parseInt(time[2]) || 0 );
    return theTime.getTime();
}
```

Ready Bake Code

Here's some ready bake code that just takes a string with the format like 1am or 3pm and converts it to a time in milliseconds.

Don't worry about this code; it uses regular expressions, which you'll learn later in your JavaScript education. For now, just go with it!

```javascript
var nextShowing = getNextShowing(movie1);
alert(nextShowing);
nextShowing = getNextShowing(movie2);
alert(nextShowing);
```

Now we use the function by calling getNextShowing and use the string it returns in an alert.

And let's do it again with movie2.

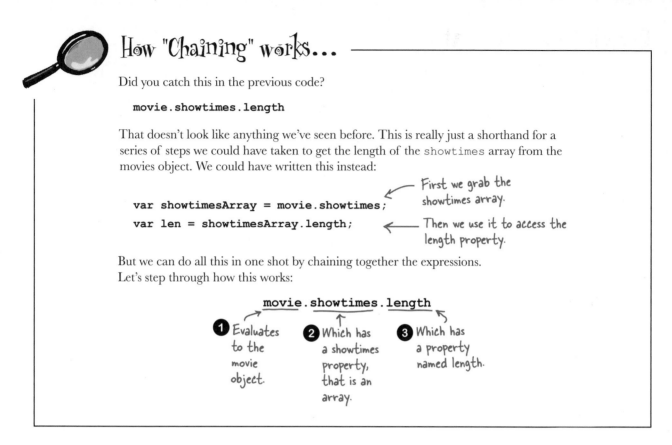

How "Chaining" works...

Did you catch this in the previous code?

```
movie.showtimes.length
```

That doesn't look like anything we've seen before. This is really just a shorthand for a series of steps we could have taken to get the length of the `showtimes` array from the movies object. We could have written this instead:

```
var showtimesArray = movie.showtimes;
var len = showtimesArray.length;
```

First we grab the showtimes array.

Then we use it to access the length property.

But we can do all this in one shot by chaining together the expressions. Let's step through how this works:

```
movie.showtimes.length
```

1 Evaluates to the movie object.

2 Which has a showtimes property, that is an array.

3 Which has a property named length.

Testing at the drive-in

Get the code on the previous page typed in and let's give it a test run. You'll see that the `getNextShowing` function takes whatever movie it is handed and figures out the next showing time. Feel free to create some new movie objects of your own and give them a test drive too. We did, at our own local time of 12:30pm:

```
var banzaiMovie = {
    title: "Buckaroo Banzai",
    genre: "Cult classic",
    rating: 5,
    showtimes: ["1:00pm", "5:00pm", "7:00pm"]
}

var nextShowing = getNextShowing(banzaiMovie);
alert(nextShowing);
```

> **http://localhost**
> Next showing of Buckaroo Banzai is 1:00pm
>
> [OK]

Note: our code isn't quite "production code" quality; if you run it after the last movie showing you'll get null. Try again the next day. ☺

Objects can have behavior too...

You didn't think objects were just for storing numbers, strings and arrays did you? Objects are active, they can do things. Dogs don't just sit there: they bark, run, play catch and a dog object should too! Given everything you've learned in this chapter, you're all set to add behavior to your objects. Here's how we do that:

```
var fido = {
    name: "Fido",
    weight: 40,
    breed: "Mixed",
    loves: ["walks", "fetching balls"]
    bark: function() {
        alert("Woof woof!");
    }
};
```

← We can add a function directly to our object like this.

↑ Rather than saying this is a "function in the object," we just say this is a method. They're the same thing, but everyone refers to object functions as methods.

↖ Notice we're making use of an anonymous function and assigning it to the bark property of the object.

When an object has a function in it, we say that object has a method.

To call a method on a object we use the object name along with the method using our dot notation, and supply any arguments needed.

fido.bark();

We tell an object to do something by calling methods on it. In this case we're calling fido's bark method.

Meanwhile back at Webville Cinema...

Now that your knowledge of objects is expanding we can go back and
improve the cinema code. We've already written a `getNextShowing`
function that takes a movie as an argument, but we could instead make this
part of the movie object by making it a method. Let's do that:

```
var movie1 = {
    title: "Plan 9 from Outer Space",
    genre: "Cult Classic",
    rating: 5,
    showtimes: ["3:00pm", "7:00pm", "11:00pm"],

    getNextShowing: function(movie) {
        var now = new Date().getTime();

        for (var i = 0; i < movie.showtimes.length; i++) {
            var showtime = getTimeFromString(movie.showtimes[i]);
            if ((showtime - now) > 0) {
                return "Next showing of " + movie.title + " is " + movie.showtimes[i];
            }
        }
        return null;
    }
};
```

We've taken our code and placed it in a
method of the movie1 object with the
property name getNextShowing.

But we know that can't be quite right...

We actually can't just throw the function in this object because
`getNextShowing` takes a movie argument, and what we really want is to call
`getNextShowing` like this:

```
var nextShowing = movie1.getNextShowing();
```

No argument should be needed here, it's clear which movie
we want the next showing of, that is, we want movie1.

Alright, so how do we fix this? We've got to remove the parameter from the
`getNextShowing` method definition, but then we need to do something with all
the references to `movie.showtimes` in the code because, once we remove the
parameter, `movie` will no longer exist as a variable. Let's take a look...

Let's get the movie parameter out of there...

We've taken the liberty of removing the `movie` parameter, and all the references to it. Which leaves us with this code:

```
var movie1 = {
    title: "Plan 9 from Outer Space",
    genre: "Cult Classic",
    rating: 5,
    showtimes: ["3:00pm", "7:00pm", "11:00pm"],

    getNextShowing: function() {
        var now = new Date().getTime();

        for (var i = 0; i < showtimes.length; i++) {
            var showtime = getTimeFromString(showtimes[i]);
            if ((showtime - now) > 0) {
                return "Next showing of " + title + " is " + showtimes[i];
            }
        }
        return null;
    }
};
```

We've highlighted the changes below...

This all looks pretty reasonable, but we need to think through how the getNextShowing method will use the showtimes property...

...we're used to either local variables (which showtimes isn't) and global variables (which showtimes isn't). Hmmmm....

Oh, and here's another one, the title property.

Now what?

Alright, here's the conundrum: we've got these references to the properties `showtimes` and `title`. Normally in a function we're referencing a local variable, a global variable, or a parameter of the function, but `showtimes` and `title` are *properties* of the `movie1` object. Well maybe this just works... it seems like JavaScript might be smart enough to figure this out?

Nope. It doesn't work. Feel free to give it a test drive; JavaScript will tell you the showtimes and title variables are undefined. How can that be?

Okay, here's the deal: these variables are properties of an object, but we aren't telling JavaScript which object. You might say to yourself, "Well, obviously we mean THIS object, this one right here! How could there be any confusion about that?" And, yes, we want the properties of this very object. In fact, there's a keyword in JavaScript named `this`, and that is exactly how you tell JavaScript you mean *this object we're in*.

Now, the situation is actually a little more complicated than it appears here, and we're going to get to that in a second, but for now we're going to add the `this` keyword and get this code working.

Adding the "this" keyword

Let's add `this` each place we specify a property, so that we're telling JavaScript we want the property in *this* object:

```
var movie1 = {
    title: "Plan 9 from Outer Space",
    genre: "Cult Classic",
    rating: 5,
    showtimes: ["3:00pm", "7:00pm", "11:00pm"],

    getNextShowing: function() {
        var now = new Date().getTime();

        for (var i = 0; i < this.showtimes.length; i++) {
            var showtime = getTimeFromString(this.showtimes[i]);
            if ((showtime - now) > 0) {
                return "Next showing of " + this.title + " is " + this.showtimes[i];
            }
        }
        return null;
    }
};
```

Here we've added a `this` keyword before every property to signify we want the movie1 object reference.

A test drive with "this"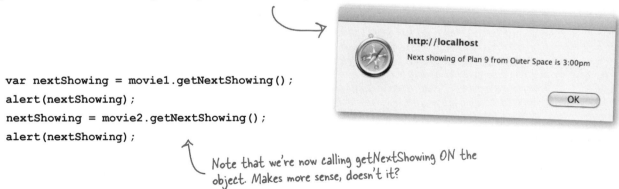

Go ahead and type in the code above and also add the `getNextShowing` function to your `movie2` object (just copy and paste it in). Then make the changes below to your previous test code. After that give it a spin! Here's what we got:

```
var nextShowing = movie1.getNextShowing();
alert(nextShowing);
nextShowing = movie2.getNextShowing();
alert(nextShowing);
```

> **http://localhost**
> Next showing of Plan 9 from Outer Space is 3:00pm
>
> [OK]

Note that we're now calling getNextShowing ON the object. Makes more sense, doesn't it?

It seems like we're duplicating code with all the copying and pasting of the getNextShowing method. Isn't there a better way?

Ah, good eye.

You have great instincts if you recognized that we are duplicating code when we copy `getNextShowing` into more than one movie object. One of the aims of "object-oriented" programming is to maximize code reuse—here we're not reusing any code, in fact we're creating every object as a one-off, and our movie objects just happen to be the same by convention (and copying and pasting!). Not only is that a waste, it can be error prone.

There's a much better way to do this using a *constructor*. What's a constructor? It's just a special function we're going to write that can create objects for us, and make them all the same. Think of it like a little factory that takes the property values you want to set in your object, and then hands you back a nice new object with all the right properties and methods.

Let's create a constructor...

How to create a constructor

Let's make a constructor for dogs. We already know what we want our dog objects to look like: they have name, breed and weight properties, and they have a bark method. So what our constructor needs to do is take the property values as parameters and then hand us back a dog object all ready to bark. Here's the code:

A constructor function looks a lot like a regular function. But by convention, we give the name of the function a capital letter.

The parameters of the constructor take values for the properties we want our object to have.

The property names and parameter names don't have to be the same, but they often are—again, by convention.

Here, we're initializing the properties of the object to the values that were passed to the constructor.

We can include the bark method in the object we're constructing by initializing the bark property to a function value, just like we've been doing.

We need to use "this.weight" and "this.name" in the method to refer to the properties in the object, just as we have before.

```javascript
function Dog(name, breed, weight) {
    this.name = name;
    this.breed = breed;
    this.weight = weight;
    this.bark = function() {
        if (this.weight > 25) {
            alert(this.name + " says Woof!");
        } else {
            alert(this.name + " says Yip!");
        }
    };
}
```

Notice how the syntax differs from object syntax. These are statements, so we need to end each one with a ";" just like we normally do in a function.

So let's walk though this again to make sure we've got it. Dog is a constructor function and it takes a set of arguments, which just happen to be the initial values for the properties we want: name, breed and weight. Once it has those values, it assigns properties using the `this` keyword. It also defines our bark method. The result of all this? The Dog constructor returns an new object. Let's see how to actually use the constructor.

> Don't worry about building all those objects yourself; we'll construct them for you.

Now let's use our constructor

Now that we've got our factory built, we can use it to create some dogs. There's only one thing we haven't told you, which is that you need to call a constructor function in a special way by putting the keyword new before the call. Here are some examples:

To create a dog, we use the new keyword with the constructor.

And then call it just like any function.

```
var fido = new Dog("Fido", "Mixed", 38);

var tiny = new Dog("Tiny", "Chawalla", 8);

var clifford = new Dog("Clifford", "Bloodhound", 65);
```

We're creating three different Dog objects by passing in different arguments to customize each dog.

```
fido.bark();

tiny.bark();

clifford.bark();
```

Once we've got the objects, we can call their bark methods to make each Dog bark.

Let's review what's going on here one more time: we're creating three different dog objects, each with its own properties, using the new keyword with the Dog constructor that we created. The constructor returns a Dog object customized with the arguments we passed in.

Next, we call the bark method on each one—notice that we're sharing the same bark method across all dogs, and when each dog barks, this points to the dog object that made the call. So if we call the bark method on fido, then, in the bark method, this is set to the fido object. Let's look a little closer at how that happens.

http://localhost
Fido says Woof!

http://localhost
Tiny says Yip!

http://localhost
Clifford says Woof!

OK

How does this **really work?**

Anytime we put this in the code of a method it will be interpreted as a reference to the object the method was called on. So, if we call fido.bark, then this is going to reference fido. Or, if we call it on our dog object tiny then this is going to reference tiny within that method call. How does this know which object it is representing? Let's see:

① Let's say we've got a dog object assigned to fido:

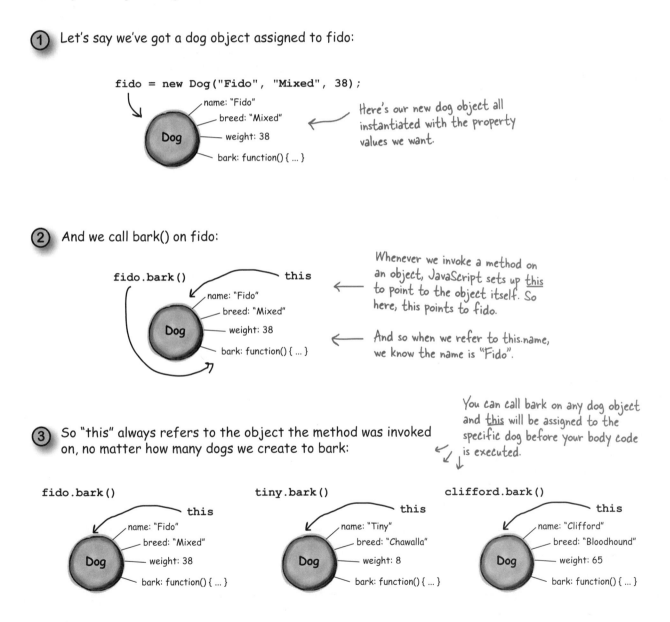

fido = new Dog("Fido", "Mixed", 38);

name: "Fido"
breed: "Mixed"
Dog
weight: 38
bark: function() { ... }

Here's our new dog object all instantiated with the property values we want.

② And we call bark() on fido:

fido.bark()   this

name: "Fido"
breed: "Mixed"
Dog
weight: 38
bark: function() { ... }

Whenever we invoke a method on an object, JavaScript sets up this to point to the object itself. So here, this points to fido.

And so when we refer to this.name, we know the name is "Fido".

You can call bark on any dog object and this will be assigned to the specific dog before your body code is executed.

③ So "this" always refers to the object the method was invoked on, no matter how many dogs we create to bark:

fido.bark()   this

name: "Fido"
breed: "Mixed"
Dog
weight: 38
bark: function() { ... }

tiny.bark()   this

name: "Tiny"
breed: "Chawalla"
Dog
weight: 8
bark: function() { ... }

clifford.bark()   this

name: "Clifford"
breed: "Bloodhound"
Dog
weight: 65
bark: function() { ... }

Code Magnets

A working Movie constructor function was on the fridge, but some of the magnets fell on the floor. Can you help get it back together? Be careful, some extra magnets may have already been on the ground and might distract you.

```
function _____(_____, _____, rating, showtimes) {
    this.title = _____;
    this.genre = genre;
    this._____ = rating;
    this.showtimes = _____;
    this.getNextShowing = function() {
        var now = new Date().getTime();
        for (var i = 0; i < _____.length; i++) {
            var showtime = getTimeFromString(this._____[i]);
            if ((showtime - now) > 0) {
                return "Next showing of " + _____ + " is " + this.showtimes[i];
            }
        }
    } _____
}
```

Use these magnets to complete the code.

```
title          Movie          Woof          rating
  function                              this.showtimes
          showtimes
                    bark()                        genre
  this.title      ,                                      this
                                                      ;
```

there are no
Dumb Questions

Q: What's the real difference between a function and a method? After all, if they're the same thing why call them something different?

A: By convention, if an object has a function we call that a method. They both work the same way, except that you invoke an object's method using the dot operator, and a method can use `this` to access the object on which the method is invoked. Think of a function as a standalone piece of code you can invoke, and a method as behavior that is attached to a specific object.

Q: So when I create objects with a constructor and those objects have a method, then all of those objects share the same code for that method?

A: That's right, and that's one of the advantages of object-oriented programming: you can create the code for that class of objects (say all your dog objects) in one place and all the dogs share it. Now the way you make it specific to each dog is with your properties and using `this` to access those properties.

Q: Can I set `this` to a value of my choosing, and if I do, will that mess things up?

A: No, you can't set `this` to anything. Remember, `this` is a keyword, not a variable! It looks and acts a bit like one, but it's not a variable.

Q: Does `this` have a value outside of an object method?

A: No, if you're not invoking an object method, then `this` is undefined.

Q: So the way to think about `this` is when I invoke a method on an object, the value of `this` is set to that object the entire time the method is being evaluated?

A: Within the body of the object, yes, `this` will always be the object itself. There are some advanced cases where it may not be true; for instance, things get more complicated when you have objects within objects, and if you start doing that, you'll need to look up the semantics, but this is a good general rule.

Q: I've heard that in object-oriented programming I can have classes of objects and they can inherit from each other. Like, I could have a mammals class that both dog and cat inherit from. Can I do that in JavaScript?

A: You can. JavaScript uses something called prototypal inheritance, which is an even more powerful model than strictly class-based models. Getting into prototypal inheritance is a little beyond the scope of this book, but who knows, we could be convinced to write more on JavaScript.

Q: So when we say new Date(), we're using a constructor, right?

A: Yes, good catch! Date is a built-in constructor in JavaScript. When you say `new Date()`, you get a Date object with a bunch of useful methods you can use to manipulate the date.

Q: What's the difference between objects we write out ourselves and ones we create with a constructor?

A: The main difference is how you create them. Objects you write out yourself using curly braces and comma separated properties are known as "object literals." You literally type them into your code! If you want another one like it, you have to type it in yourself and make sure it's got the same properties. Objects created by a constructor are created by using `new` and a constructor function, which returns the object. You can use the constructor function to create many objects that have the same properties, but different property values if you want.

Code Magnets

A working Movie constructor function was on the fridge, but some of the magnets fell on the floor. Can you help get it back together? Be careful, some extra magnets may have already been on the ground and might distract you.

This is a constructor so we're using "Movie" for the name.

```
function  Movie  (  title  ,  genre  , rating, showtimes) {
    this.title = _ title _ ;
    this.genre = genre;
    this. rating = rating;
    this.showtimes = _ showtimes _ ;
    this.getNextShowing = function() {
        var now = new Date().getTime();
        for (var i = 0; i < _ this.showtimes .length; i++) {
            var showtime = getTimeFromString(this. showtimes [i]);
            if ((showtime - now) > 0) {
                return "Next showing of  this.title + " is " + this.showtimes[i];
            }
        }
    } ;
}
```

We pass in values for the properties we want to customize: title, genre, rating and showtimes...

... and initialize the properties.

To refer to properties in the object, we need to use the <u>this</u> keyword.

Don't forget to end this statement with a semicolon!

Leftover magnets.

| function | this.showtimes | Woof |
| bark() | , | this |

Test drive your constructor right off the factory floor

Now that you've got a Movie constructor, it's time to make some Movie objects!
Go ahead and type in the Movie constructor function and then add the code
below and take your constructor for a spin. We think you'll agree this a much
easier way to create objects.

First we'll create a movie object for the movie Buckaroo Banzai (one of our cult classic favorites). We pass in the values for the parameters.

```
var banzaiMovie = new Movie("Buckaroo Banzai",
                            "Cult Classic",
                            5,
                            ["1:00pm", "5:00pm", "7:00pm", "11:00pm"]);
```

Notice we can put the array value for showtimes right in the function call.

```
var plan9Movie = new Movie("Plan 9 from Outer Space",
                           "Cult Classic",
                           2,
                           ["3:00pm", "7:00pm", "11:00pm"]);
```

And next, Plan 9 from Outer Space...

```
var forbiddenPlanetMovie = new Movie("Forbidden Planet",
                                     "Classic Sci-fi",
                                     5,
                                     ["5:00pm", "9:00pm"]);
```

And of course, Forbidden Planet.

```
alert(banzaiMovie.getNextShowing());
alert(plan9Movie.getNextShowing());
alert(forbiddenPlanetMovie.getNextShowing());
```

Once we've got all our objects created, we can call the getNextShowing method and alert the user for the next showing times.

http://localhost
Next showing of Forbidden Planet is 5:00pm
OK

http://localhost
Next showing of Plan 9 from Outer Space is 3:00pm
OK

http://localhost
Next showing of Buckaroo Banzai is 1:00pm
OK

Congrats, you've made it through functions and objects! Now that you know all about them, and before we end the chapter, let's take a few moments to check out JavaScript objects in the wild; that is, in their native habitat, the browser!

Now, you might have started to notice...

...that objects are all around you. For instance, document and window are objects, as are the elements we get back from document.getElementById. And, these are just a few of many objects we'll be encountering—when we get to the HTML5 APIs, we'll be seeing objects everywhere!

Let's take a second look at some of the objects you've been using all along in this book:

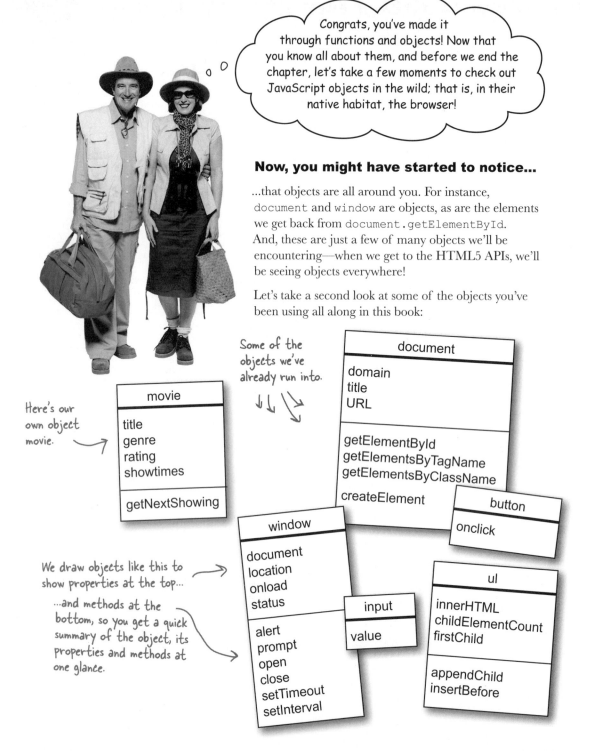

Here's our own object movie.

movie

title
genre
rating
showtimes

getNextShowing

Some of the objects we've already run into.

document

domain
title
URL

getElementById
getElementsByTagName
getElementsByClassName
createElement

button

onclick

window

document
location
onload
status

alert
prompt
open
close
setTimeout
setInterval

We draw objects like this to show properties at the top...

...and methods at the bottom, so you get a quick summary of the object, its properties and methods at one glance.

input

value

ul

innerHTML
childElementCount
firstChild

appendChild
insertBefore

What is the window object anyway?

When you're writing code for the browser, the `window` object is always going to be part of your life. The window object represents both the global environment for your JavaScript programs and the main window of your app, and as such, it contains many core properties and methods. Let's take a look at it:

Here's our window object with a few notable properties and methods you'll want to know about. There are many more...

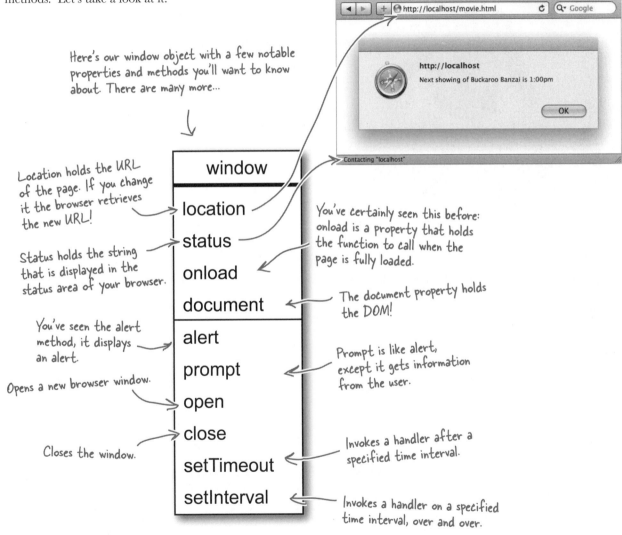

Location holds the URL of the page. If you change it the browser retrieves the new URL!

Status holds the string that is displayed in the status area of your browser.

You've certainly seen this before: onload is a property that holds the function to call when the page is fully loaded.

The document property holds the DOM!

You've seen the alert method, it displays an alert.

Prompt is like alert, except it gets information from the user.

Opens a new browser window.

Closes the window.

Invokes a handler after a specified time interval.

Invokes a handler on a specified time interval, over and over.

We've been writing "alert", not "window.alert"... how does the browser know we want the window alert method?

Window is the global object.

It may seem a little weird, but the window object acts as your global environment, so the names of any properties or methods from window are resolved even if you don't prepend them with `window`.

In addition, any global variables you define are also put into the window namespace, so you can reference them as `window.myvariable`.

A closer look at window.onload

One thing we've used often so far in this book is a `window.onload` event handler. By assigning a function to the `window.onload` property, we can ensure our code isn't run until the page is loaded and the DOM is completely set up. Now, there's a lot going on in the `window.onload` statement, so let's have another look and it will all start to come together for you:

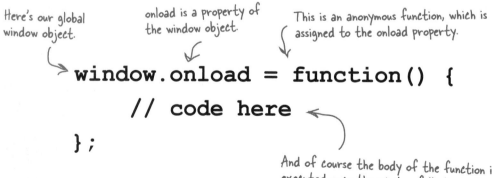

Here's our global window object.

onload is a property of the window object.

This is an anonymous function, which is assigned to the onload property.

```
window.onload = function() {
    // code here
};
```

And of course the body of the function is executed once the window fully loads the page and invokes our anonymous function!

Another look at the document object

The document object is another familar face; it's the object we've been using to access the DOM. And, as you've just seen, it is actually a property of the window object. Of course we haven't used it like window.document because we don't need to. Let's take a quick peek under the covers to see its more interesting properties and methods:

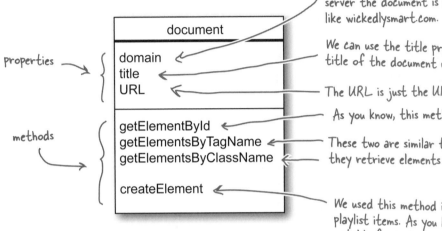

The domain property is the domain of the server the document is being served from, like wickedlysmart.com.

We can use the title property to get the title of the document using document.title.

The URL is just the URL of the document.

As you know, this method grabs an element by its id.

These two are similar to getElementById, except they retrieve elements using tags and classes.

We used this method in Chapter 3 to create new playlist items. As you know it creates elements suitable for inclusion in the DOM.

properties → { domain, title, URL }

methods → { getElementById, getElementsByTagName, getElementsByClassName, createElement }

document

A closer look at document.getElementById

We promised in the begining of this chapter that you'd understand document.getElementById by the end of the chapter. Well, you made it through functions, objects, and methods, and now you're ready! Check it out:

document is the document object, a built-in JavaScript object that gives you access to the DOM.

```
var div = document.getElementById("myDiv");
```

getElementById is a method that...

... takes one argument, the id of a <div> element, and returns an element object.

What was a confusing looking string of syntax now has a lot more meaning, right? Now, that div variable is also an object: an element object. Let's take a closer look at that too.

One more object to think about: your element objects

We shouldn't forget when we're working with methods like `getElementById` that the elements they return are also objects! Okay, you might not have realized this, but now that you know, you might be starting to think everything in JavaScript is an object, and, well, you're pretty much right.

You've already seen some evidence of element properties, like the `innerHTML` property; let's look at some of the more notable properties and methods:

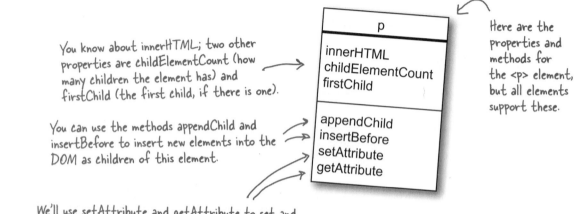

You know about innerHTML; two other properties are childElementCount (how many children the element has) and firstChild (the first child, if there is one).

You can use the methods appendChild and insertBefore to insert new elements into the DOM as children of this element.

We'll use setAttribute and getAttribute to set and get attributes, like "src", "class" and "id", in elements.

Here are the properties and methods for the <p> element, but all elements support these.

p
innerHTML childElementCount firstChild
appendChild insertBefore setAttribute getAttribute

there are no Dumb Questions

Q: Since window is the global object, that means I can use its properties and all of its methods without specifying `window` first right?

A: That's right. And whether you prepend the window object's properties and methods with `window` is up to you. For things like alert, everyone knows what that is, and no one uses window with it. On the other hand, if you're using the lesser known properties or methods you might want to to make your code more easily understandable, and use `window`.

Q: So, technically, I could write `onload = init` instead of `window.onload = init`, right?

A: Yes. But we don't recommend it in this particular case, because there are a lot of objects that have onload properties, so your code is going to be much clearer if you use `window.` in front of `onload`.

Q: The reason we don't say `window.onload = init()` is because that would call the function, instead of using its value?

A: That's right. When you use parentheses after the function name, like init(), you saying you want to *call* the function init. If you use its name without parentheses, then you're assigning the function value to the `onload` property. It's a subtle difference when you're typing it in, but the ramifications are large, so pay careful attention.

Q: **Which of the two ways of creating a window.onload handler is better, using a function name or an anonymous function?**

A: One isn't better than the other, they both do basically the same thing: set the value of `window.onload` to a function that will run when the page has loaded. If you need to call `init` from another function later in your program for some reason, then you'll need to define an `init` function. Otherwise, it doesn't matter which way you do it.

Q: **What's the difference between built-in objects like window and document, and the ones we make?**

A: One difference is that built-in objects follow the guidelines set by specifications, so you can refer to the W3C specifications to understand all their properties and methods. In addition, many of the built-in objects, like String, may have properties that are immutable and can not be changed. Other than that, objects are objects. The nice thing about built-in objects is they're already built for you.

> Yes, String is an object! Check out a good JavaScript reference to get all the details of its properties and methods.

Congrats! You've completed our tour of objects, and made it through several chapters of JavaScript bootcamp. Now it's time to use all that knowledge to program with HTML5 and all the new JavaScript APIs, starting in the very next chapter!

You're leaving this chapter knowing more about objects and functions than many people out there. Of course, you can always learn more and we encourage you to explore (after you finish this book)!

So take a little R&R after this chapter, but before you go please take a quick look at the bullet points, and do the crossword to make it all stick.

BULLET POINTS

- To create a function, use the function keyword with parentheses to hold parameters, if there are any.

- Functions can be named, or be anonymous.

- Naming rules for functions are the same as naming rules for variables.

- The body of a function goes between curly braces, and contains statements that do the work of the function.

- A function can return a value with the return statement.

- To invoke (or call) a function, use its name and pass any arguments it needs.

- JavaScript uses pass-by-value parameter passing.

- When you pass an object, like a dog, as an argument to a function, the parameter gets a copy of the **reference** to the object.

- Variables defined in functions, including parameters, are known as local variables.

- Variables defined outside of functions are known as global variables.

- Local variables are not visible outside the function in which they are defined. This is known as the scope of a variable.

- If you declare a local variable with the same name as a global variable, the local variable shadows the global variable.

- When you link to multiple JavaScript files from your page, all the global variables are defined in the same global space.

- If you assign a new variable without using the var keyword, that variable will be global, even if you are first assigning it in a function.

- Functions are values that can be assigned to variables, passed to other functions, stored in arrays, and assigned to object properties.

- Objects are collections of properties.

- You access an object's properties using dot notation or the [ ] notation.

- If you use [ ] notation, enclose the property's name as a string; for example, myObject["name"].

- You can change a property's value, delete properties, or add new properties to an object.

- You can enumerate an object's properties using a for-in loop.

- A function assigned to an object property is referred to as a method.

- A method can use a special keyword, `this`, to refer to the object on which it was invoked.

- A constructor is a function that makes objects.

- The job of a constructor is to create a new object and initialize its properties.

- To invoke a constructor to create an object, use the new keyword. For example, new Dog().

- We've already been using several objects in this book, including document, window, and various element objects.

- The window object is the global object.

- The document object is one of window's properties.

- The document.getElementById method returns an element object.

HTML5cross

It's been a whirlwind chapter of functions, objects, properties and methods—so there's lots to make stick. Sit back, relax, and work the rest of your brain a little. Here's your Chapter 4 crossword puzzle.

Across

1. These variables are only available in functions.
4. The true global object.
6. The _____ object represents the DOM.
11. Arguments are passed by _____.
12. Use this keyword to start a function definition.
14. Functions without return statements return this.
15. A function in an object.
17. Functions without a name.
18. What you supply in your function definition.

Down

2. This kind of function makes objects.
3. Functions might or might not include this kind of statement.
5. Stringing together properties and function calls with the dot operator.
7. A property in window that we assign to a handler function.
8. What you supply in your function call.
9. The _____ operator lets you access an object's properties and methods.
10. By convention, constructors have a name with an _____ first letter.
13. Refers to the current object in an object method.
16. Variable scope that is visible everywhere.

Sharpen your pencil
Solution

Use your knowledge of functions and passing arguments to parameters to evaluate the code below. After you've traced through the code, write the value of each variable below. Here's our solution.

```
function dogsAge(age) {
    return age * 7;
}


var myDogsAge = dogsAge(4);


function rectangleArea(width, height) {
    var area = width * height;
    return area;
}

var rectArea = rectangleArea(3, 4);

function addUp(numArray) {
    var total = 0;
    for (var i = 0; i < numArray.length; i++) {
        total += numArray[i];
    }
    return total;
}

var theTotal = addUp([1, 5, 3, 9]);

function getAvatar(points) {
    var avatar;
    if (points < 100) {
        avatar = "Mouse";
    } else if (points > 100 && points < 1000) {
        avatar = "Cat";
    } else {
        avatar = "Ape";
    }
    return avatar;
}
var myAvatar = getAvatar(335);
```

Write the value of each variable here...

myDogsAge = 28

rectArea = 12

theTotal = 18

myAvatar = Cat

HTML5cross Solution

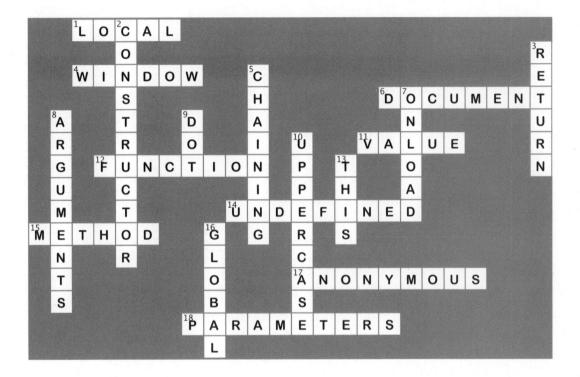

5 making your html location aware

Geolocation

Isn't it amazing how all this new technology is bringing everyone closer together?

Wherever you go, there you are. And sometimes knowing where you are makes all the difference (especially to a web app). In this chapter we're going to show you how to create web pages that are **location aware**—sometimes you'll be able to pinpoint your users down to the corner they're standing on, and sometimes you'll only be able to determine the area of town they're in (but you'll still know the town!). Heck, sometimes you won't be able to determine anything about their location, which could be for technical reasons, or just because they don't want you being so nosy. Go figure. In any case, in this chapter we're going to explore a JavaScript API: Geolocation. Grab the best location-aware device you have (even if it's your desktop PC), and let's get started.

> Your users are now on the move with mobile devices that are location aware. The best apps are going to be the ones that can enhance users' experiences using their location.

Location, Location, Location

Knowing where your users are can add a lot to a web experience: you can give them directions, make suggestions about where they might go, you can know it's raining and suggest indoor activities, you can let your users know who else in their area might be interested in some activity. There's really no end to the ways you can use location information.

With HTML5 (and the Geolocation JavaScript-based API) you can easily access location information in your pages. That's said, there are a few things to know about location before we get started. Let's check it out...

there are no Dumb Questions

Q: I heard Geolocation isn't a real API?

A: Geolocation is not considered a first-class member of the existing HTML5 standard, but that said, it is a standard of the W3C, widely supported and pretty much everyone includes Geolocation in the list of important HTML5 APIs. And it most certainly is a **real** JavaScript API!

Q: Is the Geolocation API the same as the Google Maps API?

A: No. They are completely different APIs. The Geolocation API is solely focused on getting you information about your position on the Earth. The Google Maps API is a JavaScript library offered by Google that gives you access to all their Google Maps functionality. So, if you need to display your users location in a map, Google's API gives you a convenient way to implement that functionality.

Q: Isn't it a privacy concern to have my device reveal my location?

A: The Geolocation specification specifies that any browser must have the express permission of the user to make use of their location. So, if your code makes use of the Geolocation API, the first thing the browser will do is make sure it is okay with the user to share her location.

Q: How well supported is Geolocation?

A: Very well supported; in fact, it's available in almost every modern browser including desktop and mobile. You'll want to be sure you're using the latest version of your browser; if you are, then you're probably good to go.

The Lat and Long of it...

To know where you are, you need a coordinate system, and you need one on the Earth's surface. Luckily we have such a thing, and it uses latitude and longitude together as a coordinate system. Latitude specifies a north/south point on the Earth, and longitude, an east/west point. Latitude is measured from the equator, and longitude is measured from Greenwich, England. The job of the geolocation API is to give us the coordinates of where we are at any time, using these coordinates:

← *The Royal Observatory in Greenwich, to be precise.*

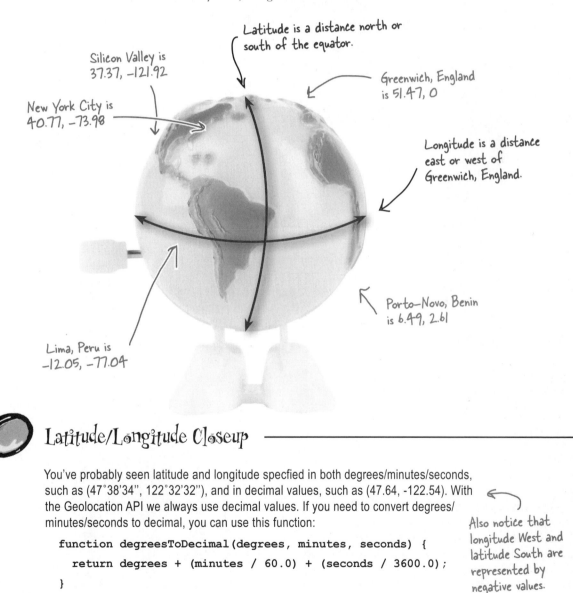

Latitude is a distance north or south of the equator.

Silicon Valley is 37.37, -121.92

New York City is 40.77, -73.98

Greenwich, England is 51.47, 0

Longitude is a distance east or west of Greenwich, England.

Lima, Peru is -12.05, -77.04

Porto-Novo, Benin is 6.49, 2.61

Latitude/Longitude Closeup

You've probably seen latitude and longitude specfied in both degrees/minutes/seconds, such as (47°38'34", 122°32'32"), and in decimal values, such as (47.64, -122.54). With the Geolocation API we always use decimal values. If you need to convert degrees/minutes/seconds to decimal, you can use this function:

```
function degreesToDecimal(degrees, minutes, seconds) {
    return degrees + (minutes / 60.0) + (seconds / 3600.0);
}
```

Also notice that longitude West and latitude South are represented by negative values.

How the Geolocation API determines your location

You don't have to have the newest smartphone to be location aware. Even desktop browsers are joining the game. You might ask, how would a desktop browser determine its location if it doesn't have GPS or any other fancy location technologies? Well, all browsers (in devices and on your desktop) are using a few different ways to determine where you are, some more accurate than others. Let's take a look:

> I scored the newest smartphone and I've got GPS built right into the phone. Talk about accuracy!

> Nothing fancy here in the office... we just have our desktop browsers. But my IP address can be mapped to a location, which is sometimes quite accurate.

IP Address

Location information based on your IP address uses an external database to map the IP address to a physical location. The advantage of this approach is that it can work anywhere; however, often IP addresses are resolved to locations such as your ISP's local office. Think of this method as being reliable to the city or sometimes neighborhood level.

GPS

Global Positioning System, supported by many newer mobile devices, provides extremely accurate location information based on satellites. Location data may include altitude, speed and heading information. To use it, though, your device has to be able to see the sky, and it can take a long time to get a location. GPS can also be hard on your batteries.

My phone is old school. No GPS on this baby. But through cell tower triangulation, my phone's got a pretty good idea of where I am, and the browser can make use of this.

Cell Phone

Cell phone triangulation figures out your location based on your distance from one or more cell phone towers (obviously the more towers, the more accurate your location will be). This method can be fairly accurate and works indoors (unlike GPS); it also can be much quicker than GPS. Then again, if you're in the middle of nowhere with only one cell tower, your accuracy is going to suffer.

I'm on the move from coffee shop to coffee shop with my laptop and wireless subscriptions. You know where I am by triangulating all those wireless carriers. Seems to work pretty well.

WiFi

WiFi positioning uses one or more WiFi access points to triangulate your location. This method can be very accurate, works indoors and is fast. Obviously it requires you are *somewhat* stationary (perhaps drinking a venti iced tea at a coffee house).

It's cool we've got so many ways to know where we are. How am I going to know which method my device is using?

You're not.

The short answer is "you're not," as the browser implementation is going to determine how location is determined. But the good news is the browser can use *any* of these means to determine your location. In fact, a smart browser might first use cell phone triangulation, if it is available, to give you a rough idea of location, and then later give you a more accurate location with WiFi or GPS.

We'll see that you don't need to worry about how the location is being determined, and we'll focus more on the accuracy of your location instead. Based on the accuracy, you can determine how useful the location is going to be for you. Stay tuned—we'll get back to accuracy a little bit later.

Sharpen your pencil

Think about your existing HTML pages and applications (or ones that you want to create); how might you incorporate location information into them?

☐   Allow my users to share with others that are nearby.

☐   Let my users more easily find local resources or services.

☐   Keep track of where my user does something.

☐   Give my users directions from where they are.

☐   Use location to determine other demographics of my users.

☐   ....

☐   ....

☐   ....

☐   ....

Your ideas here!

Just where are you anyway?

Well, of course *you* know where you are, but let's see where your *browser* thinks you are. To do that we'll just create a little HTML:

> All the usual stuff at the top, including a link to the file where we'll put our JavaScript, myLoc.js, and a stylesheet, myLoc.css to make it all look pretty.

```
<!doctype html>
<html>
<head>
  <meta charset="utf-8">
  <title>Where am I?</title>
  <script src="myLoc.js"></script>
  <link rel="stylesheet" href="myLoc.css">
</head>
<body>
  <div id="location">
    Your location will go here.
  </div>
</body>
</html>
```

> We're going to write our geolocation code in myLoc.js.

> And you're going to use this <div> to output your location.

> Put all this HTML in a file named myLoc.html.

Now let's create `myLoc.js` and write a little code; we're going to do this quickly and then come back and dissect it all. Add this to your `myLoc.js` file:

> We're calling the function getMyLocation as soon as the browser loads the page.

```
window.onload =  getMyLocation;

function getMyLocation() {
    if (navigator.geolocation) {
        navigator.geolocation.getCurrentPosition(displayLocation);
    } else {
        alert("Oops, no geolocation support");
    }
}
```

> This is how we check to make sure the browser supports the Geolocation API; if the navigator.geolocation object exists, then we have it!

> If it does, then we call the getCurrentPosition method and pass in a handler function, displayLocation. We'll implement this in just a sec.

> The displayLocation function is the handler that's going to get its hands on the location.

> If the browser does NOT support geolocation, then we'll just pop up an alert to the user.

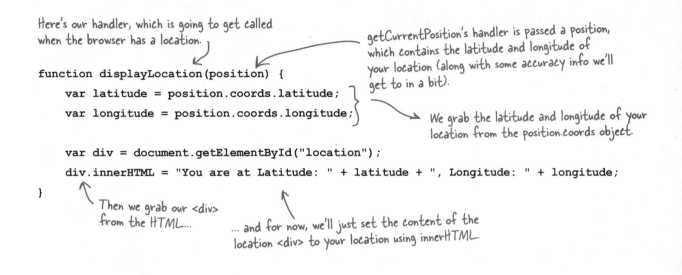

Here's our handler, which is going to get called when the browser has a location.

getCurrentPosition's handler is passed a position, which contains the latitude and longitude of your location (along with some accuracy info we'll get to in a bit).

```
function displayLocation(position) {
    var latitude = position.coords.latitude;
    var longitude = position.coords.longitude;

    var div = document.getElementById("location");
    div.innerHTML = "You are at Latitude: " + latitude + ", Longitude: " + longitude;
}
```

We grab the latitude and longitude of your location from the position.coords object.

Then we grab our <div> from the HTML...

... and for now, we'll just set the content of the location <div> to your location using innerHTML.

Test drive your location

Get this code typed in and take your new location-aware page for a test drive.

When you run a Geolocation web app for the first time, you'll notice a request in the browser asking for your permission to use your location. This is a browser security check, and you're free to tell the browser no. But assuming you want to test this web app, you'll want to click Allow or Yes. When you do, the app should show you your location, like this:

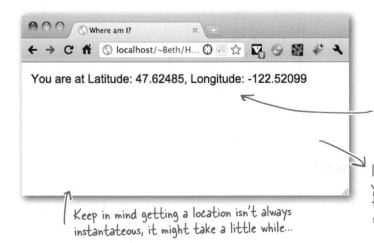

The request for permission may look a little different depending on the browser you're using, but will look something like this.

Here's your location! Your location will obviously be different from ours (if it's not we're going to get really worried about you).

If you're not getting your location, and assuming you've double checked for typos and that kind of thing, hold on for a few pages and we'll give you some code to debug this...

Keep in mind getting a location isn't always instantateous, it might take a little while...

> If your browser supports the Geolocation API, you'll find a geolocation property in the navigator object.

What we just did...

Now that we've got some geolocation code up and running (and, again, if you're not seeing a location yet, hold on, we're getting to some debugging techniques in just a sec), let's walk through the code in a little more detail:

1 The first thing you need to know if you're going to write geolocation code is "does this browser support it?" To do that we make use of the fact that browsers have a geolocation property in their navigation object only if geolocation is supported.

So we can test to see if the geolocation property exists, and if so make use of it; otherwise, we'll let the user know:

```
if (navigator.geolocation) {

    ...

} else {
    alert("Oops, no geolocation support");
}
```

We can use a simple test to see if geolocation is there (if it's not then navigator.geolocation evaluates to null and the condition will fail).

If it is there, we can make use of it, and if not, we'll let the user know.

2 Now, if there is a navigator.geolocation property, we're going to make some more use of it. In fact, the navigator.geolocation property is an object that contains the entire geolocation API. The main method the API supports is getCurrentPosition, which does the work of getting the browser's location. Let's take a closer look at this method, which has three parameters, the second two of which are optional:

Remember, APIs are just objects with properties and methods! Now aren't you glad you did all the JavaScript training up front!

The successHandler is a function that is called if the browser is able to successfully determine your location.

The errorHandler is another function, that is called if something goes wrong and the browser can't determine your location.

```
getCurrentPosition(successHandler, errorHandler, options)
```

These two parameters are optional, which is why we didn't need them before.

The options parameter allows you to customize the way geolocation works.

3 Now let's take a look at our call to the getCurrentPosition method. For now, we're supplying just the successHandler argument to handle a successful attempt to get the browser location. We'll look at the case when the browser fails to find a location in a bit.

Remember chaining from Chapter 4? We're using the navigator object to get access to the geolocation object, which is just a property of navigator.

```
if (navigator.geolocation) {

    navigator.geolocation.getCurrentPosition(displayLocation);

}
```

And we're calling the geolocation object's getCurrentPosition method with one argument, the success callback.

If and when geolocation determines your location, it will call displayLocation.

Did you notice we're passing a function to another function here? Remember from Chapter 4 that functions are values, so we can do that, no problem.

4 Now let's look at the success handler, displayLocation. When displayLocation is called, the geolocation API passes it a position object that contains information about the browser's location, including a coordinates object that holds the latitude and longitude (as well as a few other values we'll talk about later).

position is an object that's passed into your success handler by the geolocation API.

```
function displayLocation(position) {
    var latitude = position.coords.latitude;
    var longitude = position.coords.longitude;

    var div = document.getElementById("location");
    div.innerHTML = "You are at Latitude: " + latitude + ", Longitude: " + longitude;
}
```

The position object has a coords property that holds a reference to the coordinates object...

... and the coordinates object holds your latitude and longitude.

And this part we're sure you can do in your sleep by now: we're just taking the coordinate information, and displaying it in a <div> in the page.

How it all fits together

Now that we've gone through the code, let's see
how it all works at runtime:

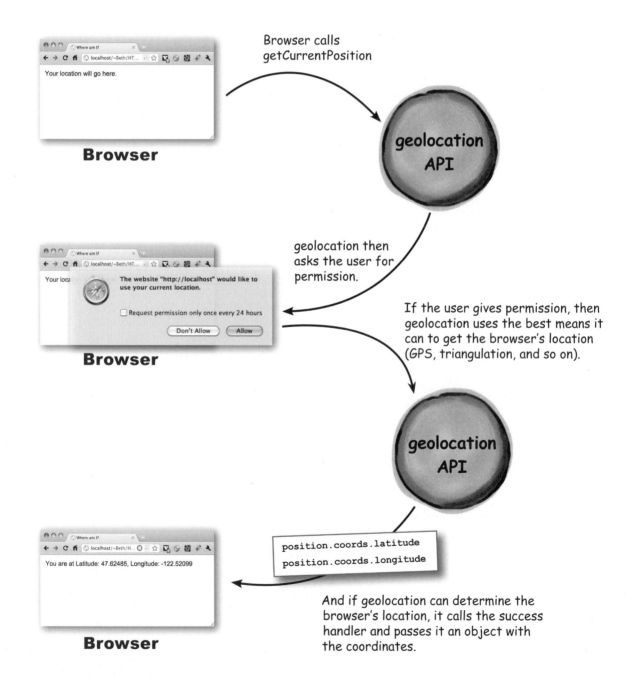

Browser

Browser calls
getCurrentPosition

geolocation API

geolocation then
asks the user for
permission.

Browser

The website "http://localhost" would like to
use your current location.

☐ Request permission only once every 24 hours

Don't Allow   Allow

If the user gives permission, then
geolocation uses the best means it
can to get the browser's location
(GPS, triangulation, and so on).

geolocation API

```
position.coords.latitude
position.coords.longitude
```

You are at Latitude: 47.62485, Longitude: -122.52099

Browser

And if geolocation can determine the
browser's location, it calls the success
handler and passes it an object with
the coordinates.

Test Drive Diagnostics

When it comes to Geolocation, not every test drive is going to be successful, and even if your first test was successful, down the road something is going to go wrong. To help, we've created a little diagnostic test for you that you can add right into your code. So, if you're having trouble, here's your answer, and even if you're not, one of your users is going to have an issue and you're going to want to know how to handle that in your code. So, add the code below, and if you're having issues, kindly fill out the diagnostic form at the end once you've diagnosed the problem:

To create the diagnostic test we're going to add an error handler to the getCurrentPosition method call. This handler is going to get called anytime the Geolocation API encounters a problem in determining your location. Here's how we add it:

Add a second argument to your getCurrentPosition call named displayError. This is a function that is going to be called when geolocation fails to find a location.

```
navigator.geolocation.getCurrentPosition(displayLocation, displayError);
```

Now we need to write the error handler. To do that you need to know that geolocation passes an error object to your handler that contains a numeric code describing the reason it couldn't determine the location of your browser. Depending on the code, it might also provide a message giving further information about the error. Here's how we can use the error object in the handler:

Here's our new handler, which is passed an error by the Geolocation API.

```
function displayError(error) {
    var errorTypes = {
        0: "Unknown error",
        1: "Permission denied by user",
        2: "Position is not available",
        3: "Request timed out"
    };
    var errorMessage = errorTypes[error.code];
    if (error.code == 0 || error.code == 2) {
        errorMessage = errorMessage + " " + error.message;
    }
    var div = document.getElementById("location");
    div.innerHTML = errorMessage;
}
```

The error object contains a code property that has a number from 0 to 3. Here's a nice way to associate an error message with each code in JavaScript:

We create an object with three properties named zero to three. These properties are strings with an error message we want to associate with each code.

And using the error.code property, we assign one of those strings to a new variable, errorMessage.

In the case of errors zero and two, there is sometimes additional information in the error.message property, so we add that to our errorMessage string.

And then we add the message to the page to let the user know.

Before we run the test, let's take a closer look at the types of errors we can get.

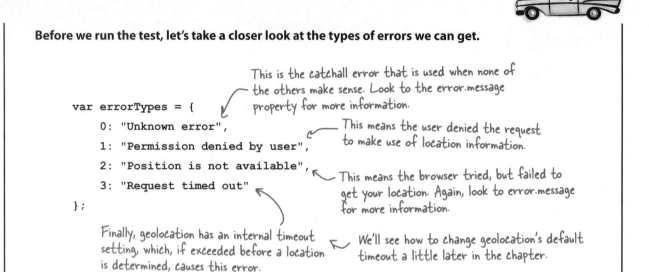

This is the catchall error that is used when none of the others make sense. Look to the error.message property for more information.

```
var errorTypes = {
    0: "Unknown error",
    1: "Permission denied by user",
    2: "Position is not available",
    3: "Request timed out"
};
```

This means the user denied the request to make use of location information.

This means the browser tried, but failed to get your location. Again, look to error.message for more information.

Finally, geolocation has an internal timeout setting, which, if exceeded before a location is determined, causes this error.

We'll see how to change geolocation's default timeout a little later in the chapter.

When you've got the diagnostic test typed in, go ahead and give it a try. Obviously if you receive a location then everything is working and you won't see any of the errors. You can force an error by denying the browser's request to use your location. Or you might get creative and, say, move indoors with your GPS phone while turning off your network. In the worst case, if you wait for a long time without getting a location or an error message, most likely you're waiting on a long timeout value to, well, time out. We'll see how to shorten that timeout duration a little later in the chapter.

My Location
localhost/~Beth/HT...
Unknown error

My Location
localhost/~Beth/HT...
Timed out

My Location
localhost/~Beth/HT...
Permission denied by user

Your Diagnostic Results Here

☐ I did not give permission for my location to be used.

☐ My position wasn't available.

☐ After a few seconds, I got a message indicating there was a request timeout.

☐ Nothing happened at all, no location and no error alert.

☐ Something else _____

Watch it!

To test your geolocation code on a mobile device, you're going to want a server.

Unless you have a means of loading your HTML, JavaScript and CSS files directly onto your mobile device, the easiest way to test them is to place them on a server (take a peek at the next chapter to see how to set up your own server if you want) and access them there. If you've got a server and you want to do that, we encourage you to do so. On the other hand, if that doesn't work for you, we've made sure the code is available on the Wickedly Smart servers so that you can test on your mobile devices. That said, we encourage you to follow along with the code on your desktop, and once you have it working there, then test on your mobile device using the server (your own or Wickedly Smart).

For the first Test Drive (including the error diagnostic), point your device to http://wickedlysmart.com/hfhtml5/chapter5/latlong/myLoc.html.

there are no Dumb Questions

Q: The latitude and longitude returned by the app for my location aren't quite right, why is that?

A: There are a variety of ways that your device and the location service provider calculate your position, and some are more accurate than others. GPS is often the most accurate. We're going to look at a way to determine the accuracy estimate that the location service gives back as part of the position object so you can see how accurate to expect the location data to be.

Revealing our secret location...

Now that you've got the basics out of the way, let's do something more interesting with location. How about we see how far you are from our secret writing location at Wickedly Smart HQ? To do that we need the HQ coordinates and we need to know how to calculate distance between two coordinates. First, let's add another `<div>` to use in the HTML:

Wickedly Smart Head Quarters is at 47.62485, -122.52099.

```
    ⋮
<body>
  <div id="location">
    Your location will go here.
  </div>
  <div id="distance">
   Distance from WickedlySmart HQ will go here.
  </div>
</body>
</html>
```

Add this new `<div>` to your HTML.

Some Ready Bake Code: computing distance

Ever wanted to know how to compute the distance between two points on a sphere? You'll find the details fascinating, but they're a little outside the scope of this chapter. So, we're going to give you some **Ready Bake Code** that does just that. To compute the distance between two coordinates most everyone uses the Haversine equation; you'll find it implemented below. Feel free to use it anywhere you need to know the distance between two coordinates:

This function takes two coordinates, a start coodinate and a destination coordinate, and returns the distance in kilometers between them.

```
function computeDistance(startCoords, destCoords) {
    var startLatRads = degreesToRadians(startCoords.latitude);
    var startLongRads = degreesToRadians(startCoords.longitude);
    var destLatRads = degreesToRadians(destCoords.latitude);
    var destLongRads = degreesToRadians(destCoords.longitude);

    var Radius = 6371; // radius of the Earth in km
    var distance = Math.acos(Math.sin(startLatRads) * Math.sin(destLatRads) +
                   Math.cos(startLatRads) * Math.cos(destLatRads) *
                   Math.cos(startLongRads - destLongRads)) * Radius;


    return distance;
}


function degreesToRadians(degrees) {
    var radians = (degrees * Math.PI)/180;
    return radians;
}
```

We'll see more of this function in the Canvas chapter.

Add this to your myLoc.js file.

We want to compute the distance from you to us, as the crow flies.

Writing the code to find the distance

Now that we've got a function to compute the distance between two coordinates, let's define our (that is, the authors') location here at the WickedlySmart HQ (go ahead and type this in too):

```
var ourCoords =  {
        latitude: 47.624851,
        longitude: -122.52099
};
```

Here we're going to define a literal object for the coordinates of our location at the Wickedly Smart HQ. Add this as a global variable at the top of your myLoc.js file.

And now let's write the code: all we need to do is pass the coordinates of your location and our location to the `computeDistance` function:

```
function displayLocation(position) {
    var latitude = position.coords.latitude;
    var longitude = position.coords.longitude;


    var div = document.getElementById("location");
    div.innerHTML = "You are at Latitude: " + latitude + ", Longitude: " + longitude;

    var km = computeDistance(position.coords, ourCoords);
    var distance = document.getElementById("distance");
    distance.innerHTML = "You are " + km + " km from the WickedlySmart HQ";
}
```

Here we're passing the coordinates of your position and also our coordinates to computeDistance.

And then we take the results and update the contents of the distance <div>.

Location-enabled test drive

Now let's give this new code a test drive. Go ahead and finish adding the code to `myLoc.js` and then reload `myLoc.html` in your browser. You should see your location and also your distance from us.

Your location and distance will obviously be different depending on where you are in the world.

> Where am I?
> ← → C ⓘ localhost:/~Beth/HT...
> You are at Latitude: 47.624851, Longitude: -122.52099
> You are 0 km from the WickedlySmart HQ

Try online: http://wickedlysmart.com/hfhtml5/chapter5/distance/myLoc.html

You know, seeing my location as 34.20472, -90.57528 is great, but a map would really come in handy right now!

Mapping your position

As we told you up front, the Geolocation API is pretty simple—it gives you a way to find (and as you'll see, track, as well) where you are, but it doesn't provide you with any tools to visualize your location. To do that we need to rely on a third-party tool, and as you might guess, Google Maps is by far the most popular tool for doing that. Obviously Google Maps isn't part of the HTML5 spec, but it does interoperate well with HTML5, and so we don't mind a little diversion here and there to show you how to integrate it with the Geolocation API. If you want to be diverted, you can start by adding this to the head of your HTML document and then we'll work on adding a map to your page:

```
<script src="http://maps.google.com/maps/api/js?sensor=true"></script>
```

This is the location of the Google Maps JavaScript API.

Make sure you type this exactly as is, including the sensor query parameter (the API won't work without this). We're using sensor=true because our code is using your location. If we were just using the map without your location, we'd type sensor=false.

How to add a Map to your Page

Now that you've linked to the Google Map API, all the functionality of Google Maps is available to you through JavaScript. But, we need a place to put our Google Map, and to do that we need to define an element that is going to hold it.

```
            :
            :
<body>
  <div id="location">
    Your location will go here.
  </div>
  <div id="distance">
   Distance from WickedlySmart HQ will go here.
  </div>
  <div id="map">
  </div>
</body>
</html>
```

Here's the <div>. Note we've defined some style in myLoc.css that sets the map <div> to 400px by 400px with a black border.

Getting ready to create a map...

To create the map we need two things: a latitude and longitude (and we know how to get those), and we need a set of options that describe how we want the map created. Let's start with the latitude and longitude. We already know how to get them with the Geolocation API, but the Google API likes them bundled up in its own object. To create one of those objects we can use a constructor supplied by Google:

Don't forget, constructors start with an uppercase letter.

```
var googleLatAndLong = new google.maps.LatLng(latitude, longitude);
```

google.maps precedes all the methods of the Google Maps API.

Here's the constructor, which takes our lat and long and returns a new object that holds them both.

Google gives us some options we can set to control how the map is created. For instance, we can control how far zoomed in or out the initial map view is, where the map is centered, and the type of map, like a road-style map, a satellite view, or both. Here's how we create the options:

The zoom option can be specified 0 to 21. Experiment with the zoom: bigger numbers correspond to being zoomed in more (so you see more detail). 10 is about "city" sized.

```
var mapOptions = {
    zoom: 10,
    center: googleLatAndLong,
    mapTypeId: google.maps.MapTypeId.ROADMAP
};
```

Here's our new object we just created. We want the map to be centered on this location.

You can also try SATELLITE and HYBRID as options here.

Displaying the Map

Let's put all this together in a new function, `showMap`, that takes a set of coordinates and displays a map on your page:

```
var map;
```

We're declaring a global variable map, that is going to hold the Google map after we create it. You'll see how this gets used in a bit.

```
function showMap(coords) {
    var googleLatAndLong =
            new google.maps.LatLng(coords.latitude,
                                   coords.longitude);
    var mapOptions = {
        zoom: 10,
        center: googleLatAndLong,
        mapTypeId: google.maps.MapTypeId.ROADMAP
    };
    var mapDiv = document.getElementById("map");
    map = new google.maps.Map(mapDiv, mapOptions);
}
```

We use our latitude and longitude from the coords object...

...and use them to create a google.maps.LatLng object.

We create the mapOptions object with the options we want to set for our map.

And finally, we grab the map <div> from the DOM and pass it and the mapOptions to the Map constructor to create the google.maps.Map object. This displays the map in our page.

We're assigning the new Map object to our global variable map.

Here's another constructor from Google's API, which takes an element and our options and creates and returns a map object.

Go ahead and add this code to your JavaScript file at the bottom. And now we just need to tie it into our existing code. Let's do that by editing the `displayLocation` function:

```
function displayLocation(position) {
    var latitude = position.coords.latitude;
    var longitude = position.coords.longitude;

    var div = document.getElementById("location");
    div.innerHTML = "You are at Latitude: " + latitude + ", Longitude: " + longitude;

    var km = computeDistance(position.coords, ourCoords);
    var div = document.getElementById("distance");
    distance.innerHTML = "You are " + km + " km from the WickedlySmart HQ";

    showMap(position.coords);
}
```

We'll call showMap from displayLocation after we've updated the other <div>s on the page.

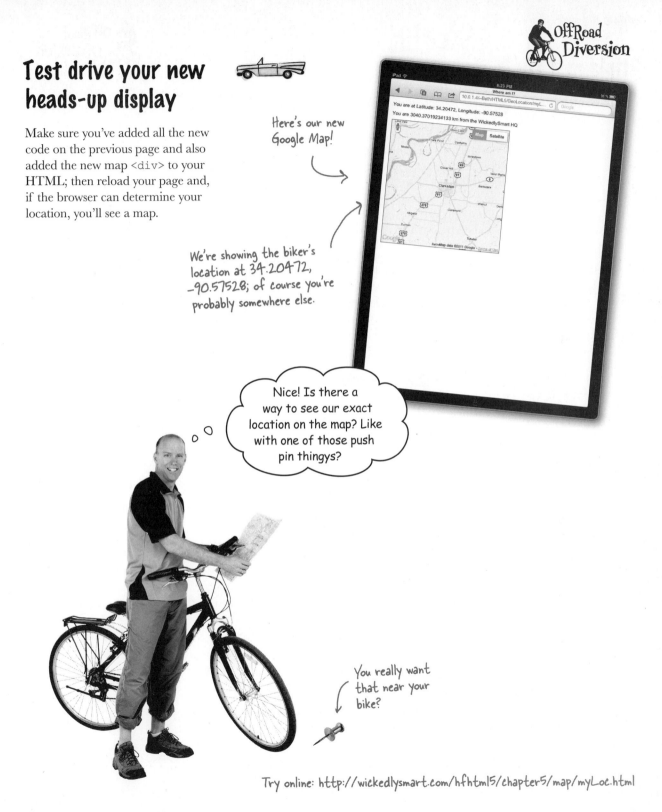

Test drive your new heads-up display

Make sure you've added all the new code on the previous page and also added the new map <div> to your HTML; then reload your page and, if the browser can determine your location, you'll see a map.

Here's our new Google Map!

We're showing the biker's location at 34.20472, -90.57528; of course you're probably somewhere else.

Nice! Is there a way to see our exact location on the map? Like with one of those push pin thingys?

You really want that near your bike?

Try online: http://wickedlysmart.com/hfhtml5/chapter5/map/myLoc.html

Sticking a Pin in it...

It *would* be more useful if you could see exactly where you're located on the map. If you've used Google Maps, then you're probably familiar with the push pins used to mark the location of items you search for. For example, if you search for Space Needle in Seattle, WA, you'll get a map with a pin near the Space Needle area in the city, and if you click on the pin, you'll see an information window with more details about the item. Well, push pins are called markers, and they are one of the many things offered in the Google Maps API.

Adding a marker with a pop-up information window requires a little code because you have to create the marker, the information window, and a handler for the click event on the marker (which opens the information window). Given we're on a diversion, we're going to cover this fairly quickly, but at this point in the book, you've got everything you need to keep up!

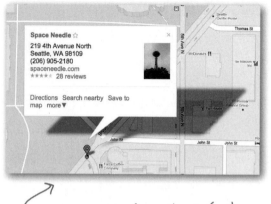

When you search for an item in Google Maps, you'll see a red pin marking the spot of the search result.

① **We're going to start by creating a new function, addMarker, and then use the Google API to create a marker:**

The addMarker function takes a map, a google-style latitude and longitude, a title for the marker, and also some content for the info window.

```
function addMarker(map, latlong, title, content) {

    var markerOptions = {

        position: latlong,

        map: map,

        title: title,

        clickable: true

    };

    var marker = new google.maps.Marker(markerOptions);

}
```

We create an options object with the latitude and longitude, the map, the title, and whether or not we want the marker to be clickable...

...we set it to true here because we want to be able to display an info window when it is clicked.

Then we create the marker object by using yet another constructor from Google's API, and pass it the markerOptions object we created.

② Next we're going to create the info window by defining some options specific to it, and then create a new InfoWindow object with the Google API. Add the code below to your addMarker function:

```
function addMarker(map, latlong, title, content) {
    :
```
⟵ ———— Our other code is still here, we're just saving some trees...

```
    var infoWindowOptions = {
```
Now we're going to define some options for the info window.

```
        content: content,
```
⟵ ——— We need the content...

```
        position: latlong
```
⟵ ... and the latitude and longitude.

```
    };

    var infoWindow = new google.maps.InfoWindow(infoWindowOptions);
```
And with that we create the info window.

```
    google.maps.event.addListener(marker, "click", function() {
```
Next we'll use the Google Maps addListener method to add a "listener" for the click event. A listener is just like a handler, like onload and onclick, that you've already seen.

```
        infoWindow.open(map);
```
We pass the listener a function that gets called when the user clicks on the marker.

```
    });
```
When the marker is clicked, this function is called and the infoWindow opens on the map.

```
}
```

③ Now all that's left to do is call the addMarker function from showMap, making sure we pass in all the right arguments for the four parameters. Add this to the bottom of your showMap function:

```
var title = "Your Location";
var content = "You are here: " + coords.latitude + ", " + coords.longitude;
addMarker(map, googleLatAndLong, title, content);
```

We pass in the map and googleLatAndLong objects we created using the Google maps API...

... and a title string, and a content string for the marker.

Testing the marker

Get all the code for `addMarker` added, update `showMap` to call `addMarker` and reload the page. You'll see a map with a marker with your location on it.

Try clicking on the marker. You'll get a pop-up window with your latitude and longitude.

This is great, because now you know exactly where you are (just in case you were lost or something...)

Here's what our map with the marker and info window pop-up looks like.

Try online: http://wickedlysmart.com/hfhtml5/chapter5/marker/myLoc.html

The other cool things you can do with the Google Maps API

We've only scratched the surface of what you can do with the Google Maps API, and although this API is way beyond the scope of this book, you're well on your way to being able to tackle it on your own. Here are some things you can consider using it for, and some pointers to where to start.

Controls: By default, your Google map includes several controls, like the zoom control, the pan control, a control to switch between Map and Satellite view, and even the Street View control (the little pegman above the zoom control). You can access these controls programmatically from JavaScript to make use of them in your applications.

Services: Ever looked up directions in Google Maps? If so, then you've used the Directions service. You have access to directions, as well as other services, like distance and street view through the Google Maps services APIs.

Overlays: Overlays provide another view on top of a Google map; say, a heat map overlay. If you're commuting, you can check traffic congestion with the traffic overlay. You can create custom overlays, like custom markers, your photos, and pretty much anything else you can imagine, using the Google Maps overlay APIs.

All this is available through the Google Maps JavaScript API. To take your experiments further, check out the documentation at:

```
http://code.google.com/apis/maps/documentation/javascript/
```

Geolocation Exposed

This week's interview:
A conversation with a wannabe HTML5 API

Head First: Welcome Geolocation. I gotta say right up front, I'm a bit surprised to see you here.

Geolocation: Why's that?

Head First: You're not even "officially" part of the HTML5 spec and here you are, you're the first API that's been given a chapter! What's up with that?

Geolocation: Well, you're right that I'm defined in a specification that's separate from the HTML5 specification, but I *am* an official specification of the W3C. And, just look around, any mobile device worth its salt has me already implemented in its browser. I mean what good is a mobile web app without me?

Head First: So what kind of web apps are making use of you?

Geolocation: Really, it's most of the apps people are using on the move; from apps that let you update your status and include geo information, to camera apps that record where pictures are taken, to social apps that find local friends or allow you to "check in" at various locations. Heck, people are even using me to record where they cycle or run or eat or to get where they're going.

Head First: Your API seems a bit simplistic, I mean you've got, what, a couple of methods and properties total?

Geolocation: Small and simple is powerful. Do you see many complaints about me out there? Nope. I've got what every developer needs and location-aware apps are getting cranked out by the dozen a day. Plus, small equals quick and easy to learn, right? Maybe that's why I'm the first API with his very own chapter?

Head First: Let's talk about support.

Geolocation: That's a short topic because I'm supported in almost every browser, on desktop and mobile.

Head First: Okay, so one thing I've always wanted to ask you: what good are you on a device that doesn't have GPS?

Geolocation: There's a big misconception that I'm somehow dependent on GPS. There are other great ways to determine location today through cell phone triangulation, using IP addresses, and so on. If you have GPS, great, and in fact I can help you even more; but if not, there are lots of ways to get location.

Head First: Help even more?

Geolocation: If you've got a good enough mobile device I can give you altitude, direction, speed, all kinds of things.

Head First: Say none of those methods work, that is, GPS, IP address, triangulation, then what good are you?

Geolocation: Well, I can't always guarantee you're going to get a location, but that's okay because I do give you a nice way to handle failures gracefully. All you have to do is give me an error handler and I'll call it if I have a problem.

Head First: Good to know. Well, that's all we have time for. Thank you, Geolocation, for being here and congrats for getting promoted to a real W3C standard.

Meanwhile back at the Geolocation API...

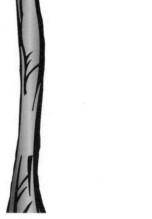

We've already travelled a fair distance with the Geolocation API: we've determined our location, computed distances to other locations, handled the error states of the API and even added a map using the Google Maps API. But it's not time to rest yet, we're just to the point of getting into the interesting parts of the API. We're also at that point between knowing about the API, and having mastery over it, so let's keep moving!

One thing we need to do before going on is to take a closer look at the API itself. We've talked about it enough, but we've never actually *looked at it*. As we've been saying, the API is actually really simple, having just three methods: `getCurrentPosition` (which you know something about), `watchPosition` (which you'll find out about soon enough), and `clearWatch` (which, you guessed it, is related to `watchPosition`). Before getting to these two new methods, let's take another look at `getCurrentPosition` and at some related objects, like the `Position` and `Coordinates` objects. You're going to find a few new things there you didn't know about.

Geolocation
getCurrentPosition watchPosition clearWatch

The methods that are part of the Geolocation API.

The error handler is called when the browser can't determine its location. As we've seen there are many possible reasons for that.

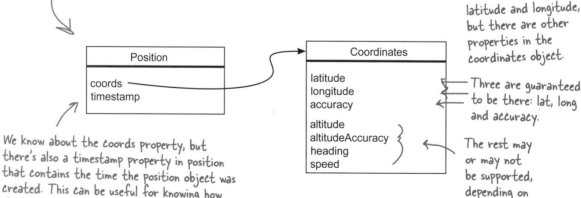

getCurrentPosition(successHandler, errorHandler, positionOptions)

Remember, the success handler (or callback) is called when a location is determined, and it is passed a <u>position</u> object.

And we have another parameter we haven't used yet that allows us to fine-tune the behavior of geolocation.

We know about latitude and longitude, but there are other properties in the coordinates object.

Position
coords timestamp

Coordinates
latitude longitude accuracy
altitude altitudeAccuracy heading speed

Three are guaranteed to be there: lat, long and accuracy.

The rest may or may not be supported, depending on your device.

We know about the coords property, but there's also a timestamp property in position that contains the time the position object was created. This can be useful for knowing how old the location is.

Can we talk about your accuracy?

Finding your location isn't an exact science. Depending on the method the browser uses, you may know only the state, city, or city block you're on. Then again, with more advanced devices you might know your location to within 10 meters, complete with your speed, heading and altitude.

So how do we write code, given this situation? The designers of the Geolocation API have made a nice little contract with us: every time they give us a location they'll also give us the accuracy, in meters, of the location, to within a 95% confidence level. So, for instance, we might know our location with 500 meters accuracy, which means that we can be pretty darn sure we can count on the location as long as we factor in a radius of 500 meters. And for 500 meters, we'd be safe, for instance, giving city or neighborhood recommendations, but we might not want to provide street by street driving directions. In any case, it is obviously up to your app to figure out how it wants to make use of the accuracy data.

Enough talk, let's find out what your accuracy looks like in your current location. As you've just seen, the accuracy information is part of the coordinates object. Let's pull it out and use it in the `displayLocation` function.

```
function displayLocation(position) {
    var latitude = position.coords.latitude;
    var longitude = position.coords.longitude;
    var div = document.getElementById("location");

    div.innerHTML = "You are at Latitude: " + latitude + ", Longitude: " + longitude;
    div.innerHTML += " (with " + position.coords.accuracy + " meters accuracy)";

    var km = computeDistance(position.coords, ourCoords);
    var div = document.getElementById("distance");
    distance.innerHTML = "You are " + km + " km from the WickedlySmart HQ";
    showMap(position.coords);
}
```

Here we use the accuracy property of position, and append onto the end of the <div>'s innerHTML.

Accuracy Test

Make sure you've got this one liner added to your code, and load the page. Now you can see how accurate your location is. Be sure to try this on any device you have.

Try online: http://wickedlysmart.com/hfhtml5/chapter5/accuracy/myLoc.html

"Wherever you go, there you are"

The orgin of this phrase has been hotly debated. Some claim the first real mention of it was in the film *Buckaroo Banzai*, others draw its origin from Zen Buddhist text, still others cite various books, movies and popular songs. No matter the source, it's here to stay, and even more so after this chapter because we're going to turn it into a little web app named "Wherever you go, there you are." Yes, there is an app for that! But, we're going to need a little participation from you, the reader, because for this one you'll have to (excuse us for saying this) get off your butt and move around a little.

What we're going to do is extend our current code so that it tracks your movements in real time. To do that we're going to bring everything together, including last two methods in the Geolocation API, and create an app that tracks you, in near real time.

Where do you come in on the debate? Is the saying a product of the Banzai Institute, or are the origins in Zen literature?

How we're going to track your movements

You've already received a heads up that the Geolocation API has a `watchPosition` method. This method does what it says: it watches your movements and reports your location back as your location changes. The `watchPosition` method actually looks just like the `getCurrentPosition` method, but behaves a little differently: it repeatedly calls your success handler each time your position changes. Let's see how it works.

① Your app calls watchPosition, passing in a success handler function.

② watchPosition sits in the background and constantly monitors your position.

Browser

position.coords.latitude
position.coords.longitude

④ watchPosition continues to monitor your position (and report it to your success handler) until you clear it by calling clearWatch.

③ When your position changes, watchPosition calls your success handler function to report your new position.

Getting the app started

We're going to use our previous code as a starting point; first we're going to add a couple of buttons to the HTML so that we can start and stop the tracking of your location. Why do we need the buttons? Well, first of all, users don't want to be tracked all the time and they usually want some control over that. But there's another reason: constantly checking your position is an energy-intensive operation on a mobile device and if it's left on all the time, it will cause your battery life to suffer. So, first, we'll update the HTML to add a form and two buttons: one to start watching your position and one to stop.

Tracking a user in real time can be a real battery drainer. Make sure you give the user information about their tracking, and some control over it, too.

```html
<!doctype html>
<html>
<head>
  <meta charset="utf-8">
  <title>Wherever you go, there you are</title>
  <script src="myLoc.js"></script>
  <link rel="stylesheet" href="myLoc.css">
</head>
<body>
  <form>
    <input type="button" id="watch" value="Watch me">
    <input type="button" id="clearWatch" value="Clear watch">
  </form>
  <div id="location">
    Your location will go here.
  </div>
  <div id="distance">
    Distance from WickedlySmart HQ will go here.
  </div>
  <div id="map">
  </div>
</body>
</html>
```

We're adding a form element with two buttons, one to start the watch, with an id of "watch", and one to clear the watch, with an id of "clearWatch".

We're going to reuse our old <div>s to report on the real-time location information.

We'll come back and worry about the Google map in a bit...

Reworking our old code...

So now we need to add button click handlers for the two buttons. We'll add them to the getMyLocation function only if there is geolocation support. And, since we're going to control all the geolocation tracking using the two buttons, we'll remove the existing call to getCurrentPosition from getMyLocation. Let's go ahead and remove that code, and add two handlers: watchLocation for the watch button, and clearWatch for the clear button:

If the browser supports geolocation, we'll add our button click handlers. No point in adding them if geolocation isn't supported.

```
function getMyLocation() {
    if (navigator.geolocation) {
        navigator.geolocation.getCurrentPosition(displayLocation,displayError);
        var watchButton = document.getElementById("watch");
        watchButton.onclick = watchLocation;
        var clearWatchButton = document.getElementById("clearWatch");
        clearWatchButton.onclick = clearWatch;
    }
    else {
        alert("Oops, no geolocation support");
    }
}
```

We're going to call watchLocation to start the watch, and clearWatch to stop it.

Writing the watchLocation handler

At this point, here's what we're trying to do: when the user clicks on the watch button, they want to start tracking their position. So, we'll use the the geolocation.watchPosition method to start watching their position. The geolocation.watchPosition method has two parameters, a success handler and an error handler, so we'll reuse the ones we already have. It also returns a watchId, which can be used at any time to cancel the watching behavior. We're going to stash the watchId in a global variable, which we'll use when we write the click handler for the clear button. Here's the code for the watchLocation function and the watchId, go ahead and add this code to myLoc.js:

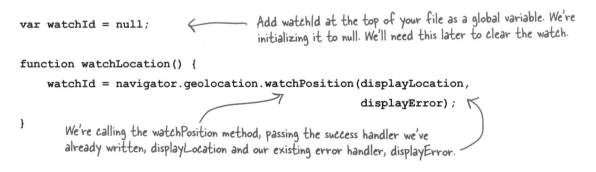

```
var watchId = null;

function watchLocation() {
    watchId = navigator.geolocation.watchPosition(displayLocation,
                                            displayError);
}
```

Add watchId at the top of your file as a global variable. We're initializing it to null. We'll need this later to clear the watch.

We're calling the watchPosition method, passing the success handler we've already written, displayLocation and our existing error handler, displayError.

Writing the clearWatch handler

Now let's write the handler to clear the watching activity. To do that we need to take the `watchId` and pass it to the `geolocation.clearWatch` method.

```
function clearWatch() {
    if (watchId) {
        navigator.geolocation.clearWatch(watchId);
        watchId = null;
    }
}
```

Make sure there's a watchId and then...

...call the geolocation.clearWatch method, passing in the watchId. This stops the watching.

We still need to make a small update to displayLocation...

There's one small change we need to make and it involves the Google Maps code we previously wrote. In this code we call `showMap` to display the Google Map. Now, `showMap` creates a new map in your page, and that is something you only want to do one time. But remember, when you start watching your location with `watchPosition`, `displayLocation` is going to get called every time there is an update to your position.

To make sure we only call `showMap` once, we'll first test to see if the map exists and if it doesn't, we'll call `showMap`. Otherwise, `showMap` has already been called (and has already created the map) and we don't need to call it again.

```
function displayLocation(position) {
    var latitude = position.coords.latitude;
    var longitude = position.coords.longitude;

    var div = document.getElementById("location");
    div.innerHTML = "You are at Latitude: " + latitude + ", Longitude: " + longitude;
    div.innerHTML += " (with " + position.coords.accuracy + " meters accuracy)";

    var km = computeDistance(position.coords, ourCoords);
    var distance = document.getElementById("distance");
    distance.innerHTML = "You are " + km + " km from the WickedlySmart HQ";

    if (map == null) {
        showMap(position.coords);
    }
}
```

If we haven't called showMap already, then call it, otherwise we don't need to call it every time displayLocation is called.

Time to get moving!

Make sure you've got all the new code typed in and reload your page, `myLoc.html`. Now, to truly test this page you're going to need to "relocate" to have your position updated. So take a walk, jump on your bike, get in the car, or use whatever your favorite mode of transportation might be.

It almost goes without saying that if you're running this on your desktop, this app is going to be pretty boring (since you can't take it with you), so you really need to use a mobile device for this test. And, if you need help getting to a hosted version with your mobile device, we've placed a copy of this code at: `http://wickedlysmart.com/hfhtml5/chapter5/watchme/myLoc.html`.

Here's our test run...

These numbers will update as you move around.

Note the map is just going to center on your initial location, for now...

Try online: http://wickedlysmart.com/hfhtml5/chapter5/watchme/myLoc.html

there are no
Dumb Questions

Q: How can I control the rate at which the browser is providing updates of my location when using watchPosition?

A: You can't. The browser determines what the optimal update rate is and decides when you've changed positions.

Q: Why does my location change a few times when I first load the page, even though I'm sitting still?

A: Remember we said the browser may use a few methods to determine your location? Depending on the method (or methods) the browser is using to determine your location, the accuracy of the location may change over time. In general the accuracy gets better, but sometimes (say, you've just driven into a rural area with only one cell tower) it may get worse. And you can always use the accuracy property in the position.coords object to keep an eye on accuracy.

Q: Can I use the altitude and altitudeAccuracy properties of the coordinates object?

A: These properties are not guranteed to be supported (and obviously are going to be supported on only high-end mobile devices), so you'll have to make sure your code handles the case where they aren't.

Q: What are heading and speed?

A: Heading is the direction you're traveling in and speed is how fast you're going. Think about if you're in a car heading north on Interstate 5 at 55mph. Your heading is north, and your speed is 55mph. If you are in your car in the parking lot at Starbuzz Coffee, then your speed is 0 and you have no heading (because you're not moving).

Q: When I map the distance from my location to your location, it's a lot longer than is being reported in the app, why?

A: Remember, our distance function is computing the distance "as the crow flies." Your mapping tool is most likely giving you the driving distance.

Sharpen your pencil

Below you'll find an alternative implementation for displayLocation. Can you guess what it does? Take a look and write your answer below. If you're feeling adventurous, try it out!

```
distance.innerHTML = "You are " + km + " km from the WickedlySmart HQ";
if (km < 0.1) {
  distance.innerHTML = "You're on fire!";
} else {
  if (prevKm < km) {
    distance.innerHTML = "You're getting hotter!";
  } else {
    distance.innerHTML = "You're getting colder...";
  }
}
prevKm = km;
```

Write what you think this does here. → ....

You've got some Options...

So far we've stayed away from the third parameter of `getCurrentPosition` (and `watchPosition`): the `positionOptions` parameter. With this parameter we can control how geolocation computes its values. Let's look at the three parameters along with their default values:

```
var positionOptions = {

    enableHighAccuracy: false,

    timeout: Infinity,

    maximumAge: 0

}
```

First we have a property that enables high accuracy, we'll talk about what that means in a sec...

The timeout option controls how long the browser gets to determine its location. By default this is set to infinity meaning the browser gets all the time it needs).

You can reset this to a value in milliseconds, say 10000, this gives the browser ten seconds to find a location, otherwise the error handler is called.

Finally, the maximumAge option sets the oldest age a location can be before the browser needs to recalculate the location. By default this is zero, which means the browser will always have to recalculate its location (every time getCurrentPosition is called).

Can we talk about your accuracy, again?

We've already seen that each position handed to us by the Geolocation API has an accuracy property. But, we can also tell the Geolocation API that we'd like only the most accurate result it can get. Now, this is only meant as a hint to the browser, and in fact, different implementations may do different things with the hint. And, while this option doesn't sound like a big deal, it has lots of implications. For instance, if you don't care that your results are super accurate—you might be just fine knowing that your user is in Baltimore—the API might be able to tell you that very quickly and very cheaply (in terms of power consumption). If, on the other hand, you need to know the street your user is on, that's fine, but the API might then have to fire up GPS, and use lots of power to get that information. With the `enableHighAccuracy` option, you're telling the API you need the most accurate location it can get, even if it is costly. Just keep in mind, using this option doesn't *guarantee* the browser can give you a more accurate location.

The world of timeouts and maximum age...

Let's review once again what the `timeout` and `maximumAge` options are:

timeout: this option tells the browser how **long** it gets to determine the user's location. Note that if the user is prompted to approve the location request, the timeout doesn't start until they've accepted. If the browser can't determine a new location within the number of milliseconds specified in the timeout, the error handler is called. *By default, this option is set to Infinity.*

maximumAge: this option tells the browser how **old** the location can be. So, if the browser has a location that was determined sixty seconds go, and maximumAge is set to 90000 (90 seconds), then a call to `getCurrentPosition` would return the existing, cached position (the browser would not try to get a new one). But if the maximumAge was set to 30 seconds, the browser would be forced to determine a new position.

> So by using maximumAge I can really tune how often my browser recalculates or determines my position. I can see how using that can make my app faster and more power efficient. What about timeout? How can I use it to improve things?

You're right on with your thinking on maximumAge. For timeout, think about it like this: when you're using maximumAge so you get an old (cached) result, as long as that result is younger than the maximumAge you specified, this works really well to optimize the performance of your app. But what happens when the position's age exceeds the maximumAge? Well, the browser goes off and tries to get a new one. But, what if you don't care *that much*—say you'll take a new location if it has it, but otherwise, you don't need it right now. Well, you could set timeout to 0, and if there is a result that passes the maximumAge test, great, here it is, otherwise the call will fail immedately and call your error handler (with an error code of `TIMEOUT`). That's just one example of the creative ways you can use `timeout` and `maximumAge` to tune the behavior of your application.

WHO DOES WHAT?

Below you'll see a few options for the geolocation API.
For each option, match it to its behavior.

`{maximumAge:600000}`

I want only cached positions less than 10 minutes old. If there aren't any cached positions less than 10 minutes old, I ask for a new position, but only if I can get one in 1 second or less.

`{timeout:1000, maximumAge:600000}`

I'll use a cached position if the browser has one that's less than 10 minutes old, otherwise, I want a fresh position.

`{timeout:0, maximumAge:Infinity}`

I want only fresh positions. The browser can take as long it wants to get me one.

`{timeout:Infinity, maximumAge:0}`

I want only cached positions. I'll take one of any age. If there is no cached position at all, then I call the error handler. No new positions for me! I'm for offline use.

How to specify options

One of the nice things about JavaScript is that if we want to specify a set of options in an object, we can just type in a literal object, right into the middle of our method call. Here's how you do that: let's say we want to enable high accuracy and also set the maximum age of the location to be 60 seconds (or 60,000 milliseconds). We could create options like this:

```
var options = {enableHighAccuracy: true, maximumAge: 60000};
```

Are you starting to see that JavaScript really rocks? Well, at least we think it does. ☺

And then pass `options` to either `getCurrentPosition` or `watchPosition`, like this:

```
navigator.geolocation.getCurrentPosition(
                displayLocation,
                displayError,
                options);
```

Here, we're just passing our options along using the options variable.

Or, we could just write the options object inline, like this:

```
navigator.geolocation.getCurrentPosition(
                displayLocation,
                displayError,
                {enableHighAccuracy: true, maximumAge: 60000});
```

You'll see this technique used a lot in JavaScript code.

Here are the options, written as a literal object right in the function call! Some would argue this is easier and more readable as code.

Now that you know the options, what they do, and how to specify them, we should use them. We're going to do that, but remember, these are meant to tune *your* application, which will have its own unique requirements. These options are also affected by your device, browser implementation and network, so you'll need to play on your own to fully explore them.

Test Drive Diagnostics Checkup

When you ran the diagnostics before, did you get the test case where you waited and waited and nothing happened? That's most likely because of the infinite timeout. In other words the browser will wait forever to get a location as long as it doesn't encounter some error condition. Well, now you know how to fix that, because we can force the Geolocation API to be a little more expedient by setting its timeout value. Here's how:

```
function watchLocation() {
    watchId = navigator.geolocation.watchPosition(
                displayLocation,
                displayError,
                {timeout:5000});
}
```

By setting timeout to 5000 milliseconds (5 seconds) you're making sure the browser doesn't sit there forever trying to get a location.

Give it a try and feel free to adjust the option values.

~~DON'T~~ TRY THIS AT HOME
(PUSHING GEO TO THE LIMIT)

Wouldn't it be fun to see how fast your browser can find your location? We could make it as hard for your browser as we can:

- let's ask it to enable high accuracy,
- let's not allow it to use a cache (by setting maximumAge to 0)
- let's time it by setting the timeout option to 100, and then increase the timeout every time it fails.

Warning: we don't know if all devices and their batteries are up to this, so use at your own risk!

Here's what the intial options are going to look like:

```
{enableHighAccuracy: true, timeout:100, maximumAge:0}
```
← We'll start here...

```
{enableHighAccuracy: true, timeout:200, maximumAge:0}
```
← and if that fails give it more time...

```
{enableHighAccuracy: true, timeout:300, maximumAge:0}
```
← and so on...

Now check out the code on the next page, you'll find it quite interesting. Go ahead and type it in—you can just add it to your JavaScript in `myLoc.js`. Try it on your various devices and record your results here:

device here ↘

↓ time here

ON _____ FOUND IN _____ milliseconds

ON _____ FOUND IN _____ milliseconds

ON _____ FOUND IN _____ milliseconds

ON _____ FOUND IN _____ milliseconds

Try online: http://wickedlysmart.com/hfhtml5/chapter5/speedtest/speedtest.html

```
var options = { enableHighAccuracy: true, timeout:100, maximumAge: 0 };
window.onload = getMyLocation;
function getMyLocation() {
    if (navigator.geolocation) {
        navigator.geolocation.getCurrentPosition(
            displayLocation,
            displayError,
            options);
    } else {
        alert("Oops, no geolocation support");
    }
}
function displayError(error) {
    var errorTypes = {
        0: "Unknown error",
        1: "Permission denied",
        2: "Position is not available",
        3: "Request timeout"
    };
    var errorMessage = errorTypes[error.code];
    if (error.code == 0 || error.code == 2) {
        errorMessage = errorMessage + " " + error.message;
    }
    var div = document.getElementById("location");
    div.innerHTML = errorMessage;
    options.timeout += 100;
    navigator.geolocation.getCurrentPosition(
        displayLocation,
        displayError,
        options);
    div.innerHTML += " ... checking again with timeout=" + options.timeout;
}
function displayLocation(position) {
    var latitude = position.coords.latitude;
    var longitude = position.coords.longitude;
    var div = document.getElementById("location");
    div.innerHTML = "You are at Latitude: " + latitude +
                    ", Longitude: " + longitude;
    div.innerHTML += " (found in " + options.timeout + " milliseconds)";
}
```

Start by initializing our options with a timeout of 100, and a maximumAge of 0.

Do the usual here, with displayLocation and displayError as our success and error handlers, and passing in options as the third paramter.

We'll do the error handler first.

This code here is the same...

But in the case of a failure, we're going to increase the timeout option by 100ms and try again. We'll let the user know we're re-trying as well.

When the browser successfully gets your position, we'll let the user know how long it took.

Let's finish this app!

When you sit back and think about it, with just a little HTML and JavaScript you've created a web app that not only can determine your location, but it can also track and display it in *near real time*. Wow, HTML sure has grown up (and so have your skills!).

But, speaking of this app, don't you think it needs just a little bit of polish to finish it off? For instance, we could show your position on the map as you move around, and we could even go further and show where you've been too, to create a path through the map.

Let's write a function to keep the map centered on your location as you move around, and drop a new marker each time we get a new position:

What we're going to do to finish this app!

Okay, we're going to call this function scrollMapToPosition and we're going to pass it a position's coordinates.

The coordinates are going to be your latest new position, so we're going to center the map on that location, and drop a marker there too.

```
function scrollMapToPosition(coords) {
    var latitude = coords.latitude;
    var longitude = coords.longitude;
    var latlong = new google.maps.LatLng(latitude, longitude);

    map.panTo(latlong);

    addMarker(map, latlong, "Your new location", "You moved to: " +
                            latitude + ", " + longitude);
}
```

First let's grab the new lat and long, and create a google.maps. LatLng object for them.

The panTo method of the map takes the LatLng object and scrolls the map so your new location is at the center of the map.

Finally, we'll add a marker for your new location using the addMarker function we wrote earlier, passing in the map, the LatLng object, a title and some content for the new marker.

Integrating our new function

Now, all we need to do is update the `displayLocation` function to call `scrollMapToPosition` each time your position changes. Remember that the first time `displayLocation` is called, we're calling `showMap` to create the map and display a marker for your initial location. Each time after that we just need to call `scrollMapToPosition` to add a new marker and re-center the map. Here's the code change:

```
function displayLocation(position) {
    var latitude = position.coords.latitude;
    var longitude = position.coords.longitude;
    var div = document.getElementById("location");
    div.innerHTML = "You are at Latitude: " + latitude
                    + ", Longitude: " + longitude;
    div.innerHTML += " (with " + position.coords.accuracy + " meters accuracy)";
    var km = computeDistance(position.coords, ourCoords);
    var distance = document.getElementById("distance");
    distance.innerHTML = "You are " + km + " km from the WickedlySmart HQ";

    if (map == null) {
        showMap(position.coords);
    } else {
        scrollMapToPosition(position.coords);
    }
}
```

The first time displayLocation is called, we need to draw the map and add the first marker.

After that, all we need to do is add a new marker to the existing map.

And one more time...

Reload your page and start moving around... is your map following you? You should see a trail of markers being added to your map as you move (unless you're sitting at your desktop!).

So, we submit this application as solid proof that "wherever you go, there you are."

Our trail of markers on a recent trip from Wickedly Smart HQ to the secret underground lair...oh wait, we shouldn't have said that...

Try online: http://wickedlysmart.com/hfhtml5/chapter5/watchmepan/myLoc.html

Code Magnets

Before we conclude this chapter, we thought you might want to really polish up this app. You might have noticed (under some circumstances) that there are just a few too many markers being added to the map when you're watching your position?

What's happening is that watchPosition is detecting movement frequently, so it's calling the displayLocation success handler every few steps or so. One way to fix that is to add some code so we have to move some significant distance, say 20 meters for testing purposes, before we create a new marker.

We already have a function that will compute the distance between two coordinates (computeDistance), so all we need to do is save our position each time displayLocation is called, and check to see if the distance between the previous position and the new position is greater than 20 meters before calling scrollMapToPosition. You'll find some of the code below to do that; it's your job to finish it. Watch out, you'll have to use some magnets more than once!

Whoa, can you say marker explosion?

```
var _____;
function displayLocation(position) {
    var latitude = position.coords.latitude;
    var longitude = position.coords.longitude;
    var div = document.getElementById("location");
    div.innerHTML = "You are at Latitude: " + latitude + ", Longitude: " + longitude;
    div.innerHTML += " (with " + position.coords.accuracy + " meters accuracy)";
    var km = computeDistance(position.coords, ourCoords);
    var distance = document.getElementById("distance");
    distance.innerHTML = "You are " + km + " km from the WickedlySmart HQ";
    if (map == null) {
        showMap(position.coords);
        prevCoords = _____;
    } else {
        var meters = _____(position.coords, prevCoords) * 1000;
        if (_____ > _____) {
            scrollMapToPosition(position.coords);
            _____ = _____;
        }
    }
}
```

| computeDistance |

| meters |

| prevCoords = null; |

| position.coords | | 20 | | prevCoords |

BULLET POINTS

- Geolocation is not "officially" part of the HTML5 specification, but it's considered part of the "family" of HTML5 specs.

- There are a variety of ways to determine your location, depending on the device you have.

- GPS is a more accurate method of getting your location than cell tower triangulation or network IP.

- Mobile devices without GPS can use cell tower triangulation to determine location.

- The Geolocation API has three methods and a few properties.

- The primary method in the Geolocation API is getCurrentPosition, a method of the navigator.geolocation object.

- getCurrentPosition has one required parameter, the success handler, and two optional parameters, the error handler, and the options.

- A position object is passed to the success handler with information about your location, including your latitude and longitude.

- The position object contains a coords property, which is a coordinates object.

- The coordinates object has properties including latitude, longitude and accuracy.

- Some devices may support the other coordinates properties: altitude, altitudeAccuracy, heading, and speed.

- Use the accuracy property to determine how accurate your location is in meters.

- When getCurrentPosition is called, your browser must verify that you have given permission to share your location.

- watchPosition is a method of the geolocation object that monitors your location and calls a success handler when your location changes.

- Like getCurrentPosition, watchPosition has one required parameter, a success handler, and two optional parameters, an error handler and options.

- Use clearWatch to stop monitoring your location.

- When watchPosition is used, your device will require more energy, so your battery life may be shortened.

- The third parameter, options, for getCurrentPosition and watchPosition, is an object with properties you set to control the behavior of the Geolocation API.

- The maximumAge property determines whether getCurrentPosition will use a cached position, and if so, how old that position can be before a fresh position is required.

- The timeout property determines how much time getCurrentPosition has to get a fresh position before the error handler is called.

- The enableHighAccuracy property gives a hint to devices to spend more effort getting a highly accurate location if possible.

- You can use the Geolocation API with the Google Maps API to place your location on a map.

HTML5cross

You've traveled quite far in this chapter with your first JavaScript API. Make it stick with this crossword.

Across

4. Longitude is measured from _____, England.
7. Accuracy has implications for your app because it can affect _____ life.
8. If you say no when your browser asks you to share your location, your error handler will be called with an _____ code of 1.
9. "Wherever you go, there you are" was mentioned in the movie _____.
10. Don't give driving directions to someone if your coordinates don't have a good _____.
11. The secret location of the _____ HQ is 47.62485, -122.52099.

Down

1. Re-center your map using the_____ method.
2. Old Skool devices without GPS use cell tower _____ to determine your location.
3. The latitude, longitude of _____ is 40.77, -73.98.
5. You'll never get a cached location if you set _____ to 0.
6. You can use the _____ equation to find the distance between two coordinates.

Code Magnets

It's your job to finish the code below, so we only display a new marker if we've traveled more than 20 meters since the last marker was added. Use the fridge magnets to complete the code. Watch out, you'll have to use some of them more than once! Here's our solution.

```
var    prevCoords = null;
function displayLocation(position) {
    var latitude = position.coords.latitude;
    var longitude = position.coords.longitude;
    var div = document.getElementById("location");
    div.innerHTML = "You are at Latitude: " + latitude + ", Longitude: " + longitude;
    div.innerHTML += " (with " + position.coords.accuracy + " meters accuracy)";
    var km = computeDistance(position.coords, ourCoords);
    var distance = document.getElementById("distance");
    distance.innerHTML = "You are " + km + " km from the WickedlySmart HQ";
    if (map == null) {
        showMap(position.coords);
        prevCoords = position.coords ;
    }
    else {
        var meters = computeDistance (position.coords, prevCoords) * 1000;
        if ( meters  >  20 ) {
            scrollMapToPosition(position.coords);
            prevCoords = position.coords ;
        }
    }
}
```

Much better!

Try online: http://wickedlysmart.com/hfhtml5/chapter6/final/myLoc.html

Sharpen your pencil
Solution

Below you'll find an alternative implementation for displayLocation. Can you guess what it does? Take a look and write your answer below. If you're feeling adventurous, try it out! Here's our solution.

```
distance.innerHTML = "You are " + km + " km from the WickedlySmart HQ";
if (km < 0.1) {
  distance.innerHTML = "You're on fire!";
} else {
  if (prevKm < km) {
    distance.innerHTML = "You're getting hotter!";
  } else {
    distance.innerHTML = "You're getting colder...";
  }
}
prevKm = km;
```

This code turns our app into a Hot/Cold game. It displays a "getting hotter" message if you're moving closer to the WickedlySmart HQ, or "getting colder" if you're moving farther away. If you're within 0.1 km of the HQ, then the message is, "You're on fire!"

Write what you think this does here.

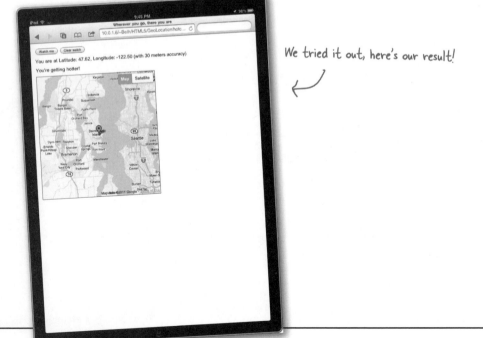

We tried it out, here's our result!

WHO DOES WHAT? SOLUTION

Below you'll see a few options for the geolocation API.
For each option, match it to its behavior.

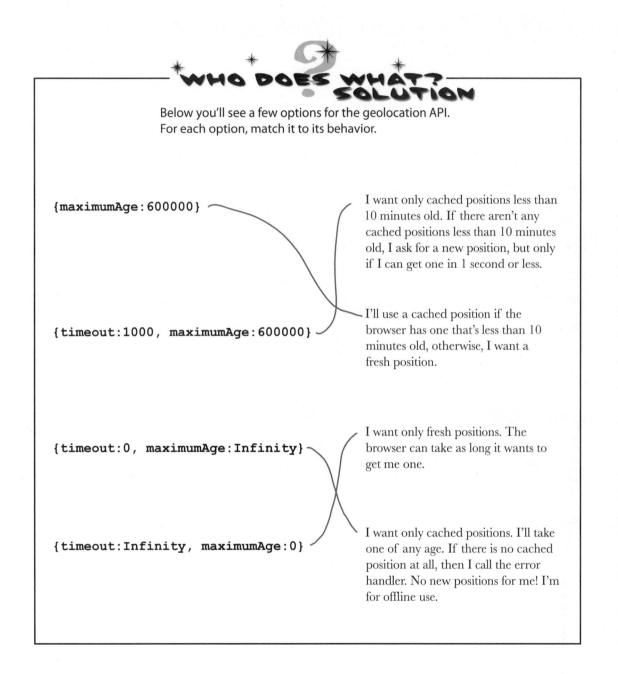

`{maximumAge:600000}`

`{timeout:1000, maximumAge:600000}`

`{timeout:0, maximumAge:Infinity}`

`{timeout:Infinity, maximumAge:0}`

I want only cached positions less than 10 minutes old. If there aren't any cached positions less than 10 minutes old, I ask for a new position, but only if I can get one in 1 second or less.

I'll use a cached position if the browser has one that's less than 10 minutes old, otherwise, I want a fresh position.

I want only fresh positions. The browser can take as long it wants to get me one.

I want only cached positions. I'll take one of any age. If there is no cached position at all, then I call the error handler. No new positions for me! I'm for offline use.

HTML5cross Solution

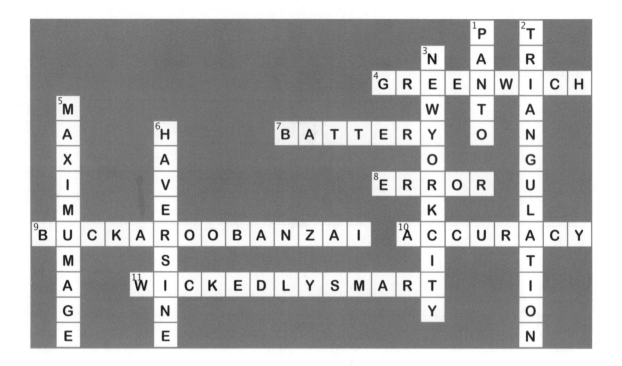

6 talking to the web

Extroverted Apps

> If only I'd known reaching out and touching a web service could be so much fun...

You've been sitting in your page for too long. It's time to get out a little, to talk to web services, to gather data and to bring it all back so you can build better experiences mixing all that great data together. That's a big part of writing modern HTML5 applications, but to do that you've got to *know how* to talk to web services. In this chapter we're going to do just that, and incorporate some data from a real web service right in your page. And, after you've learned how to do that you'll be able to reach out and touch any web service you want. We'll even fill you in on the hippest new lingo you should use when talking to web services. So, come on, you're going to use some more APIs, the communications APIs.

Mighty Gumball wants a Web app

Check out the new Web-enabled MG2200 gumball machine. It's going to revolutionize the biz.

This just in: Mighty Gumball, Inc., an innovative company that builds and deploys *real gumball machines*, has contacted us for some help. If you're not up on them, they've recently network-enabled their gumball machines to track sales in near real time.

You might remember them from our book Head First Design Patterns, when we helped them design their server-side code.

Now it almost goes without saying that Mighty Gumball are gumball experts, not software developers, and so they'd like our help building an app to help them monitor gumball sales.

Here's what they sent over:

CEO, MightyGumball

Mighty Gumball, Inc.
Where the Gumball Machine
is Never Half Empty

Thanks for helping! Here's the way we think the gumball machine realtime sales tool should work and we're hoping you can implement this for us! Let us know if you have any questions!

Oh, we'll send over some specs for the web service soon.

— Mighty Gumball Engineers

Mobile and desktop devices get sales from a real-time server through a web service.

We want you to write this part, using HTML5 of course!

Our server on the Web

All our gumball machines reporting into the central server.

Before we get started, take a little time to think through how you might design an app that retrieves data from a web service and then keeps a web page updated based on the data. Don't worry that you don't know how to retrieve the data yet, just think through the high level design. Draw a pic, label it, write out pseudo-code for any code you might need. Think of this as a warm-up, just to get your brain going...

Engineering Notes

Mighty Gumball, Inc.
Where the Gumball Machine
is Never Half Empty

How do we get the data from the web service to our web page?

Once we've got the data, how do we update the page?

What kinds of problems might we have with getting data from a remote server?

A little more background on Mighty Gumball

You probably need a little background beyond Mighty Gumball's short note. Here's what we've got: first, they've got gumball machines all over the country sending sales reports to a Mighty Gumball server, which combines all those reports and makes them available through a web service. And, second, they're asking us to build a web app that displays the sales in a browser for the Gumball Sales team. And, most likely they want this report to be updated as the sales change over time. Here's the view from 10,000 feet:

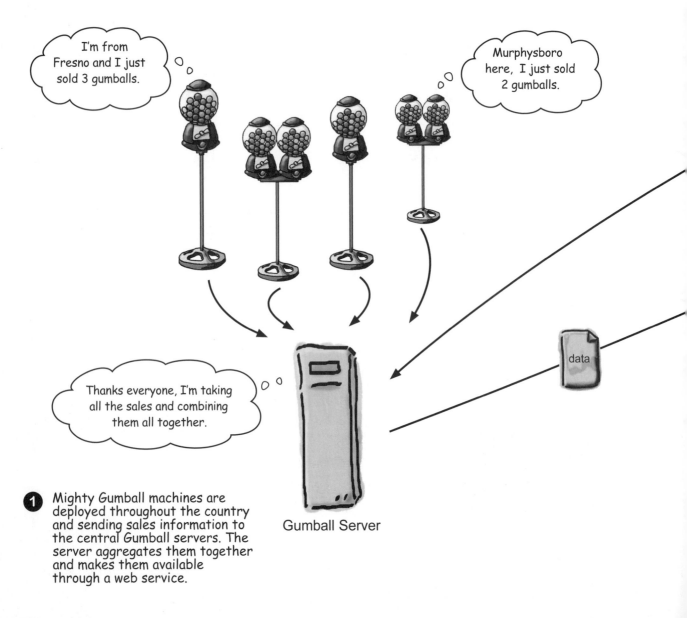

1. Mighty Gumball machines are deployed throughout the country and sending sales information to the central Gumball servers. The server aggregates them together and makes them available through a web service.

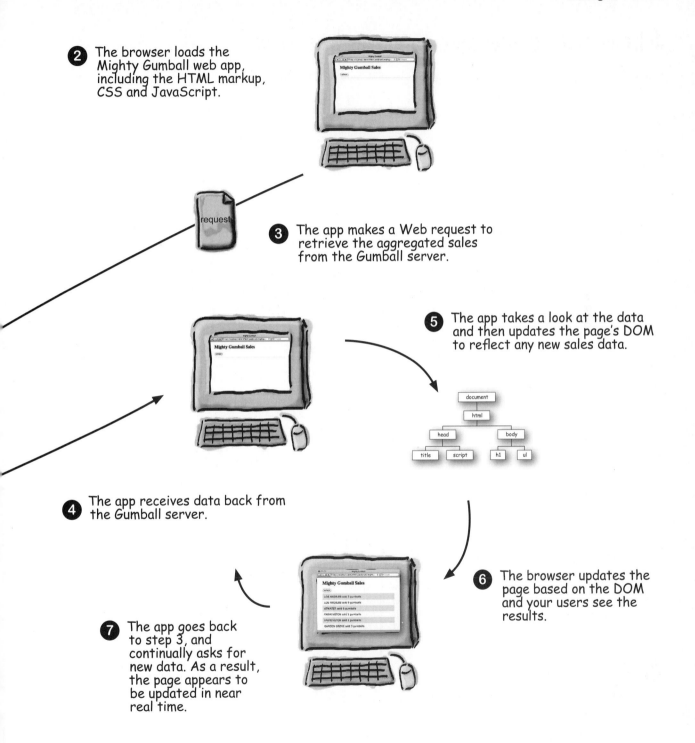

2 The browser loads the Mighty Gumball web app, including the HTML markup, CSS and JavaScript.

3 The app makes a Web request to retrieve the aggregated sales from the Gumball server.

5 The app takes a look at the data and then updates the page's DOM to reflect any new sales data.

4 The app receives data back from the Gumball server.

6 The browser updates the page based on the DOM and your users see the results.

7 The app goes back to step 3, and continually asks for new data. As a result, the page appears to be updated in near real time.

Just a quick start...

While we're waiting on those specs from Mighty Gumball, let's get some HTML going.

You're probably getting the idea we don't need a lot of HTML markup to get a web app off the ground, and you're right. All we need is a place to put our sales reports as they come in, and we'll let JavaScript do the rest. Go ahead and get this typed in, and then we'll take a look at how to retrieve things via the Web.

```html
<!doctype html>
<html lang="en">
<head>
<title>Mighty Gumball (JSON)</title>
<meta charset="utf-8">
<script src="mightygumball.js"></script>
<link rel="stylesheet" href="mightygumball.css">
</head>
<body>
<h1>Mighty Gumball Sales</h1>
<div id="sales">

</div>
</body>
</html>
```

Just your standard HTML5 head and body.

We've gone ahead and linked to a JS file knowing we'll be writing some JavaScript soon!

And we set up our CSS to style the Mighty Gumball sales report so it looks good for the CEO.

Here's a placeholder for where we're going to put the sales data. Each sale item will be added as a <div> here.

Turn the engine over...

Go ahead and type in the code above, load it into your favorite browser and give it a try it before proceeding. And remember, you can download the CSS (and the other code for this chapter) from http://wickedlysmart.com/hfhtml5.

So how do we make requests to web services?

Let's step back for a sec... you already know how a browser requests a page from a web server—it makes an HTTP request to the server, which returns the page along with other metadata that (typically) only the browser sees. What you might not know is that the browser can also *retrieve data* with HTTP from a web server in the same way. Here's how that works:

Browsers can request data from applications on the server, like the Mighty Gumball application that aggregates all the sales data.

Here's a server just waiting on requests from browsers.

"I need the aggregated gumball data."

request

"Sure here you go"

data

The server returns its data.

Web Server

It helps to look a little more closely at the request we make to the server and the response that comes back. The request takes care of telling the server what data we're after (which we sometimes refer to as the "resource" we're after), while the response contains metadata and, if all goes well, the data we requested:

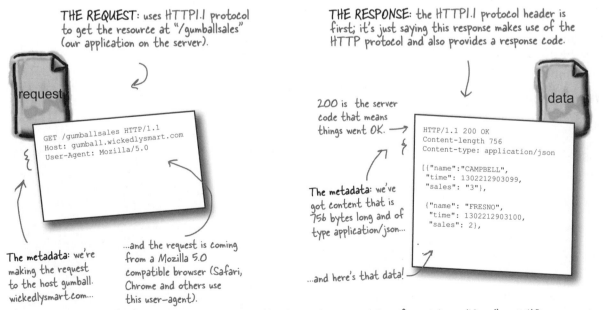

THE REQUEST: uses HTTP1.1 protocol to get the resource at "/gumballsales" (our application on the server).

request

```
GET /gumballsales HTTP/1.1
Host: gumball.wickedlysmart.com
User-Agent: Mozilla/5.0
```

The metadata: we're making the request to the host gumball. wickedlysmart.com...

...and the request is coming from a Mozilla 5.0 compatible browser (Safari, Chrome and others use this user-agent).

THE RESPONSE: the HTTP1.1 protocol header is first; it's just saying this response makes use of the HTTP protocol and also provides a response code.

200 is the server code that means things went OK.

data

```
HTTP/1.1 200 OK
Content-length 756
Content-type: application/json

[{"name":"CAMPBELL",
 "time": 1302212903099,
 "sales": "3"},

{"name": "FRESNO",
 "time": 1302212903100,
 "sales": 2},
```

The metadata: we've got content that is 756 bytes long and of type application/json...

...and here's that data!

Note: This pattern of retrieving data using XMLHttpRequest is commonly referred to as "Ajax" or XHR.

How to make a request from JavaScript

Okay, so we know we can retrieve data with HTTP, but how? We're going to write a little code to create an actual HTTP request and then ask the browser to make the request on our behalf. After it's made the request, the browser will then hand us back the data it receives. Let's step through making an HTTP request:

 To kick things off, we'll start with a **URL**. After all, we need to tell the browser **where** to get the data we're after:

The ".json" signifies a format for exchanging data, we'll come back to this in a bit

Here's our URL at someserver.com.

```
var url = "http://someserver.com/data.json";
```

And let's stash the URL in a variable, url, which will use in a sec.

2 Next we'll create a **request object**, like this:

XMLHttpRequest

```
var request = new XMLHttpRequest();
```

We're assigning the request object to the variable request.

And we use the XMLHttpRequest constructor to create a new request object. We'll talk about the "XML" part of that in a bit

A brand new XMLHttpRequest object.

3 Next we need to tell the request object which URL we want it to retrieve along with the kind of request it should use (we'll use the standard HTTP GET request like we saw on the previous page). To do this, we'll use the request object's open method. Now "open" sounds like a method that not only sets these values in the request object, but also opens the connection and retrieves the data. It doesn't. Despite the name, open just sets up the request with a URL and tells the request object the kind of request to use so that XMLHttpRequest can verify the connection. Here's how we call the open method:

The updated XMLHttpRequest object that knows where it's going

XMLHttpRequest

method: GET
URL: "http://..."

```
request.open("GET", url);
```

This sets up a request for us, using an HTTP GET request, which is the standard means of retrieving HTTP data.

And also sets up the request to use the URL stored in our url variable.

④ Okay here's the important part, and the trick of how XMLHttpRequest works: when we finally ask our XMLHttpRequest object to retrieve data, it's going to go off on its own and get the data. It might take a 90 milliseconds (quite a while in compute time), or, on a slow day, it might take ten seconds (an eternity in compute time). So rather than just waiting around for the data, we're going to provide a handler that is called when the data arrives. Here's how you set up the handler (this should look somewhat familiar):

Our request object

```
request.onload = function() {
    if (request.status == 200) {
        alert("Data received!");
    }
};
```

When the browser gets an answer from the remote web service, it calls this function.

The handler first needs to check if the return code is 200, or "OK", and then it can do something with the data. For now we'll just alert the user the data is here. We'll fill this in with more meaningful code soon.

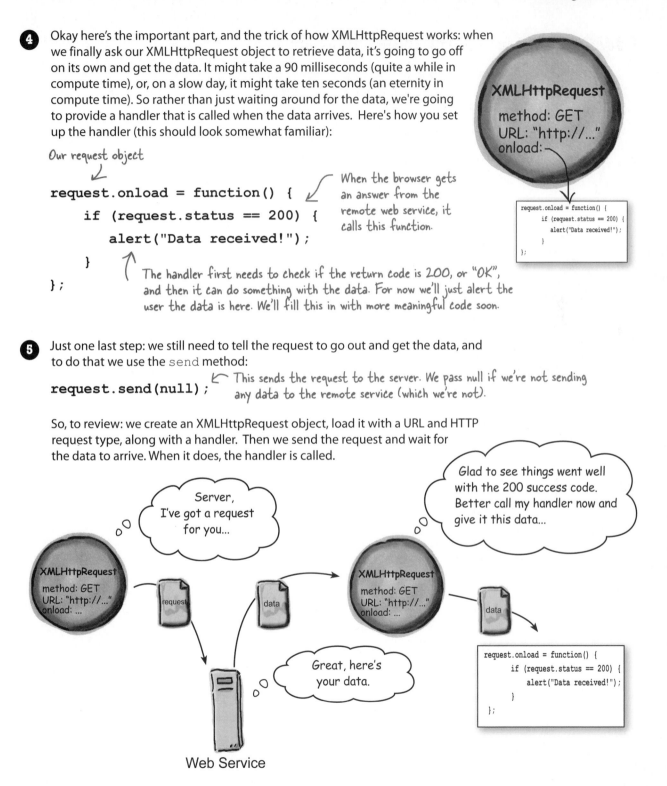

XMLHttpRequest
method: GET
URL: "http://..."
onload:

```
request.onload = function() {
    if (request.status == 200) {
        alert("Data received!");
    }
};
```

⑤ Just one last step: we still need to tell the request to go out and get the data, and to do that we use the send method:

```
request.send(null);
```

This sends the request to the server. We pass null if we're not sending any data to the remote service (which we're not).

So, to review: we create an XMLHttpRequest object, load it with a URL and HTTP request type, along with a handler. Then we send the request and wait for the data to arrive. When it does, the handler is called.

Server, I've got a request for you...

Glad to see things went well with the 200 success code. Better call my handler now and give it this data...

XMLHttpRequest
method: GET
URL: "http://..."
onload: ...

request

data

XMLHttpRequest
method: GET
URL: "http://..."
onload: ...

data

Great, here's your data.

```
request.onload = function() {
    if (request.status == 200) {
        alert("Data received!");
    }
};
```

Web Service

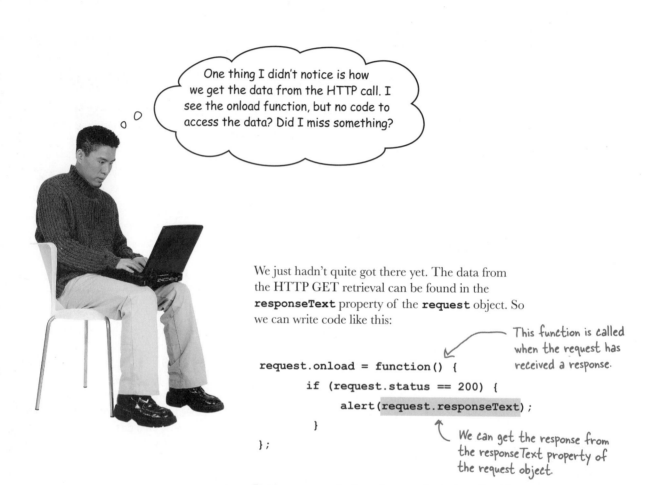

One thing I didn't notice is how we get the data from the HTTP call. I see the onload function, but no code to access the data? Did I miss something?

We just hadn't quite got there yet. The data from the HTTP GET retrieval can be found in the **responseText** property of the **request** object. So we can write code like this:

This function is called when the request has received a response.

```
request.onload = function() {
    if (request.status == 200) {
        alert(request.responseText);
    }
};
```

We can get the response from the responseText property of the request object.

But hang on, we're just about to the point of writing some real code that uses **request.responseText.**

Code Magnets

A new web service at *http://wickedlysmart.com/ifeelluckytoday* returns either "unlucky" or "lucky" each time you hit it. The logic is based on a secret and ancient algorithm we can't reveal, but it's a great service to let users know if they are lucky or not on a given day.

We need your help to create a reference implementation to show others how they might include it in their site. You'll find the skeleton code below; help us fill in the details using the magnets. Be careful, you may not need all the magnets. We've already done one for you.

```
window.onload = function () {

    var url = "http://wickedlysmart.com/ifeelluckytoday";

    var request = _____

    _____ {

        if (_____) {

            displayLuck(_____);

        }

    };
                                                    ⬅ Your magnets go here!
    _____

    _____

}

function displayLuck(luck) {

    var p = document._____("luck");

    P._ innerHTML _ = "Today you are " + luck;

}
```

Feel lucky today?
Wanna be sure?
Use the service!

Magnets:

- `new TextHttpRequest();`
- `request.create("GET", url);`
- `var i = 0;`
- `request.responseText`
- `request.send(null);`
- `request.open("GET", url);`
- `request.onload = function()`
- `myLuckyText`
- `new XMLHttpRequest();`
- `request.status == 200`
- `getElementById`

Code Magnets Solution

A new web service at *http://wickedlysmart.com/ifeelluckytoday* returns either "unlucky" or "lucky" each time you hit it. The logic is based on a secret and ancient algorithm we can't reveal, but it's a great service to let users know if they are lucky or not on a given day.

We need your help to create a reference implementation to show others how they might include it in their site. You'll find the code skeleton below; help us fill in the details using the magnets. Be careful, you may not need all the magnets. Here's our solution.

```javascript
window.onload = function () {

    var url = "http://wickedlysmart.com/ifeelluckytoday";

    var request = new XMLHttpRequest();
    request.onload = function() {
        if ( request.status == 200 ) {
            displayLuck( request.responseText );
        }
    };
    request.open("GET", url);
    request.send(null);
}

function displayLuck(luck) {
    var p = document.getElementById("luck");
    p.innerHTML = "Today you are " + luck;
}
```

Your magnets go here!

Feel lucky today?
Wanna be sure?
Use the service!

Leftover magnets

```javascript
var i = 0;
request.create("GET", url);
myLuckyText
new TextHttpRequest();
```

XMLHttpRequest Exposed

This week's interview:
Confessions of an HTTP Request Object

Head First: Welcome XMLHttpRequest, we're glad you could fit us into your busy schedule. Tell us about how you fit into building web apps.

XMLHttpRequest: I started this whole trend for bringing outside data into your web page. Heard of Google Maps? GMail? That was all me. In fact, it wouldn't have been possible without me.

Head First: How so?

XMLHttpRequest: Until I arrived, people were building a web page on the server side and baking everything into the page as they created it. I allow you to go out and get data *after* the page is built. Think about Google Maps: it updates what's on the page every time you adjust your location on the map, without having to reload the whole page.

Head First: So, you've been a successful guy. What's your secret?

XMLHttpRequest: I'm humble, oh, and simple. Give me a URL and I'll go get the data for you. Not much more to me than that.

Head First: That's all there is to it?

XMLHttpRequest: Well, you do have to tell me what to do with the data after I've retrieved it. You can just give me a handler function—a callback of sorts—and when I get the data, I'll throw it at your handler to do whatever it wants with the data.

Head First: What kinds of data are we talking about here?

XMLHttpRequest: The Web is full of data these days; weather, maps, social data about people and friends, geolocation data about what's nearby... really, just about any data set you can think of is making its way onto the Web in a form that works with me.

Head First: And this is all XML data, right? I mean your first name is XML.

XMLHttpRequest: Really? You're a professional and that's where you wanna take this interview? You did your homework and all you can say is "you're all about XML, right?" Let me set you straight. Sure, there was a time I mostly retrieved XML, but the world is moving on. Nowadays, I retrieve all kinds of data. Sure, some XML, but more and more I'm getting requests for JSON.

Head First: Really? What's JSON and why is it getting so popular?

XMLHttpRequest: JSON is JavaScript Object Notation and it has a number of advantages—size, readability, the fact that it is native to the most popular programming language on the Web: my friend JavaScript, of course.

Head First: But isn't it the case that the format really shouldn't matter to you? Users should be able to request XML or JSON or teletype for all you care. No?

XMLHttpRequest: <silence>

Head First: Well, it seems I've hit on a sore spot. That's okay, we've got to go to break... So, XMLHttpRequest, I think we've got more time with you later in this chapter?

XMLHttpRequest: Yes, unfortunately I see that in my schedule...

Move over XML, meet JSON

You might (or might not) remember that XML was going to save us all—a data format that was human readable and machine parseable, a data format that was going to support all the data needs of the world. And when XMLHttpRequest was first developed, XML was indeed the way we all exchanged data (thus, the name XMLHttpRequest).

Well, along the way XML apparently slipped on a banana peel thrown by JSON. Who's JSON? Just the latest and greatest data format, born out of JavaScript, and being adopted across the Web in the browser and on the server side. And might we add, it's quickly become the *format of choice* for HTML5 apps?

So, what's so great about JSON? Well, it's pretty darn human-readable, and it can be parsed quickly and easily straight into JavaScript values and objects. Unlike XML, it's so cute and cuddly... anyway, can you tell we like it just a little? You'll be seeing a lot of JSON in this book. We're going to use it to exchange JavaScript data over the network, to store data in a local store with the Web Storage API, and as part of another way to access web data (more on that shortly).

But wait a sec, network data exchange formats... storage formats... that's complex stuff, right? No worries, ~~over the next ten pages we're going to make you an expert~~ you already know practically everything about JSON you need to. To use JSON you just need to understand JavaScript objects (which you do, big time) and two simple method calls. Here's how it all works:

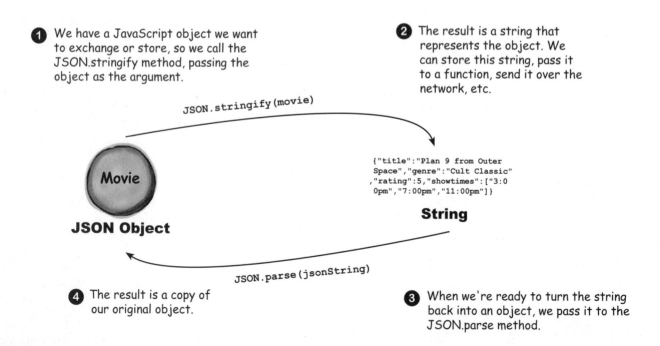

1 We have a JavaScript object we want to exchange or store, so we call the JSON.stringify method, passing the object as the argument.

2 The result is a string that represents the object. We can store this string, pass it to a function, send it over the network, etc.

JSON.stringify(movie)

Movie

JSON Object

{"title":"Plan 9 from Outer Space","genre":"Cult Classic","rating":5,"showtimes":["3:00pm","7:00pm","11:00pm"]}

String

JSON.parse(jsonString)

4 The result is a copy of our original object.

3 When we're ready to turn the string back into an object, we pass it to the JSON.parse method.

A quick example using JSON

(1) Let's run through a quick example that converts an object into its JSON string format. We'll start with an object you already understand, the Movie object from Chapter 4. Not everything can be converted into a JSON string—for instance, methods—but all the basic types, like numbers, strings, and arrays, are supported. Let's create an object and then stringify it:

> There are actually a few other restrictions, but we won't worry about those now.

```
var plan9Movie = new Movie("Plan 9 from Outer Space","Cult Classic", 2,
                           ["3:00pm", "7:00pm", "11:00pm"]);
```

> Here's a nice movie object complete with strings, numbers and an array.

(2) Once you've got an object, you can convert it into the JSON string format with the JSON.stringify method. Let's see how this works... (feel free to try this by opening your Chapter 4 movie code back up and adding the following code to the bottom of your script):

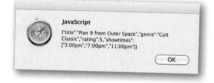

```
var jsonString = JSON.stringify(plan9Movie);
alert(jsonString);
```

> Here's the result, a string version of the object displayed in the alert.

(3) Now we've got a JSON string that represents our movie object. At this point we could take this string and do any number of things with it, like send it over HTTP to a server. We can also receive a JSON string from another server. Let's say a server gave us this string; how would we turn it back into an object we can do something with? Just use JSON.stringify's sister method: JSON.parse. Like this:

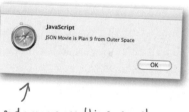

```
var jsonMovieObject = JSON.parse(jsonString);
alert("JSON Movie is " + jsonMovieObject.title);
```

> Ah, and now we use this as a real *object*, accessing its properties.

 **BRAIN POWER**

Try this URL. What do you see?

`http://search.twitter.com/search.json?q=hfhtml5`

Note: Firefox will ask you to open or save a file. You can open with TextEdit, Notepad, or any basic text editor.

> Hey! The specs just arrived!! Turn the page!

The specs just arrived!

Gumball Server Specs

Mighty Gumball, Inc.
Where the Gumball Machine
is Never Half Empty

Thanks for taking this on!!!

We've got all the sales from the Gumball machines aggregated and being served from our central server at:

`http://gumball.wickedlysmart.com/`

We've chosen JSON as our data format and if you hit the above URL, you'll get back an array of JSON objects that look like this:

```
[{"name":"CAMPBELL",
  "time": 1302212903099,
  "sales": 3},

 {"name": "FRESNO",
  "time": 1302212903100,
  "sales": 2},

    . . .
 ]
```

← The name of the city; we're just testing California right now.

The time in milliseconds when this report came in.

# of gumballs sold since last report.

A second city, FRESNO.

And more cities will be here...

Make sure you do this! → Go ahead and type this URL into your browser to see the values coming back. You should see one or more of these objects in an array.

You can also add a lastreporttime parameter to the end of the URL and you'll get only the reports since that time. Use it like this:

Just specify a time in milliseconds. ↓

`http://gumball.wickedlysmart.com/?lastreporttime=1302212903099`

We've got hundreds of gumball machines reporting in right now, in fact you should see reports about every 5-8 seconds on average. That said, this is our production server so test your code locally first!

Thanks again for your help!! And remember "the gumball machine is never half empty," as our CEO says.

— Mighty Gumball Engineers

Let's get to work!

We've got our specs from Mighty Gumball and you've done your training on XMLHttpRequest and JSON. You should be all ready to get some code written and to get a first cut of the Gumball App running.

```html
<!doctype html>
<html lang="en">
    <head>
        <title>Mighty Gumball (JSON)</title>
        <meta charset="utf-8">
        <script src="mightygumball.js"></script>
        <link rel="stylesheet" href="mightygumball.css">
    </head>
    <body>
        <h1>Mighty Gumball Sales</h1>
        <div id="sales">

        </div>
    </body>
</html>
```

Now, remember we've already laid out some HTML to work from, which links to a file called `mightygumball.js`. That's what we're going to start writing our code now. Remember too that we've already left a spot in the HTML where we're going to put the gumball sales data, right into the `<div>` we labeled with an id of "sales." So let's put everything together and write some code.

Writing an onload handler function

We're sure this is old hat for you now, but we're going to write an onload handler that gets invoked when the HTML is fully loaded; we're also going to go ahead and fire off an HTTP request to get the sales data. When the data comes back we'll ask the `XMLHttpRequest` to call the function `updateSales` (which we'll write in just a sec):

```javascript
window.onload = function() {
    var url = "http://localhost/sales.json";
    var request = new XMLHttpRequest();
    request.open("GET", url);
    request.onload = function() {
        if (request.status == 200) {
            updateSales(request.responseText);
        }
    };
    request.send(null);
}
```

We're going to test on a local file first (like the Mighty Gumball engineers suggested!) to make sure everything's working. We'll talk more about this in one sec...

We set up the XMLHttpRequest by creating the object, calling the open method with our URL and then setting the onload property to a function.

We check to make sure everything is OK, and then...

... when the data has completed loading, this function is called.

Finally, we send the request.

If you're using Opera or IE 8 or older, we recommend you test with another browser. We'll talk about how to support Opera and older IE browsers later.

Watch it!

Displaying the gumball sales data

Now we need to write the handler, `updateSales`. Let's make this easy and just go with the simplest implementation possible, we can always make it better later:

```
function updateSales(responseText) {

    var salesDiv = document.getElementById("sales");

    salesDiv.innerHTML = responseText;

}
```

We'll grab the <div> already put in the HTML and use it as a place for the data.

And set the div's content to the whole chunk of data. We'll deal with parsing it in a minute... Let's test this first.

Watch Out, Detour Ahead!

It's time for another test drive, but we have a little detour to take care of first. The Mighty Gumball engineers asked us to test locally before hitting their production server, which is a good idea. But to do that we need the data to live on a server so that XMLHttpRequest can use the HTTP protocol to retrieve it.

In terms of servers you've got a few choices:

- If your company has servers that are available for testing, use those.

- Or, you can use a third-party hosting service like GoDaddy, Dreamhost or one of many other hosting companies.

- Finally, you can set up a server right on your own machine. In that case your URLs are going to look something like:

```
http://localhost/mightygumball.html
```

The files can also be placed in a subdirectory, like http://localhost/gumball/mightygumball.html

Check out the next page for tips and pointers. Keep in mind, hosting environments differ a fair bit, so we can't write a general guide to these. So, may the force be with you, and if you don't have easy access to a server already, setting up a server on your local machine may be your best choice!

Detour

How to set up your own Web Server

How you set up your local hosting really depends on what kind of operating system you're using. Check out the tips below for OS X (otherwise known as the Mac), the PC and Linux. You'll find other options on the next page.

I'm a Mac

Setting up a web server on the Mac is easy. Go to > System Preferences, and then choose Sharing. In the panel on the left, make sure Web Sharing is checked:

☑ Web Sharing

Once you've turned Web Sharing on (or if you already have it on), you'll see some information about how to access your local server. You should be able to use localhost instead of the IP address (which tends to change if you're using a DHCP router, so localhost will work better for you). By default, your files are served from `http://localhost/~YOUR_USERNAME/`, which serves files from your `YOUR_USERNAME/Sites/` folder, so you'll probably want to set up a subfolder there for Mighty Gumball.

I'm a PC

Installing your own web server on Windows is easier than it used to be thanks to the Microsoft Web Platform Installer (also known as Web PI). The current version is available for Windows 7, Windows Vista SP2, Windows XP SP3+, Windows Server 2003 SP2+, Windows Server 2008, and Windows Server 2008 R2, and you can download it from here: `http://www.microsoft.com/web/downloads/platform.aspx`.

Another option is to install the open source WampServer, which comes with Apache, PHP and MySQL for web application development. It's easy to install and manage.

You can download WampServer from: `http://www.wampserver.com/en/`.

There are a few other open source solutions out there if you look, so you've got lots of options.

I'm a ~~total geek~~ Linux Distribution

Let's face it, you already know what you're doing. Right? Apache is usually installed by default, so check your distribution documentation.

How to set up your own Web Server, continued

Detour

Ah, you want to *really* host your pages? Excellent, there's no substitute for having your pages hosted on the real Web. Check out the tips below and have fun!

3rd Party Hosting...

If you don't want to set up your own server, you can always use a remote server, but you'll need to host your HTML, JavaScript and CSS, as well as the JSON file, all on the same server (we'll talk later about why this is crucial) in order to follow along with this example.

Most hosting services will give you FTP access to a folder where you can put all these files. If you have access to a server like this, upload all the files and substitute your server name wherever you see `localhost` in the following pages.

Head–First–HTML5		hfhtml5	
Name		**Name**	
.DS_Store		chapter1	
chapter3		chapter2	
chapter6		chapter3	
.git		chapter4	
chapter1		chapter5	
chapter7		chapter6	
chapter9		chapter7	
chapter8		chapter8	
chapter5		chapter9	
chapter4		chapter10	
chapter2			
README.txt			
global			

your stuff. (13 items)   their stuff. (10 items)

Status: Idle

You can use an FTP program like Transit, Cyberduck or WinSCP to get your files uploaded if you don't want to use command line FTP.

We've put together a list of hosting providers in case you need a recommendation, but they're easy to find; just search for "web hosting" and you'll find lots to choose from. Our list is at `http://wickedlysmart.com/hfhtml5/hosting/hosting.html`. And let us know if you get an HTML5 web site up online; we'd love to see it!

Back to the code

At this point we're expecting you've got your own server up and running—that could be a server running on your local machine (what we're doing) or a server somewhere else you have access to. In either case you're going to place your HTML and JavaScript files on the server and then point your browser to the HTML file. You're also going to need the Mighty Gumball sales data test file there too, so we're going to give you a simple data file to place on your server. To your application it will look just like it's being generated from Mighty Gumball's near-real-time server, and it gives you a way to test your code without hitting the Mighty Gumball server. Here's what the file looks like; it's named `sales.json` and it's included with the code for the book (or you can type it in if you enjoy that kind of thing):

```json
[{"name":"ARTESIA","time":1308774240669,"sales":8},
 {"name":"LOS ANGELES","time":1308774240669,"sales":2},
 {"name":"PASADENA","time":1308774240669,"sales":8},
 {"name":"STOCKTON","time":1308774240669,"sales":2},
 {"name":"FRESNO","time":1308774240669,"sales":2},
 {"name":"SPRING VALLEY","time":1308774240669,"sales":9},
 {"name":"ELVERTA","time":1308774240669,"sales":5},
 {"name":"SACRAMENTO","time":1308774240669,"sales":7},
 {"name":"SAN MATEO","time":1308774240669,"sales":1}]
```

We're going to use "sales.json" for testing before we hit the real production server with the real-time sales data.

Go ahead and put this file on your server and then make sure you update your JavaScript to the URL for this file. Ours is `http://localhost/gumball/sales.json`:

It helps to first test this URL in your browser to make sure it works.

```javascript
window.onload = function() {
    var url = "http://localhost/gumball/sales.json";
    var request = new XMLHttpRequest();
    request.open("GET", url);
    request.onload = function() {
        if (request.status == 200) {
            updateSales(request.responseText);
        }
    };
    request.send(null);
}
```

Make sure this is pointing to the right URL.

Let's test this already!

It's been a long road but we're finally ready to test this code!

Just make sure you've got the HTML, JavaScript, JSON—and don't forget your CSS—files on the server. Go ahead and enter the URL of your HTML file into your browser (ours is `http://localhost/gumball/mightygumball.html`), press return...

Mighty Gumball

`http://localhost/gumball/mightygumball.html`

Mighty Gumball Sales

[{"name":"ARTESIA","time":1308774240669,"sales":8},{"name":"LOS ANGELES","time":1308774240669,"sales":2}, {"name":"PASADENA","time":1308774240669,"sales":8}, {"name":"STOCKTON","time":1308774240669,"sales":2}, {"name":"FRESNO","time":1308774240669,"sales":2},{"name":"SPRING VALLEY","time":1308774240669,"sales":9}, {"name":"ELVERTA","time":1308774240669,"sales":5}, {"name":"SACRAMENTO","time":1308774240669,"sales":7},{"name":"SAN MATEO","time":1308774240669,"sales":1}]

↑
Not pretty, but the data is there.

Remember we're sending an HTTP request to get the data in sales.json, which we're just dumping into the <div> for now. Looks like it worked!

If you're having trouble, check each file independently through your browser and make sure it is accessible. Then double-check your URLs.

Nice! That took a lot of work. We had to understand how to do HTTP requests and also set up the server, but it works! I'm already thinking of all the great apps I can build to make use of all the web services out there, now that I know how to talk to them.

Impressing the client...

We've done a lot of heavy lifting to get this app working, and that's great, but Mighty Gumball is going to be a lot more impressed if it looks good too. Here's what we're going for...

What we have

Mighty Gumball

http://localhost/gumball/mightygumball.html

Mighty Gumball Sales

[{"name":"ARTESIA","time":1308774240669,"sales":8},{"name":"LOS ANGELES","time":1308774240669,"sales":2},
{"name":"PASADENA","time":1308774240669,"sales":8},
{"name":"STOCKTON","time":1308774240669,"sales":2},
{"name":"FRESNO","time":1308774240669,"sales":2},{"name":"SPRING VALLEY","time":1308774240669,"sales":9},
{"name":"ELVERTA","time":1308774240669,"sales":5},
{"name":"SACRAMENTO","time":1308774240669,"sales":7},{"name":"SAN MATEO","time":1308774240669,"sales":1}]

At the moment we're just dumping a JSON array right into the browser. Somewhat effective but ugly. And what a waste, there is a whole data structure just waiting to be used more effectively!

What we want

Mighty Gumball

http://localhost/gumball/mightygumball.html

Mighty Gumball Sales

ARTESIA sold 8 gumballs

LOS ANGELES sold 2 gumballs

PASADENA sold 8 gumballs

STOCKTON sold 2 gumballs

FRESNO sold 2 gumballs

SPRING VALLEY sold 9 gumballs

ELVERTA sold 5 gumballs

SACRAMENTO sold 7 gumballs

SAN MATEO sold 1 gumballs

Here we've used the JSON array and created a nice display from it. It's that last 10% that can make the difference between amateur and professional, don't ya think?

Here's what we need to do to improve our display:

1. First we need to take the data we got back from our XMLHttpRequest object (which is just a JSON string) and convert it into a true JavaScript object.

2. Then we can walk through the resulting array and add new elements to the DOM, one per sales item in the array.

Reworking our code to make use of JSON

Let's follow those two steps and get this code in shape:

 First we need to take the data we got from the XMLttpRequest object (which is just a JSON string) and convert it into a true JavaScript object.

To do that, let's update the updateSales function by first deleting the line that sets the <div> content to the responseText string, and convert the responseText from a string to its equivalent JavaScript using JSON.parse.

```
function updateSales(responseText) {

    var salesDiv = document.getElementById("sales");

    salesDiv.innerHTML = responseText;                    We don't need this line anymore.

    var sales = JSON.parse(responseText);
}
```

Take the response and use JSON.parse to convert it
into a JavaScript object (in this case it will be an
array), and assign it to the variable sales.

② Now let's walk through the resulting array and add new elements to the DOM, one per sales item in the array. In this case we are going to create a new <div> for each item:

```
function updateSales(responseText) {
    var salesDiv = document.getElementById("sales");
    var sales = JSON.parse(responseText);
    for (var i = 0; i < sales.length; i++) {              Iterate through each item in the array.
        var sale = sales[i];
        var div = document.createElement("div");          For each item create a <div>, and give it
        div.setAttribute("class", "saleItem");            the "saleItem" class (used by CSS).
        div.innerHTML = sale.name + " sold " + sale.sales + " gumballs";
        salesDiv.appendChild(div);                        Set the <div>'s contents with innerHTML,
    }                                                     and then add it as a child of the sales <div>.
}
```

The Home Stretch...

You already know what this one is going to look like, but go ahead and make these changes. Take one more careful look at the code on the previous page and make sure you've got it all down. Then go ahead, reload that page.

See, we told you it would look like this!

Mighty Gumball Sales

ARTESIA sold 8 gumballs
LOS ANGELES sold 2 gumballs
PASADENA sold 8 gumballs
STOCKTON sold 2 gumballs
FRESNO sold 2 gumballs
SPRING VALLEY sold 9 gumballs
ELVERTA sold 5 gumballs
SACRAMENTO sold 7 gumballs
SAN MATEO sold 1 gumballs

Testing has gone well, you guys are ready to use Mighty Gumball's live production servers now. Good luck!

Moving to the Live Server

Mighty Gumball asked us to test locally, and we have. Now we're ready to move on to testing against the real server. This time, rather than retrieving a static JSON data file, we'll be retrieving JSON that is generated dynamically from the Mighty Gumball servers. We do need to update the URL that XMLHttpRequest is using and change it to point to Mighty Gumball. Let's do that:

Here's their server URL. Change this and make sure it's saved.

```
window.onload = function() {
    var url = "http://gumball.wickedlysmart.com";
    var request = new XMLHttpRequest();
    request.open("GET", url);
    request.onload = function() {
        if (request.status == 200) {
            updateSales(request.responseText);
        }
    };
    request.send(null);
}
```

Ajay, the Quality Assurance Guy

A Live Test Drive...

Make sure your URL change is saved in your `mightygumball.js` file on your server, if you want to keep retrieving your HTML from there, or to your local hard drive if you are using localhost. From there you know what to do: point your browser to your HTML file and watch the live, beautiful, real data from all those people around the world buying Mighty Gumballs!

> Houston, we have a problem! Come quick, we're getting no sales data since we changed to the live servers!

Mighty Gumball Sales

← What?! We're not seeing any data!

Ajay, the Upset Quality Assurance Guy

Yikes!

And everything was looking so good; we figured by this time we'd be sipping Perrier and celebrating another successful project with Mighty Gumball. Now the whole thing could go down in flames. Okay, we're getting a little overly dramatic, but what the heck? This should have worked!

Deep breath. Okay, there's a logical explanation...

Note to Editor: actually we thought we'd be cashing a fat advance check and shipping this book! Now we've got to write our way out of another fine mess!

It's a cliffhanger!

We're not seeing any data in our page. It was all working fine until we moved to the live server...

Will we **find** the problem?

Will we **fix** it?

Stay tuned... we'll answer these questions, and more...

And in the meantime, see if you can come up with ideas for what went wrong and how we can fix it.

BULLET POINTS

- To get HTML files or data from a server, the browser sends an HTTP request.

- An HTTP response includes a response code that indicates if there was an error with the request.

- The HTTP response code 200 means the request had no errors.

- To send an HTTP request from JavaScript, use the XMLHttpRequest object.

- The XMLHttpRequest object's onload handler handles getting the response from the server.

- The JSON response to an XMLHttpRequest is placed in the request's responseText property.

- To convert the responseText string to JSON, use the JSON.parse method.

- XMLHttpRequest is used in applications to update content, such as maps and email, without requiring a page reload.

- XMLHttpRequest can be used to retrieve any kind of text content, such as XML, JSON, and more.

- XMLHttpRequest Level 2 is the most recent version of XMLHttpRequest, but the standard is still in development.

- To use XMLHttpRequest, you must serve files and request data from a server. You can set up a local server on your own machine for testing, or use a hosting solution.

- The XMLHttpRequest onload property isn't supported by older browsers, like IE8 and lower, and Opera 10 and lower. You can write code to check for the browser version and provide an alternative for older browsers.

XMLHttpRequest Exposed Part 2

This week's interview:
Internet Explorer, and "Did you say JSON?"

Head First: Welcome back to the second part of the interview, XMLHttpRequest. I wanted to ask you about browser support—are you available in only the newer browsers only?

XMLHttpRequest: The guys don't call me "old man" for nothing; I've been supported by browsers since 2004. In Internet years I'm a senior citizen.

Head First: Well, what about obsolescence, do you worry about that?

XMLHttpRequest: I'm someone who reinvents himself every decade or so. Right now, we're all working on the second version of XMLHttpRequest, known as Level 2. In fact, most modern browsers already support Level 2.

Head First: Impressive. What is different with Level 2?

XMLHttpRequest: Well, for one thing, support for more event types, so you can do things like track the progress of a request, and write more elegant code (in my opinion).

Head First: Speaking of browser support...

XMLHttpRequest: Okay, here it comes....wait for it...

Head First: We've heard through the grapevine that you and IE don't really get along...

XMLHttpRequest: ...and there it is...if you want the answer to that, all you have to do is read every interview I've ever given. But apparently, you missed it. Are you kidding me? This whole XMLHttpRequest business started with IE.

Head First: Yeah, but what about ActiveXObject and XDomainRequest? Have you heard those names before?

XMLHttpRequest: Those are my nicknames! That's what they call me at Microsoft! Okay, I agree it is a pain that we have different names for me, but they all do the same thing. It's easily handled with a little more code, and in terms of the recent Microsoft browsers, version 9 and later, everything is good. If this is news to your readers, I'm happy to stay after the interview to make sure their code works on older versions of IE.

Head First: That's very kind, we'll make sure that makes it into this chapter somewhere.

XMLHttpRequest: Hey, I'm a nice guy, I wouldn't leave your readers hanging on this.

Head First: We'll take your word for it. Another question: you mentioned JSON and that you are a big fan of it. Do you worry at all about, well, JSONP?

XMLHttpRequest: What me? Worry?

Head First: Word on the street is a lot people are using it in place of you.

XMLHttpRequest: Okay, sure, with JSONP you can retrieve data, but it's just a clever hack. I mean, think of the convoluted code you have to write, and what about security?

Head First: Hey, I'm not overly technical, all I know is a lot of people say it gets them around problems you can't solve. Anyway, that's all we have time for.

XMLHttpRequest: Heh, well at least you got the "not overly technical" part right.

Watch it!

The XMLHttpRequest onload property isn't supported by older versions of browsers, but there's an easy workaround.

We've been using request.onload to define a function that is called when the request finishes getting the data from the server. This a feature of XMLHttpRequest Level 2 (think of it as "version 2"). XMLHttpRequest Level 2 is still pretty new, so many users may still be using browsers that don't support it. In particular, IE 8 (and lower), and Opera 10 (and lower) support only XMLHttpRequest Level 1. The good news is that the new features of XMLHttpRequest Level 2 are enhancements, so you can continue to use only the features of version 1 in all browsers without any problems; it just means your code isn't quite as elegant. Here's the code to use XMLHttpRequest Level 1:

Most of the code to use XMLHttpRequest Level 1 is the same...

```
function init() {

    var url = "http://localhost/gumball/sales.json";

    var request = new XMLHttpRequest();

    request.onreadystatechange = function() {

        if (request.readyState == 4 && request.status == 200) {

            updateSales(request.responseText);

        }

    };

    request.open("GET", url);

    request.send(null);

}
```

... But there is no request. onload property in Level 2, so you'll need to use the onreadystatechange property instead.

And then check the readyState to make sure the data has completed loading. If readyState is 4, you know it's done.

Everything else is basically the same.

You could also check for other readyState and status values if you want to check for various errors.

Remember, we left you with a cliffhanger? A bug.

We had all the code working just fine using our local server, but as soon as we moved to the live server on the Web, it failed!

What we expected:

Here's what our page looks like when we run the code using our local server to serve the sales data from `http://localhost/gumball/sales.json`.

What we got:

Here's what our page looks like when we run the code using the live Mighty Gumball server to serve the sales data from `http://gumball.wickedlysmart.com`.

So, what do we do now?!

Why, let's do what we always do, pull the crew together for a quick cubicle conversation. We're sure that together, all of us (including a few fictional characters) can figure this out! Frank? Jim? Joe? Where are you? Oh, there you are on the next page...

Ajay, the Quality Assurance Guy, got pretty upset.

I don't know what's going on with this code, Jim, but it just isn't working for me.

Jim: Do you have the correct URL?

Frank: Yep, and in fact, I typed it into the browser to make sure I see the sales data we're expecting, and it worked fine. I don't get it...

Joe: I peeked at the JavaScript console in Chrome and I see something about access control and origins or domains.

Frank: Errrrr?

Jim   Frank   Joe

Guys, where were you on the Starbuzz Coffee project? Remember we had a problem with the same behavior. I bet you've got cross-domain issues because you're requesting data from a server that is different than where your page came from. The browser thinks that is a security issue.

Hmmmm, maybe you could refresh our memory on the browser security issues?

Judy

What Browser Security Policy?

Okay, it's embarassing to hit this kind of snag—just think of the position we're putting you readers in—but Judy's right, the browser does enforce some security around your `XMLHttpRequest` HTTP requests and that can cause some issues.

So what is this policy? Well, it's a browser policy, and it says you can't retrieve data from a domain that is different from the domain the page itself was served from. Say you're running the site for DaddyWarBucksBank.com and someone has hacked into your systems and inserted a bit of JavaScript that takes the user's personal information and does all kinds of interesting things with it by communicating with the server HackersNeedMoreMoney. com. Sounds bad right? Well, to stop that sort of thing, browsers prevent you from making `XMLHttpRequests` to domains other than the original domain the page was served from.

Let's take a look at what is okay, and what isn't:

Acceptable Behavior for JavaScript code:

1 First the user (through the browser) makes a request for an HTML page (and, of course, any associated JavaScript and CSS):

Your browser makes a request for a page from GoodDomain.com.

request

HTML

Browser

Server happily serves you your page.

GoodDomain.com

2 The page needs some data from GoodDomain.com so it makes a XMLHttpRequest for the data:

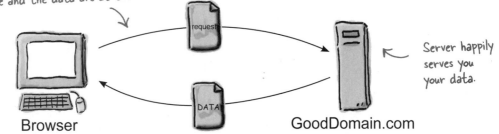

This request to get data from GoodDomain.com succeeds because the page and the data are at the same domain.

request

DATA

Browser

Server happily serves you your data.

GoodDomain.com

Unacceptable Behavior for JavaScript code:

Now let's see what happens when your page hosted at GoodDomain.com tries to make a request for data using XMLHttpRequest to BadDomain.com instead.

 Just like before, the browser makes a request for a page on GoodDomain.com. This may include JavaScript and CSS files that are also hosted at GoodDomain.com.

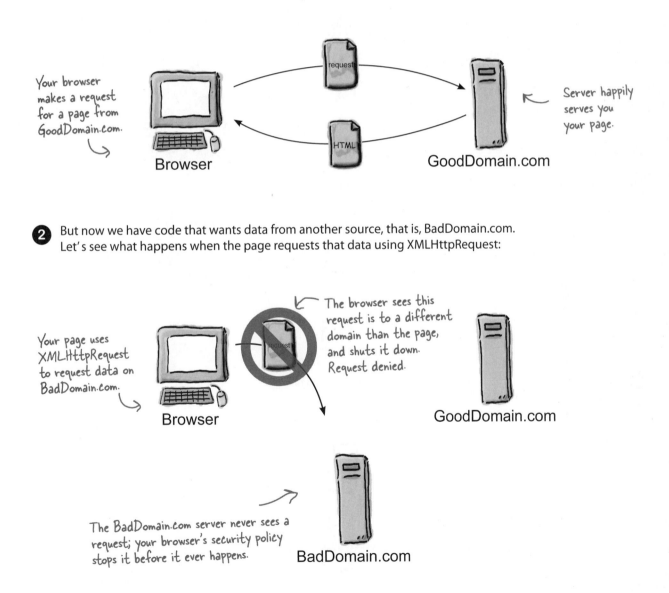

② But now we have code that wants data from another source, that is, BadDomain.com. Let's see what happens when the page requests that data using XMLHttpRequest:

Nice job, all this code and this won't even work? Can't we just copy our files to the Mighty Gumball servers?

Usually the answer is yes.

Say you were a developer working on code for Mighty Gumball, then you'd typically have access to their servers (or to people who could deploy files to the servers for you), and you could place all your files there and avoid any cross-domain issues. In this case, however (and we do hate to break your suspension of disbelief), you're *not* actually working for Mighty Gumball, you're readers of this book, and we can't think of a way to have a couple hundred-thousand people copy their files to the Mighty Gumball servers.

At least not on the budget the editor has given us!

So where does that leave us? Have we reached a dead end? No, we've still got a few options. Let's step through them...

XMLHttpRequest
Police.

So, what are our options?

We gotta be honest with you, we knew all along that the `XMLHttpRequest` cross-origin request would fail. But, as we just said, when you're building apps you've often got access to the server and so this isn't an issue (and if you're building apps largely dependent on your own data, using `XMLHttpRequest` is usually the best way to do it).

But at this point we can hear you saying "that's great, but how can we get this code working already?" Well, we've got a couple ways to make that happen:

 Plan 1: Use our hosted files.

We've already put files on our server for you and placed the files at:

```
http://gumball.wickedlysmart.com/gumball/gumball.html
```

Go ahead and give it a try by pointing your browser to this URL and you'll be able to see the same code you typed in so far in action and working.

(2) Plan 2: Use another way to get the data.

So, `XMLHttpRequest` is a great way to get data into your apps when that data is hosted at the same domain as your app, but what if you need to really get data from a third party? Say you need data from Google or Twitter for instance? In those cases we really do have to break through this problem and find another approach.

As it turns out there is another way, based on JSON, known as JSONP (if you're curious it stands for "JSON with Padding"; we agree that sounds weird, but we'll walk through it in just a sec). Get your jetpack on because the way it works is a little "from another planet" if you know what we mean.

JSONP, guys, this is our chance to get ahead of Judy, for once.

Joe: Totally! But, what is it?

Jim: Sounds like it is another way to get data from web services into our apps.

Frank: I'm useless here, I'm just the creative guy.

Jim: Frank, I don't think this is that bad. I quickly google'd JSONP and basically it is a way of getting the `<script>` tag to do the work of retrieving the data.

Joe: Huh, is that legit?

Jim: Totally legit—a lot of big services are supporting it, like Twitter.

Frank: Sounds like a hack.

Joe: Well yeah, that's what I was getting at. I mean, how can using the `<script>` tag be a kosher way of getting data? I don't even get how that would work.

Jim: I'm only a little way into understanding it myself. But think about it this way: when you use a `<script>` element, it is retrieving code for you right?

Joe: Right...

Jim: Well, what if you put data in that code?

Joe: Okay, wheels are turning...

Frank: Yeah, you mean hamster wheels...

Grasshopper, sit.
Often what I teach,
you already inherently
know...

HTML5 Guru: ...and this
is one of those times.
Grasshopper, look at the this code:

```
alert("woof");
```

What does it do?

This code is located at this URL.

Web Developer: When you evaluate it, assuming it is
running in a browser, it will display an alert saying "woof".

Guru: Ah, yes. Create your own simple HTML file and put a
<script> element in it, in the body, like this:

```
<script src="http://wickedlysmart.com/hfhtml5/chapter6/dog.js">
</script>
```

Guru: What does it do?

Web Developer: It loads the page, which loads the
JavaScript from dog.js from wickedlysmart.com, which calls
the alert function, and I see an alert with "woof" displayed by
the browser.

Guru: So a JavaScript file, served from another domain, can
call a function within your browser?

Web Developer: Well, now that you put it that way, yes
Guru, I guess that is what is happening. The dog.js file at
wickedlysmart.com, once retrieved, calls alert in my browser.

Guru: You'll find another file at:
http://wickedlysmart.com/hfhtml5/chapter5/dog2.js with
the JavaScript:

```
animalSays("dog", "woof");
```

Guru: What does it do?

Web Developer: It's similar to dog.js, but it calls a function animalSays. It also has two arguments not one: the animal type, and the animal sound.

Guru: Write the function animalSays and add it in a <script> element in the head of your HTML file, above the <script> element that points to wickedlysmart.

Web Developer: How's this?

```
function animalSays(type, sound) {
    alert(type + " says " + sound);
}
```

Guru: Very good, you're progressing well. Now, change your other <script> reference, the one that points to dog.js, to point to dog2.js and reload the page in your browser.

Web Developer: I get an alert that says "dog says woof".

Guru: Take a look at http://wickedlysmart.com/hfhtml6/chapter5/cat2.js, change your <script> reference to point to cat2.js and try that.

```
animalSays("cat", "meow");
```

Web Developer: I get an alert that says "cat says meow".

Guru: So not only can a JavaScript file that was served from another domain call any function it wants in your code, but it can also pass us any data it wants?

Web Developer: I don't see any data really, just two arguments.

Guru: And arguments aren't data? What if we change the arguments to look like this:

```
var animal = {"type": "cat", "sound": "meow"};
animalSays(animal);
```
← cat3.js

Web Developer: Now the function animalSays is passing one argument that happens to be an object. Hmm, I can certainly see how that object starts to look like data.

Guru: Can you rewrite animalSays so it uses the new object?

Web Developer: I'll give it a try...

Web Developer: How's this?

```
function animalSays(animal) {
    alert(animal.type + " says " + animal.sound);
}
```

Guru: Very good. Change your reference to http://wickedlysmart.com/hfhtml5/chapter6/dog3.js and try it. Try http://wickedlysmart.com/hfhtml5/chapter6/cat3.js too.

Web Developer: Yes, both work as you would expect with my new function.

Guru: What if you change the name of animalSays to updateSales?

Web Developer: Guru, I don't see how animals are related to gumball sales?

Guru: Work with me here. What if we rename dog3.js to sales.js, and rewrite it like this:

```
var sales = [{"name":"ARTESIA","time":1308774240669,"sales":8},
             {"name":"LOS ANGELES","time":1308774240669,"sales":2}];

updateSales(sales);
```

Web Developer: I think I'm starting to get it. We are passing data through the JavaScript file we're referencing, rather than using XMLHttpRequest to retrieve it ourselves.

Guru: Yes, Grasshopper. But don't miss the forest for the trees. Are we not also getting it from another domain? Something that is forbidden by XMLHttpRequest.

Web Developer: Yes, it appears that way. This seems truly like magic.

Guru: There is no magic, the <script> element has always worked like this. The answer was within you all along. Now please go meditate on how this works to make it stick.

Web Developer: Yes master. "Make it stick"... you know that phrase sounds so familiar but I can't quite place it.

ZEN MOMENT

Using JavaScript to retrieve data is something you have to become one with. Grab a sheet of paper or use the inside cover of this book. Draw a server that hosts your HTML & JavaScript files. Also draw a server at another domain that has the files dog3.js and cat3.js. Now go through the steps the browser uses to get and use the object in each file. When you think you've got it, we'll go through it all again together.

Meet JSONP

You've probably figured out that JSONP is a way to retrieve JSON objects by using the <script> tag. It's also a way of retrieving data (again, in the form of JSON objects) that avoids the same-origin security issues we saw with XMLHttpRequest.

Let's step through how JSONP works over the next few pages:

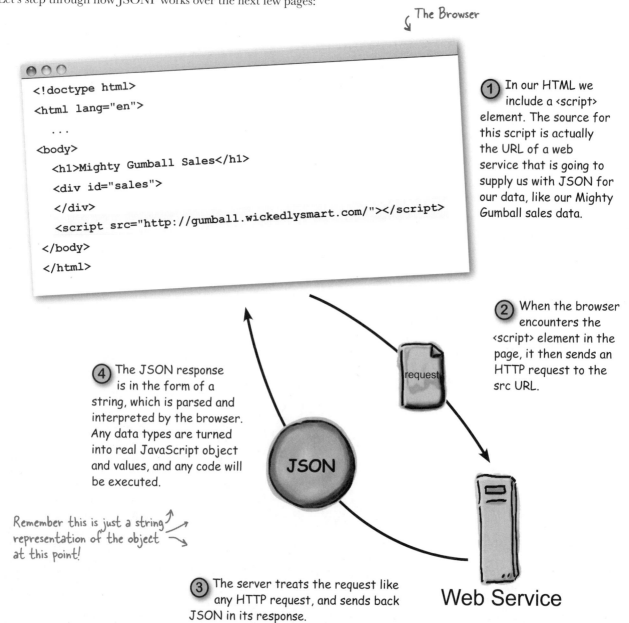

The Browser

```
<!doctype html>
<html lang="en">
   . . .
<body>
   <h1>Mighty Gumball Sales</h1>
   <div id="sales">
   </div>
   <script src="http://gumball.wickedlysmart.com/"></script>
</body>
</html>
```

① In our HTML we include a <script> element. The source for this script is actually the URL of a web service that is going to supply us with JSON for our data, like our Mighty Gumball sales data.

② When the browser encounters the <script> element in the page, it then sends an HTTP request to the src URL.

request

④ The JSON response is in the form of a string, which is parsed and interpreted by the browser. Any data types are turned into real JavaScript object and values, and any code will be executed.

Remember this is just a string representation of the object at this point!

JSON

③ The server treats the request like any HTTP request, and sends back JSON in its response.

Web Service

But what is the "P" in JSONP for?

OK, the first thing you need to know about JSONP is it has a dumb and non-obvious name: "JSON with Padding." If we had to name it, we'd call it something like "JSON with a Callback" or "get me some JSON and execute it when you get it back" or, well, really just about anything other than JSON with Padding.

But, all the padding amounts to is wrapping a function around the JSON before it comes back in the request. Here's how that works:

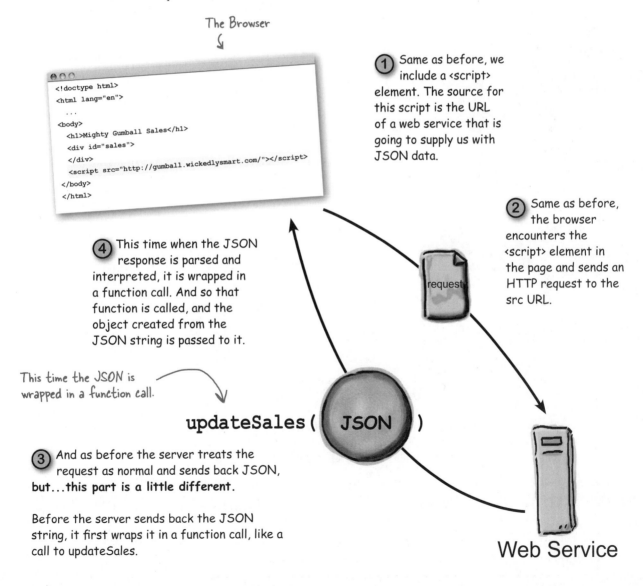

The Browser

```
<!doctype html>
<html lang="en">
  ...
<body>
  <h1>Mighty Gumball Sales</h1>
  <div id="sales">
  </div>
  <script src="http://gumball.wickedlysmart.com/"></script>
</body>
</html>
```

① Same as before, we include a <script> element. The source for this script is the URL of a web service that is going to supply us with JSON data.

② Same as before, the browser encounters the <script> element in the page and sends an HTTP request to the src URL.

④ This time when the JSON response is parsed and interpreted, it is wrapped in a function call. And so that function is called, and the object created from the JSON string is passed to it.

This time the JSON is wrapped in a function call.

updateSales(JSON)

③ And as before the server treats the request as normal and sends back JSON, **but...this part is a little different.**

Before the server sends back the JSON string, it first wraps it in a function call, like a call to updateSales.

Web Service

> I see how to use the <script> tag to make the browser go retrieve JavaScript, and how the server can put its data in that JavaScript. What about the function name though? How does the web service know the right function name is? Like, how does the Mighty Gumball web service know to call updateSales? What if I have another service and I want it to call, say, updateScore, or alert, or whatever?

Web services let you specify a callback function.

In general, web services allow you to specify what you want the function to be named. Although we didn't tell you, Mighty Gumball is already supporting a way to do this. Here's how it works: when you specify your URL, add a parameter on the end, like this:

`http://gumball.wickedlysmart.com/?callback=updateSales`

Here's the usual URL we've been using.

And here we've added a URL parameter, callback, that says to use the function updateSales when the JavaScript is generated.

MightyGumball will then use `updateSales` to wrap the JSON formatted object before sending it back to you. Typically, web services name this parameter `callback`, but check with your web service documentation to make sure that's what they're using.

BRAIN POWER

Try these URLs: what do you see in the response?

`http://search.twitter.com/search.json?q=hfhtml5&callback=myCallback`

`http://search.twitter.com/search.json?q=hfhtml5&callback=justDoIt`

`http://search.twitter.com/search.json?q=hfhtml5&callback=updateTweets`

Note: Firefox will ask you to open or save a file. You can open with TextEdit, Notepad, or any basic text editor.

Guys, we've got this. It took us a while to wrap our heads around using a <script> element to hit a web service, but now it almost seems easier than using XMLHttpRequest.

Jim: Well, almost.

Joe: I think this actually allows us to delete some code.

Frank: And I'm ready to make it all look good when you're done.

Jim: So Joe, code-wise, what do you have in mind?

Joe: With XMLHttpRequest we were retrieving a string. Using JSONP, the script tag is going to parse and evaluate the code coming back, so by the time we get our hands on the data it will be a JavaScript object.

Jim: Right, and with XMLHttpRequest we were using JSON.parse to convert the string into an object. We can just get rid of that?

Joe: Yup. That's my story and I'm sticking to it.

Jim: What else?

Joe: Well obviously we need to insert the `<script>` element.

Jim: I was wondering about that. Where do we put it?

Joe: Well, the browser is going to control when it loads, and we want the page to be loaded first, so we can update the DOM when `updateSales` is called. The only way I can think of dealing with that is to put the `<script>` at the bottom of the page in the body of the HTML.

Jim: Yeah, sounds like a good guess. We should look into that a little more. But for starters let's try it.

Joe: Okay, I want to get this code working! Let's get this code in!

Frank: You guys better hurry, I bet Judy's already got her own version in the works.

Let's update the Mighty Gumball web app

It's time to update your Mighty Gumball code with JSONP. Other than removing
the existing code that deals with the XMLHttpRequest call, all the changes are
minor. Let's make those changes now:

What we need to do:

 Remove our XMLHttpRequest code.

② Make sure the updateSales function is ready
to receive an object, not a string (as it was
with the XMLHttpRequest).

③ Add the <script> element to do the actual
data retrieval.

 All the code in our onload function was code involved in the XMLHttpRequest,
so we can just delete it. We'll keep the onload function around in case we need
it a little later. For now it will do nothing. Open up your mightygumball.js file
and make these changes:

```
window.onload = function() {
    var url = "http://gumball.wickedlysmart.com";
    var request = new XMLHttpRequest();
    request.open("GET", url);
    request.onload = function() {
        if (request.status == 200) {
            updateSales(request.responseText);
        }
    };
    request.send(null);
}
```

*For now, just delete all the
code in this function.*

② Next, remember that when we use the <script> element, we're telling the browser that it needs to retrieve JavaScript, and so the browser retrieves it, parses it and evaluates it. That means by the time it gets to your updateSales function, the JSON is no longer in string form, but is a first-class JavaScript object. When we used XMLHttpRequest, the data came back in the form of a string. Right now, updateSales assumes it is getting a string, so let's change that so that it handles an object, not a string:

```
function updateSales(responseText) {
function updateSales(sales) {
    var salesDiv = document.getElementById("sales");
    var sales = JSON.parse(responseText);
    for (var i = 0; i < sales.length; i++) {
        var sale = sales[i];
        var div = document.createElement("div");
        div.setAttribute("class", "saleItem");
        div.innerHTML = sale.name + " sold " + sale.sales + " gumballs";
        salesDiv.appendChild(div);
    }
}
```

Remove responseText and rewrite the line with a parameter named sales.

And we can delete the JSON.parse call too.

And that's it: we've now got a function ready to handle our data.

③ And finally, let's add the <script> element to do the actual data retrieval.

```
<!doctype html>
<html lang="en">
<head>
  <title>Mighty Gumball</title>
  <meta charset="utf-8">
  <script src="mightygumball.js"></script>
  <link rel="stylesheet" href="mightygumball.css">
</head>
<body>
  <h1>Mighty Gumball Sales</h1>
  <div id="sales">
  </div>
  <script src="http://gumball.wickedlysmart.com/?callback=updateSales"></script>
</body>
</html>
```

This is the link to the Mighty Gumball web service. We're using the callback parameter and specifying our function, updateSales, so the web service wraps the JSON in a function call to updateSales.

Test drive your new JSONP-charged code

If you've made all your changes, it's time for a test drive. Reload `mightygumball.html` into your browser. You're now loading Mighty Gumball sales data using your web app and JSONP. The page should look the same as when you were getting the sales data from the local file, but you know that it's using a whole different method of getting the data.

Here's what we see when we reload the Mighty Gumball page. You'll get different cities and sales because this is real data.

> Yes! The Mighty Gumball CEO should be happy with this. Time to par-tay.

> Nice work, boys.

> JSONP seems like one big security hole to me!

It's not any more or less secure than using <script> to load JavaScript.

It's true: if you make a JSONP request to a malicious web service, the response could include JavaScript code you're not expecting and the browser will execute it.

But it's no different than including JavaScript by linking to libraries hosted on other servers. Any time you link to JavaScript, whether it's to a library in the <head> of your document, or using JSONP, you need to be sure you trust that service. And if you're writing a web app that uses authentication to give the user access to sensitive data, it's probably best not to use third party libraries or JSON data hosted on other servers at all.

So choose the web services you link to carefully. If you're using an API like Google, Twitter, Facebook or one of the many other well-known web services out there, you're safe. Otherwise, caution is advised.

In our case, we know the Mighty Gumball engineers personally and we know they'd never put anything malicious in their JSON data, so you're safe to proceed.

Fireside Chats

Tonight's talk: XMLHttpRequest and JSONP

Tonight, we have two popular methods of retrieving data from your browser.

XMLHttpRequest:	**JSONP:**
No offense meant, but aren't you kind of a hack? I mean your purpose is to retrieve code, and people are using you to do requests for data.	
	Hack? I'd call it elegance. We can use the same means of retrieving code and data. Why have two ways of doing it?
But all you're doing is throwing some data in with code. And there's no way for you to make your requests directly from JavaScript code; you've got to use an HTML `<script>` element. Seems very confusing for your users.	
	Hey, it works, and it allows people to write code that retrieves JSON from services like Twitter and Google and a lot of others. How are you going to do that with XMLHttpRequest given your security restrictions. I mean you're still stuck on the old days, "XML," heh.
Hey XML is still in wide use, don't knock it. And you can retrieve JSON just fine with me.	
	Sure, if you want to always JSON.parse the result.
At least with me you're in control of what data gets parsed into JavaScript. With you it just happens.	
	That's an advantage—by the time my users get their data, it's all nicely parsed for them. Look, I have a lot of respect for you, you made this whole way of writing apps happen, but the problem is you're too restrictive. Today, in this world of web services, we need to be able to make requests to other domains.
Well you can go ahead and use a hack, like JSON-With-Padding—heh, dumb name—or, you can use the right thing, XMLHttpRequest and grow with it as it evolves. After all, people are working on making me more flexible while still secure.	
	Sure people are working on new ways, but my users have real needs today—they can't wait for you to figure out all your cross-domain issues.

XMLHttpRequest:

I had nothing to do with the name Ajax, so don't ask me! By the way, you never said how you are secure?

All I can say is if you don't need to go get someone else's data, like Twitter or Google, and you're writing your own web service and client, stick with me. I've got more security and I'm more straightforward to use.

Yeah yeah, mishmash.

Come on, it doesn't take that much code to support me going all the way back to IE5.

Yeah, well there's more to it than that, and have you ever tried to do something iterative, where you need to retrieve something over and over? Like that Mighty Gumball thing they've been working on. How are they going to make that work?

Here's my impression of your readers having just heard the sentence you just said: "Say what?"

JSONP:

And there's nothing dumb about "padding," it just means that when a user makes a web service request it also asks it to add a little prefix, like "updateSales()", on to the result. And what were they calling you for a while? Ajax? Isn't that a bathroom cleaner?

Coders have always needed to be careful. If you're retrieving code from another server, yeah you need to know what you're doing. But the answer isn't to just say "don't do it."

Hello? No one is writing services that don't use outside data. Ever heard the name "mashup?"

Hey, at least I'm consistently supported everywhere, I'd hate to have to write XMLHttpRequest code that worked across old browsers.

Haha, for me it takes ZERO code. Just a simple HTML tag.

Hey, it's not that bad. You just need to use write a new `<script>` element into the DOM to do another request.

HEAD FIRST:

Thanks guys! I'm afraid we're out of time!

You came up a little short. I thought I was going to see a constantly updated stream of sales from my gumball machines. Sure, I could hit refresh on my browser, but then I see only the newest reports, and only when I manually refresh. That's not what I want!

BRAIN POWER

He's right, we need to change our app so that it is updating the display with new sales at some regular interval (say, every ten seconds). Right now we're just putting a <script> element into the page that initiates the request to the server only one time. Can you think of any way to use JSONP to continually retrieve new sales reports?

Hint: using the DOM we can insert a new <script> element into the page. Could that work?

Guys, I just heard the Mighty Gumball CEO isn't exactly happy with your first version?

Jim: Yeah, he wants the data to be continually updated in the display.

Judy: That does make sense. I mean one big advantage of a web app is you don't have to refresh it like a web page.

Joe: Fair enough, and obviously we know how to replace old sales data with new sales data in the page using the DOM. But we're not sure yet how to handle the JSONP part.

Judy: Remember, you can use the DOM with the `<script>` element too. In other words, you can create a new `<script>` element in the DOM any time you want to retrieve more data.

Jim: Okay, right over my head. Can you say that again?

Joe: I think I sort of get it. Right now, we're putting the `<script>` element statically in the HTML markup by just typing it in. We could instead create a new `<script>` element with JavaScript code, and add it to the DOM. The only part I'm not sure of is, will the browser do another retrieval when we create the new `<script>` element?

Judy: It sure will.

Jim: I see, so we're creating a new `<script>` element any time we want the browser to do a JSONP-type operation for us.

Judy: Right! Sounds like you're getting it. And you know how to do it over and over?

Jim: Well, uh, we're not there yet, we were still thinking about the JSONP.

Judy: You know all about handler functions by now, you know like `onload` or `onclick`. You can set up a timer to call a function handler at a specified interval using the `setInterval` method in JavaScript.

Joe: So, let's get that set up and get the dynamic JSONP working ASAP for the Gumball CEO.

Jim: Oh, is that all you want? We better get on it!

Improving Mighty Gumball

As you can see we have a little more work to do, but it's not going to be too bad. Basically, we wrote our first version so that it grabs the latest sales reports from Mighty Gumball and displays them, *once*. Our bad, because almost any web app these days should continuously monitor data and update the app in (near) real time.

Here's what we need to do:

 We're going to remove the JSONP <script> element from the Mighty Gumball HTML, because we won't be using that any more.

② We need to set up a handler to handle making the JSONP request every few seconds. We'll take Judy's advice and use JavaScript's setInterval method.

③ Then we need to implement our JSONP code in the handler, so that each time it is called it makes a request to get the latest Mighty Gumball sales reports.

Step 1: Taking care of the script element...

We're going to be using a new way to invoke our JSONP requests, and so let's go ahead and remove the <script> element from our HTML.

```html
<!doctype html>
<html lang="en">
<head>
  <title>Mighty Gumball</title>
  <meta charset="utf-8">
  <script src="mightygumball.js"></script>
  <link rel="stylesheet" href="mightygumball.css">
</head>
<body>
  <h1>Mighty Gumball Sales</h1>
  <div id="sales">
  </div>
  <script src="http://gumball.wickedlysmart.com/?callback=updateSales"></script>
</body>
</html>
```

You can go ahead and delete this element from your HTML file.

Step 2: Now it's time for the timer

Okay, we're progressing from retrieving the sales reports once, to retrieving them every so often, say every three seconds. That might be too fast or slow depending on the application, but for Mighty Gumball we're going to start with three seconds.

Now, to do something every three seconds we need to have a function we can call every three seconds. And, as Judy mentioned, we can use the `setInterval` method in the `window` object to do this; here's what it looks like:

```
setInterval(handleRefresh, 3000);
```

The setInterval method takes a handler and a time interval.

Here's our handler function, which we'll define in a sec.

And here's our time interval, expressed in milliseconds. 3000 milliseconds = 3 seconds.

So every 3,000 milliseconds JavaScript will invoke your handler, in this case the `handleRefresh` function. Let's write a simple handler and give it a try:

```
function handleRefresh() {
    alert("I'm alive");
}
```

Every time this is called (which will be every three seconds), we'll throw up the alert "I'm alive."

Now we just need some code to set up the `setInterval` call, which we'll add to the onload function so it gets set up right after the entire page is loaded:

```
window.onload = function() {
    setInterval(handleRefresh, 3000);
}
```

This is our old onload function, which had nothing in it after we deleted the XMLHttpRequest code.

And all we need to do is add our call to setInterval, which, when the init function is run, will start a timer that fires every three seconds and calls our function handleRefresh.

Let's give this a try and then when we know it's working—that is, when we see our our handler being invoked every three seconds—we'll implement the JSONP code.

A time-driven test drive

This should be fun. Make sure you've typed in the `handleRefresh` function and also made the changes to the `onload` handler. Save everything and load it into your browser. You'll see a stream of alerts, and you'll have to close your browser window to stop it!

http://localhost

I'm alive

OK

Here's what we get!

Sharpen your pencil

Now that you know about setInterval (not to mention XMLHttpRequest and JSONP), think of ways you could use them in other web applications. List those here:

Check and update progress on a task and display it.

See if any new comments have been posted on a topic.

Update a map if any friends have shown up nearby.

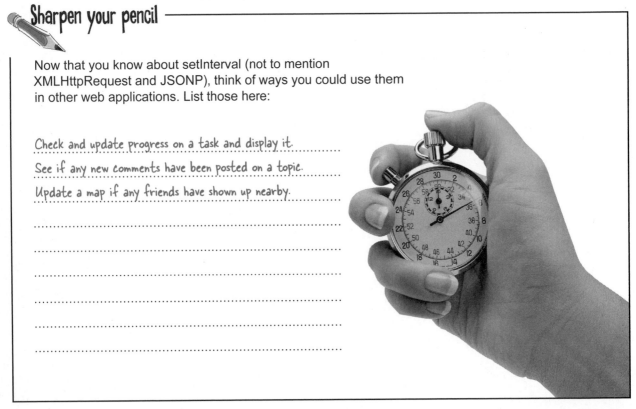

Step 3: Reimplementing JSONP

We still want to use JSONP to retrieve our data, but we need a way to do it whenever our refresh handler is called, not just at page load time. That's where the DOM comes in—the great thing about the DOM is that we can *insert new elements* into the DOM *at any time*, <u>even `<script>` elements</u>. So, we should be able to insert a new `<script>` element any time we want to make a JSONP call. Let's work up some code using everything we know about the DOM and JSONP to do this.

First, let's set up the JSONP URL

This is the same URL we used with our previous script element. Here we'll assign it to a variable for later use. Delete the alert out of your handler and add this code:

We're back in our
handleRefresh function.

Here, we're setting up the JSONP URL
and assigning it to the variable url.

```
function handleRefresh() {
    var url = "http://gumball.wickedlysmart.com?callback=updateSales";
}
```

Next, let's create a new script element

Now, instead of having the <script> element in our HTML, we're going to build a <script> element using JavaScript. We need to create the element, and then set its src and id attributes:

```
function handleRefresh() {
    var url = "http://gumball.wickedlysmart.com?callback=updateSales";

    var newScriptElement = document.createElement("script");
    newScriptElement.setAttribute("src", url);
    newScriptElement.setAttribute("id", "jsonp");
}
```

First, we create a new
script element...

... and set the src attribute of
the element to our JSONP URL.

And we'll give this script an id so
we can easily get it again, which
we'll need to, as you'll see.

The setAttribute method might look new to you (we've only mentioned it in passing so far), but it's pretty easy to see what it does. The setAttribute method allows you to set the attributes of an HTML element, like the src and id attributes or a number of others including class, href and so on.

How do we insert the script into the DOM?

We're almost there, we just need to insert our newly created script element. Once we do that the browser will see it and do its thing, causing the JSONP request to be made. Now, to insert the script requires a little bit of planning and forethought; let's see how this is going to work:

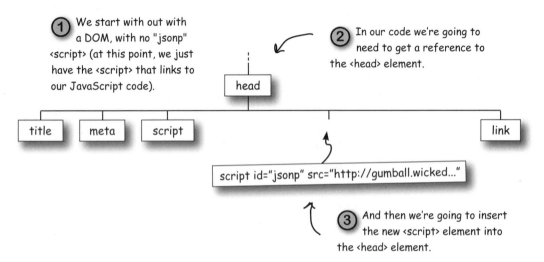

① We start with out with a DOM, with no "jsonp" \<script\> (at this point, we just have the \<script\> that links to our JavaScript code).

② In our code we're going to need to get a reference to the \<head\> element.

head

title   meta   script   link

script id="jsonp" src="http://gumball.wicked..."

③ And then we're going to insert the new \<script\> element into the \<head\> element.

Once we've inserted the script, the browser will see the new script in the DOM and go retrieve what's at the URL in the src attribute. Now, we've also got a second use case. Let's look at it.

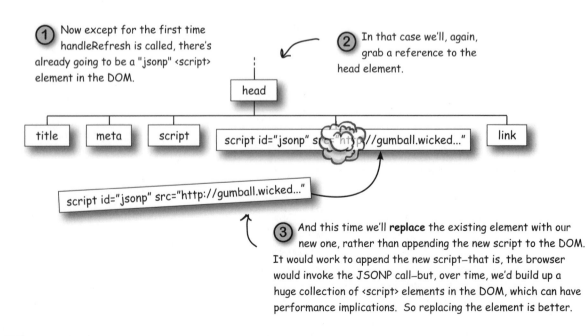

① Now except for the first time handleRefresh is called, there's already going to be a "jsonp" \<script\> element in the DOM.

② In that case we'll, again, grab a reference to the head element.

head

title   meta   script   script id="jsonp" src="http://gumball.wicked..."   link

script id="jsonp" src="http://gumball.wicked..."

③ And this time we'll **replace** the existing element with our new one, rather than appending the new script to the DOM. It would work to append the new script—that is, the browser would invoke the JSONP call—but, over time, we'd build up a huge collection of \<script\> elements in the DOM, which can have performance implications. So replacing the element is better.

Now let's write the code to insert the script into the DOM

Now that we know the steps, let's check out the code. We'll do this in two steps too: first we'll show the code to add a new script, then the code to replace a script:

```
function handleRefresh() {
    var url = "http://gumball.wickedlysmart.com?callback=updateSales";

    var newScriptElement = document.createElement("script");
    newScriptElement.setAttribute("src", url);
    newScriptElement.setAttribute("id", "jsonp");

    var oldScriptElement = document.getElementById("jsonp");
    var head = document.getElementsByTagName("head")[0];
    if (oldScriptElement == null) {
        head.appendChild(newScriptElement);
    }
}
```

We're first going to get the reference to the <script> element. If doesn't exist, we'll get back null. Notice we're counting on it having the id "jsonp."

Next we're going to get a reference to the <head> element using a new document method. We'll come back to how this works. but for now just know it gets a reference to the <head> element.

Now that we have a reference to the <head> element, we check to see if there is already a <script> element, and if there isn't (if its reference is null) then we go ahead and append the new <script> element to the head.

Okay, let's check out the code that replaces the script element if it already exists. We'll just show the conditional if statement, which is where all the new code is:

Here's our conditional again, remember it is just checking to see if a <script> element already exists in the DOM.

```
if (oldScriptElement == null) {
    head.appendChild(newScriptElement);
} else {
    head.replaceChild(newScriptElement, oldScriptElement);
}
```

If there is already a <script> element in the head, then we just replace it. You can use the replaceChild method on the <head> element and pass it the old and new scripts to do that. We'll look a little more closely at this new method in a sec.

getElementsByTagName Up Close

This is the first time you've seen the getElementsByTagName method, so let's take a quick up close look. It's similar to getDocumentById, except that it returns an array of elements that match a given tag name.

getElementsByTagName returns all the elements in the DOM with this tag.

```
var arrayOfHeadElements = document.getElementsByTagName("head");
```

In this case it returns an array of head elements.

Once you have the array, you can get the first item in it using index 0:

```
var head = arrayOfHeadElements[0];
```

Returns the first head element in the array (and there should be only one, right?).

Now we can combine these two lines, like this:

```
var head = document.getElementsByTagName("head")[0];
```

We get the array and then index into the array to get the first item in one step.

In our code example, we're always using the first <head> element but you can use this method on any tag, like <p>, <div> and so on. And usually you'll get more than one of those back on the array.

replaceChild Up Close

Let's also look at the replaceChild method because you haven't seen that before. Call the replaceChild method on the element in which you want to replace a child, passing in the references to both the new and old children. The method simply replaces the old child with the new one.

The replaceChild method tells the <head> element to replace one of its children, oldScriptElement, with a new child, newScriptElement.

Our new <script> element

The <script> that's already in the page.

```
head.replaceChild(newScriptElement, oldScriptElement);
```

there are no
Dumb Questions

Q: Why can't I just replace the data in the src attribute instead of replacing the whole <script> element?

A: If you replace just the src attribute with the new URL, the browser doesn't see it as a new script, and so it doesn't make the request to retrieve the JSONP. To force the browser to make the request, we have to create this whole new script. This is a technique known as "script injection."

Q: What happens to the old child when I replace it?

A: It's removed from the DOM. What happens from there depends on you: if you've still got a reference to it stored in a variable somewhere you can continue to use it (in whatever way might make sense). However if you don't, the JavaScript runtime might eventually reclaim the memory the element is taking up in your browser.

Q: What if there is more than one <head> element? Your code seems to depend on there being only one head when you index by zero in the array returned by getElementsByTag?

A: By definition, an HTML file has only one <head> element. That said, sure, someone could type two into an HTML file. In that case your results may vary (and that's what you get for not validating your HTML!), but as usual, the browser will do its very best to do the right thing (what that is, just may depend on the browser).

Q: Can I stop the interval timer after I start it?

A: You sure can. The setInterval method actually returns an id that identifies the timer. By storing the id in a variable you can then pass it to the clearInterval method at any time to stop the timer. Closing your browser also stops the timer.

Q: How can I know the parameters a web service uses? And if it supports JSON and JSONP?

A: Most web services publish a public API that includes the ways you can access the service as well as all the things you can do with the service. If you're using a commercial API you might need to get this documentation directly from the provider. For many public APIs you'll most likely find the information you need through a web search or on the organization's developer section of their web site. You can also visit sites like programtheweb.com, which documents the growing list of APIs out there.

Q: XMLHttpRequest is obviously older than HTML5, but what about JSON and JSONP? Are they part of HTML5? Do I need HTML5 to use them?

A: We'd call JSON and JSONP contemporaries of HTML5. While neither one is defined by an HTML5 specification, they are in heavy use by HTML5 applications and are a core part of building web apps. So, when we say HTML = Markup + JavaScript APIs + CSS, well, JSON and JSONP are very much part of that picture (as are requests using HTTP with XMLHttpRequest).

Q: Do people still use XML? Or is everything JSON now?

A: One truism in the computer industry is that nothing ever dies, and so we're sure we'll have XML for a long time to come. That said, we'd also say JSON has momentum right now and so lots of new services are being created using JSON. You'll often find that many web services support a variety of data formats including XML, JSON and many others (like RSS). JSON has the advantage that it is based directly on JavaScript and JSONP gets us around cross domain issues.

We almost forgot: watch out for the dreaded browser cache

We're almost ready to go here, but there's a small detail we need to take care of, and it's one of those "if you've never done it before, how would you know you need to address it" kind of issues.

Most browsers have an interesting property in that if you retrieve the same URL over and over (like our JSONP request will), the browser ends up caching it for efficiency, and so you just get the same cached file (or data) back over and over. Not what we want.

Luckily there is an easy and old-as-the-Web cure for this. All we do is add a random number onto the end of the URL, and then the browser is tricked into thinking it's a new URL the browser's never seen before. Let's fix our code by changing the URL line above to:

You'll find this code at the top of your handleRefresh function.

Change your URL declaration above to look like this.

```
var url = "http://gumball.wickedlysmart.com/?callback=updateSales" +
          "&random=" + (new Date()).getTime();
```

We're adding a new, "dummy" parameter on the end of the URL. The web server will just ignore it, but it's enough to fake out the browser.

We create a new Date object, use the getTime method of the Date object to get the time in milliseconds, and then add the time to the end of the URL.

With this new code, the generated URL will look something like this:

This part should look familiar...

And here's the random parameter.

```
http://gumball.wickedlysmart.com?callback=updateSales&random=1309217501707
```

This part will change each time to defeat caching.

Go ahead and replace the `url` variable declaration in your `handleRefresh` function with the code and then we'll be ready for a test drive!

One more TIME test drive

Alright, surely we've thought of everything this time. We should be all ready. Make sure you've got all the code in since the last test drive, and reload the page. Wow, we're seeing continuous updates!

Wait a sec... are you seeing what we're seeing? What are these duplicates? That's not good. Hmmm. Maybe we're retrieving too fast and getting reports we've already retrieved?

Duplicates!

How to remove duplicate sales reports

If you take a quick look back at the Gumball Specs on page 228, you'll see that you can specify a last report time parameter in the request URL, like this:

You can also add a lastreporttime parameter to the end of the URL and you'll get only the reports since that time. Use it like this:

`http://gumball.wickedlysmart.com/?lastreporttime=1302212903099`

Just specify a time in milliseconds.

That's a great, but how do we know the time of the last report we've retrieved? Let's look at the format of the sales reports again:

```
[{"name":"LOS ANGELES","time":1309208126092,"sales":2},
 {"name":"PASADENA","time":1309208128219,"sales":8},
 {"name":"DAVIS CREEK","time":1309214414505,"sales":8}
 ...]
```

Each sales report has the time it was reported.

I see where you're going with this; we can keep track of the time of the last report, and then use that when we make the next request so that the server doesn't give us reports we've already received?

You got it.

And to keep track of the last sales report received we're going to need to make some additions to the updateSales function, where all the processing of the sales data happens. First, though, we should declare a variable to hold the time of the most recent report:

```
var lastReportTime = 0;
```

↙ The time can't be less then zero, so let's just set it to 0 for starters.

Put this at the top of your JavaScript file, <u>outside</u> any function.

And let's grab the time of the most recent sale in updateSales:

```
function updateSales(sales) {
    var salesDiv = document.getElementById("sales");
    for (var i = 0; i < sales.length; i++) {
        var sale = sales[i];
        var div = document.createElement("div");
        div.setAttribute("class", "saleItem");
        div.innerHTML = sale.name + " sold " + sale.sales +
            " gumballs";
        salesDiv.appendChild(div);
    }
    if (sales.length > 0) {
        lastReportTime = sales[sales.length-1].time;
    }
}
```

If you look at the sales array, you'll see that the most recent sale is the last one in the array. So here we're assigning that to our variable lastReportTime.

We need to make sure there IS an array though; if there are no new sales, then we'd get back an empty array and our code here would cause an exception.

Updating the JSON URL to include the lastreporttime

Now that we're keeping track of the last reported sales time, we need to make sure we're sending it to Mighty Gumball as part of the JSON request. To do that, we'll edit the `handleRefresh` function, and add the `lastreporttime` query parameter like this:

```
function handleRefresh() {
    var url = "http://gumball.wickedlysmart.com" +
                "?callback=updateSales" +
                "&lastreporttime=" + lastReportTime +
                "&random=" + (new Date()).getTime();
    var newScriptElement = document.createElement("script");
    newScriptElement.setAttribute("src", url);
    newScriptElement.setAttribute("id", "jsonp");
    var oldScriptElement = document.getElementById("jsonp");
    var head = document.getElementsByTagName("head")[0];
    if (oldScriptElement == null) {
        head.appendChild(newScriptElement);
    }
    else {
        head.replaceChild(newScriptElement, oldScriptElement);
    }
}
```

We've split up the URL into several strings that we're concatenating together...

... and here's the lastreporttime parameter with its new value.

Test drive lastReportTime

Let's take the `lastreporttime` query parameter for a test run and see if it solves our duplicate sales reports problem. Make sure you type in the new code, reload the page, and click that refresh button.

We did it! And Mighty Gumball is super happy with their new web app.

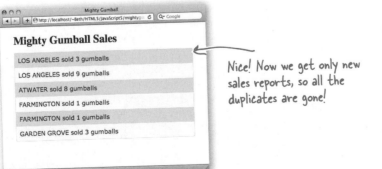

Mighty Gumball Sales

LOS ANGELES sold 3 gumballs

LOS ANGELES sold 9 gumballs

ATWATER sold 8 gumballs

FARMINGTON sold 1 gumballs

FARMINGTON sold 1 gumballs

GARDEN GROVE sold 3 gumballs

Nice! Now we get only new sales reports, so all the duplicates are gone!

You've outdone yourselves! This works great and now I can totally keep up with sales at my desk or when I'm mobile. I'm starting to really think there is something to these web apps. Just think what we're going to be able to do with gumball machines, JSON, and all those HTML5 APIs!

BULLET POINTS

- XMLHttpRequest does not allow you to request data from a different server than the one from which your HTML and JavaScript are being served. This is a browser security policy designed to prevent malicious JavaScript from getting access to your web pages and a user's cookies.

- An alternative to XMLHttpRequest for accessing data hosted by web services is JSONP.

- Use XMLHttpRequest when your HTML and JavaScript are hosted on the same machine as your data.

- Use JSONP when you need to access data hosted by a web service on a remote server (assuming that web service supports JSONP). A web service is a web API that is accessed by HTTP.

- JSONP is a method of retrieving data by using the <script> element.

- JSONP is JSON data wrapped in JavaScript; typically, a function call.

- The function call that wraps the JSON data in JSONP is referred to as a "callback."

- Specify the callback function as a URL query parameter in a JSONP request.

- JSONP is no more (or less) secure than linking to JavaScript libraries using the <script> element. Use caution whenever you link to third-party JavaScript.

- Specify the <script> element to make the JSONP request by adding it directly to your HTML, or by writing the <script> element to the DOM using JavaScript.

- Use a random number on the end of your JSONP request URL if you are making the request multiple times so the browser doesn't cache the response.

- The method replaceChild replaces an element in the DOM with another element.

- setInterval is a timer that calls a function at a specified interval. You can use setInterval to make repeated JSONP requests to a server to retrieve new data.

HTML5cross

Wow, you got your apps talking to the Web in this chapter!
Time for some left-brain activity to help it all sink in.

Across

2. The pattern of using XMLHttpRequest to get data from servers is sometimes called _____.

5. _____ is the latest Mighty Gumball Web-enabled gumball machine.

8. XMLHttpRequest made fun of JSONP's _____.

10. The Guru teaches Grasshopper that function arguments are also _____.

12. We were _____ to get twenty-five pages into the chapter before discovering the browser security policy.

15. One of XMLHttpRequest's nicknames at Microsoft.

16. JSONP stands for "JSON with _____".

Down

1. JSONP uses a _____

3. JSONP uses these types of objects.

4. Format we all thought would save the world.

6. _____ has a JSONP Web service.

7. This chapter had one of these in the middle.

9. Mighty Gumball is testing the MG2200 in _____

11. _____ reminded Frank, Jim, and Joe about the cross-domain security issues with XMLHttpRequest.

13. It's easy to set up a local server on a _____.

14. _____, the QA guy, was upset when the request to the production Gumball server failed.

A Special Message
from Chapter 7...

While we've got you thinking about JSONP, we'd love to have your help in the Canvas chapter.

We're working with Twitter's JSONP API and building out a service that allows you to put any tweet on a t-shirt.

We like to say "if it's worth tweeting, it's worth printing on a t-shirt."

TweetShirt.com founder

HTML5cross Solution

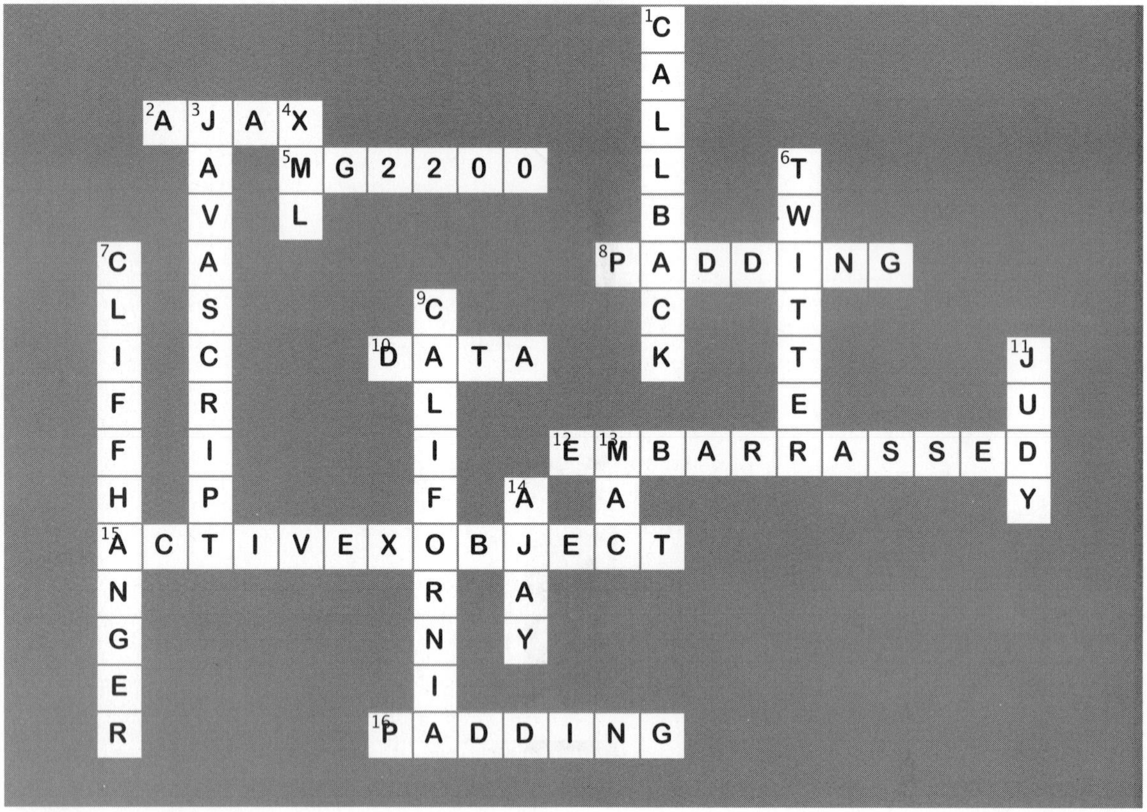
1 CALLBACK
2 AJAX
3 JAVASCRIPT
4 XML
5 MG2200
6 TWITTER
7 CLIFFHANGER
8 PADDING
9 CALIFORNIA
10 DATA
11 JUDY
12 EMBARRASSED
13 MAC
14 AJAY
15 ACTIVEXOBJECT
16 PADDING

7 bringing out your inner artist

The Canvas

Yeah, sure, markup is nice and all, but there's nothing like getting your hands in and painting with fresh, pure pixels.

HTML's been liberated from being just a "markup" language.

With HTML5's new canvas element, you've got the power to create, manipulate and destroy *pixels*, right in your own hands. In this chapter we'll use the canvas element to bring out your inner artist—no more talk about HTML being all semantics and no presentation; with canvas we're going to paint and draw with color. Now it's *all* about presentation. We'll tackle how to place a canvas in your pages, how to draw text and graphics (using JavaScript, of course), and even how to handle browsers that don't support the canvas element. And canvas isn't just a one-hit wonder; you're going to be seeing a lot more of canvas in other chapters in this book.

Okay, "destroy" might be a little overly dramatic.

↖ In fact we hear <canvas> and <video> have been sharing more than just web pages... we'll get into the juicy details later.

Our new start-up: TweetShirt

Our motto is "if it's worth tweeting on Twitter, it's worth wearing on a t-shirt."

After all, half the battle of calling yourself a journalist is being willing to put your words in print, so what better place than printing on your or someone else's chest? At least that's our start-up pitch, and we're sticking to it.

Now, there's only one thing that stands in the way of getting this start-up off the ground: we need a nice web app that lets customers create a custom t-shirt design, featuring one of their recent tweets.

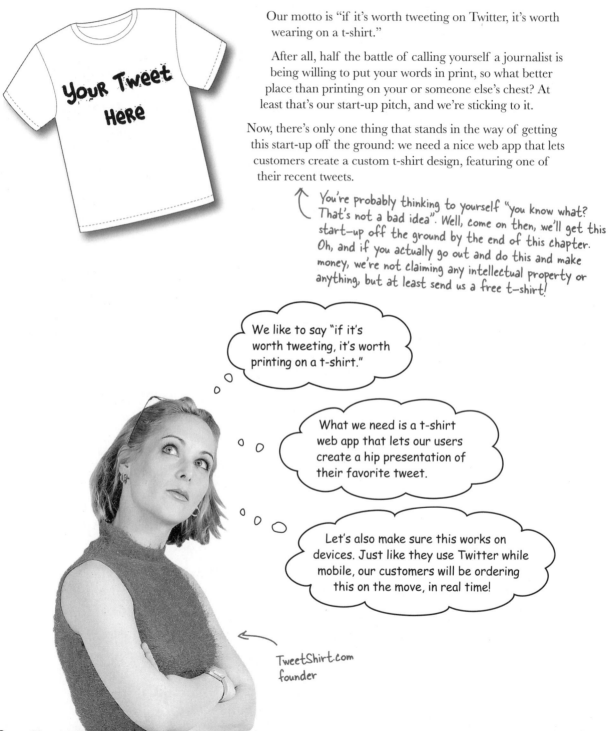

You're probably thinking to yourself "you know what? That's not a bad idea". Well, come on then, we'll get this start-up off the ground by the end of this chapter. Oh, and if you actually go out and do this and make money, we're not claiming any intellectual property or anything, but at least send us a free t-shirt!

We like to say "if it's worth tweeting, it's worth printing on a t-shirt."

What we need is a t-shirt web app that lets our users create a hip presentation of their favorite tweet.

Let's also make sure this works on devices. Just like they use Twitter while mobile, our customers will be ordering this on the move, in real time!

TweetShirt.com founder

Checking out the "comps"

After exhaustive iterative design and extensive focus group testing we've got a comp (otherwise known as an initial visual design) ready for you to review, let's take a look:

Yeah right, come on we're a start-up, we did this on a napkin at Starbuzz Coffee.

Here's the t-shirt design.

Here's the tweet the user chose nicely displayed on the shirt.

Allow user to choose background color. Here they've chosen white.

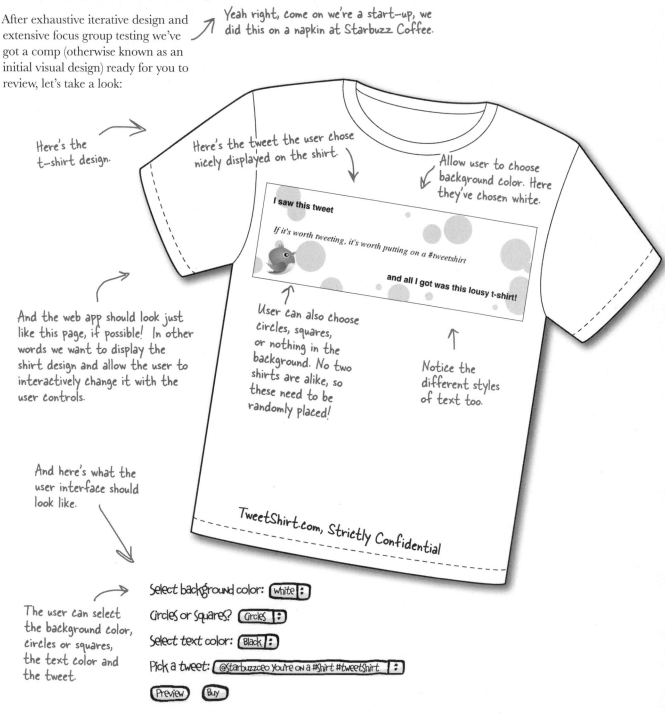

I saw this tweet

If it's worth tweeting, it's worth putting on a #tweetshirt

and all I got was this lousy t-shirt!

TweetShirt.com, Strictly Confidential

And the web app should look just like this page, if possible! In other words we want to display the shirt design and allow the user to interactively change it with the user controls.

User can also choose circles, squares, or nothing in the background. No two shirts are alike, so these need to be randomly placed!

Notice the different styles of text too.

And here's what the user interface should look like.

The user can select the background color, circles or squares, the text color and the tweet.

Select background color: [White ▼]

Circles or Squares? [Circles ▼]

Select text color: [Black ▼]

Pick a tweet: [@starbuzzceo You're on a #shirt #tweetShirt ▼]

(Preview) (Buy)

BRAIN POWER

Take another look at the requirements on the previous page. How do you think you can accomplish this using HTML5? Remember, one requirement is making sure your site works across as many device formats and sizes as possible?

Check all the possibilities below (and then circle the best answer):

☐   Just use Flash, it works on most browsers.

☐   Take a look at HTML5 and see if there are any new technologies that might help (hint: there might be one named canvas).

☐   Write a custom application for every device, that way you know the exact experience you're going to get.

☐   Just compute the image on the server side and deliver a custom image back to the browser.

there are no Dumb Questions

Q: Well seriously, why not Flash, or a custom application for that matter?

A: Flash is a great technology, and you certainly could use it. Right now, though, the industry is heading toward HTML5, and as we write this, you'd have trouble running your Flash app on all devices, including some very popular ones.

An app may be a great choice if you really need an experience that is totally customized to the device. Keep in mind that developing a custom application for a variety of devices is expensive.

With HTML5 you get great support across mobile devices and the desktop, and you can often create an application by using a single technology solution.

Q: I like the idea of creating the image on the server. That way I can write one piece of code and images work on all devices. I know a little PHP so I should be able to pull this off.

A: That's another way you could go, but the disadvantages are that if you have a zillion users, you are going to have to worry about scaling those servers to meet the demand (versus each user's client dealing with generating the preview of the t-shirt). You're also going to have a much more interactive and seamless experience if you write it for the browser instead.

How? Well, we're glad you asked...

Let's drop in on the TweetShirt crew...

You've heard the requirements and you've got a basic design for the user experience, so now comes the tough part, making it work. Let's listen in and see where this is all going...

↖ Frank, Judy and Joe

Joe: I thought this was going to be simple until I saw those circles in the background.

Frank: What do you mean, that's just an image...

Judy: No no, the founder wants those circles to be random; so the circles on my shirt will be different from yours. Same with the squares.

Frank: That's okay, in the past we've done it by generating an image on the server side.

Joe: Yeah, I know, but that didn't work out so well; remember having to pay all those server fees to Amazon?

Frank: Uh, yeah. Nevermind.

Joe: And in any case, we want this thing to be instant gratification, you know, no long trips back to the server. So, let's do it all on the client-side if we can.

Judy: Guys, I think we can, I've been looking at the canvas stuff in HTML5.

Frank: Canvas? Remember I'm just the design guy, fill me in.

Judy: You must have heard of the canvas, Frank—it's a new element in HTML5 that creates an drawable region for 2D shapes, text and bitmap images.

Frank: It sounds like an `<img>` tag. We just place it on the page with a width and height and the browser does the rest.

Judy: Not a bad comparison, we do define a width and height for the canvas, but in this case what gets drawn on the canvas is specified with JavaScript code.

Joe: Well, where does markup come into that? Can we tell the canvas in JavaScript to "put this `<h1>` element here"?

Judy: Nope, after you place the canvas in the page you leave the markup world behind; in JavaScript we're placing points, lines, paths, images and text. It's really a low level API.

Joe: Well, as long as it can pull off those random circles I'm good. Okay, enough talking, let's have a look at it!

How to get a canvas into your web page

Frank was right, in some ways a canvas is like an `<img>` element. You add a canvas like this:

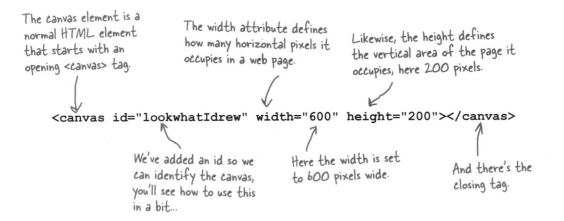

The canvas element is a normal HTML element that starts with an opening `<canvas>` tag.

The width attribute defines how many horizontal pixels it occupies in a web page.

Likewise, the height defines the vertical area of the page it occupies, here 200 pixels.

`<canvas id="lookwhatIdrew" width="600" height="200"></canvas>`

We've added an id so we can identify the canvas, you'll see how to use this in a bit...

Here the width is set to 600 pixels wide.

And there's the closing tag.

And the browser allocates some space in the page for the canvas, with the width and height you specified.

In this case, a width of 600 and a height of 200.

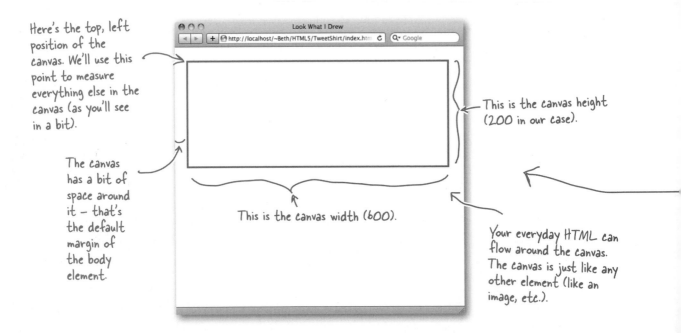

Here's the top, left position of the canvas. We'll use this point to measure everything else in the canvas (as you'll see in a bit).

The canvas has a bit of space around it – that's the default margin of the body element.

This is the canvas width (600).

This is the canvas height (200 in our case).

Your everyday HTML can flow around the canvas. The canvas is just like any other element (like an image, etc.).

Test drive your new canvas

Time for you to get this working in your own web page. Go ahead and type in the code below into a new file and then load it in your browser:

```
<!doctype html>
<html lang="en">
<head>
    <title>Look What I Drew</title>
    <meta charset="utf-8">
</head>
<body>

<canvas id="lookwhatIdrew" width="600" height="200"></canvas>

</body>
</html>
```

Type this in and give it a try.

What gives? My page is blank!

What she sees...

...and what you probably see too!

We drew these lines to explain how the canvas fits in a page, for illustration purposes only. They aren't really there (unless you draw them yourself).

Turn the page to find out more...

How to see your canvas

Unless you draw something in the canvas, you're not going to see it. It is simply a space in the browser window for you to draw in. We're going to draw in the canvas very soon, but for now, what we really want is evidence that the canvas is actually in our page.

There is another way we can see the canvas... if we use CSS to style the <canvas> element so we can see the border, we'll be able to see it in the page. Let's add a simple style that adds a 1-pixel-wide black border to the canvas.

```
<!doctype html>
<html lang="en">
<head>
    <title>Look What I Drew</title>
    <meta charset="utf-8">
    <style>
      canvas {
        border: 1px solid black;
      }
    </style>
</head>
<body>
<canvas id="lookwhatIdrew" width="600" height="200"></canvas>
</body>
</html>
```

We've added a style for the canvas that just puts a 1px black border on it, so we can see it in the page.

Much better! Now we can see the canvas. Next, we need to do something interesting with it...

Look What I Drew

there are no
Dumb Questions

Q: Can I only have one canvas per page?

A: No, you can have as many as you like (or that the browser or your users can handle). Just give each a unique id and you can draw on each as a separate canvas. You'll see how to use the canvas id in a moment.

Q: Is the canvas transparent?

A: By default, yes, the canvas is transparent. You can draw in the canvas to fill it with colored pixels; you'll see how to do that later in the chapter.

Q: If it's transparent, that means I could position it on top of another element to, say, draw something over an image or anything else on the page, right?

A: That's right! That's one of the cool things about canvas. It gives you the ability to add graphics anywhere on your page.

Q: Can I use CSS to set the width and height of the canvas instead of the width and height attributes on the element?

A: You can, but it works a little differently from how you might expect. By default, a canvas element is 300px wide and 150px high. If you don't specify the width and height attributes in the canvas tag, that's what you get. If you then specify a size in CSS, say 600px by 200px, the 300 x 150 canvas is *scaled* to fit that size, and so is everything that's drawn in the canvas. It's just like scaling an image by specifying a new width and height that is larger or smaller than the real width and height of the image. If you scale it up, you'll get some pixelation in the image, right?

The same thing happens with the canvas. A 300px wide canvas that becomes 600px wide has the same number of pixels stretched into twice the size, so it'll look kind of chunky. However, if you use the width and height attributes in the element, you're setting the dimensions of the canvas to be bigger (or smaller) than 300 x 150 and everything drawn in that canvas will be drawn normally. So, we recommend specifying the width and height in the tag attributes, and not setting those properties in CSS unless you really mean to scale the canvas.

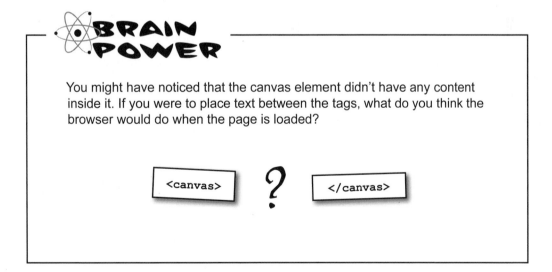

BRAIN POWER

You might have noticed that the canvas element didn't have any content inside it. If you were to place text between the tags, what do you think the browser would do when the page is loaded?

`<canvas>`   ?   `</canvas>`

Drawing on the Canvas

Right now we've got a blank canvas staring us in the face. Rather than sit here with a case of JavaScript-writers-block, we're just going to go for it and put a nice black-filled rectangle on our canvas. To do that we've got to decide where it goes and how big to make it. How about we put it at the location x=10 pixels and y=10 pixels and make it 100 pixels high and wide? Works for us.

Now let's check out some code that does this:

Let's start with just our standard HTML5.

```
<!doctype html>

<html lang="en">

<head>

    <title>Look What I Drew</title>

    <meta charset="utf-8" />

    <style>

        canvas { border: 1px solid black; }

    </style>

    <script>

        window.onload = function() {

            var canvas = document.getElementById("tshirtCanvas");

            var context = canvas.getContext("2d");

            context.fillRect(10, 10, 100, 100);

        };

    </script>

</head>

<body>

    <canvas width="600" height="200" id="tshirtCanvas"></canvas>

</body>

</html>
```

We'll keep our CSS border in for now.

Here's our onload handler; we'll start drawing after the page is fully loaded.

To draw on the canvas we need a reference to it. Let's use getElementById to get it from the DOM.

Hmm, this is interesting, we apparently need a "2d" context from the canvas to actually draw....

We're using the 2d context to draw a filled rectangle on the canvas.

These numbers are the x, y position of the rectangle on the canvas.

And we've also got the width and height (in pixels).

Also interesting that a rectangle fill method doesn't take a fill color... more on that in a sec.

Ah, and we can't forget our canvas element. We're specifying a canvas that is 600 pixels wide and 200 pixels high, and has an id of "tshirtCanvas".

A little Canvas test drive...

Go ahead and type this code in (or grab it from `http://wickedlysmart.com/hfhtml5`) and load it into your browser. Assuming you're using a modern browser you should see something like we do:

Here's our 100 x 100 rectangle, positioned at 10, 10 in the canvas.

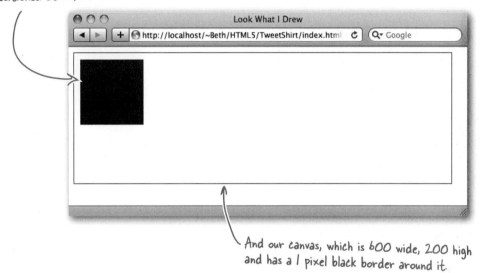

And our canvas, which is 600 wide, 200 high and has a 1 pixel black border around it.

A closer look at the code

That was a great little test run, but let's dive in a little deeper:

 In our markup, we define a canvas and give it an id, using the `<canvas>` tag. The first thing you need to do to draw into that canvas is to get a handle on the canvas object in the DOM. As usual we do this with the `getElementById` method:

```
var canvas = document.getElementById("tshirtCanvas");
```

With a reference to the canvas element assigned to the `canvas` variable, we now have to go through a bit of "protocol" before we draw on the canvas. We need to ask the canvas to give us a context to draw on. And in this case, we specifically want a 2D context. The context returned by the canvas is assigned to the `context` variable:

```
var context = canvas.getContext("2d");
```

This is a bit of protocol we have to follow before we can start drawing on the canvas.

Now, with the context in hand, we can use it to draw onto the canvas, which we do by calling the `fillRect` method. This method creates a rectangle starting at the x, y position of 10, 10 and that is 100 pixels wide and high.

Note, we're calling the fillRect method on the context, not the canvas itself.

```
context.fillRect(10, 10, 100, 100);
```

Try this out and you should see a black rectangle appear. Try changing the values for x, y, width, and height and see what happens.

Can you think of a way to use a canvas element if your browser supports it and if not, to just display a message like "Hey, you, yes you, upgrade your browser!!"?

there are no
Dumb Questions

Q: How does the canvas know to make the rectangle black?

A: Black is the default fill color for a canvas. Of course, you can change this using the fillStyle property, as we'll show you shortly.

Q: What if I wanted a rectangle outline, not a filled rectangle?

A: To get just the outline of a rectangle, you'd use the strokeRect function instead of fillRect. You'll learn more about stroking later in the chapter.

Q: What is a 2d context, and why can't I just draw right on the canvas?

A: The canvas is the graphical area displayed in the web page. The context is an object associated with the canvas that defines a set of properties and methods you can use to draw on the canvas. You can even save the state of the context and then restore it later, which comes in handy at times. You'll see many of these context properties and methods in the rest of this chapter.

The canvas was designed to support more than one interface; 2d, 3d, and others we haven't even thought of yet. By using a context, we can work with different interfaces within the same element, canvas. You can't draw right on the canvas because you need to specify which interface you're using by choosing a context.

Q: Does that mean there is a "3d" context too?

A: Not yet. There are a few competing and emerging standards for this, but nothing that looks like a frontrunner yet. Stay tuned on this one; in the mean time take a look at WebGL and the libraries that use it, like SpiderGL, SceneJS and three.js.

Serious Coding

Wondering how you can detect whether your browser supports canvas or not, in code?

Well of course you can, and we should point out that so far we've just been assuming our browser supports canvas. But in any production code you should test to make sure you have support.

All you have to do is test to see if the getContext method exists in your canvas object (the one you get back from getElementById):

First we grab a reference to a canvas element in the page.

```
var canvas =
    document.getElementById("tshirtCanvas");
if (canvas.getContext) {
    // you have canvas
} else {
    // sorry no canvas API support
}
```

Then we check for the existance of the getContext method. Note, we're not calling it, we're just seeing if it has a value.

If you want to test for canvas support without having to have a canvas already in your markup, you can create a canvas element on the fly, using all the techniques you already know. Like this:

```
var canvas =
    document.createElement("canvas");
```

Be sure to check out the appendix for information about an open source library you can use to test for all the functionality in HTML5 in a consistent way.

When I try this in Internet Explorer, I'm seeing nothing where the canvas element should be. What's the story?

IE supports canvas only in versions 9 and later, so you should code your page to let your users know.

Here's the deal: if you really really need to support canvas functionality in Internet Explorer (again, pre-version 9), then you can check out the Explorer Canvas Project and other similar efforts as a way to use a plug-in to get this functionality.

For now though, let's just assume you'd like to let your users know they are missing out on your great canvas content. Let's take a look at how to do this ...

And perhaps you can suggest that they upgrade to IE9!

Failing gracefully

So, the truth is, out there somewhere, in another place and time, a user is going to visit your site and not have support for the canvas element. Would you like to send them a kind message saying that they really should upgrade? Here's how:

Just your typical, everyday canvas element.

```
<canvas id="awesomecontent">
    Hey you, yes YOU, upgrade your browser!!
</canvas>
```

Put the message you want displayed to your users who don't have a canvas-capable browser.

How does this work? Well, any time a browser sees an element it doesn't recognize it displays any text contained within it as a default behavior. So, when non-capable browsers see the `<canvas>` element, they just display "Hey you, yes YOU, upgrade your browser!!" Capable browsers, on the other hand, conveniently ignore any text between the canvas tags and so won't display the text.

Thank you HTML5 standards guys (and girls) for making this easy!

```
Hey you, yes
YOU, upgrade
your browser!!
```

And, as you already know, another way to handle browsers that don't support canvas is to use JavaScript to detect if the browser knows about the element. This gives you a bit more flexibility to give your users a different experience in case their browsers don't support it; for instance, you could redirect them to a different page or display an image instead.

> Now that we know how to
> make rectangles, we can use that
> to make squares on the canvas, right?
> We need to figure out how to get them
> randomly placed on the t-shirt, and in
> the user-chosen color.

Frank: Sure, but also we need the user interface for the user to specify all this. I mean we've got the mock-up, but we need to implement it.

Judy: You're right Frank. Not much point in going further without the interface.

Joe: Isn't that just HTML?

Frank: Yeah, I guess so. But, given we're trying to do this all on the client-side, how is this going to work? For instance, where does the form get submitted? I'm just not sure I understand how this all fits together.

Joe: Frank, we can just call a JavaScript function when the user clicks the preview button, and then we can display the shirt design in the canvas.

Frank: That makes sense, but how do we access the values in the form if it is all client side?

Judy: The same way we always access the DOM; we can use `document.getElementById` to grab the form values. You've done that before.

Frank: You guys lost me way back.

Joe: That's okay, let's step through this together. We'll start with the big picture.

TweetShirt: the Big Picture

Before we jump into a big implementation job, let's step back and look at the big picture. We're going to build this web app out of a *canvas element* along with some form elements that act as the user interface, and behind the scenes we're going to make everything happen with JavaScript and the *canvas API*.

Here's what it looks like:

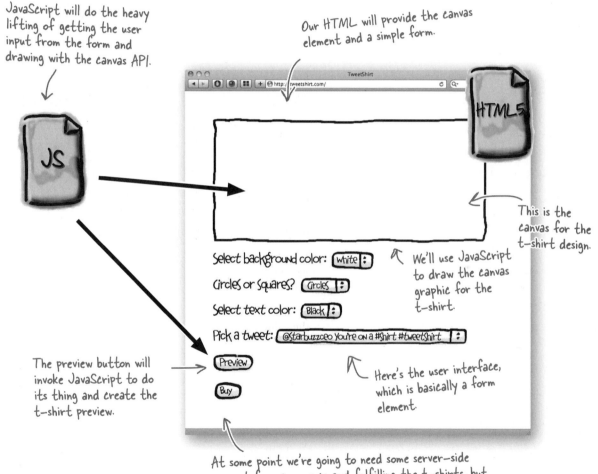

JavaScript will do the heavy lifting of getting the user input from the form and drawing with the canvas API.

Our HTML will provide the canvas element and a simple form.

This is the canvas for the t-shirt design.

We'll use JavaScript to draw the canvas graphic for the t-shirt.

The preview button will invoke JavaScript to do its thing and create the t-shirt preview.

Here's the user interface, which is basically a form element.

Select background color: [White ⇕]

Circles or Squares? [Circles ⇕]

Select text color: [Black ⇕]

Pick a tweet: [@Starbuzzceo You're on a #Shirt #tweetShirt ⇕]

(Preview)

(Buy)

At some point we're going to need some server-side support for ecommerce and fulfilling the t-shirts, but hey, we have to leave some work for your start-up! Don't forget to send us a free t-shirt. A few founder's shares would be even better.

Below, you'll find the form for the t-shirt interface. Your job is to play like you're the browser and to render the interface. After you're done, compare your interface to the one on the previous page to see if you did it correctly.

```html
<form>
<p>
    <label for="backgroundColor">Select background color:</label>
    <select id="backgroundColor">
        <option value="white" selected="selected">White</option>
        <option value="black">Black</option>
    </select>
</p>
<p>
    <label for="shape">Circles or squares?</label>
    <select id="shape">
        <option value="none" selected="selected">Neither</option>
        <option value="circles">Circles</option>
        <option value="squares">Squares</option>
    </select>
</p>
<p>
    <label for="foregroundColor">Select text color:</label>
    <select id="foregroundColor">
        <option value="black" selected="selected">Black</option>
        <option value="white">White</option>
    </select>
</p>
<p>
    <label for="tweets">Pick a tweet:</label>
    <select id="tweets">
    </select>
</p>
<p>
    <input type="button" id="previewButton" value="Preview">
</p>
</form>
```

Render your interface here. Draw the web page as it will look with the form elements on the left.

BE the Browser, again

Now that you have an interface, execute these JavaScript statements and write in the value for each interface element. Check your answer with our solution at the end of the chapter.

Assume you've used the interface to pick the values for your t-shirt.

```
var selectObj = document.getElementById("backgroundColor");
var index = selectObj.selectedIndex;
var bgColor = selectObj[index].value;        ...........................................
```

```
var selectObj = document.getElementById("shape");
var index = selectObj.selectedIndex;
var shape = selectObj[index].value;          ...........................................
```

```
var selectObj = document.getElementById("foregroundColor");
var index = selectObj.selectedIndex;
var fgColor = selectObj[index].value;        ...........................................
```

First, let's get the HTML in place

Enough talk! Let's build this thing. Before we do anything else, we just need a simple HTML page. Update your `index.html` file so it looks like this:

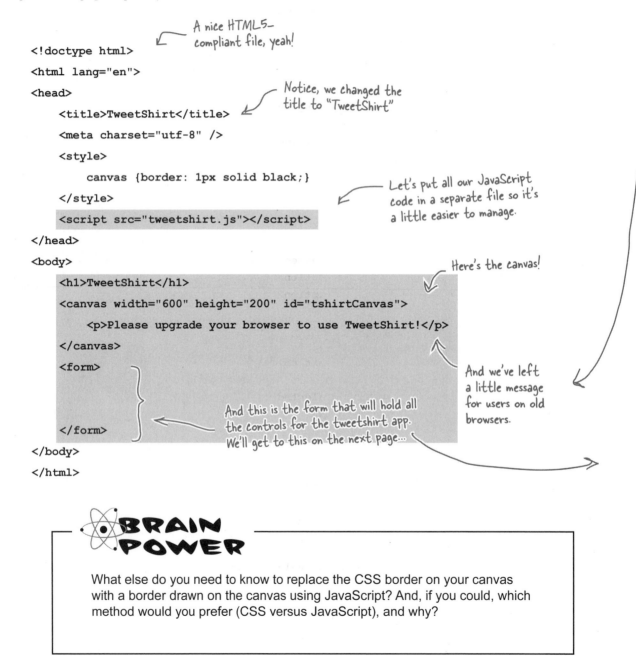

A nice HTML5-compliant file, yeah!

```
<!doctype html>
<html lang="en">
<head>
    <title>TweetShirt</title>
    <meta charset="utf-8" />
    <style>
        canvas {border: 1px solid black;}
    </style>
    <script src="tweetshirt.js"></script>
</head>
<body>
    <h1>TweetShirt</h1>
    <canvas width="600" height="200" id="tshirtCanvas">
        <p>Please upgrade your browser to use TweetShirt!</p>
    </canvas>
    <form>



    </form>
</body>
</html>
```

Notice, we changed the title to "TweetShirt"

Let's put all our JavaScript code in a separate file so it's a little easier to manage.

Here's the canvas!

And we've left a little message for users on old browsers.

And this is the form that will hold all the controls for the tweetshirt app. We'll get to this on the next page...

BRAIN POWER

What else do you need to know to replace the CSS border on your canvas with a border drawn on the canvas using JavaScript? And, if you could, which method would you prefer (CSS versus JavaScript), and why?

Now, let's add the <form>

Okay, let's now add the user interface so we can start writing some code to create t-shirts. You've seen this code before, but we added some annotations just to make everything clear; as you type in the code, make sure you check out our annotations:

All this code goes in between the <form> tags you set up on the previous page.

```
<form>
<p>
    <label for="backgroundColor">Select background color:</label>
    <select id="backgroundColor">
        <option value="white" selected="selected">White</option>
        <option value="black">Black</option>
    </select>
</p>
<p>
    <label for="shape">Circles or squares?</label>
    <select id="shape">
        <option value="none" selected="selected">Neither</option>
        <option value="circles">Circles</option>
        <option value="squares">Squares</option>
    </select>
</p>
<p>
    <label for="foregroundColor">Select text color:</label>
    <select id="foregroundColor">
        <option value="black" selected="selected">Black</option>
        <option value="white">White</option>
    </select>
</p>
<p>
    <label for="tweets">Pick a tweet:</label>
    <select id="tweets">
    </select>
</p>
<p>
    <input type="button" id="previewButton" value="Preview">
</p>
</form>
```

Here's where the user selects the background color for the tweet shirt design. The choices are black or white. Feel free to add your own colors.

We're using another selection control here for choosing circles or squares to customize the design. The user can also choose neither (which should result in a plain background).

Another selection for choosing the color of the text. Again, just black or white.

Here's where all the tweets go. So why's it empty? Ah, we'll be filling in that detail later (hint: we need to get them live from Twitter, after all this is a web app, right?!).

And last, a button to preview the shirt.

If you're used to forms, you might have noticed that this form doesn't have an action attribute (which means the button won't do anything when it's clicked). We're going to handle all that in just a bit...

Time to get computational, with JavaScript

Markup is great, but it's the JavaScript that brings the TweetShirt web application together. We're going to put some code into `tweetshirt.js`. Right now, we want to take the baby step of just putting random squares on the shirt. But before we even get to that, we need to enable our preview button, so it calls a JavaScript function when you click it.

Create a tweetshirt.js file and add this.

Start by getting the previewButton element.

```javascript
window.onload = function() {
    var button = document.getElementById("previewButton");
    button.onclick = previewHandler;
};
```

Add a click handler to this button so that when it is clicked (or touched on a mobile device), the function previewHandler is called.

So now when the preview button is clicked, the `previewHandler` function is going to be called, and that's our chance to update the canvas to represent the shirt the user is designing. Let's begin writing `previewHandler`:

Start by getting the canvas element and asking for its 2d drawing context.

```javascript
function previewHandler() {
    var canvas = document.getElementById("tshirtCanvas");
    var context = canvas.getContext("2d");

    var selectObj = document.getElementById("shape");
    var index = selectObj.selectedIndex;
    var shape = selectObj[index].value;

    if (shape == "squares") {
        for (var squares = 0; squares < 20; squares++) {
            drawSquare(canvas, context);
        }
    }
}
```

Now we need to see what shape you chose in the interface. First we get the element with the id of "shape".

Then we find out which item is selected (squares or circles) by getting the index of the selected item, and assigning its value to the variable shape.

And if the value of shape is "squares", then we need to draw some squares. How about 20 of them?

To draw each square we're relying on a new function named drawSquare, which we're going to have to write. Notice that we're passing both the canvas and the context to drawSquare. You'll see in a bit how we make use of those.

there are no
Dumb Questions

Q: How does the selectedIndex work?

A: The selectedIndex property of a selection form control returns the number of the option you have chosen from the pulldown menu. Every list of options is turned into an array and each option is in the array in order. So, say you have an selection list with these options: "pizza", "doughnut", "granola bar". If you selected "doughnut", the selectedIndex would be 1 (remember, JavaScript arrays start at 0).

Now, you probably don't want just the index; you want the value of the option at that index (in our case, "doughnut"). To get the value of the option, you first use the index to get the element of the array; this returns an option *object*. To get the *value* of that object, you use the value property, which returns the string in the value attribute of the option.

Pseudo-code Magnets

Use your pseudo-magical coding powers to arrange the pseudo code below. We need to write the pseudo-code for the drawSquare function. This function takes a canvas and context and draws one randomly sized square on the canvas. Check your answer at the end of the chapter before you go on.

We did this one for you.

```
function drawSquare (           ,  context  ) {




}
```

Your magnets go here!

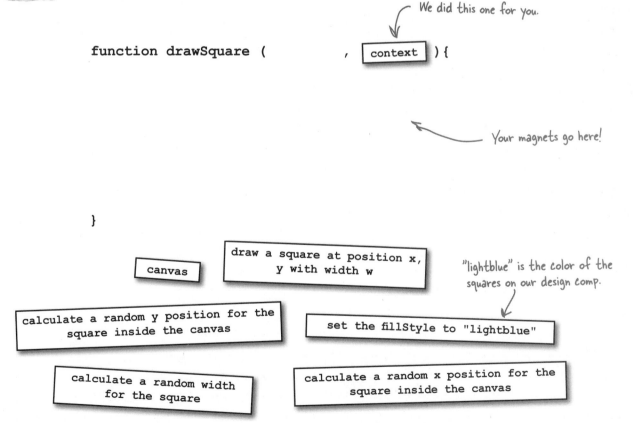

canvas	draw a square at position x, y with width w

"lightblue" is the color of the squares on our design comp.

calculate a random y position for the square inside the canvas	set the fillStyle to "lightblue"

calculate a random width for the square	calculate a random x position for the square inside the canvas

Writing the drawSquare function

Now that you've done all the hard work of figuring out the pseudo-code, let's use what we already know to write `drawSquare`:

Here's our function, which has two parameters: the canvas and the context.

We're using Math.random() to create random numbers for the width and the x,y position of the square. More on this in a moment....

```
function drawSquare(canvas, context) {
    var w = Math.floor(Math.random() * 40);
    var x = Math.floor(Math.random() * canvas.width);
    var y = Math.floor(Math.random() * canvas.height);
    context.fillStyle = "lightblue";
    context.fillRect(x, y, w, w);
}
```

Here we need a random width, and x and y position for the square.

We chose 40 as the largest square size so the squares don't get too big.

The x & y coordinates are based on the width and height of the canvas. We choose a random number between 0 and the width and height respectively.

We're going to make the squares a nice light blue using the fillStyle method, we'll look at this method more closely in a sec...

And finally, we draw the actual square with fillRect.

Head First HTML with CSS & XHTML has a good chapter on color if you need a refresher.

How did we figure out what numbers to multiply each `Math.random` value by to get our square width and x, y position? In the case of the width of the rectangle, we chose 40 because it's a nice small size with respect to the canvas size. Because this is a square, we used the same value for the height. And, we chose the width and height of the canvas as the basis for choosing x and y values so our square stays within the boundaries of the canvas.

Feel free to specify a value other than 40 in your own code!

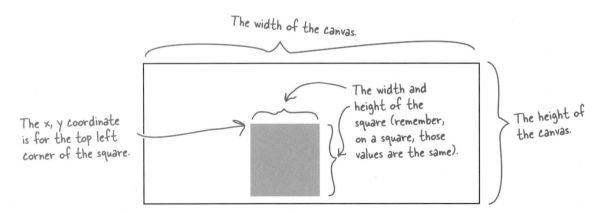

The width of the canvas.

The x, y coordinate is for the top left corner of the square.

The width and height of the square (remember, on a square, those values are the same).

The height of the canvas.

Time for a test drive!

Okay, after all that typing, let's give all this code a test run. Go ahead and open your TweetShirt index.html file in your browser. Press preview and you should see random blue squares.

Here's what we see:

Nice that's just the look we want!

> Uh, wait a sec, if you keep pressing the preview button you get a LOT of squares. That's not right!

He's right, we've got a slight problem. Press your preview button a bunch of times and you'll see something like this.

Why are we seeing the old squares and the new squares when we preview?

This is actually kind of a cool effect... but it's not what we wanted. We want the new squares to *replace* the old squares each time we press preview (just like we'll also want the new tweet to replace the old tweet when we get the tweets working, too).

The key here is to remember that we're painting pixels on the canvas. When you press preview, you're getting the canvas and drawing squares on it. Whatever is already on the canvas just gets painted right over with the new pixels!

But no worries. You already know everything you need to know to fix this right now. Here's what we're going to do:

(1) Get the selected background color from the "backgroundColor" select object.

(2) Fill the background color of the canvas using fillStyle and fillRect, each time before we start drawing squares.

Sharpen your pencil

To make sure we see only new squares in the canvas each time we click preview, we need to fill the background of the canvas with the background color the user has selected from the "backgroundColor" select menu. First, let's implement a function to fill the canvas with that color. Fill in the blanks below to complete the code. Check your answer with our solution at the end of the chapter before you go on.

```
function fillBackgroundColor(canvas, context) {

    var selectObj = document.getElementById("_____");

    var index = selectObj.selectedIndex;

    var bgColor = selectObj.options[index].value;

    context.fillStyle = _____;

    context.fillRect(0, 0, _____, _____);

}
```

Hint: What you get out of the selected option will be a string color you can use just like you used "lightblue" for the squares.

Hint: we want to fill the WHOLE canvas with the color!

Add the call to fillBackgroundColor

You have the `fillBackgroundColor` function ready to go; now we just need to make sure we call it from `previewHandler`. We're going to add that as the very first thing we do so we get a nice, clean background before we start adding anything else to the canvas.

```
function previewHandler() {
    var canvas = document.getElementById("tshirtCanvas");
    var context = canvas.getContext("2d");
    fillBackgroundColor(canvas, context);

    var selectObj = document.getElementById("shape");
    var index = selectObj.selectedIndex;
    var shape = selectObj[index].value;

    if (shape == "squares") {
        for (var squares = 0; squares < 20; squares++) {
            drawSquare(canvas, context);
        }
    }
}
```

We're adding the call to fillBackgroundColor before we draw our squares so it covers up the previous drawing, and gives us a clean background for our new drawing.

Another quick test drive to make sure our new fillBackgroundColor function works...

Add the new code to your `tweetshirt.js` file, reload your browser, select a background color, select squares, and click preview. Click it again. This time you should see only new squares each time you preview.

Select background color: [White ↕]

Circles or squares? [Squares ↕]

Select text color: [Black ↕]

Pick a tweet: [↕]

[Preview]

Now we get only the new squares for each preview.

BRAIN POWER

Count the squares in a few different previews. Do you ever see less than 20 squares? You might.

Why would this happen? What could you do to fix this problem? (After all, you don't want customers cheated out of their 20 squares, do you?)

A JavaScript CloseUp

Let's take a closer look at fillStyle since this is the first time you've seen it. fillStyle is a property of the context that holds the color for any drawing you do to the canvas.

Just like fillRect, fillStyle is something we control through the context.

But unlike fillRect, fillStyle is a property, not a method. So we set it, rather than call it.

And what we set it to is a color. You can use the same color formats you use in CSS. So you can use color names, like lightblue, or values like #ccceff or rgb(0, 173, 239). Try it!

```
context.fillStyle = "lightblue";
```

Note that unlike in CSS, you must put quotes around the value if you're not using a variable.

there are no Dumb Questions

Q: I was expecting we'd set the background color of the squares and the canvas by passing in a color value to fillRect. I don't really get how fillStyle works. How does it affect what fillRect does?

A: Great question. This is a little different from how you might be used to thinking of things. Remember, the context is an object that controls access to the canvas. What you're doing with fillStyle and fillRect is first setting a property that tells the canvas, "Whatever you draw next should be in this color". So anything you fill with color (like with fillRect) after setting the fillStyle will use that color, until you change the color again by setting fillStyle to a different color.

Q: Why does the color need quotes around it, when the property values in CSS don't? I don't use quotes when I'm setting the background-color of an element, for instance.

A: Well, CSS is a different language from JavaScript, and CSS doesn't expect quotes. But if you don't use quotes around the color, JavaScript will think that the color name is a variable instead of a string, and will try to use the value of the variable for the color.

Say you have a variable fgColor = "black". You could write context.fillstyle = fgColor, and it would work because the value of fgColor is "black".

But context.fillStyle = black won't work because black isn't a variable (unless you set it up that way, which might be a bit confusing). You'll know you've made this mistake because you'll get a JavaScript error that says something like "Can't find variable: black". (Don't worry, we all make that mistake at least once.)

Q: Okay, I give up. Why were we seeing less than 20 squares sometimes?

A: The x, y and width of the squares are all random. Some squares might obscure other squares. A square might have an x, y position of 599, 199 so you'd only be able to see one pixel of that square (because the rest of the square would be off the canvas). Some squares might be 1 pixel wide, and some squares might even be 0 pixels wide because the Math.random method can return 0. Or you might generate two squares of exactly the same size and location.

But for this application it's all part of the randomness, so we think it's fine. For another application we might need to ensure this doesn't happen.

Meanwhile, back at TweetShirt.com...

Jim

Frank

Not bad, you know this is already starting to look like the boss's design.

Jim: I know, and I'm impressed with how little code this took. Just think if we did this the old, server-side way, we'd still be getting our server up.

Frank: And it seems like we're in a good position to knock out the circles in the design too; after all, they are just like the squares.

Jim: I agree, where's Judy? She probably knows the API for the circles already. Then again, it's probably just a matter of calling the `fillCircle` method.

Frank: Sounds right to me! Who needs Judy, we've got this!

And, a couple of hours later...

Frank: I don't know what's going on, I've double checked everything, but, no matter what I do, when I call `fillCircle`, I get nothing on the canvas.

Judy: Well, show me your `fillCircle` method.

Frank: What do you mean by my method? I don't have one, I'm using the method in the canvas's API directly.

Judy: The canvas API doesn't have a `fillCircle` method.

Frank: Er, I *assumed* it did because we have a `fillRect`...

Judy: Yeah, well you know what that ass-u-me stuff gets us. Come on, pull up a browser—you can always find the API at: `http://dev.w3.org/html5/2dcontext/`.

...Anyway, drawing a circle is a little more complex than calling a single method. You need to learn about paths and arcs first.

Jim, entering: Judy, did Frank tell you about how we nailed the circle?

Frank: Uh yeah, Jim, *enoughway ithway ethay irclecay!*

> ↖ We recommend the translation services of piglatin.bavetta.com.

Drawing with Geeks

Before digging into circles, we need to talk about paths and arcs. Let's start with paths, and draw some triangles. If we want to draw a triangle on the canvas, there's no `fillTriangle` method, but we can create a triangle anyway by first creating a *path* in the shape of a triangle, and then *stroking* over it to draw a triangle on the canvas.

What does that mean? Well, say you wanted to be really careful drawing on the canvas, you might take a pencil and trace a light shape (let's just call it a path) on the canvas. You trace it so lightly that only you can see it. Then, after you're satisfied with your path, you take a pen (with a thickness and color of your choosing) and you use that to stroke over the path so everyone can see your triangle (or whatever shape you traced with the pencil).

That's just how drawing arbitary shapes with lines works on the canvas. Let's draw a triangle and see how this works:

I can create any paths you want.

We use the beginPath method to tell the canvas we're starting a new path.

```
context.beginPath();
context.moveTo(100, 150);
```

We use the moveTo method to move the "pencil" to a specific point on the canvas. You can think of the pencil as being put down at this point.

Here we're putting the pencil down at x = 100 and y = 150. This is the first point on the path.

The lineTo method traces a path from the pencil's current location to another point on the canvas.

```
context.lineTo(250, 75);
```

The pencil was at 100, 150, and here we're extending the path from there to the point x=250, y=75.

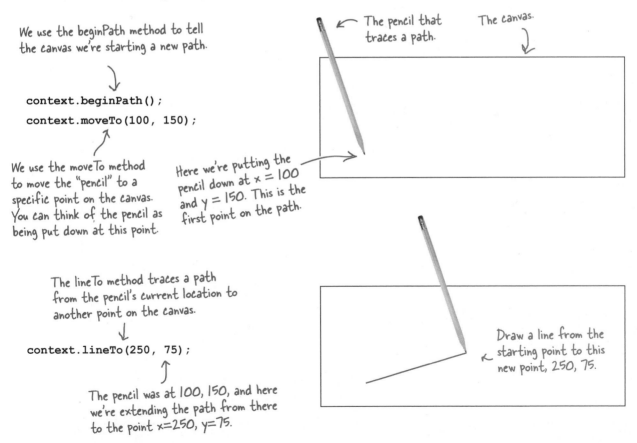

The pencil that traces a path.

The canvas.

Draw a line from the starting point to this new point, 250, 75.

We've got the first side of the triangle, now we need two more. Let's use lineTo again for the second side:

```
context.lineTo(125, 30);
```

Here we're tracing from the current pencil position (250, 75) to a new position, x = 125, y = 30. That completes our second line.

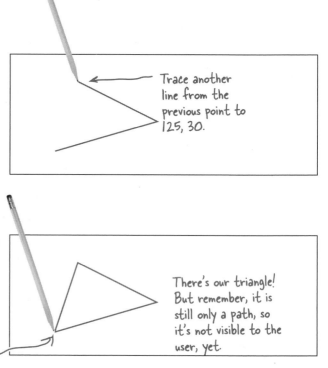

Trace another line from the previous point to 125, 30.

We're almost there! All we need to do now is to trace one more line to finish the triangle. And to do that, we're just going to close the path with the closePath method.

```
context.closePath();
```

The closePath method connects the starting point of the path (100, 150) to the last point in the current path (125, 30).

There's our triangle! But remember, it is still only a path, so it's not visible to the user, yet.

So you have a path! Now what?

Exercise You use the path to draw lines and fill in your shape with color, of course! Go ahead and create a simple HTML5 page with a canvas element and type in all the code so far. Give it a test run, too.

```
context.beginPath();
context.moveTo(100, 150);
context.lineTo(250, 75);
context.lineTo(125, 30);
context.closePath();
```

Here's the code so far.

```
context.lineWidth = 5;

context.stroke();

context.fillStyle = "red";

context.fill();
```

....

....

....

....

And here's some new code. Go ahead and annotate this with what you think it does. Load the page. Were you right? Check your answers at the end of the chapter.

> Just to keep us on track here, I thought we were trying to draw circles? What does all this path stuff have to do with drawing circles?

To create a circle, we first create a path.

We're about to show you how to trace a circle as a path. And, once you know how to do that, you can make any kind of circle you like.

Here's a bit more detail for you. You know how to start a path, right? Like we've been doing, you use this code:

```
context.beginPath();
```

Now, what we haven't told you yet is there is another method in the context object named `arc`:

```
context.arc(150, 150, 50, 0, 2 * Math.PI, true);
```

What does that do? Ah, we'll spend the next page or so finding out the details. But, as you might expect, it traces a path along a circle.

Do you happen to remember from geometry class that the circumference of a circle = 2πR? Just put that in the back of your mind for a sec...

Breaking down the arc method

Let's dive right into the arc method and check out its parameters.

`context.arc(x, y, radius, startAngle, endAngle, direction)`

The whole point of the arc method is to specify how we want to trace a path along a circle. Let's see how each parameter contributes to that:

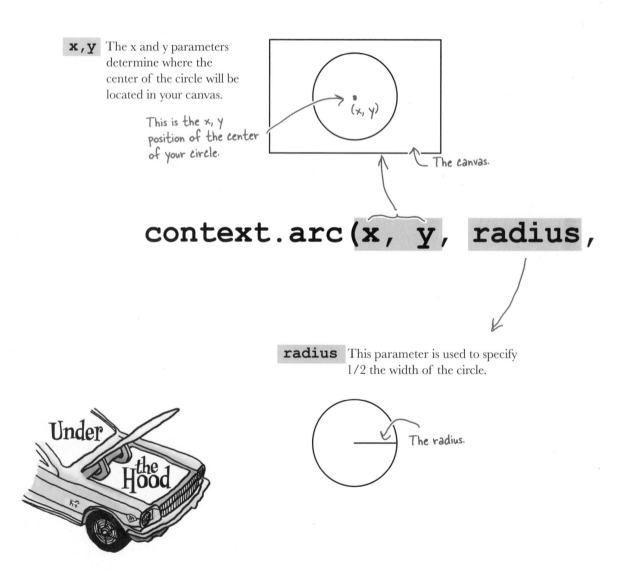

x,y The x and y parameters determine where the center of the circle will be located in your canvas.

This is the x, y position of the center of your circle.

(x, y)

The canvas.

context.arc(**x, y, radius**,

radius This parameter is used to specify 1/2 the width of the circle.

The radius.

Under the Hood

direction determines if we are creating the arc path in a counterclockwise or clockwise direction. If direction is true, we go counterclockwise; if it's false, we go clockwise.

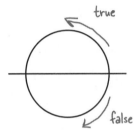

true

false

If direction is true, we trace the arc going counter-clockwise. If it is false we trace clockwise.

startAngle, endAngle, direction)

startAngle, endAngle The start angle and end angle of the arc determine where your arc path starts and stops on the circle.

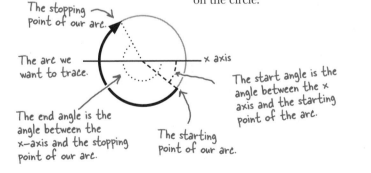

The stopping point of our arc.

The arc we want to trace.

x axis

The end angle is the angle between the x-axis and the stopping point of our arc.

The starting point of our arc.

The start angle is the angle between the x axis and the starting point of the arc.

Important Point Below!

Don't skip this. Angles can be measured in the negative direction (counterclockwise from the x-axis) or in the positive direction (clockwise from the x-axis). This is *not* the same as the direction parameter for the arc path! (You'll see on the next page.)

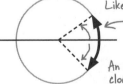

An angle measured going counterclockwise from the x-axis is negative. Like −35 degrees.

An angle measured going clockwise from the x-axis is positive. Like 45 degrees.

A little taste of using the arc

What we need right now is a good example. Let's say that you want to trace an arc over a circle that is centered at x=100, and y=100 and you want the circle to be 150 pixels wide (or, a radius of 75). And, the path you want to trace is just 1/4 of the circle, like this:

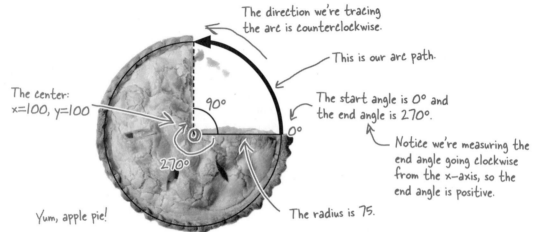

The direction we're tracing the arc is counterclockwise.

This is our arc path.

The start angle is 0° and the end angle is 270°.

Notice we're measuring the end angle going clockwise from the x–axis, so the end angle is positive.

The center: x=100, y=100

90°

0°

270°

Yum, apple pie!

The radius is 75.

Now let's create an arc method call that traces this path:

1 We start with the x, y point of the center of the circle: 100, 100.

```
context.arc(100, 100, __, __, _____, ____);
```

2 Next, we need the radius of the circle, 75.

```
context.arc(100, 100, 75, __, _____, ____);
```

3 What about our start and end angles? Well, the start angle is 0 because the starting point is at 0 degrees from the x axis. The end angle is the angle between the x-axis and the stopping point of our arc. Since our arc is a 90 degree arc, our end angle is 270 degrees (90+270 = 360). (Note that if we'd measured in the negative, or counterclockwise direction instead, our end angle would be -90 degrees.)

```
context.arc(100, 100, 75, 0, degreesToRadians(270), ____);
```

We'll come back to this in a sec. It just converts degrees (which we're used to), into radians (which the context seems to prefer).

4 Finally, we're tracing the arc in a counterclockwise direction, so we use true.

```
context.arc(100, 100, 75, 0, degreesToRadians(270), true);
```

I say degree, you say radian

We all talk about circle angles every day: "nice 360 dude," or "I was heading down that path and I did a complete 180," or, ...well, you get the picture. The only problem is, we think in *degrees*, but the canvas context thinks in *radians*.

> Nice 360 dude!
> Oh, I mean Nice 2π
> Radians dude!

A radian is just another measure of an angle. One radian equals 180/3.14159265... (or 180 divided by π).

Now, we could tell you that:

```
360 degrees = 2Pi radians
```

and you're good to go if you want to compute radians in your head from now on. Or, if for some reason you'd rather not do that in your head, here's a handy function that will do the work for you:

```
function degreesToRadians(degrees) {
    return (degrees * Math.PI)/180;
}
```

You might remember seeing this briefly in the Geolocation chapter.

To get radians from degrees, you multiply by π and divide by 180.

Use this function whenever you want to think in degrees, but get radians for drawing an arc.

On page 313, you saw us use 2*Math. PI to specify the end angle of a circle. You could do that... or just use degreesToRadians(360).

BE the Browser

Interpret the call to the arc method and sketch out all the values on the circle, including the path the method creates.

```
context.arc(100, 100, 75, degreesToRadians(270), 0, true);
```

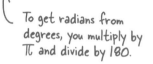

Annotate this circle with all the arguments and then draw the path this method call creates.

Hint: what is left in the pie after eating this?

Back to writing the TweetShirt circle code

Now that you know how to draw circles, it's time to get back to TweetShirt and add a new function, `drawCircle`. We want to draw 20 random circles, just like we did for squares. To draw those circles we need to first determine that the user has selected circles from the shape menu. Let's add that to the previewHandler function.

Edit your `tweetshirt.js` file and add the new code below.

```
function previewHandler() {
    var canvas = document.getElementById("tshirtCanvas");
    var context = canvas.getContext("2d");
    fillBackgroundColor(canvas, context);

    var selectObj = document.getElementById("shape");
    var index = selectObj.selectedIndex;
    var shape = selectObj[index].value;

    if (shape == "squares") {
        for (var squares = 0; squares < 20; squares++) {
            drawSquare(canvas, context);
        }
    } else if (shape == "circles") {
        for (var circles = 0; circles < 20; circles++) {
            drawCircle(canvas, context);
        }
    }
}
```

This code looks almost identical to the code to test for squares. If the user has chosen circles rather than squares then we draw 20 circles with the drawCircle function (which we now need to write).

We're passing the canvas and context to the drawCircle function, just like we did with drawSquares.

⚛ BRAIN POWER

What start angle and end angle do you use to draw a complete circle?

What direction do you use: counterclockwise or clockwise? Does it matter?

A: You draw a circle with a start angle of 0° and an end angle of 360°. It doesn't matter what direction you use since you're drawing a complete circle.

Writing the drawCircle function...

Now let's write the `drawCircle` function. Remember, here we just need to draw one random circle. The other code is already handling calling this function 20 times.

```
function drawCircle(canvas, context) {
    var radius = Math.floor(Math.random() * 40);
    var x = Math.floor(Math.random() * canvas.width);
    var y = Math.floor(Math.random() * canvas.height);


    context.beginPath();
    context.arc(x, y, radius, 0, degreesToRadians(360), true);


    context.fillStyle = "lightblue";
    context.fill();
}
```

Just like we did for squares, we're using 40 for the maximum radius size to keep our circles from getting too big.

And, again, the x & y coordinates of the center of the circle are based on the width and height of the canvas. We choose random numbers between 0 and the width and height respectively.

We're using "lightblue" as our fillStyle again, and then filling the path with context.fill().

We use an end angle of 360° to get a full circle. We draw counterclockwise around the circle, but for a circle, it doesn't matter which direction we use.

... and test drive!

So go ahead and type this in (and don't forget to add the degreesToRadians function too), save, and load it in your browser. Here's what we see (given these are random circles—yours will look a little different):

Intermission

A Little Cookie Break

Whew! That was a fun set of pages we just went through. We don't know about you, but we're ready for some cookies. How about taking a short cookie break? But, don't think we aren't going to give you something fun to do while you're having them (check on the exercise to the right).

So, sit back, have a little break, and nibble on this while you give your brain and stomach something else to do for a bit. Then come on back and we'll finish off the TweetShirt code!

To the right you'll find a smiley face (or a chocolate chip cookie smiley face if you prefer). The code below to draw the smiley face is almost done; we just need your help to finish it up. With all the work you've done in this chapter, you've got all you need to complete this. You can always check your answer at the end of the chapter when you're finished.

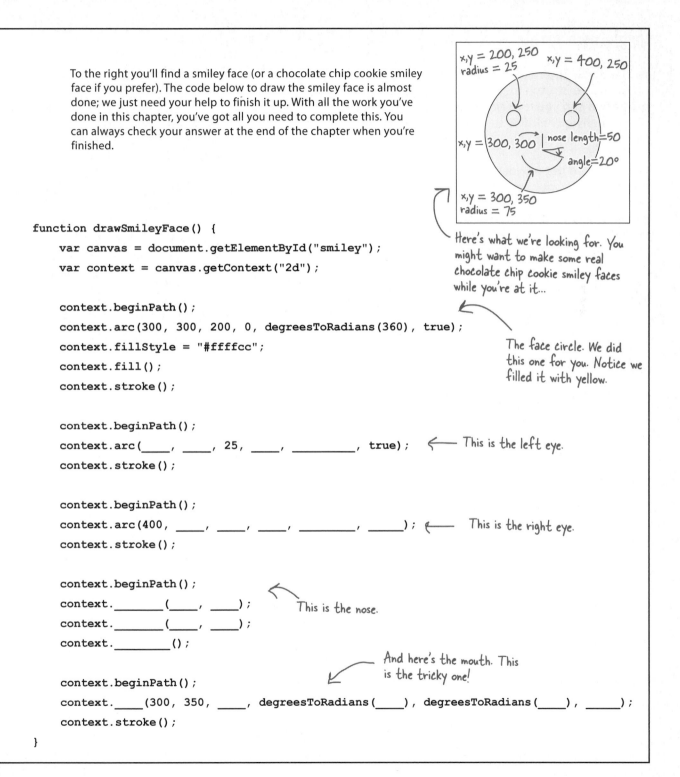

x,y = 200, 250
radius = 25

x,y = 400, 250

x,y = 300, 300 | nose length=50

angle=20°

x,y = 300, 350
radius = 75

Here's what we're looking for. You might want to make some real chocolate chip cookie smiley faces while you're at it...

```
function drawSmileyFace() {
    var canvas = document.getElementById("smiley");
    var context = canvas.getContext("2d");

    context.beginPath();
    context.arc(300, 300, 200, 0, degreesToRadians(360), true);
    context.fillStyle = "#ffffcc";
    context.fill();
    context.stroke();

    context.beginPath();
    context.arc(____, ____, 25, ____, _____, true);
    context.stroke();

    context.beginPath();
    context.arc(400, ____, ____, ____, _____, ____);
    context.stroke();

    context.beginPath();
    context._____(____, ____);
    context._____(____, ____);
    context._____();

    context.beginPath();
    context.____(300, 350, ____, degreesToRadians(____), degreesToRadians(____), ____);
    context.stroke();
}
```

The face circle. We did this one for you. Notice we filled it with yellow.

← This is the left eye.

← This is the right eye.

This is the nose.

And here's the mouth. This is the tricky one!

Welcome back...

You're back, you're rested, refreshed, and we're on the home stretch to getting this start-up off the ground. When you look at all the work we've done, all we really have left is to display the tweets and the other text in the canvas preview.

Now, to get a get a tweet on the canvas we first need some of your recent tweets to choose from, and we're going to use JSONP to do it. If you remember Chapter 6, you already know how to do this. If you need to, go back to Chapter 6 for a quick refresher. All we're going to do is:

> Speaking of goodies, remember that JSONP code we baked in Chapter 6? It's time to pull it out of the oven.

① Add a <script> at the bottom of the tweetshirt. html file to make a call to the Twitter JSONP API. We're going to ask for the most recent status updates of a specified user.

② Implement a callback to get the tweets that Twitter sends back. We'll use the name of this callback in the URL for the <script> in Step 1.

Here's our HTML file for TweetShirt.

Imagine your head element here, and your form here (we wanted to save a few trees).

```
<html>
...
<body>
    <form>
    ...
    </form>
    <script src="http://twitter.com/statuses/user_timeline/wickedsmartly.json?callback=updateTweets">
    </script>
</body>
</html>
```

Here's our JSONP call; this works by retrieving the JSON created by calling the Twitter URL, and then passing that JSON to the callback function (which we'll define in just a sec).

Here's the Twitter API call. We're asking for a user timeline which will give us recent statuses.

Change this to your username, or someone else's if you like.

And here's the callback function where the JSON will be passed back.

Type this all on one line in your text file (it's too long to fit on one line in the book).

There's a lot going on here. If this is only vaguely familiar, please do have a look back at how JSONP works, in Chapter 6.

Getting your tweets

We've already done the hard work, which is getting the tweets from Twitter. Now we need to add them to the tweets `<select>` element in the `<form>` of our page. Just to review again: when the callback function is called (in our case, the function `updateTweets`), Twitter hands it a response that contains JSON formatted tweets.

Twitter's response is an array of tweets. Each tweet has a ton of data in it; the piece we're going to use is the text of the tweet.

Edit your `tweetshirt.js` file and add the `updateTweets` function at the bottom. Here's the code:

Here's our callback.

Which is passed a response containing the tweets from the user timeline as an array of tweets.

We grab a reference to the tweets selection from the form.

```
function updateTweets(tweets) {
    var tweetsSelection = document.getElementById("tweets");

    for (var i = 0; i < tweets.length; i++) {
        tweet = tweets[i];
        var option = document.createElement("option");
        option.text = tweet.text;
        option.value = tweet.text.replace("\"", "'");

        tweetsSelection.options.add(option);
    }

    tweetsSelection.selectedIndex = 0;
}
```

For each tweet in the array of tweets, we:

Get a tweet from the array.

Create a new option element.

Set its text to the tweet.

And set its value to the same text, only we've processed the string a little to replace double quotes with single quotes (so we can avoid formatting issues in the HTML).

We then take the new option, and add it to the tweet selection in the form.

And, finally, we make sure the first tweet is the selected tweet by setting the selectedIndex of the `<select>` to 0 (the first option element contained within it).

After we've done this for each tweet, we have a `<select>` element that contains an option for each tweet.

Test driving Tweets

Let's do a quick test drive. Make sure you've got all the code added to `tweetshirt.js` and `index.html`. Also make sure you're using a Twitter username that has recent tweets in your script src URL (so you'll be sure you see some tweets!). Load the page and click on the tweets selection. Here's what we see:

Here's the tweets menu with REAL tweets in it. Cool!

> Guys, this is great. We have squares and circles and Jim's got us hooked up to Twitter! What's next?

Frank's tablet.

Jim: We're almost there. We need to nail down all the text we need to display. We've got the two messages: the "I saw this tweet" and "and all I got was this lousy t-shirt!" and also the tweet the user has chosen to display. Now we've got to figure out how to display it, not to mention apply some styling to the text.

Frank: I'm assuming we can throw some text in the canvas and then apply some CSS to it?

Joe: I don't think it works like that. The canvas is a drawing area, I don't think we can place text and style it, we have to draw text onto the canvas.

Jim: Well, this time I learned my lesson and I've already checked out the API for text.

Joe: Good, I haven't looked yet; how does it look?

Jim: Remember that arc method? We have to custom draw all our text using that.

Frank: Are you kidding me? I guess I'll be working all weekend now.

Jim: Gotcha! No seriously, there is a `fillText` method that takes the text to draw on the canvas along with the x, y position of where to draw it.

Joe: That sounds pretty straightforward. What about the differences in style? If I remember the comp, the tweet text is italic, and the rest of the text is bold.

Jim: We need to look a bit more, there are various methods for setting alignment and fonts and fill styles, but I'm not not quite sure how to use them.

Frank: And to think maybe I could have helped, but no CSS?

Jim: Sorry, like Joe said, this is an API for drawing onto a canvas, it doesn't make use of HTML or CSS styling in any way.

Joe: Well, lets pull up the API and take a look and then we can try getting the "I saw a tweet" text on the canvas. Come on Frank, join us, this can't be too bad and I'm sure we can use your knowledge of fonts, styles and all that.

Frank: Sure thing, I'm here for you!

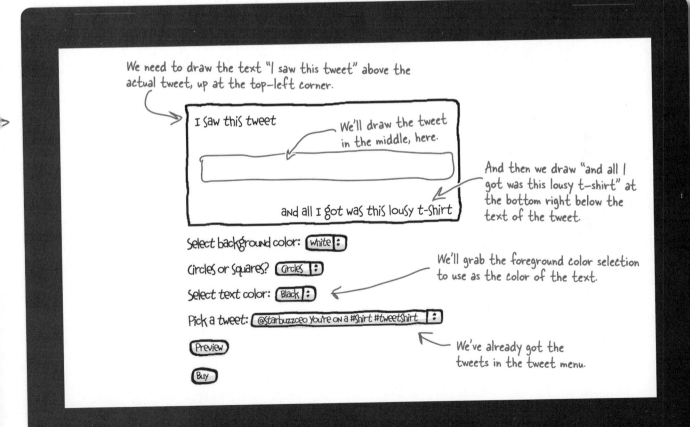

One thing that confuses me about drawing text in canvas is that we've always stressed that content is separate from presentation. With canvas it seems like they are the same thing. What I mean is, they don't seem to be separate.

That's a really good point.

Now let's work through why it's set up this way. Remember that canvas is designed to give you a way to present graphics within the browser. Everything in the canvas is considered presentation, not content. So while you usually think of text—and certainly tweets—as content, in this case, you've got to think of it as presentation. It's part of the design. Like an artist who uses letterforms as part of her artwork, you're using tweets as part of the artwork of your t-shirt design.

One of the main reasons that separating presentation and content is a good idea is so that the browser can be smart about how it presents the content in different situations: for example, an article from a news web site is presented one way on a big screen and a different way on your phone.

For our t-shirt design, we want what's in the canvas to be more like an image: it should be displayed the same way no matter how you are viewing it.

So, let's get the text on the canvas and get this start-up rolling!

Code Magnets

It's time for your first experiment with canvas text. Below we've started the code for drawText, the method we're going to call to draw all the text onto the preview canvas. See if you can finish up the code to draw "I saw this tweet" and "and all I got was this lousy t-shirt!" on the canvas, we'll save drawing the actual tweet for later. Make sure you check your answer with the solution at the end of the chapter before you go on.

```
function drawText(canvas, context) {

    var selectObj = document.getElementById("_____");

    var index = selectObj.selectedIndex;

    var fgColor = selectObj[index].value;

    context._____ = fgColor;

    context._____ = "bold 1em sans-serif";

    context._____ = "left";

    context._____(_"_____, 20, 40);
```

Hint: This is the x, y position for the "I saw this tweet" text.

```
    // Get the selected tweet from the tweets menu
    // Draw the tweet
```

For right now, we're just putting comments in where the code to draw the tweet text will be.

Hint: We'll be using an italic serif font for the tweet, but we want this one to be bold sans-serif.

```
    context.font = "_____";

    context._____ = "_____";

    context._____("and all I got was this lousy t-shirt!",

    _____, _____);
```

Hint: we want to position the text in the bottom-right corner.

```
}
```

We want to draw this text at 20 from the right side of the canvas, and 40 from the bottom of the canvas, so it balances the top line of text.

foregroundColor

fillStyle   fillText   bold 1em sans-serif   fillText   font

textAlign   canvas.width-20   right   textAlign   canvas.height-40

fillCircle   fillRect   "I saw this tweet"   left

Canvas Text Up Close

Now that you've had a chance to draw your first text in the canvas, it's time to take a closer look at the text methods and properties available in the canvas API. As you found out in the exercise this is a fairly low-level API—you have to tell the context what text to draw, what position to use, and what font to use.

In this Up Close segment we'll examine the alignment, font, and baseline properties, and the fill and stroke methods in detail so you'll be a canvas text expert by the time you turn the page!

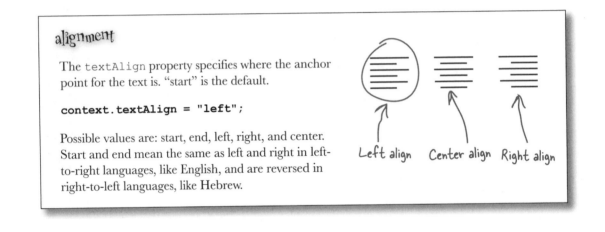

alignment

The `textAlign` property specifies where the anchor point for the text is. "start" is the default.

```
context.textAlign = "left";
```

Possible values are: start, end, left, right, and center. Start and end mean the same as left and right in left-to-right languages, like English, and are reversed in right-to-left languages, like Hebrew.

Left align   Center align   Right align

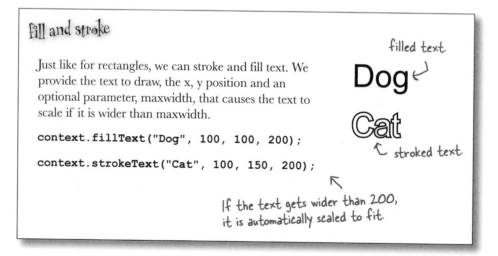

fill and stroke

Just like for rectangles, we can stroke and fill text. We provide the text to draw, the x, y position and an optional parameter, maxwidth, that causes the text to scale if it is wider than maxwidth.

```
context.fillText("Dog", 100, 100, 200);

context.strokeText("Cat", 100, 150, 200);
```

filled text.

Dog

Cat
↖ stroked text.

If the text gets wider than 200, it is automatically scaled to fit.

font

To set the font properties, you can use the same format you're used to using in CSS, which is handy. If you specify every property value, you'll include: font style, weight, size, and family, in that order.

```
context.font = "2em Lucida Grande";
context.fillText("Tea", 100, 100);
context.font = "italic bold 1.5em Times, serif";
context.fillText("Coffee", 100, 150);
```

⟶ Tea

⟶ *Coffee*

The spec recommends that you use vector fonts only (bitmap fonts may not display very well).

> See! I KNEW CSS had to come into this somehow!!!

baseline

The `textBaseline` property sets the alignment points in the font and determines the line your letters sit on. To see how the line affects the text, try drawing a line at the same x, y point you draw a text.

```
context.beginPath();
context.moveTo(100, 100);
context.lineTo(250, 100);
context.stroke();
context.textBaseline = "middle";
context.fillText("Alphabet", 100, 100);
```

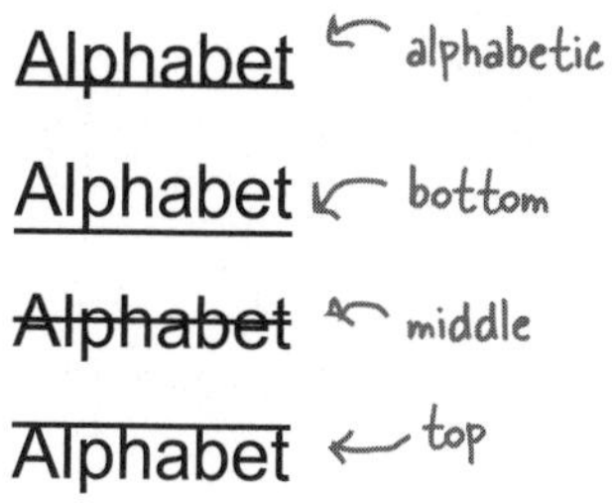

Alphabet ⟵ alphabetic

Alphabet ⟵ bottom

Alphabet ⟵ middle

Alphabet ⟵ top

Possible values are: top, hanging, middle, alphabetic, ideographic, and bottom. The default is alphabetic. Experiment with the different values to find what you need (and check out the spec for more details).

Giving drawText a spin

Now that you've got more of the API in your head, go ahead and get the code you created in the Magnet Code exercise typed in— here it is with the magnets nicely translated to code:

```
function drawText(canvas, context) {
    var selectObj = document.getElementById("foregroundColor");
    var index = selectObj.selectedIndex;
    var fgColor = selectObj[index].value;

    context.fillStyle = fgColor;
    context.font = "bold 1em sans-serif";
    context.textAlign = "left";
    context.fillText("I saw this tweet", 20, 40);



    context.font = "bold 1em sans-serif";
    context.textAlign = "right";
    context.fillText("and all I got was this lousy t-shirt!",
        canvas.width-20, canvas.height-40);
}
```

We're going to put the code that draws the tweet text here in a sec...

After you've got it typed in, update your `previewHandler` function to call the `drawText` function, and give it a test drive by loading it in your browser. You should see something like we do:

Here's the text. We've got sans-serif text in bold at the correct location.

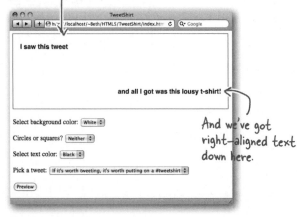

And we've got right-aligned text down here.

Sharpen your pencil

Take a shot at completing the drawText function. You need to get the selected tweet, set the font to an italic serif font that's slightly (1.2em) bigger than than the default, make sure the text is aligned left, and position it at x = 30, y = 100. This is the last step before we see the TweetShirt!

Write your code above, and don't peek at the next page! (Really!)

Completing the drawText function

Here's our solution code. How does it compare to yours? If you haven't already typed your code in, go ahead and type in the code below (or your version if you prefer), and reload your index.html. We'll show you our test drive on the next page.

```
function drawText(canvas, context) {
    var selectObj = document.getElementById("foregroundColor");
    var index = selectObj.selectedIndex;
    var fgColor = selectObj[index].value;

    context.fillStyle = fgColor;
    context.font = "bold 1em sans-serif";
    context.textAlign = "left";
    context.fillText("I saw this tweet", 20, 40);

    selectObj = document.getElementById("tweets");
    index = selectObj.selectedIndex;
    var tweet = selectObj[index].value;
    context.font = "italic 1.2em serif";
    context.fillText(tweet, 30, 100);

    context.font = "bold 1em sans-serif";
    context.textAlign = "right";
    context.fillText("and all I got was this lousy t-shirt!",
        canvas.width-20, canvas.height-40);
}
```

We don't need to align the tweet text to the left; the alignment is still set from up here.

We grab the selected option from the tweet menu.

Set the font to italic serif, just a tad bigger...

... and draw it at position 30, 100.

Hurry up and press preview, Frank. I want to see this TweetShirt!

A quick test drive and then ~~LUNCH~~ LAUNCH!

We hope you're seeing what we're seeing! Nice huh? Give the interface a real bit of quality assurance testing: try all the combinations of colors and shapes, or swap out the username for another you like.

Feel like you're ready to launch this for real? Let's do it!

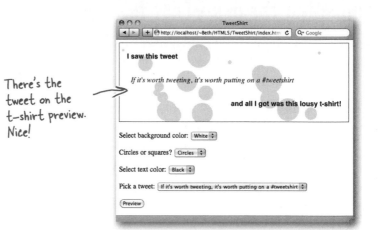

There's the tweet on the t-shirt preview. Nice!

Yes! It works. We're ready to launch!!

Guys, I hate to burst your bubble, but you're not done yet. You're supposed to put an image of the Twitter bird on the t-shirt too!

Remember the TweetShirt founder?

Uh guys, I sorta did a little work on my own and I have the image code already for the Twitter bird...

Here, let me walk you through it...

1 The first thing we need is an image. We've put an image named `twitterBird.png` in the TweetShirt folder. To get that into the canvas we first need a JavaScript image object. Here's how we get one:

```
var twitterBird = new Image();
twitterBird.src = "twitterBird.png";
```

Create a new image object.

And set its source to be the image of the Twitter bird.

2 The next part should feel pretty natural by now; we need to draw the image on the canvas using a context method named, you guessed it, `drawImage`.

```
context.drawImage(twitterBird, 20, 120, 70, 70);
```

Using the drawImage method

Here's our image object.

And we specify the x, y location, width and height.

3 There's one other thing to know about images: they don't always load immediately, so you need to make sure that the image has fully loaded beford you draw it. How do we wait until something is loaded before we take action? We implement an onload handler:

```
twitterBird.onload = function() {
    context.drawImage(twitterBird, 20, 120, 70, 70);
};
```

Here, we're saying: when the image has loaded, then execute this function.

We draw the image to the canvas using the context's drawImage method.

Exercise

See if you can put together the drawBird function from all the pieces Judy gave us. The drawBird function takes a canvas and context, and draws the bird onto the canvas. You can assume that with this function we're placing "twitterBird.png" at the location x=20, y=120, with a width and height of 70. We've written the method declaration and the first line for you. You'll find our solution at the end of the chapter.

```
function drawBird(canvas, context) {
    var twitterBird = new Image();
```

Your code here. ➔

}

Make sure you add a call to the drawBird function in the previewHandler function.

Yet another test drive

Double check your code and get in another test drive! Wow, this is really looking polished now.

Give it a few tries; try it with circles or squares. You'll notice that we used a png with a transparent background so that the circles and squares work if they're behind the bird.

This rocks and we're well on our way to developing a cool app. But like we said, we're counting on you to implement the ecommerce and fulfillment and all that. →

TweetShirt

http://localhost/~Beth/HTML5/TweetShirt/index.htm

I saw this tweet

If it's worth tweeting, it's worth putting on a #tweetshirt

and all I got was this lousy t-shirt!

Select background color: White
Circles or squares? Circles
Select text color: Black
Pick a tweet: If it's worth tweeting, it's worth putting on a #tweetshirt
Preview

there are no
Dumb Questions

Q: We haven't seen the Image object before. You used it when you added an image to the canvas. What is this? Why didn't we create it with document.createElement("img")?

A: Good catch. Both methods you mention create image objects. The JavaScript Image constructor is arguably a more direct way to create images from JavaScript and gives us a little more control over the loading process (like giving us the ability to easily use a handler to be notified when the image is loaded).

So, our goal here is to create an image, and to make sure it's loaded before we draw it on the canvas. The Image object gives us the best path to doing that.

Q: Canvas is cool... but also kind of a pain compared to HTML. Anything more complicated than basic shapes must be really difficult to do.

A: There's no doubt about it, you're writing graphics code when you're programming canvas. Unlike the browser, which takes care of a lot of details for you, like flowing elements onto the page so you don't have to worry about drawing everything yourself, you have to tell canvas where to put everything.

Canvas gives you a lot of power to do almost any kind of graphics (currently, 2D) you can imagine, however. And we're in early days of canvas; it's likely that libraries of JavaScript code will make it easier to write graphics for canvas in the future.

Q: I noticed that for very long tweets, the tweet just disappears off the edge of the canvas. How can I fix that?

A: One way to fix it is to check to see how many characters the tweet contains and if it's greater than a certain number, split it into multiple lines and draw each line separately onto the canvas. We've included a function, splitIntoLines, in the code on wickedlysmart.com that you can use to do just that.

Q: I also noticed that some tweets have HTML entities in them, like " and &. What's that all about?

A: The Twitter API that we're using to get tweets as JSON converts characters that people post in their tweets to HTML entities. It's actually a good thing because any special characters, or even quotes, that would mess up our ability to get the tweets properly from the JSON are represented as entities. If we were displaying the tweets in HTML, those entities would be displayed in the browser as the characters you're meant to see, just like entities you add to your own page are displayed correctly in the browser. However, as you saw, in the canvas they don't look so great. Unfortunately, right now there is no function in the canvas API that will convert those entities back to their characters, so you'd have to do that yourself.

Q: Can you do anything fancy in canvas, like put dropshadows on text or shapes?

A: Yes! There are lots of fancy things you can do with canvas and dropshadows is certainly one of them. As you'd expect, you create a shadow by setting properties on the context. For instance, to set the blur size of the shadow, you set context.shadowBlur. You can set the position of the shadow with context.shadowOffsetX and context.shadowOffsetY, and the color with context.shadowColor.

Other things you can do with canvas you might want to check into are things like drawing gradients, rotating shapes, and putting rounded corners on rectangles.

Q: What other interesting things can I do with canvas?

A: A lot! We'll cover a couple more ways to use canvas in later chapters, and you'll definitely want to check out the canvas API for more: http://dev.w3.org/html5/2dcontext/.

Q: Is all this canvas stuff going to work on my mobile device too? Or am I going to have to rewrite it for mobile users?

A: If your mobile device has a modern browser (devices like Android, iPhone and iPad all do), then this will work just fine (the sizing of the page might be off, but the functionality will work. The nice thing about canvas is, because you're drawing with raw pixels, what you draw will look the same everywhere (or, everywhere on browsers that support canvas). Fortunately, modern smart devices like Android, iPhone and iPad all have sophisticated browsers that have most of the functionality of desktop browsers.

I was thinking it would be great to be able to save a t-shirt and the location and position of all its squares. Is there a canvas save method for that?

No, that requires a little extra work.

The canvas is really meant to be a simple drawing surface. When you draw a shape, the canvas just sees it as pixels. The canvas isn't aware of the specifics of what you're drawing, and it doesn't keep track of any shapes. It simply creates the pixels you ask it to create. (If you're familiar with the graphics terms "bitmap" and "vector" drawing, you'll recognize what canvas is doing as "bitmap" drawing).

If you'd like to treat the rectangles in your canvas as a set of objects that you can save and maybe even move or manipulate, you need to maintain the information about the shapes and paths as you create them on the canvas. You can store this data in JavaScript objects. For instance, if you're keeping track of the random circles we've drawn on the TweetShirt canvas, you'd need to save the x, y location, the circle radius and color in order to be able to recreate that circle.

This sounds like a good project for you.. ;)

Congrats team, you did it! And it even works on my iPad, so this is perfect for customers on the go. I'm thrilled. We're throwing a TweetShirt launch party, so come join us.

The TweetShirt founder also wanted to pass along that she's happy to see the web app works on her iPad and iPhone too! If she's happy, we're happy.

review of canvas

BULLET POINTS

- Canvas is an element you place in your page to create a drawing space.

- The canvas has no default style or content until you provide it (so you won't see it on the page until you draw something in it or add a border with CSS).

- You can have more than one canvas on your page. Of course, you'll need to give each one a unique id to access each using JavaScript.

- To specify the size of the canvas element, use the width and height attributes on the element.

- Everything you put in canvas is drawn using JavaScript.

- To draw on the canvas, you first need to create a context. Currently, a 2D context is your only option, although other context types may exist in the future.

- A context is needed to draw in the canvas because it provides a specific kind of interface (e.g., 2D versus 3D). You'll be able to choose from more than one kind of interface to draw on a canvas.

- You access the canvas by using context properties and methods.

- To draw a rectangle in the canvas, use the context. fillRect method. This creates a rectangle filled with color.

- To create a rectangle outline, use strokeRect instead of fillRect.

- Use fillStyle and strokeStyle to change the default fill and stroke color, which is black.

- You can specify colors using the same format as you use with CSS (e.g., "black", "#000000", "rgb(0, 0, 0)". Remember to put quotes around the value of the fillStyle.

- There is no fillCircle method. To draw a circle in canvas, you need to draw an arc.

- To create arbitrary shapes or arcs, you first need to create a path.

- A path is a invisible line or shape you create that defines a line or area on the canvas. You can't see the path until you stroke or fill it.

- To create a triangle, create a path using beginPath, then use moveTo and lineTo to draw the path. Use closePath to join two points on the path.

- To draw a circle, create an arc that is 360 degrees. Your start angle is 0, and your end angle is 360 degrees.

- Angles are specified in canvas using radians, not degrees, so you need to convert from degrees to radians to specify your start and end angles.

- 360 degrees = 2Pi radians.

- To draw text in canvas, use the fillText method.

- When you draw text in canvas, you need to specify the position, style, and other properties using context properties.

- When you set a context property, it applies to all the drawing that follows until you change the property again. For example, changing the fillStyle will affect the color of shapes and text you draw after setting the fillStyle.

- Add an image to your canvas with the drawImage method.

- To add an image, you first need to create an image object and make sure it's completely loaded.

- Drawing on canvas is like doing "bitmap" drawing in graphics programs.

THE WEBVILLE INQUIRER

We have the scoop, <canvas> and <video> are an item after all!

Webville—You'll hear it here first

After an exclusive interview we can report that <canvas> and <video> have been doing more than just sharing the same web pages. Yeah, you got it... let's just say they've been mixing their content together.

By Troy Armstrong
INQUIRER STAFF WRITER

<Video> says, "It's true, we've formed a tight relationship. You see, I'm a pretty simple guy; I know how to display video, and I do that very well. But that's pretty much all I do. With <canvas>, everything has changed. I'm dressing up in custom controls, I'm filtering my video content, I'm displaying multiple videos at once."

We asked <canvas> to comment. Is she the woman behind the <video> tag? <Canvas> told us, "Well, <video> does very well on his own, you know decoding all those video codecs, maintaining his frames-per-second, all that, it's a very big job, and I could never do it. But with me he has a way to escape his normal, dare I say, "boring" way of playing back video. I give him a means to explore all kinds of creative possibilities of mixing video into the Web experience."

Well, who would have guessed? I guess we've got some interesting things in store ahead from the partnership that is <canvas>+<video>!

The fallout from this revelation can be expected to continue well into the video chapter, when the budding relationship will be exposed to public scrutiny.

Local resident Heidi Musgrove was shocked to learn the truth about the two elements.

HTML5cross

We're looking forward to checking out the <canvas> and <video> scoop in the next chapter. In the meantime, cement your new canvas knowledge with a quick crossword and perhaps a cup of tea.

Across

4. Everything on the canvas is _____ .
5. We _____ aligned the "and all I got was this lousy t-shirt!" text.
6. The property we set to fill a shape with a color.
7. You can tell when something has finished loading using an _____ handler.
9. The non-existent context method Jim tried to use to create circles.
12. Draw a circle with an _____ .
14. How we make the path of a shape visible.
15. Want to know which option is selected? You might need this property.
16. An invisible line you create to draw a shape.

Down

1. Best place for a good tweet.
2. This context method creates a rectangle.
3. Canvas and _____ go well together.
8. There are 360 _____ in a circle.
9. Use this method to draw text on the canvas.
10. We think in degrees, canvas thinks in _____ .
11. An object with methods and properties to draw on a canvas.
13. To move your path pencil to point 100, 100, use _____ (100, 100);

BE the Browser Solution

Now that you have an interface, execute these JavaScript statements and write in the value for each interface element.

Assume you've used the interface to pick the values for your t-shirt.

```
var selectObj = document.getElementById("backgroundColor");
var index = selectObj.selectedIndex;
var bgColor = selectObj[index].value;                    white
```

```
var selectObj = document.getElementById("shape");
var index = selectObj.selectedIndex;
var shape = selectObj[index].value;                      circles
```

```
var selectObj = document.getElementById("foregroundColor");
var index = selectObj.selectedIndex;
var fgColor = selectObj[index].value;          black
```

Notice that for each menu option value, we get the select element the option is contained in, find the selected option with the selectedIndex property, and the get the value of the selected option.

Remember that the value of the option may be different than the text you see in the controls; in our case, it's just the case of the first letters of the text.

Look at the HTML again to see the values of the options if you need to.

Here are the values we picked in the TweetShirt interface to create the answers above.

Select background color: [White ♦]

Circles or squares? [Neither ♦]

Select text color: [Black ♦]

Pick a tweet: [♦]

(Preview)

Pseudo-code Magnets Solution

Use your pseudo-magical coding powers to arrange the pseudo code below. We need to write the pseudo-code for the drawSquare function. This function takes a canvas and context and draws one randomly sized square on the canvas. Here's our solution.

We did this one for you.

```
function drawSquare ( canvas , context ) {

    calculate a random width
          for the square

    calculate a random x position for the
          square inside the canvas

    calculate a random y position for the
          square inside the canvas

    set the fillStyle to "lightblue"

    draw a square at position x,
          y with width w

}
```

Your magnets go here!

Sharpen your pencil Solution

To make sure we see only new squares in the canvas each time we click preview, we need to fill the background of the canvas with the background color the user has selected from the "backgroundColor" select menu. First, let's implement a function to fill the canvas with that color. Fill in the blanks below to complete the code. Here's our solution.

```
function fillBackgroundColor(canvas, context) {

    var selectObj = document.getElementById("backgroundColor");

    var index = selectObj.selectedIndex;

    var bgColor = selectObj.options[index].value;

    context.fillStyle = bgColor;

    context.fillRect(0, 0, canvas.width, canvas.height);

}
```

All we're doing to create a background color is drawing a rectangle that fills the entire canvas with a color.

BE the Browser Solution

Interpret the call to the arc method and sketch out all the values on the circle, including the path the method creates.

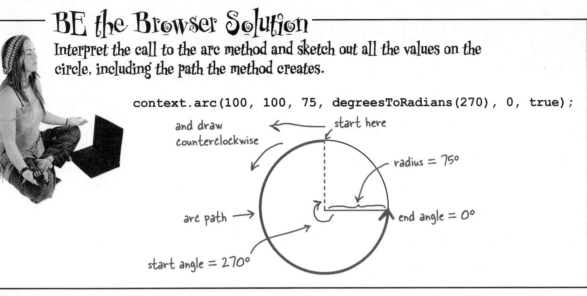

```
context.arc(100, 100, 75, degreesToRadians(270), 0, true);
```

and draw counterclockwise

start here

radius = 75°

arc path →

end angle = 0°

start angle = 270°

So you have a path! Now what?

Exercise Solution

You use the path to draw lines and fill in your shape with color, of course! Go ahead and create a simple HTML5 page with a canvas element and type in all the code so far. Give it a test run, too.

```
context.beginPath();
context.moveTo(100, 150);
context.lineTo(250, 75);
context.lineTo(125, 30);
context.closePath();
```

← Here's the code so far.

```
context.lineWidth = 5;
```
Set the width of line to draw over the path.

```
context.stroke();
```
Draw over the path with the line.

```
context.fillStyle = "red";
```
Set the color to fill the triangle with to red.

```
context.fill();
```
Fill the triangle with red.

When we load our triangle page, here's what we get (we made a 300 x 300 canvas to draw in).

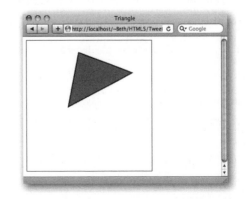

Intermission Solution

Time to practice your new arc and path drawing skills to create a smiley face. Fill in the blanks below with the code you need to complete the smiley face. We've given you some hints about where the eyes, nose and mouth should go in the diagram.

Here's our solution:

```
function drawSmileyFace() {
    var canvas = document.getElementById("smiley");
    var context = canvas.getContext("2d");


    context.beginPath();
    context.arc(300, 300, 200, 0, degreesToRadians(360), true);
    context.fillStyle = "#ffffcc";
    context.fill();
    context.stroke();


    context.beginPath();
    context.arc(200, 250, 25, 0, degreesToRadians(360), true);
    context.stroke();


    context.beginPath();
    context.arc(400, 250, 25, 0, degreesToRadians(360), true);
    context.stroke();


    context.beginPath();
    context.moveTo(300, 300);
    context.lineTo(300, 350);
    context.stroke();


    context.beginPath();
    context.arc(300, 350, 75, degreesToRadians(20), degreesToRadians(160), false);
    context.stroke();
}
```

Smiley Face
http://localhost/~Beth/HTML5/TweetShirt/smiley.html

x,y = 200, 250
radius = 25

x,y = 400, 250

x,y = 300, 300
nose length=50

angle=20°

x,y = 300, 350
radius = 75

The face circle. We did this one for you. Notice we filled it with yellow.

This is the left eye. The center of the circle is at x=200, y=250, the radius is 25, the starting angle is 0, and the ending angle is Math.PI * 2 radians (360 degrees). We stroke the path so we get the outline of the circle (but no fill).

This is the right eye. Just like the left eye, except it's at x=400. We use counterclockwise (true) for the direction (it doesn't matter for a complete circle).

This is the nose. We use moveTo(300,300) to move the pen to x=300, y=300 to start the line. Then we use lineTo(300,350) because the nose is 50 long. Then we stroke the path.

To get a more realistic smile, we start and end the edge of the mouth at 20 degrees below the x-axis. That means the starting angle is 20°, and the ending angle is 160°.

The direction is clockwise (false) because we want the mouth in a smile. (Remember, the starting point is to the right of the mouth center.

Code Magnets Solution

It's time for your first experiment with canvas text. Below we've started the code for drawText, the method we're going to call to draw all the text onto the preview canvas. See if you can finish up the code to draw "I saw this tweet" and "and all I got was this lousy t-shirt!" on the canvas, we'll save drawing the actual tweet for later. Here's our solution.

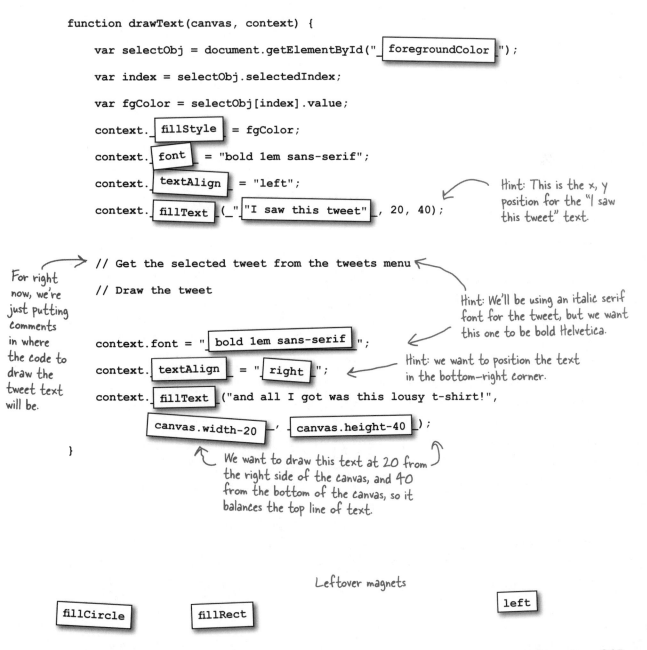

```
function drawText(canvas, context) {

    var selectObj = document.getElementById(" foregroundColor ");

    var index = selectObj.selectedIndex;

    var fgColor = selectObj[index].value;

    context. fillStyle  = fgColor;

    context. font  = "bold 1em sans-serif";

    context. textAlign  = "left";

    context. fillText (_" "I saw this tweet" , 20, 40);
```

Hint: This is the x, y position for the "I saw this tweet" text.

```
    // Get the selected tweet from the tweets menu

    // Draw the tweet
```

For right now, we're just putting comments in where the code to draw the tweet text will be.

Hint: We'll be using an italic serif font for the tweet, but we want this one to be bold Helvetica.

```
    context.font = " bold 1em sans-serif ";

    context. textAlign  = " right ";

    context. fillText ("and all I got was this lousy t-shirt!",

        canvas.width-20 , canvas.height-40 );
```

Hint: we want to position the text in the bottom-right corner.

We want to draw this text at 20 from the right side of the canvas, and 40 from the bottom of the canvas, so it balances the top line of text.

```
}
```

Leftover magnets

```
fillCircle        fillRect                    left
```

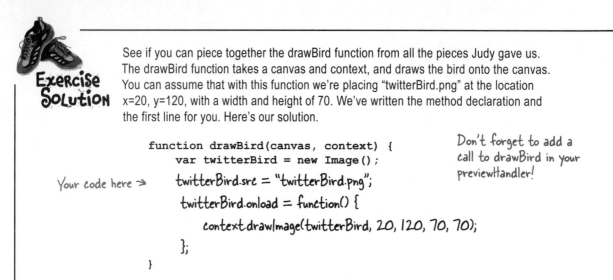

See if you can piece together the drawBird function from all the pieces Judy gave us. The drawBird function takes a canvas and context, and draws the bird onto the canvas. You can assume that with this function we're placing "twitterBird.png" at the location x=20, y=120, with a width and height of 70. We've written the method declaration and the first line for you. Here's our solution.

```
function drawBird(canvas, context) {
    var twitterBird = new Image();
```

Your code here →

```
    twitterBird.src = "twitterBird.png";
    twitterBird.onload = function() {
        context.drawImage(twitterBird, 20, 120, 70, 70);
    };
}
```

Don't forget to add a call to drawBird in your previewHandler!

HTML5cross Solution

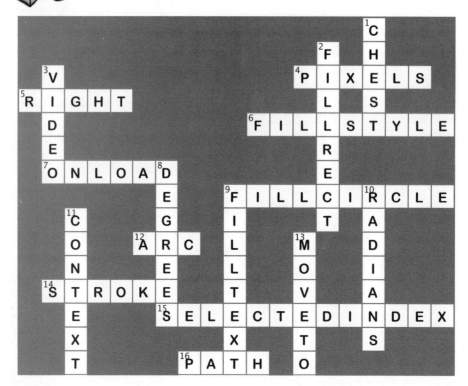

TweetShirt Easter egg

So, you've made the perfect TweetShirt preview—now what? Well, if you really want to make a t-shirt out of your design, you can! How? Here's a little extra bonus to add to your code—a TweetShirt "easter egg" if you will—that will make an image out of your design, all ready for you to upload to a site that will print an image on a t-shirt for you (there are plenty of them on the Web).

How can we do this? It's simple! We can use the `toDataURL` method of the **canvas** object. Check it out:

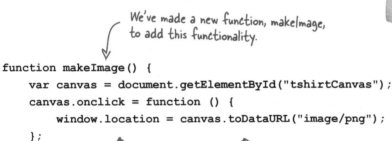

We've made a new function, makeImage, to add this functionality.

```
function makeImage() {
    var canvas = document.getElementById("tshirtCanvas");
    canvas.onclick = function () {
        window.location = canvas.toDataURL("image/png");
    };
}
```

We grab the canvas object...

And add an event handler so that when you click on the canvas, it creates the image.

We set the browser window location to the image that's generated, so you'll see a browser page with just the image in it.

We're asking canvas to create a png image of the pixels drawn on the canvas.

Note that png is the only format that must be supported by browsers, so we recommend you use it.

Now, just add a call to `makeImage` in the window onload function and your canvas is now enabled to make an image when you click on it. Give it a try. And let us know if you make a tshirt!

```
window.onload = function() {
    var button = document.getElementById("previewButton");
    button.onclick = previewHandler;
    makeImage();
}
```

Call makeImage to add the click event handler to the canvas, and your easter egg is complete.

Watch it! **Some browsers won't let you grab an image from the canvas if you're running the code from file://.**

Run this code from localhost:// or a hosted server if you want it to work across all browsers.

8 not your father's tv

Video
...with special guest star "Canvas"

We don't need no plug-in. After all, video is now a first-class member of the HTML family—just throw a <video> element in your page and you've got instant video, even across most devices. But video is *far more* than *just an element*, it's also a JavaScript API that allows us to control playback, create our own custom video interfaces and integrate video with the rest of HTML in totally new ways. Speaking of *integration*... remember there's that *video and canvas connection* we've been talking about—you're going to see that putting video and canvas together gives us a powerful new way to *process video* in real time. In this chapter we're going to start by getting video up and running in a page and then we'll put the JavaScript API through its paces. Come on, you're going to be amazed what you can do with a little markup, JavaScript and video & canvas.

Meet Webville TV

Webville TV—all the content you've been waiting for, like *Destination Earth*, *The Attack of the 50' Woman*, *The Thing*, *The Blob*, and it wouldn't be beyond us to throw in a few '50s educational films. What else would you expect in Webville? But that's just the content, on the technology side would you expect anything less than HTML5 video?

Of course, that's just the vision, we have to build Webville TV if we want it to be a reality. Over the next few pages we're going to build Webville TV from the ground up using HTML5 markup, the video element and a little JavaScript here and there.

Webville TV built with 100% HTML5 technology.

Coming to a browser near you soon!

The HTML, let's get it done...

Hey this is Chapter 8, no lollygagging around! Let's jump right in and create some HTML:

```html
<!doctype html>
<html lang="en">
<head>
  <title>Webville TV</title>
  <meta charset="utf-8">
  <link rel="stylesheet" href="webvilletv.css">
</head>
<body>
<div id="tv">
   <div id="tvConsole">
      <div id="highlight">
          <img src="images/highlight.png" alt="highlight for tv">
      </div>
      <div id="videoDiv">
          <video controls autoplay src="video/preroll.mp4" width="480" height="360"
                 poster="images/prerollposter.jpg" id="video">
          </video>
      </div>
   </div>
</div>
</body>
</html>
```

Pretty standard HTML5.

Don't forget the CSS file to make it all look nice.

Just a little image to help make it look like a television set.

And here's our <video> element for playing our video. We'll take a closer look in a sec...

Plug that set in and test it out...

You need to make sure of a few things here: first, make sure you've got the code above typed into a file named `webvilletv.html`; second, make sure you've downloaded the CSS file, and finally, make sure you've also downloaded the video files and placed them in a directory named `video`. After all that, load the page and sit back and watch.

If you're having issues, turn the page!

Here's what we see. Notice if you hover your mouse over the screen you get a set of controls, which you can use to pause, play, set the audio or seek around in the video.

Download everything from http://wickedlysmart.com/hfhtml5

I'm not seeing any video. I've triple checked the code and I have the video in the right directory. Any ideas?

Yes, it's probably the video format.

While the browser makers have agreed on what the `<video>` element and API look like in HTML5, not everyone can agree on the *actual format* of the video files themselves. For instance if you are on Safari, H.264 format is favored, if you're on Chrome, WebM is favored, and so on.

By the time you read this, these formats could be more widely supported across all browsers. So if your video's working, great. Always check the Web to see the latest on this unfolding topic. And we'll come back for more on this topic shortly.

In the code we just wrote, we're assuming H.264 as a format, which works in Safari, Mobile Safari and IE9+. If you're using another browser then look in your `video` directory and you'll see three different types of video, with three different file extensions: ".mp4", ".ogv", and ".webm" (we'll talk more about what these mean in a bit).

For Safari you should already be using .mp4 (which contains H.264).

For Google Chrome, use the .webm format by replacing your src attribute with:

```
src="video/preroll.webm"
```

If you're using Firefox or Opera, then replace your src attribute with:

```
src="video/preroll.ogv"
```

And if you're using IE8 or earlier, you're out of luck—wait a sec, this is Chapter 8! How could you still be using IE8 or earlier? Upgrade! But if you need to know how to supply fallback content for your IE8 users, hang on, we're getting to that.

Give this a try to get you going, and we're coming back to all this in a bit.

How does the video element work?

At this point you've got a video up and playing on your page, but before we move on, let's step back and look at that video element we used in our markup:

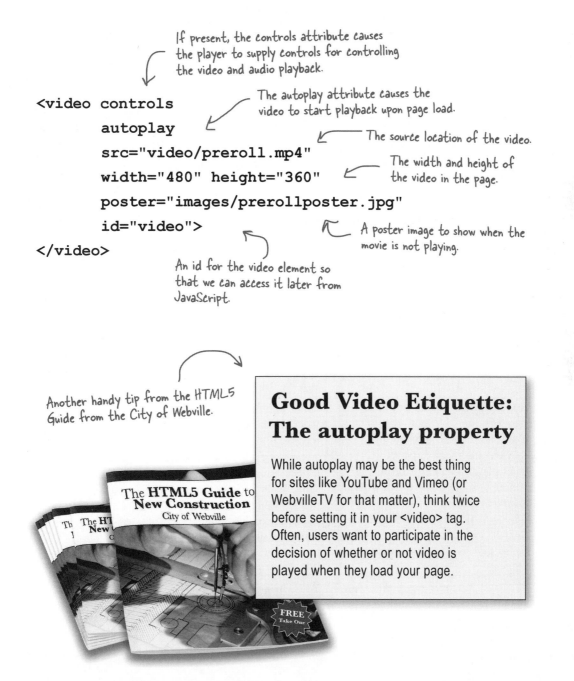

If present, the controls attribute causes the player to supply controls for controlling the video and audio playback.

The autoplay attribute causes the video to start playback upon page load.

The source location of the video.

The width and height of the video in the page.

```
<video controls
       autoplay
       src="video/preroll.mp4"
       width="480" height="360"
       poster="images/prerollposter.jpg"
       id="video">
</video>
```

A poster image to show when the movie is not playing.

An id for the video element so that we can access it later from JavaScript.

Another handy tip from the HTML5 Guide from the City of Webville.

The **HTML5 Guide** to
New Construction
City of Webville

FREE
Take One

Good Video Etiquette: The autoplay property

While autoplay may be the best thing for sites like YouTube and Vimeo (or WebvilleTV for that matter), think twice before setting it in your <video> tag. Often, users want to participate in the decision of whether or not video is played when they load your page.

Closely inspecting the video attributes...

Let's look more closely at some of the more important video attributes:

controls

The controls attribute is a **boolean** attribute. It's either there or it's not. If it is there, then the browser will add its built-in controls to the video display. This varies by browser, so check out each browser to see what they look like. Here's what they look like in Safari.

src is what video file is used here.

src

The src attribute is just like the `<img>` element's src—it is a URL that tells the video element where to find the source file. In this case, the source is video/preroll.mp4. (If you downloaded the code for this chapter, you'll find this video and two others in the video directory).

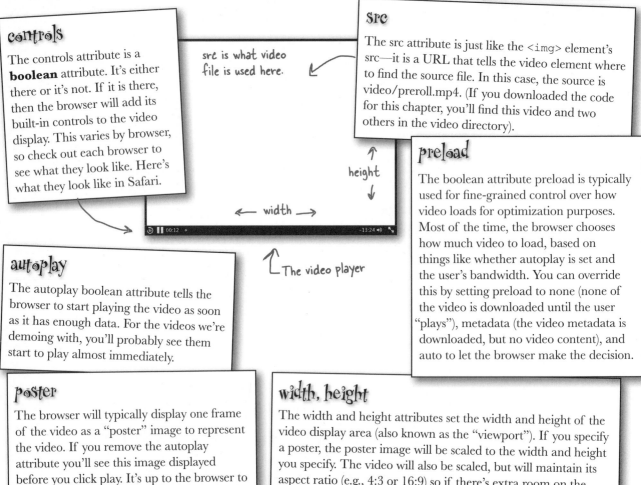

↑ height ↓

← width →

⌐ *The video player*

preload

The boolean attribute preload is typically used for fine-grained control over how video loads for optimization purposes. Most of the time, the browser chooses how much video to load, based on things like whether autoplay is set and the user's bandwidth. You can override this by setting preload to none (none of the video is downloaded until the user "plays"), metadata (the video metadata is downloaded, but no video content), and auto to let the browser make the decision.

autoplay

The autoplay boolean attribute tells the browser to start playing the video as soon as it has enough data. For the videos we're demoing with, you'll probably see them start to play almost immediately.

poster

The browser will typically display one frame of the video as a "poster" image to represent the video. If you remove the autoplay attribute you'll see this image displayed before you click play. It's up to the browser to pick which frame to show; often, the browser will just show the first frame of the video... which is often black. If you want to show a specific image, then it's up to you to create an image to display, and specify it by using the poster attribute.

width, height

The width and height attributes set the width and height of the video display area (also known as the "viewport"). If you specify a poster, the poster image will be scaled to the width and height you specify. The video will also be scaled, but will maintain its aspect ratio (e.g., 4:3 or 16:9) so if there's extra room on the sides, or the top and bottom, the video will be letter-boxed or pillar-boxed to fit into the display area size. You should try to match the native dimensions of the video if you want the best performance (so the browser doesn't have to scale in real time).

Pillar-boxing ↘   ↙ Letter-boxing

loop

Another boolean attribute, loop automatically restarts the video after it finishes playing.

The controls look different on every browser; at least with solutions like Flash I had consistent looking controls.

Yes, the controls in each browser are different with HTML video.

The look and feel of your controls is dictated by those who implement the browsers. They do tend to look different in different browsers and operating systems. In some cases, for instance, on a tablet, they have to look and behave differently because the device just works differently (and it's a good thing that's already taken care of for you). That said, we understand; across, say, desktop browsers, it would be nice to have consistent controls, but that isn't a formal part of the HTML5 spec, and in some cases, a method that works on one OS might clash with another operating system's UI guidelines. So, just know that the controls may differ, and if you really feel motivated, you can implement custom controls for your apps.

We'll do this later...

What you need to know about video formats

We wish everything was as neat and tidy as the video element and its attributes, but as it turns out, video formats are a bit of a mess on the Web. What's a video format? Think about it this way: a video file contains two parts, a video part and an audio part, and each part is encoded (to reduce size and to allow it to be played back more efficiently) using a specific encoding type. That encoding, for the most part, is what no one can agree on—some browser makers are enamored with H.264 encodings, others really like VP8, and yet others like the open source alternative, Theora. And to make all this *even more* complicated, the file that holds the video and audio encoding (which is known as a container) has its own format with its own name. So we're really talking buzzword soup here.

Anyway, while it might be a big, happy world if all browser makers agreed on a single format to use across the Web, well, that just doesn't seem to be in the cards for a number of technical, political, and philosophical reasons. But rather than open that debate here, we're just going to make sure you're reasonably educated on the topic so you can make your own decisions about how to support your audience.

Let's take a look at the popular encodings out there; right now there are three contenders trying to rule the (Web) world...

Three different video formats in use across the major browsers.

This is a container...

...that contains a video and an audio encoding of the video data.

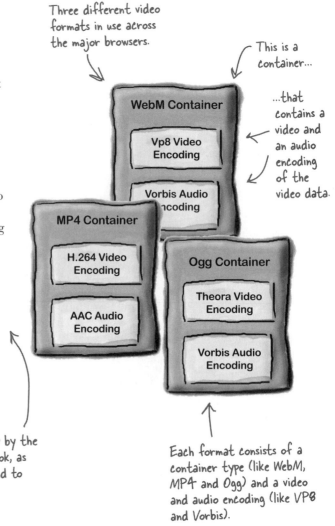

Your mileage may vary by the time you read this book, as favored encodings tend to change over time.

Each format consists of a container type (like WebM, MP4 and Ogg) and a video and audio encoding (like VP8 and Vorbis).

The HTML5 specification allows for any video format. It is the browser implementation that determines what formats are actually supported.

The contenders

The reality is, if you're going to be serving content to a wide spectrum of users you're going to have to supply more than one format. On the other hand, if all you care about is, say, the Apple iPad, you may be able to get away with just one. Today we have three main contenders—let's have a look at them:

MP4 container with H.264 Video and AAC Audio

H.264 is licensed by the MPEG-LA group.

There is more than one kind of H.264; each is known as a "profile."

MP4/H.264 is supported by Safari and IE9+. You may find support in some versions of Chrome.

WebM container with VP8 Video and Vorbis Audio

WebM was designed by Google to work with VP8 encoded videos.

WebM/VP8 is supported by Firefox, Chrome and Opera.

You'll find WebM formatted videos with the .webm extension.

Ogg container with Theora Video and Vorbis Audio

Theora is an open source codec.

Video encoded with Theora is usually contained in an Ogg file, with the .ogv file extension.

Ogg/Theora is supported by Firefox, Chrome and Opera.

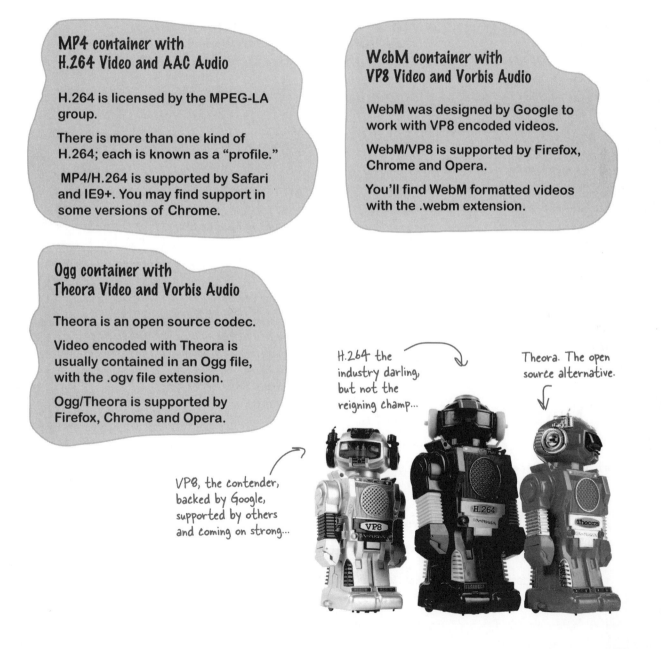

H.264 the industry darling, but not the reigning champ...

Theora. The open source alternative.

VP8, the contender, backed by Google, supported by others and coming on strong...

How to juggle all those formats...

So we know it's a messy world with respect to video format, but what to do? Depending on your audience you may decide to provide just one format of your video, or several. In either case, you can use one `<source>` element (not to be confused with the `src` *attribute*) per format inside a `<video>` element, to provide a set of videos, each with its own format, and let the browser pick the first one it supports. Like this:

Notice we're removing the src attribute from the `<video>` tag...

... and adding three source tags each with their own src attribute, each with a version of the video in a different format.

```
<video src="video/preroll.mp4" id="video"
       poster="video/prerollposter.jpg" controls
       width="480" height="360">
    <source src="video/preroll.mp4">
    <source src="video/preroll.webm">
    <source src="video/preroll.ogv">
    <p>Sorry, your browser doesn't support the video element</p>
</video>
```

This is what the browser shows if it doesn't support video.

The browser starts at the top and work its way down until it finds a format it can play.

For each source the browser loads the metadata of the video file to see if it can play it (which can be a lengthy process, although we can make it easier on the browser... see the next page).

BULLET POINTS

- The **container** is the file format that's used to package up the video, audio and metadata information. Common container formats include: MP4, WebM, Ogg and Flash Video.

- The **codec** is the software used to encode and decode a specific encoding of video or audio. Popular web codecs include: H.264, VP8, Theora, AAC, and Vorbis.

- The browser decides what video it can decode and not all browser makers agree, so if you want to support everyone, you need multiple encodings.

How to be even more specific with your video formats

Telling the browser the location of your source files gives it a selection of different versions to choose from, however the browser has to do some detective work before it can truly determine if a file is playable. You can help your browser even more by giving it more information about the MIME type and (optionally) codecs of your video files:

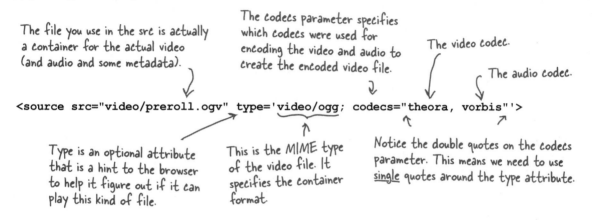

The file you use in the src is actually a container for the actual video (and audio and some metadata).

The codecs parameter specifies which codecs were used for encoding the video and audio to create the encoded video file.

The video codec.

The audio codec.

```
<source src="video/preroll.ogv" type='video/ogg; codecs="theora, vorbis"'>
```

Type is an optional attribute that is a hint to the browser to help it figure out if it can play this kind of file.

This is the MIME type of the video file. It specifies the container format.

Notice the double quotes on the codecs parameter. This means we need to use <u>single</u> quotes around the type attribute.

We can update our `<source>` elements to include the type information for all three types of video we have, like this:

```
<video id="video" poster="video/prerollposter.jpg" controls width="480" height="360">
    <source src="video/preroll.mp4" type='video/mp4; codecs="avc1.42E01E, mp4a.40.2"'>
    <source src="video/preroll.webm" type='video/webm; codecs="vp8, vorbis"'>
    <source src="video/preroll.ogv" type='video/ogg; codecs="theora, vorbis"'>
    <p>Sorry, your browser doesn't support the video element</p>
</video>
```

If you don't know the codecs parameters, then you can leave them off and just use the MIME type. It will be a little less efficient, but most of the time, that's okay.

The codecs for mp4 are more complicated than the other two because h.264 supports various "profiles," different encodings for different uses (like high bandwidth vs. low bandwidth). So, to get those right, you'll need to know more details about how your video was encoded.

If and when you do your own video encoding, you'll need to know more about the various options for the type parameters to use in your source element. You can get a lot more information on type parameters at http://wiki.whatwg.org/wiki/Video_type_parameters.

there are no
Dumb Questions

Q: **Is there any hope of getting to one container format or codec type in the next few years? Isn't this why we have standards?**

A: There probably won't be one encoding to rule them all anytime soon—as we said earlier, this topic intersects with a whole host of issues including companies wanting to control their own destiny in the video space to a complex set of intellectual property issues. The HTML5 standards committee recognized this and decided not to specify the video format in the HTML5 specification. So, while in principle HTML5 supports (or is at least agnostic to) all of these formats, it is really up to the browser makers to decide what they do and don't support.

Keep an eye on this topic if video is important to you; it will surely be an interesting one to watch over the next few years as this is all sorted out. And, as always, keep in mind what your audience needs and make sure you're doing what you can to support them.

Q: **If I want to encode my own video, where do I start?**

A: There are a variety of video capture and encoding programs out there, and which one you choose is really going to depend on what kind of video you're capturing and how you want to use the end result. Entire books have been written on video encoding, so be prepared to enter a world of all new acronyms and technology. You can start simple with programs like iMovie or Adobe Premiere Elements, which include the ability to encode your video for the Web. If you're getting into serious video work with Final Cut Pro or Adobe Premiere, these software programs include their own production tools. And, finally, if you are delivering your videos from a Content Delivery Network (CDN), many CDN companies also offer encoding services. So you've got a wide variety of choices depending on your needs.

Q: **Can I play my video back fullscreen? I am surprised there isn't a property for this in the API.**

A: That functionality hasn't yet been standardized, although you'll find ways to do it with some of the browsers if you search the Web. Some of the browsers supply a fullscreen control (for instance, on tablets) that give the video element this capability. Also note that once you've got a way to go fullscreen, what you can do with the video, other than basic playback, may be limited for security reasons (just as it is with plug-in video solutions today).

Q: **What about the volume of my video? Can I use the API to control the volume level?**

A: You sure can. The volume property can be set to an floating point value between 0.0 (sound off) to 1.0 (sound the loudest). Just use your video object to set this at any time:

```
video.volume = 0.9;
```

CASE FILE: VIDEO

YOUR NEXT MISSION:
VIDEO RECONNAISSANCE

TOP SECRET

GO OUT AND DETERMINE ███████████ THE CURRENT LEVEL OF SUPPORT FOR VIDEO IN EACH BROWSER
███████████ BELOW (HINT, HERE ARE A FEW SITES THAT KEEP UP WITH SUCH THINGS:
HTTP://EN.WIKIPEDIA.ORG/WIKI/HTML5_VIDEO, ███████████ ASSUME THE LATEST VERSION OF THE
HTTP://CANIUSE.COM/#SEARCH=VIDEO). ASSUME THE LATEST VERSION OF THE
BROWSER. FOR EACH BROWSER/FEATURE PUT A CHECKMARK IF IT IS SUPPORTED.
UPON YOUR RETURN, REPORT BACK FOR YOUR NEXT ASSIGNMENT!

iOS and Android devices (among others)
↓

Video \ Browser	Safari	Chrome	Firefox	Mobile Webkit	Opera	IE9+	IE8	IE7 or <
H.264								
WebM								
Ogg Theora								

I think Flash video is still important and I want to make sure I have a fallback if my users' browsers don't support HTML5 video.

No problem.

There are techniques for falling back to another video player if your preferred one (whether that be HTML5 or Flash or another) isn't supported.

Below you'll find an example of how to insert your Flash video as a fallback for HTML5 video, assuming the browser doesn't know how to play HTML5 video. Obviously this is an area that is changing fast, so please take a look on the Web (which is updated a lot more often than a book) to make sure you're using the latest and greatest techniques. You'll also find ways to make HTML5 the fallback rather than Flash if you prefer to give Flash video priority.

```
<video poster="video.jpg" controls>
        <source src="video.mp4">
        <source src="video.webm">
        <source src="video.ogv">
        <object>...</object>
</video>
```

Insert your <object> element inside the <video> element. If the browser doesn't know about the <video> element, the <object> will be used.

I was told there would be APIs?

As you can see, you can do a lot using markup and the `<video>` element. But the `<video>` element also exposes a rich API that you can use to implement all kinds of interesting video behaviors and experiences. Here's a quick summary of some of the methods, properties and events of the `<video>` element you might be interested in (and check the spec for a comprehensive list):

Call these Methods

play ← plays your video

pause ← pauses your video

load ← loads your video

canPlayType — helps you determine which video types you can play, programmatically

Use these Properties

videoWidth	loop
videoHeight	muted
currentTime	paused
duration	readyState
ended	seeking
error	volume

These are all properties of the `<video>` element object. Some you can set (like loop and muted); some are read only (like currentTime and error).

Catch these Events

play	abort
pause	waiting
progress	loadeddata
error	loadedmetadata
timeupdate	volumechange
ended	

And these are all events you can handle if you want by adding event handlers that are called when the event you're listening for occurs.

A little content "programming" on Webville TV

So far we've got one single video up and running on Webville TV. What we'd really like is a programming schedule that serves up a playlist of videos. Let's say we want to do this on Webville TV:

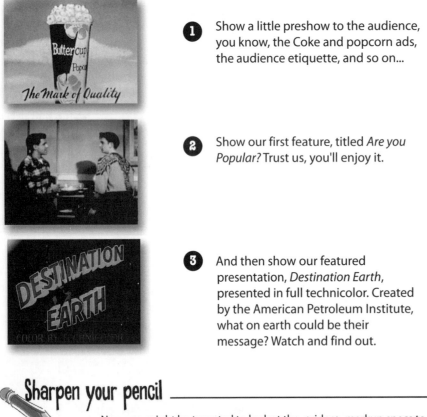

1 Show a little preshow to the audience, you know, the Coke and popcorn ads, the audience etiquette, and so on...

2 Show our first feature, titled *Are you Popular?* Trust us, you'll enjoy it.

3 And then show our featured presentation, *Destination Earth*, presented in full technicolor. Created by the American Petroleum Institute, what on earth could be their message? Watch and find out.

Sharpen your pencil

Now you might be tempted to look at the <video> markup specs to see how you specify a playlist, but for this you're going to need code because the <video> element allows you to specify only one video. If you were on a desert island and had to implement a playlist with only the browser, the <video> element, the src property, the load and play methods, and the ended event, how would you do it (you can use any JavaScript data types you like):

Just a hint: the ended event happens when a video reaches the end and stops playing. Like any event, you can have a handler called when this happens.

No peeking at the answer!!

Sharpen your pencil
Solution

Now you might be tempted to look at the <video> markup specs to see how you specify a playlist, but for this you're going to need code because the <video> element allows you to specify only one video. If you were on a desert island and had to implement a playlist with only the browser, the <video> element, the src property, the load and play methods, and the ended event, how would you do it (you can use any JavaScript data types you like)? Here's our solution:

When the page loads we set up a playlist array, start the first video playing, and set up an event handler for when it stops.

Playlist Pseudo-code

Create array of playlist videos

Get video from DOM

Set event handler on video for "ended" event

Create variable position = 0

Set video source to playlist position 0

Play the video

Here's how we're going to store the playlist, as an array. Each item is a video to play.

"preroll.mp4"

"areyoupopular.mp4"

"destinationearth.mp4"

Playlist Array

Ended Event

Every time a video finishes playing the ended event occurs...

... which calls the ended event handler.

Here's our handler to deal with video ending.

Ended Event Handler Pseudo-code

Increment position by one

Set video to next playlist position

Play the next video

When we get to the end of our playlist we can either stop, or loop around to the first video.

Implementing Webville TV's playlist

Now we're going to use JavaScript and the video API to implement the Webville TV playlist. Let's start by adding a link to a JavaScript file in `webvilletv.html`; just add this into the `<head>` element:

```
<script src="webvilletv.js"></script>
```

And delete this from your existing `<video>` element:

```
<video controls autoplay src="video/preroll.mp4" width="480" height="360"
        poster="images/prerollposter.jpg" id="video">
</video>
```

← We're removing the autoplay and src attributes from the <video> tag.

Also remove any <source> elements you might have been experimenting with.

Now, create a new file `webvilletv.js`, and let's define a few global variables and a function that will be called when the page is fully loaded:

← First let's define a variable to keep track of which video we're playing; we'll name this position.

```
var position = 0;
var playlist;      ← And we need a variable to hold the video playlist array.
var video;         ← And also a variable to hold a reference to the video element.
```

```
window.onload = function() {      ← We'll set up our playlist with three videos.
    playlist = ["video/preroll.mp4",
                "video/areyoupopular.mp4",
                "video/destinationearth.mp4"];
    video = document.getElementById("video");   ← Grab the video element.
    video.addEventListener("ended", nextVideo, false);
```

← And add a handler for the video ended event. Yes, this looks different than what we're used to—hold on one sec, we'll talk about this on the next page.

```
    video.src = playlist[position];    ← Now let's set the src for the first video.
    video.load();
    video.play();      ← And load the video and play it!
}
```

So what's up with that event handler code?

In the past we've always just assigned a handler function to be called when an event occurs to a property (like `onload` or `onclick`) like this:

```
video.onended = nextVideo;
```

However, this time we're going to do things a little differently. Why? Because at the time we're writing this, support for all the event properties on the video object are a little spotty. That's okay; that deficiency is also going to allow us to show you another way of registering for events: `addEventListener`, which is a general method supported by many objects for registering for various events. Here's how it works:

You can use the addEventListener method to add an event handler.

This is the function we're going to call when the event happens.

```
video.addEventListener("ended", nextVideo, false);
```

This is the object on which we're listening for the event.

This is the event we're listening for. Notice we don't put an "on" before the event name like we do with handlers that we set with properties (like onload).

The third parameter controls some advanced methods of getting events if it is set to true. Unless you're writing advanced code you'll always set this to false.

Other than the fact the `addEventListener` method is a little more complicated than just adding a handler by setting the property to a function, it works pretty much the same way. So let's get back to our code!

How to write the "end of video" handler

Now we just need to write the handler for the video's ended event. This handler is going to be called whenever the video player hits the end of the current video file. Here's how we write the `nextVideo` function (add it to `webvilletv.js`):

Note the handler won't be called if the user pauses the video or if the video is looping (which you can do by setting the loop property).

```
function nextVideo() {

    position++;

    if (position >= playlist.length) {

        position = 0;

    }

    video.src = playlist[position];

    video.load();

    video.play();

}
```

First, increment the position in the playlist array.

And if we hit the end of the list, we'll just loop back around by setting the position to zero again.

Now let's set the source of the player to the next video.

And finally, let's load and start the new video playing.

Another test drive...

Can you believe we're ready for a test drive? All we
did was use the API to set up a video to play, then we
made sure we had an event listener ready to handle the
situation when the video ends, which it does by starting
the next video in the playlist. Make sure you've got the
changes made to your HTML file, type in your new
JavaScript code and give it a test drive.

*Here's what we see, feel free to scrub
ahead in the video to see the video
change from one to another without
watching the whole show.*

> It works! But how do we
> decide which video format
> to play when we're using code to
> load the video source?

Good question.

When we were using multiple `source` tags we could count
on the browser to sort through one or more video formats
and decide if it could play any of them. Now that we're
using code we're just giving the video element a single
option. So how do we test to see what the browser supports
to make sure we supply the best format?

We do that using the `canPlayType` method of the video
object. `canPlayType` takes a video format and returns a
string that represents how confident the browser is that it
can play that type of video. There are three confidence
levels: probably, maybe or no confidence. Let's take a closer
look and then rework the playlist code to use this.

*Are you scratching your head saying "probably? maybe?
why doesn't it return true or false?" Us too, but we'll go
through what this means in a sec...*

How the canPlayType method works

The video object provides a method `canPlayType` that can determine how likely you are to be able to play a video format. The `canPlayType` method takes the same format description you used with the `<source>` tag and returns one of three values: the empty string, "maybe" or "probably". Here's how you call `canPlayType`:

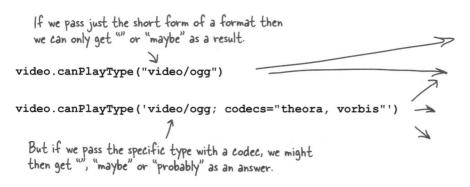

If we pass just the short form of a format then we can only get "" or "maybe" as a result.

```
video.canPlayType("video/ogg")
```

```
video.canPlayType('video/ogg; codecs="theora, vorbis"')
```

But if we pass the specific type with a codec, we might then get "", "maybe" or "probably" as an answer.

Empty string if the browser knows it can't play the video.

The string "maybe" if the browser thinks it can possibly play the video.

The string "probably" if the browser is confident it can play the video.

Notice that the browser is only confident beyond "maybe" if you include the codec parameter in the type. Also notice that there's no "I'm absolutely sure" return value. Even if the browser knows it can play a *type* of video, there's still no guarantee it can play the *actual* video; for instance, if the bitrate of the video is too high, then the browser won't be able to decode it.

Bitrate is the number of bits the browser has to process per unit of time to decode the video and display it correctly.

Putting canPlayType to use

We're going to use `canPlayType` to determine which video format to use for Webville TV videos—you already know that we have three versions of each file: MP4, WebM and Ogg, and depending on which browser you're using, some will work and some won't. Let's create a new function that returns the file extension (".mp4", ".webm" or ".ogv") that is appropriate for your browser. We're going to use only the MIME types (`"video/mp4"`, `"video/webm"` and `"video/ogg"`) and not the codecs, so the only possible returns values are "maybe" and the empty string. Here's the code:

We know we'll only get "maybe" and empty string as answers, so we'll just make sure our matching type doesn't result in an empty string.

```
function getFormatExtension() {
    if (video.canPlayType("video/mp4") != "") {
        return ".mp4";
    } else if (video.canPlayType("video/webm") != "") {
        return ".webm";
    } else if (video.canPlayType("video/ogg") != "") {
        return ".ogv";
    }
}
```

We try each of the types, and return the corresponding file extension if the browser says, "Maybe I can support that."

For most use cases, if you don't know the codecs, it's good enough to be "maybe" confident.

Integrating the getFormatExtension function

Now, we need to make some changes to the `window.onload` and
`nextVideo` functions to use `getFormatExtension`. First, we'll remove
the file extensions from the filenames in the playlist (because we're going to
figure those out using `getFormatExtension` instead), and then we'll call
`getFormatExtension` where we set the `video.src` property:

```
window.onload = function() {
    playlist = ["video/preroll",
               "video/areyoupopular",
               "video/destinationearth"];
    video = document.getElementById("video");
    video.addEventListener("ended", nextVideo, false);
    video.src = playlist[position] + getFormatExtension();
    video.load();
    video.play();
}
```

Remove the file extensions.
We're figuring these out
programmatically now.

And concatenate the result
of getFormatExtension to the
filename for the new video src.

And do the same thing in `nextVideo`:

```
function nextVideo() {
    position++;
    if (position >= playlist.length) {
        position = 0;
    }
    video.src = playlist[position] + getFormatExtension();
    video.load();
    video.play();
}
```

Same thing here; we
concatenate the result of
getFormatExtension to the
video src.

And test drive...

Add the `canPlayType` function and make the changes above, then reload
your `webvilletv.html` file. Work? Now your code is figuring out the
best format. If you want to know which video the browser chose, try
adding an alert to the `window.onload` and `nextVideo` functions; add it
at the bottom of each function, after `video.play()`:

```
alert("Playing " + video.currentSrc);
```

Which file did your browser play?

there are no
Dumb Questions

Q: If I'm programmatically setting the source of my video, and canPlayType says its a "maybe", but yet the playback fails, how can I deal with that?

A: There are a couple of ways to approach this. One is to catch the error and give the video object another source (we'll talk about catching errors at the end of this chapter). The other is to use the

DOM to write multiple source tags into the video object at once (just as if you'd typed them into your markup). That way your video object has several choices and you don't have to write more complex error handling code). We're not going to do that in this chapter, but it's a way of giving your video object multiple choices and doing it through code, not markup, if you have advanced needs.

You may need to install Quicktime to play mp4 video in Safari.

Watch it! Quicktime often comes installed by default, but if it's not, you can download it from http://www.apple.com/quicktime/download/.

Google Chrome has extra security restrictions.

Watch it! These security restrictions will prevent you from doing some video+canvas operations if you loaded the web page as a file (i.e., your URL will show file:// rather than http://), like we'll be doing in the rest of this chapter. If you try, the app won't work and you'll get no indication of why.

So, for this chapter, we recommend either using a different browser, or running your own server and running the examples from http://localhost.

Make sure your server is serving video files with the correct MIME type.

Watch it! Whether you're using your own local server, or running an app using video from a hosted server, you need to make sure that the videos are being served correctly. If they're not, they might not work properly.

If you're on a Mac or Linux using a local server, you're most likely using Apache. You can modify the httpd.conf file (if you have root access) or create a .htaccess file in the directory where your video files are stored, and add the following lines:

```
AddType video/ogg   .ogv

AddType video/mp4   .mp4

AddType video/webm  .webm
```

This tells the server how to serve files with those file extensions.

You can install Apache on Windows, and do the same thing. For IIS servers, we recommend looking in the Microsoft online documentation for "Configuring MIME types in IIS."

I keep tellin' you, it's not just about JavaScript... you've gotta see the big picture. Building web apps is about markup, CSS, and JavaScript and its APIs.

At some point we have to treat you like a real developer.

In this book we've (hopefully) helped you every step of the way—we've been there to catch you before you fall and to make sure that, in your code, your i's were dotted and your t's were crossed. But, part of being a real developer is jumping in, reading other peoples' code, making out the forest despite all the trees, and working through the complexity of how it all fits together.

Over the rest of this chapter we're going to start to let you do that. Up next we've got an example that is the closet thing to a real web app we've seen so far, and its got lots of pieces, lots of API use and code that handles lots of real details. Now, we can't step you through every single piece, explaining every nuance like we usually do (or this book will be 1200 pages); nor do we want to, because you also need to acquire the skill of putting all the pieces together, *without us*.

Don't worry, we're still here and we're going to tell you what everything does, but we want you to start to learn how to take code, read it, figure it out, and then augment it and alter it to do *what you want it to do*. So, over the next three chapters, we want you to dig into these examples, study them, and get the code in your head. Really... you're ready!

We need your help!

This just in... we just got the contract to build the **Starring You Video** software for their new video booth. What on earth is that? Oh, just the latest HTML5-enabled video messaging booth—a customer enters an enclosed video booth and shoots their own video message. They can then enhance their video using real movie effects; there's an old-time western sepia filter, a black & white film noir filter, and even an otherwordly sci-fi alien filter. Then the customer can send their message to a friend. We went ahead and commited us all to building the video interface and effects processing system for it.

There's a problem though. The video booths won't be available for another six weeks, and when they arrive the code has to be done. So, in the meantime, we're going to get a partly functional demo unit and a few test video files, and we'll write all our code using those. Then when we're done, the Starring You folks can just point the code to the just-captured real video. And of course, remember that all this has to be done using HTML5.

So, we hope you're in, because we signed the contract!

Step in, cut a video, give it a style, and send it to your friends!

Step inside the booth, let's take a look...

Below you'll see our demo unit complete with a user interface. What we've got is a video screen where users will see their video played back. They'll be able to apply a filter like "old-time western" or "sci-fi," see how it looks, and when they're happy, send it off to a friend. We don't have record capability yet, so we've got the test videos to play with. Our first job is going to be to wire everything up so the buttons work, and then write the video filters. Before we get into all that, check out the interface:

Here's the interface of the demo unit. It's got a video player right in the middle for viewing videos.

Apply your favorite effect: old-time western (sepia), film noir (extra dark) or sci-fi (inverted video).

The play, pause, loop and mute controls.

Choose a test video. Our demo unit has two to choose from.

Unpacking the Demo Unit

The demo unit just arrived via next day air and it's time to unpack it. It looks like we've got a functioning unit with some simple HTML markup & JavaScript written so far. Let's have a look at the HTML first (videobooth.html). By the way, sit back; we've got a few pages of factory code to look through, and then we'll get cracking on the *real* code.

HTML5, of course.

And all the styling is done for us! Here's the CSS file.

```html
<!doctype html>
<html lang="en">
<head>
    <title>Starring YOU Video Booth</title>
    <meta charset="utf-8">
    <link rel="stylesheet" href="videobooth.css">
    <script src="videobooth.js"></script>
</head>
<body>
<div id="booth">
    <div id="console">
        <div id="videoDiv">
            <video id="video" width="720" height="480"></video>
        </div>
        <div id="dashboard">
            <div id="effects">
                <a class="effect" id="normal"></a>
                <a class="effect" id="western"></a>
                <a class="effect" id="noir"></a>
                <a class="effect" id="scifi"></a>
            </div>
            <div id="controls">
                <a class="control" id="play"></a>
                <a class="control" id="pause"></a>
                <a class="control" id="loop"></a>
                <a class="control" id="mute"></a>
            </div>
            <div id="videoSelection">
                <a class="videoSelection" id="video1"></a>
                <a class="videoSelection" id="video2"></a>
            </div>
        </div>
    </div>
</div>
</body>
</html>
```

And here's the JavaScript file, we're going to need to write most of this. We'll take an in-depth look, but it looks they've just written the code to control the buttons on the interface so far...

Here's the main interface, we've got the console itself, which looks like it is divided into the video display and a dashboard, with three sets of buttons grouped into "effects", "controls" and "videoSelection".

They've already got a video player installed...good, we're going to need that.

Here are all the effects.

These are all just HTML anchors. We'll see how we tie into these in a sec...

And the player controls.

And the two demo videos to test with.

Inspecting the rest of the factory code

Now let's take a look at all the JavaScript code that shipped from the factory, including the code that sets up the buttons (which we just looked at in the HTML) and the code for each button handler (which, right now, just makes sure the right buttons are depressed). We'll review it all before we start adding our own code.

And now the JavaScript...

So let's crack open the JavaScript (`videobooth.js`). It looks like all the interface buttons work, they just don't do anything interesting, yet. But it's important that we understand how these are set up because the buttons are going to invoke the code we have to write (like, to play a video or to view a video with an effect filter).

Below you'll find the function that is invoked when the page is loaded. For each set of buttons (effects, controls, and the video selection), the code steps through the buttons and assigns click handlers to the anchor links. Let's take a look:

Here's the function that is invoked when the page is fully loaded.

```javascript
window.onload = function() {
    var controlLinks = document.querySelectorAll("a.control");
    for (var i = 0; i < controlLinks.length; i++) {
        controlLinks[i].onclick = handleControl;
    }

    var effectLinks = document.querySelectorAll("a.effect");
    for (var i = 0; i < effectLinks.length; i++) {
        effectLinks[i].onclick = setEffect;
    }

    var videoLinks = document.querySelectorAll("a.videoSelection");
    for (var i = 0; i < videoLinks.length; i++) {
        videoLinks[i].onclick = setVideo;
    }

    pushUnpushButtons("video1", []);
    pushUnpushButtons("normal", []);
}
```

Each for statement loops over the elements of one group of buttons.

The onclick handler for each button in the player controls is set to the handleControl handler.

And the handler for effects is set to setEffect.

And finally the handler for video selection is set to setVideo.

Once we've done all the ground work we use a helper function to visually depress the "video1" button, and the "normal" (no filter) button in the interface.

> You haven't seen `document.querySelectorAll` before; it's similar to `document.getElementsByTagName` except that you're selecting elements that match a CSS selector. The method returns an array of element objects that match the CSS selector argument.
>
> ```javascript
> var elementArray = document.querySelectorAll("selector");
> ```

Looking at the button handlers

OK, so far the JavaScript code takes care of setting up all the buttons so that if they are clicked on, the appropriate handler is called. Next, let's take a look at the actual handlers, starting with the handler for the player buttons (play, pause, loop and mute), to see what they are doing:

The first thing we do in this handler is see who called us by retrieving the id of the element that invoked the handler.

```
function handleControl(e) {
    var id = e.target.getAttribute("id");

    if (id == "play") {
        pushUnpushButtons("play", ["pause"]);

    } else if (id == "pause") {
        pushUnpushButtons("pause", ["play"]);

    } else if (id == "loop") {
        if (isButtonPushed("loop")) {
            pushUnpushButtons("", ["loop"]);
        } else {
            pushUnpushButtons("loop", []);
        }
    } else if (id == "mute") {
        if (isButtonPushed("mute")) {
            pushUnpushButtons("", ["mute"]);
        } else {
            pushUnpushButtons("mute", []);
        }
    }
}
```

Once we know the id, we know if the element was play, pause, loop or mute.

Depending on which button it was, we alter the interface to reflect the button that was pushed. For instance if pause was pushed then play shouldn't be.

We're using a helper function to make sure the onscreen button states are taken care of, it's called pushUnpushButtons, and it takes a pushed button along with an array of unpushed buttons and updates the interface to reflect that state.

Various buttons have different semantics. For instance play and pause are like true radio buttons (pushing one in pops the other one out), while mute and loop are like toggle buttons.

All this code so far is cosmetic, it just changes the look of the buttons from pressed to depressed. There is no code to do anything real, like play a video. That's what we have to write.

Now that's great and all, but where does *our code* come in? Let's think through this: when a button, like play, is pushed, not only are we going to update the interface (which the code already does), we're also going to add some code that actually *does something*, like make the video start playing. Let's go ahead and look at the other two handlers (for setting the video effects and for setting the test video), and it should be pretty obvious (if it isn't already) where our code is going to go...

The setEffect and setVideo handlers

Let's look at the other two handlers. The setEffect handler handles your choice of effect, like no effect (normal), western, film noir or sci-fi. Likewise the setVideo handler handles your choice of test video one or two. Here they are:

This works the same as the handleControl handler: we grab the id of the element that called us (the button that was clicked on) and then update the interface accordingly.

```
function setEffect(e) {
    var id = e.target.getAttribute("id");

    if (id == "normal") {
        pushUnpushButtons("normal", ["western", "noir", "scifi"]);

    } else if (id == "western") {
        pushUnpushButtons("western", ["normal", "noir", "scifi"]);

    } else if (id == "noir") {
        pushUnpushButtons("noir", ["normal", "western", "scifi"]);

    } else if (id == "scifi") {
        pushUnpushButtons("scifi", ["normal", "western", "noir"]);

    }
}
```

And here's where our code is going to go.

We'll be adding code to each case to handle implementing the appropriate special effect filter.

The same is true of setVideo; we see which button was pressed and update the interface.

```
function setVideo(e) {
    var id = e.target.getAttribute("id");
    if (id == "video1") {
        pushUnpushButtons("video1", ["video2"]);
    } else if (id == "video2") {
        pushUnpushButtons("video2", ["video1"]);
    }

}
```

We'll also be adding code here to implement switching between the two test videos.

And here are the helper functions

And for the sake of completeness (or if you're on a 11-hour flight to Fiji without Internet access and you really want to type all this in):

And remember, if you don't want to type it in, you can get all the code from http://wickedlysmart.com/hfhtml5.

pushUnpushButtons takes care of button states. The arguments are the ids of a button to push in, and one or more buttons to unpush in an array.

```
function pushUnpushButtons(idToPush, idArrayToUnpush) {
    if (idToPush != "") {
        var anchor = document.getElementById(idToPush);
        var theClass = anchor.getAttribute("class");
        if (!theClass.indexOf("selected") >= 0) {
            theClass = theClass + " selected";
            anchor.setAttribute("class", theClass);
            var newImage = "url(images/" + idToPush + "pressed.png)";
            anchor.style.backgroundImage = newImage;
        }
    }

    for (var i = 0; i < idArrayToUnpush.length; i++) {
        anchor = document.getElementById(idArrayToUnpush[i]);
        theClass = anchor.getAttribute("class");
        if (theClass.indexOf("selected") >= 0) {
            theClass = theClass.replace("selected", "");
            anchor.setAttribute("class", theClass);
            anchor.style.backgroundImage = "";
        }
    }
}

function isButtonPushed(id) {
    var anchor = document.getElementById(id);
    var theClass = anchor.getAttribute("class");
    return (theClass.indexOf("selected") >= 0);
}
```

First, check to make sure the id of the button to push is not empty.

Grab the anchor element using that id...

... and get the class attribute.

We "press" the button by adding the "selected" class to the anchor, and ...

... update the background image of the anchor element so it covers up that button with a "button pressed" image. So "pause" uses the "pausepressed.png" image.

To unpush buttons, we loop through the array of ids to unpush, grabbing each anchor...

... make sure the button is really pushed (if it is, it will have a "selected" class)...

... remove "selected" from the class...

... and remove the background image so we see the unpushed button.

isButtonPushed simply checks to see if a button is pushed. It takes the id of an anchor...

... grabs the anchor...

... gets the class of that anchor...

... and returns true if the anchor has the "selected" class.

That new demo machine  smell...test drive time!

We haven't done much writing code, but we are reading and understanding code, and that can be just as good. So load the `videobooth.html` file into your browser and check out the buttons. Give them a good testing. For extra credit, add some alerts into the handler functions. Get a good feel for how this is working. When you come back, we'll start writing some code to make the buttons work for real.

Give all those buttons a try, notice some are like radio buttons, some are like toggle buttons.

Sharpen your pencil

You'll find the solution just a couple of pages on...

Mark the buttons below with whether they are like toggle buttons (independent) or like radio buttons (pushing one in pops the other ones out). Also annotate each button with its corresponding click handler. We've done a couple for you:

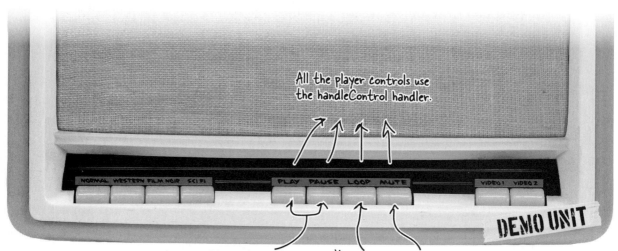

All the player controls use the handleControl handler.

Radio buttons, play and pause can't be selected at the same time.

Loop and Mute are toggle buttons, they can be used independently of any other buttons.

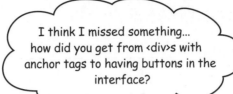

I think I missed something... how did you get from <div>s with anchor tags to having buttons in the interface?

That would be the power of CSS.

It's a shame this book isn't *Head First HTML5 Programming with JavaScript & CSS*, but then it would be 1,400 pages, wouldn't it? Of course, we could be talked into writing an advanced CSS book...

But seriously, this is the power of markup for structure and CSS for presentation (and if that is a new topic to you, check out *Head First HTML with CSS & XHTML*). What we're doing isn't that complex; here it is in a nutshell for the curious:

We set the background image of the console <div> to the booth console (no buttons).

The <video> element is in a <div> which is positioned relative to the console. Then, the <video> element is absolute positioned so it sits in the middle of the console.

We position the dashboard <div> relative to the console and then position the <div>s for each group of buttons relative to the dashboard.

Each button group <div> gets a background image for all the unpushed buttons.

Each "button" anchor is positioned within the <div> for the group, and given a width and height to match the button it corresponds to. When you click on a "button", we give that anchor a background image of a pushed in button to cover up the unpushed button.

Check out the CSS in detail if you want: videobooth.css.

DEMO UNIT

Sharpen your pencil
Solution

Mark the buttons below with whether they are like toggle buttons (independent) or like radio buttons (pushing one in pops the other ones out). Also annotate each button with its corresponding click handler. Here's our solution:

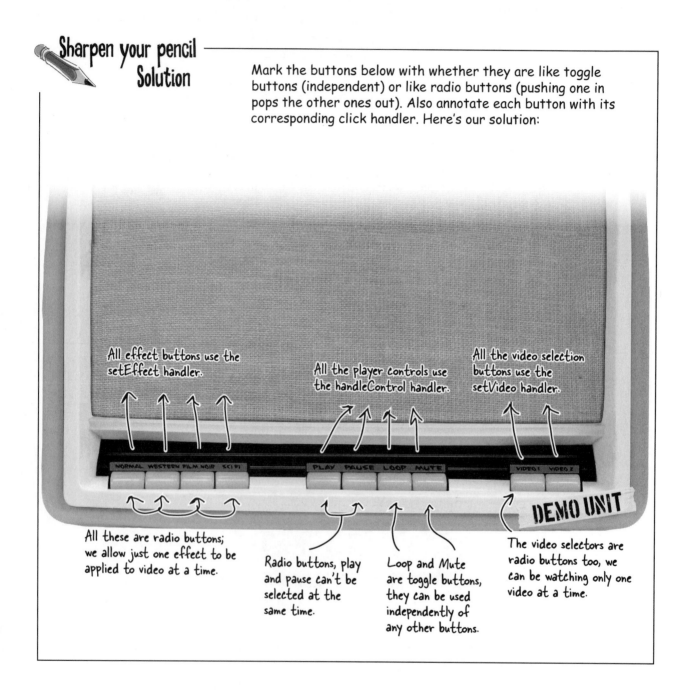

All effect buttons use the setEffect handler.

All the player controls use the handleControl handler.

All the video selection buttons use the setVideo handler.

NORMAL WESTERN FILM NOIR SCI FI   PLAY PAUSE LOOP MUTE   VIDEO 1 VIDEO 2

DEMO UNIT

All these are radio buttons; we allow just one effect to be applied to video at a time.

Radio buttons, play and pause can't be selected at the same time.

Loop and Mute are toggle buttons, they can be used independently of any other buttons.

The video selectors are radio buttons too, we can be watching only one video at a time.

Getting our demo videos ready...

Before we implement the button controls, we need video to test them with, and as you can see from the buttons, Starring You Video has sent us two demo videos. Let's go ahead and create an object to hold the two videos and then add some code for our onload handler to set up the source of the video object (just like we did for Webville TV).

We'll create this object to hold the two demo videos. We'll come back and explain more about this shortly.

```
var videos = {video1: "video/demovideo1", video2: "video/demovideo2"};
```

```
window.onload = function() {

    var video = document.getElementById("video");
    video.src = videos.video1 + getFormatExtension();
    video.load();
```

Here, we're getting the video element, and setting its source to the first video in the array with a playable extension.

Then we go ahead and load the video so if the user clicks play, it's ready to go.

```
    var controlLinks = document.querySelectorAll("a.control");
    for (var i = 0; i < controlLinks.length; i++) {
        controlLinks[i].onclick = handleControl;
    }
    var effectLinks = document.querySelectorAll("a.effect");
    for (var i = 0; i < effectLinks.length; i++) {
        effectLinks[i].onclick = setEffect;
    }
    var videoLinks = document.querySelectorAll("a.videoSelection");
    for (var i = 0; i < videoLinks.length; i++) {
        videoLinks[i].onclick = setVideo;
    }
    pushUnpushButtons("video1", []);
    pushUnpushButtons("normal", []);
}
```

READ THIS CAREFULLY!

Now before we get sloppy, remember the `getFormatExtension` function is in Webville TV, not this code! So open up `webvilletv.js` and copy and paste the function into your video booth code. One other small thing: in the video booth code we aren't keeping a global video object, so add this line to the top of your `getFormatExtension` function to make up for that:

Add this line to your getFormatExtension function at the top.

```
var video = document.getElementById("video");
```

Implementing the video controls

Alright, time to get to those buttons! Now, it's important to point out that for this project, we're going to implement *our own* video controls. That is, rather than use the built-in video controls, we're going to control the experience ourselves—so when the user needs to play, pause or mute the video, or even to loop the playback, they're going to use our custom buttons, not the built-in controls. It also means we're going to do all this *programmatically* through the API. Now, we're not going to go all the way, which would mean implementing our own video scrubber, or perhaps next and previous buttons, because those don't make sense in this application, *but we could if we needed to.* You'll find that just by implementing our small control panel you'll get the idea and be in perfect shape to take it further if you want to.

So, let's get started. How about if we start with the play button and then move to the right (to pause and then to loop and then to mute) from there? So find the handleControl handler and add this code:

Now we're going to implement all these buttons.

```
function handleControl(e) {
    var id = e.target.getAttribute("id");
    var video = document.getElementById("video");

    if (id == "play") {
        pushUnpushButtons("play", ["pause"]);
        if (video.ended) {
            video.load();
        }
        video.play();
    } else if (id == "pause") {
        pushUnpushButtons("pause", ["play"]);

    } else if (id == "loop") {
        if (isButtonPushed("loop")) {
            pushUnpushButtons("", ["loop"]);
        } else {
            pushUnpushButtons("loop", []);
        }
    } else if (id == "mute") {
        if (isButtonPushed("mute")) {
            pushUnpushButtons("", ["mute"]);
        } else {
            pushUnpushButtons("mute", []);
        }
    }
}
```

We need a reference to the video object.

This should be pretty simple. If the user has pressed play, then call the play method on the video object.

But we'll warn you, there's one edge case here about to bite us, so let's go ahead and take care of it: If we've played a video, and let that video play through to the end, then to start it playing again, we have to load it again first. We check to make sure the video ran through to the end (and wasn't just paused), because we only want to load again in that case. If it's paused, we can just play without loading.

Implementing the rest of the video controls

Let's knock out the rest of the controls—they're so straightforward they're almost going to write themselves:

```
function handleControl(e) {
    var id = e.target.getAttribute("id");
    var video = document.getElementById("video");

    if (id == "play") {
        pushUnpushButtons("play", ["pause"]);
        video.load();
        video.play();
    } else if (id == "pause") {
        pushUnpushButtons("pause", ["play"]);
        video.pause();

    } else if (id == "loop") {
        if (isButtonPushed("loop")) {
            pushUnpushButtons("", ["loop"]);
        } else {
            pushUnpushButtons("loop", []);
        }
        video.loop = !video.loop;

    } else if (id == "mute") {
        if (isButtonPushed("mute")) {
            pushUnpushButtons("", ["mute"]);
        } else {
            pushUnpushButtons("mute", []);
        }
        video.muted = !video.muted;

    }
}
```

If the user pauses the video, then use the video object's pause method.

For looping we've got a boolean property named loop in the video object. We just set it appropriately...

...and to do that we'll keep you on your toes by using the boolean "!" (not) operator, which just flips the boolean value for us.

And mute works the same way: we just flip the current value of the mute property when the button is pressed.

Another test drive!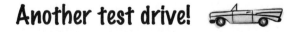

Make sure you've got all the code changes typed in. Load `videobooth.html` into your browser and give your control buttons a test. You should see video start playing, be able to pause it, mute it, or even put it in a loop. Of course, you can't select the other demo video yet or add an effect, but we're getting there!

Taking care of a loose end...

There's a little loose end we need to take care of to really make these buttons work like they should. Here's the use case: let's say you're playing a video and you don't have loop selected, and the video plays to completion and stops. As we have things implemented now, the play button will remain in the pressed position. Wouldn't it be better if it popped back up, ready to be pressed again?

Our play button isn't 100% right yet...

Using events we can easily do this. Let's start by adding a listener for the `ended` event. Add this code to the bottom of your `onload` handler:

```
video.addEventListener("ended", endedHandler, false);
```

Set a handler for the "ended" event, which is called when the video playback ends (but NOT when you pause!).

Now let's write the handler, which will be called any time the video playback stops by coming to the end of the video:

```
function endedHandler() {
    pushUnpushButtons("", ["play"]);
}
```

All we need to do is "unpush" the play button. That's it!

And another...

Okay, make the changes, save the code and reload. Now start a video and let it play to its conclusion without the loop button pressed, and at the end you should see the play button pop back out on its own.

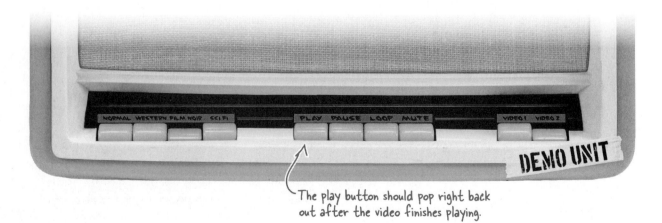

The play button should pop right back out after the video finishes playing.

Switching test videos

We already added an object to hold our two test videos, and we've even got two buttons for selecting between them. Each button is assigned the `setVideo` handler. Let's work through writing that now so we can switch between our videos:

Here's our object with the two videos, we're showing this again as a reminder, so you can see how we're going to use it...

```
var videos = {video1: "video/demovideo1", video2: "video/demovideo2"};

function setVideo(e) {                          ← And here's the handler again.
    var id = e.target.getAttribute("id");
    var video = document.getElementById("video");       ← Again, we need a reference to
                                                          the video object.

    if (id == "video1") {
        pushUnpushButtons("video1", ["video2"]);    ← Then we still update the
    } else if (id == "video2") {                       buttons in the same way we
        pushUnpushButtons("video2", ["video1"]);       were, no changes there.
    }
    video.src = videos[id] + getFormatExtension();   ← Then we use the source id of the
    video.load();                                       button (the id attribute of the
    video.play();                                       anchor) to grab the correct video
                                                        filename, and add on our browser-aware
                                                        extension. Notice we're using the [ ]
    pushUnpushButtons("play", ["pause"]);               notation with our videos object, using
}                                                       the id string as the property name.
```

Once we have the correct video path and filename, we load and play the video.

And we make sure the play button is pushed in because we start the video playing when the user clicks on a new video selection.

Switch drivers and test drive!

Make these changes to your `setVideo` function and then load your page again. You should now be able to easily switch between video sources.

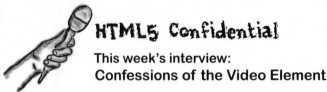

HTML5 Confidential

This week's interview:
Confessions of the Video Element

Head First: Welcome, Video. I'm going to jump right to the topic on everyone's minds, and that would be YOU and the Canvas element.

Video: Meaning?

Head First: Allegedly nights out on the town, early morning breakfasts together. Need I say more?

Video: What is there to say, Canvas and I have a great relationship. She displays her content in a very, let's say, visually appealing manner, and I'm a video workhorse. I crunch through codecs and get that video content to the browser.

Head First: Well, that's not what I was getting at, but I'll go with it. Okay, she's great at 2D display, you're great at video display. So what? What's the real connection?

Video: Like any relationship, when you put two things together and get out more than the sum of the parts, that's when you have something special.

Head First: Okay, well, can you put that in more concrete terms?

Video: It's a simple concept. If you want to do anything other than just basic video playback—that is, if you want to do any processing on your video, or custom overlays or display mulitple videos at once— then you want to use Canvas.

Head First: That all sounds great, but video requires heavy-duty processing, I mean that's a lot of data coming through. How is JavaScript, a scripting language, going to do anything real? Writing JavaScript code isn't like writing in a native language.

Video: Oh you'd be surprised... have you looked at the latest benchmarks on JavaScript? It's already fast, and getting faster every day. The industry's brightest virtual machine jockeys are working the problem and kicking butt.

Head First: Yeah, but video? Really?

Video: Really.

Head First: Can you give us some examples of things you can do with JavaScript, canvas and video?

Video: Sure, you can process video in real time, inspect the video's characteristics, grab data from video frames, and alter the video data by, say... rotating it, scaling it or even changing the pixels.

Head First: Can you walk us through how you might do that in code?

Video: Uh, I'll have to get back to you on that, just got a call from Canvas... gotta run...

It's time for special effects

Isn't it about time we add those movie effects? What we want to do is take our original video and be able to apply effects, like film noir, western, and even an otherworldly sci-fi effect. But if you look at the video API, you won't find any effects methods there, or any way to add them directly. So how are we going to add those effects?

Take a little time to think through how we might add effects to our video. Don't worry that you don't know how to process video yet, just think through the high level design.

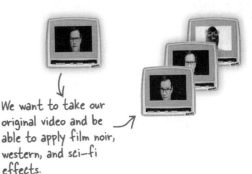

We want to take our original video and be able to apply film noir, western, and sci-fi effects.

Starring You Video
Engineering Notes...

Use this engineering note to draw a picture, label it, or write out pseudo-code for any code for your video effects. Think of this as a warm up, just to get your brain going...

How will you get your hands on the pixels that make up each frame of the video?

Once you've got the pixels, how do you process them to apply the effect?

Say you were to write a function to implement each effect, what would it look like?

How can you display the video once you've processed all its pixels to apply the effect?

Your ideas here.

The FX plan

We don't know exactly how to implement the effects yet, but here's a high level plan of attack:

 1 We know we've still got to hook up those buttons that control the effects. So we're going to do that first.

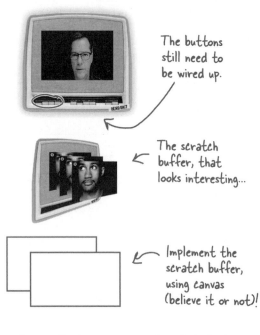

The buttons still need to be wired up.

2 We're going to learn a little about video processing and check out the "scratch buffer" technique for adding our effects.

The scratch buffer, that looks interesting...

3 We're going to implement the scratch buffer, which is going to give us a chance to see video and canvas together in action.

Implement the scratch buffer, using canvas (believe it or not)!

4 We're going to implement one function for each effect: western, film noir, and sci-fi.

```
function noir(pos, r, g, b, data) {
    . . .
}
```

We'll display the altered pixels in a, you guessed it, canvas.

 5 Finally, we're going to put it all together and test!

⚛ BRAIN POWER

Now you know we're going to implement a function that will handle each effect. Let's take film noir, for example. How are you going to take a color pixel from the video and make it black and white? Hint: every pixel has three components: red, green, and blue. If we could get our hands on those pieces, what could we do?

Time to get those effects buttons working

Alright, the easy part first: we're going to get those effects buttons
wired up and working. We'll start by creating a global variable named
`effectFunction`. This variable is going to hold a function that can take
data from the video, and apply a filter to it. That is, depending on which
effect we want, the `effectFunction` variable will hold a function that
knows how to process the video data and make it black and white, or sepia,
or inverted for sci-fi. So add this global variable to the top of your file:

```
var effectFunction = null;
```

Now we're going to set this variable anytime an effects button is clicked on. For
now, we'll use function names like `western`, `noir` and `scifi`, and we'll write
these functions in just a bit.

Here's our setEffect handler again. Remember this is called
whenever the user clicks on a effect button.

For each button
press we set the
effectFunction variable
to the appropriate
function (all of which
we still need to write).

```
function setEffect(e) {
    var id = e.target.getAttribute("id");

    if (id == "normal") {
        pushUnpushButtons("normal", ["western", "noir", "scifi"]);
        effectFunction = null;
    } else if (id == "western") {
        pushUnpushButtons("western", ["normal", "noir", "scifi"]);
        effectFunction = western;
    } else if (id == "noir") {
        pushUnpushButtons("noir", ["normal", "western", "scifi"]);
        effectFunction = noir;
    } else if (id == "scifi") {
        pushUnpushButtons("scifi", ["normal", "western", "noir"]);
        effectFunction = scifi;
    }
}
```

If the effect is no
effect, or normal,
we just use null as
the value.

Otherwise we set
effectFunction to
an appropriately
named function
that will do the
work of applying
the effect.

We still need to write these effects
functions. So, let's see how we process
video so we can apply effects to it!

Okay, with that out of the way, we're going to learn about that "scratch buffer" and
then come back and see how these functions fit in, as well as how to write them!

How video processing works

What we've done so far is given ourselves a way to assign a function to the `effectsFunction` global variable as a result of clicking on the effects buttons in the interface. For now, just take that knowledge and tuck it in the back of your brain for a little while, because we've got to work through how we're actually going to take video and process it in real time to add an effect. To do that we need to get our hands on the video's pixels, alter those pixels to achieve our desired effect, and then somehow get them back on the screen.

Now, does the video API offer some special way to process video before it is displayed? Nope. But it does give us a way to get the pixels, so we just need a way to process and display them. Wait, pixels? Display? Remember Chapter 7? The **canvas**! Ah, that's right, we did mention something about the "special relationship" that the video element and canvas have. So, let's walk through one of the ways the video and canvas elements can work together:

← The details of the scoop, finally revealed!

① The video player decodes and plays the video behind the scenes.

② Video is copied frame by frame into a (hidden) buffer canvas and processed.

Color in the original video.

Processing color to, say, B&W, in a buffer canvas.

Then we copy the processed frame from the buffer to the display canvas.

In a nutshell, we're taking each frame of video and changing it from color to B&W, and then displaying it.

③ After a frame is processed, it is copied to another display canvas to be viewed.

How to process video using a scratch buffer

Now, you might ask why we're using two canvases to process and display the video. Why not just find a way to process the video as it is decoded?

The method we're using here is a proven technique for minimizing visual glitches during intensive video and image processing: it's known as using a "scratch buffer." By processing a frame of video in a buffer and then copying it all in one fell swoop to the display canvas, we minimize visual issues.

Let's step through how our scratch buffer implementation is going to work.

 The browser decodes the video into a series of frames. Each frame is a rectangle of pixels with a snapshot of the video at a given point in time.

One frame of video.

As each frame is decoded we copy it into the canvas that is acting as a scratch buffer.

We copy the whole frame into the canvas.

This is the scratch buffer.

③ We iterate over scratch buffer,
pixel by pixel, passing each pixel to
our effects function for processing.

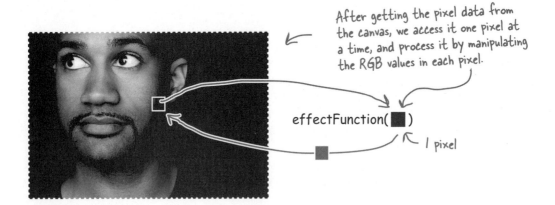

After getting the pixel data from
the canvas, we access it one pixel at
a time, and process it by manipulating
the RGB values in each pixel.

effectFunction(■)

⌐ 1 pixel

④ After all the pixels in the scratch buffer are
processed, we copy them from the scratch
buffer canvas to the display canvas.

Once the data in the scratch
buffer is processed...

... we grab the image from the
scratch buffer canvas and copy the
whole thing to the display canvas.

And of course, this
is the canvas you
actually see!

⑤ And then we repeat the process on every
frame as it is decoded by the video object.

Implementing a scratch buffer with Canvas

As you already know, to implement a scratch buffer in canvas we need two canvases: one to do our computation in, and one to display our results. To create those canvases, we'll start back in our HTML file `videobooth.html`. Open this file and find the `<div>` with the id "`videoDiv`" and add two canvas elements below the `<video>`:

```
<div id="videoDiv">

    <video id="video" width="720" height="480"></video>
    <canvas id="buffer" width="720" height="480"></canvas>
    <canvas id="display" width="720" height="480"></canvas>

</div>
```

We're adding two canvas elements, one for the buffer and one to display.

Notice they're exactly the same size as the video element.

How to position the video and canvases

Now you might be wondering about positioning these elements; we're going to position them right on top of each other. So at the bottom will be the video element, on top of that is the buffer, and on top of that, the display canvas element. We're using CSS to do it, and although we don't talk much about CSS in this book, if you open `videobooth.css` you'll see the positioning for the three elements:

```
div#videoDiv {
    position: relative;
    width: 720px;
    height: 480px;
    top: 180px;
    left: 190px;
}
video {
    background-color: black;
}
div#videoDiv canvas {
    position: absolute;
    top: 0px;
    left: 0px;
}
```

The videoDiv `<div>` is positioned relative to the element it's in (the console `<div>`), at 180px from the top and 190px from the left, which places it in the center of the console. We set the width and height equal to the width and height of the `<video>` and the two `<canvas>` elements.

The `<video>` is the first element in the videoDiv `<div>` so it's automatically positioned at the top left of the `<div>`. We set the background to black so that if we have letter-boxing or pillar-boxing, the space is black.

The two `<canvas>` elements in the videoDiv `<div>` are positioned absolutely with respect to the videoDiv (their parent), so by placing the `<canvas>` elements at 0px from the top, and 0px from the left, they are in exactly the same position as the `<video>` and the videoDiv.

Writing the code to process the video

We've got a video element, a buffer that's a canvas, and a canvas that is going to display the final video frames. And we've also got them stacked on one another so we see only the top display canvas, which will contain the video with the effect applied. To process the video we're going to use the video element's `play` event, which is called as soon as a video begins playing. Add this to the end of the `onload` handler:

```
video.addEventListener("play", processFrame, false);
```

When the video begins playing it will call the function processFrame.

The `processFrame` function is where we'll process the video pixels and get them into the canvas for display. We'll start by making sure we have access to all our DOM objects:

```
function processFrame() {
    var video = document.getElementById("video");
    if (video.paused || video.ended) {
        return;
    }
    var bufferCanvas = document.getElementById("buffer");
    var displayCanvas = document.getElementById("display");
    var buffer = bufferCanvas.getContext("2d");
    var display = displayCanvas.getContext("2d");
}
```

First grab the video object...

... and check to see if the video is still playing. If it isn't then we've got no work to do, just return.

Then grab a reference to both canvas elements and also to their contexts, we're going to need those.

How to create the buffer

To create the buffer, we need to take the current video frame, and copy it to the buffer canvas. Once we have it on the canvas, we can process the data in the frame. So, to create that buffer we do this (add this to the bottom of `processFrame`):

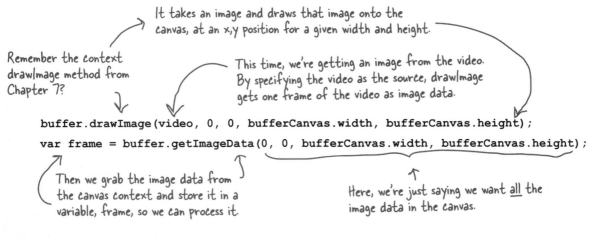

It takes an image and draws that image onto the canvas, at an x,y position for a given width and height.

Remember the context drawImage method from Chapter 7?

This time, we're getting an image from the video. By specifying the video as the source, drawImage gets one frame of the video as image data.

```
buffer.drawImage(video, 0, 0, bufferCanvas.width, bufferCanvas.height);
var frame = buffer.getImageData(0, 0, bufferCanvas.width, bufferCanvas.height);
```

Then we grab the image data from the canvas context and store it in a variable, frame, so we can process it.

Here, we're just saying we want all the image data in the canvas.

How to process the buffer

We've got our hands on a frame of video data, so let's do some processing on it! To process the frame, we're going to loop over every single pixel in the frame data and pull out the RGB color values that are stored in each pixel. Actually, each pixel has 4 values, RGB and Alpha (the opacity), but we're not going to use the Alpha. Once we've got the RGB values, we'll call the `effectFunction` (remember, that's the function we set back on page 392 and asked you to tuck in the back of your brain!) with the RGB information and the frame.

Add this code to the bottom of your `processFrame` function:

```
buffer.drawImage(video, 0, 0, bufferCanvas.width, displayCanvas.height);

var frame = buffer.getImageData(0, 0, bufferCanvas.width, displayCanvas.height);

var length = frame.data.length / 4;


for (var i = 0; i < length; i++) {
    var r = frame.data[i * 4 + 0];
    var g = frame.data[i * 4 + 1];
    var b = frame.data[i * 4 + 2];
    if (effectFunction) {
        effectFunction(i, r, g, b, frame.data);
    }
}
display.putImageData(frame, 0, 0);
```

First, we find out the length of the frame data. Notice that the data is in a property of frame, frame.data, and length is a property of frame.data. The length is actually four times longer than the size of the canvas because each pixel has four values: RGBA.

Now we loop over the data and get the RGB values for each pixel. Each pixel takes up four spaces in the array, so we grab r from the first position, g from the second, and b from the third.

Then, we call the effectFunction (if it's not null, which it will be if the "Normal" button is pressed), passing in the position of the pixel, the RGB values, and the frame.data array. The effect function will update the frame.data array with new pixel values, processed according to the filter function assigned to effectFunction.

At this point the frame data has been processed, so we use the context putImageData method to put the data into the display canvas. This method takes the data in frame and writes it into the canvas at the specified x, y position.

We've processed one frame, what next?

Yes, that's one single frame we just processed, and we want to keep processing them all as the video continues to play. We can use `setTimeout` and pass it a value of zero milliseconds to ask JavaScript to run `processFrame` again as soon as it possibly can. JavaScript won't actually run the function in *zero* milliseconds, but it will give us the next soonest time slot we can get. To do that, just add this to the bottom of your `processFrame` function:

setTimeout is just like setInterval, except that it runs only once after a specified time in milliseconds.

```
setTimeout(processFrame, 0);
```

Tells JavaScript to run processFrame again as soon as possible!

It's interesting you are using setTimeout with a time of zero. What's going on there? Shouldn't we be doing something that's tied to a video's frame rate or something?

We wish we could.

You're absolutely right: what we'd love to do is have our handler called once for every frame, but the video API doesn't give us a way to do that. It does give us an event named `timeupdate` that can be used to update a running time display of your video, but it doesn't tend to update at a granularity that you can use for processing frames (in other words, it runs at a slower rate than the video).

So instead we use `setTimeout`. When you pass zero to `setTimeout`, you're asking JavaScript to run your timeout handler as soon as it possibly can—and this leads to your handler running as frequently as it possibly can.

But might that be faster than the frame rate? Wouldn't it be better to calculate a timeout close to what is needed for the frame rate? Well, you could, but it's unlikely that the handler is going to actually get to run in lockstep with the frames of your video, so zero is a good approximation. Of course, if you are looking to enhance the performance characteristics of your app, you can always do some profiling and figure out what the optimal values are. But until we have a more specific API, that's our story.

Now we need to write some effects

Finally, we've got everything we need to write the video effects: we're grabbing each frame as it comes in, accessing the frame data pixel by pixel and sending the pixels to our effect filter function. Let's look at the *Film Noir* filter (which, in our version, is just a fancy name for black and white):

The filter function is passed the position of the pixel...

... the red, green, and blue pixel values ...

... and a reference to the frame data array in the canvas.

So the first thing we do is compute a brightness value for this pixel based on all its components (r, b and g).

```javascript
function noir(pos, r, g, b, data) {
    var brightness = (3*r + 4*g + b) >>> 3;
    if (brightness < 0) brightness = 0;
    data[pos * 4 + 0] = brightness;
    data[pos * 4 + 1] = brightness;
    data[pos * 4 + 2] = brightness;
}
```

>>> is a bitwise operator that shifts the bits in the number value over to modify the number. Explore further in a JavaScript reference book.

And then we assign each component in the canvas image to that brightness.

Remember this function is called once per pixel in the video frame!

This has the affect of setting the pixel to a grey scale value that corresponds to the pixel's overall brightness.

A film noir test drive

Add this function to `videobooth.js` and then reload your page. As soon as the video starts rolling press the Film Noir button and you'll see a brooding black & white film look. Now choose Normal again. Not bad, eh? And all in JavaScript, in real time!

Kind of amazing when you think about it.

Sharpen your pencil

This book isn't really about video processing and effects, but it sure is fun. Below we've got the western and sci-fi effects. Look through the code and make notes on the right as to how each works. Oh, and we added an extra one—what does it do?

```
function western(pos, r, g, b, data) {
    var brightness = (3*r + 4*g + b) >>> 3;
    data[pos * 4 + 0] = brightness+40;
    data[pos * 4 + 1] = brightness+20;
    data[pos * 4 + 2] = brightness-20;
}


function scifi(pos, r, g, b, data) {
    var offset =  pos * 4;
    data[offset]   = Math.round(255 - r) ;
    data[offset+1] = Math.round(255 - g) ;
    data[offset+2] = Math.round(255 - b) ;
}


function bwcartoon(pos, r, g, b, outputData) {
    var offset =  pos * 4;
    if( outputData[offset] < 120 ) {
        outputData[offset] = 80;
        outputData[++offset] = 80;
        outputData[++offset] = 80;
    } else {
        outputData[offset] = 255;
        outputData[++offset] = 255;
        outputData[++offset] = 255;
    }
    outputData[++offset] = 255;
    ++offset;
}
```

The Big Test Drive

This is it! We have this code wrapped up and ready to ship off to
Starring You Video. Go ahead and double check that you've
got all the code typed in, save, and load `videobooth.html`.
Then have fun playing around with your new app!

Sci-fi mode

Western mode

Film Noir mode

Normal mode

IN THE LABORATORY

Obviously we've only scratched the surface in terms of video processing, and we're sure you can think of more creative effects than those we came up with. Go ahead and think up a few, implement them, and document them here.

Have you invented something really cool and implemented it? Tell us about it at wickedlysmart.com and we'll feature it for other readers!

_____

_____

_____

_____

Your ideas here!

B&W Cartoon is just one of many other fun things you can do with effects.

Hey I know its almost the end of the chapter, but I keep meaning to ask this: we've been loading video from a local file, what changes if my video is hosted on the Web?

Sure, just use a web URL.

You can substitute a web URL for any of the sources we been defining locally. For instance:

```
<video src="http://wickedlysmart.com/myvideo.mp4">
```

Keep in mind there is more room for bad things to happen when you are delivering on the Web (and we'll talk about how to handle those things in a moment). Also, the bitrate of your videos starts to matter a lot more when delivering to a browser or a mobile device over the network. Like with video formats, if you're going down this road, seek out experts and educate yourself.

Great, and one more question, is there a difference between what we're doing and streaming video?

Yes, a big difference.

The term streaming often gets used like the term xerox or kleenex—as a generic term for getting video from the Web to your browser. But "progressive video" and "streaming video" are actually technical terms. In this book we've been using progressive video, which means when we retrieve the video (either locally or over the network) we're retrieving a file using HTTP, just like an HTML file or an image, and we try to decode and play it back as we retrieve it. Streaming video is delivered using a protocol that is highly tuned to delivering video in an optimal way (perhaps even altering the bitrate of the video over time as bandwidth becomes more or less available).

Streaming video probably sounds like it would provide your user with a better experience (it does), and is perhaps more efficient in terms of your user's connection and your bandwidth charges (it is). On top of all that, streaming video makes it easier to do things like protect the content of your video if you need that kind of security.

So, is there a standard for HTML5 streaming?

No.

There is no standard for streaming video with HTML5. As a matter of fact the problem isn't HTML5, there isn't really a supported standard for streaming video anywhere—but there are plenty of proprietary ones. Why? There are a number of reasons ranging from the money to be made with streaming video to the fact that many people in open source don't want to work on a protocol that could be used for DRM or other protection technologies. Like the situation with video formats, we're in a complex world with streaming video.

So what do I do if I need to stream?

There are solutions out there.

There are lots of legitimate uses for streaming video technologies, and if you have a large audience, or you have content you think needs to be protected, you should check them out: Apple's HTTP Live Streaming, Microsoft's Smooth Streaming and Adobe's HTTP Dynamic Streaming are good places to start.

There's good news on the horizon too: the standards bodies are starting to look closely at HTTP-based video streaming, so keep an eye out for developments in this area.

If only it were a perfect world...

But it's not: we have all those nasty network issues, incompatible devices and operating systems, and an increasing chance of asteroids hitting the earth. That last one we can't help with, but for the first two actually knowing you have an error is half the battle, then you can at least do something about it.

The video object has an error event, which can be thrown for a number of reasons that can be found in the `video.error` property, or more specifically in the `video.error.code` property. Let's take a look at what kinds of errors we can detect:

Errors

MEDIA_ERR_ABORTED=1

Used any time the process of getting the video over the network is aborted by the browser (possibly at a user's request).

MEDIA_ERR_NETWORK=2

Used whenever a network retrieval of the video is interrupted by a network error.

MEDIA_ERR_DECODE=3

Used whenever the decoding of a video fails. This could happen because the encoding uses features the browser can't support or because the file is corrupt.

MEDIA_ERR_SRC_NOT_SUPPORTED=4

Used when the specified video source cannot be supported because of a bad URL or because the source type isn't decodable by the browser.

Each error type also has an associated number that is the error code produced by the error event, we'll see this in just a sec...

How to use error events

Dealing with errors is complex business and how you deal with errors depends a lot on your application, and what would be appropriate for the app and your users. That said, we can at least get you started and point you in the right direction. Let's take Webville TV and give it the ability to know it has encountered an error—and if it does encounter one, give the audience a PLEASE STAND BY message.

We want to be notified when there's an error message, so we need to add a listener for the error event. Here's how we do that (add this to the onload handler in `webville.js`):

```
video.addEventListener("error", errorHandler, false);
```

When an error occurs, the errorHandler function is called.

Now we need to write the function `errorHandler`, which will check if there is an error, and if so, place our "please stand by" image on the video display by making it the poster image:

If the handler is called, we make sure there is an error by checking video.error and then we place a poster up on the video display.

```
function errorHandler() {
    var video = document.getElementById("video");
    if (video.error) {
        video.poster = "images/technicaldifficulties.jpg";
        alert(video.error.code);
    }
}
```

Optionally add this line to be able to see the error code (see the previous page for the integer stored in the code property).

Test Crash!

There are many ways for the playback of the video to fail, and to test this code you're going to make it fail. Here are a few suggestions:

- Disconnect your network at different points in playback.
- Give the player a bad URL.
- Give the player a video you know it can't decode.
- Give the player a URL that isn't even a video.
- Use software to reduce your bandwidth (it's out there, just look for it).

So get this code typed in and get testing. Remember you can map the integer in the alert dialog back to a real code by looking at the codes on page 407.

Where can you go from here?

This is where it gets exciting, because think of all you know how to do with HTML markup, with the video element and, of course, the canvas...not to mention web services, geolocation... wow. Sure, we did some cool video processing with canvas, but you can apply everything you know how to do with canvas to video. Here are just a few ideas we had, please add your own. And give yourself a pat on the back from us, you've earned it!

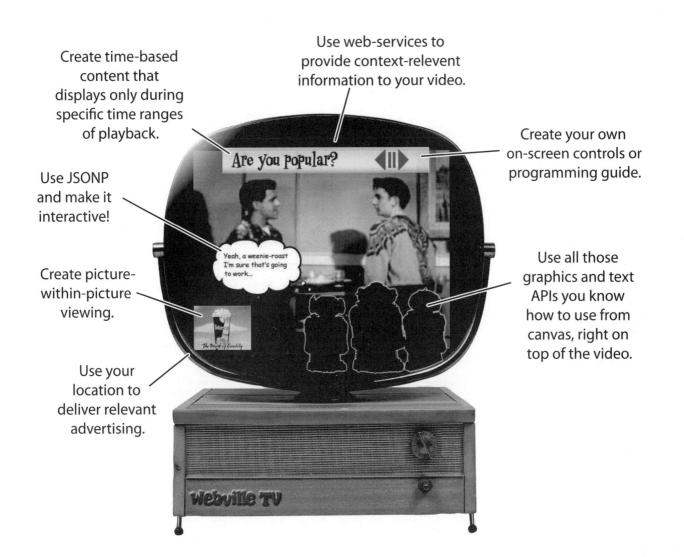

Create time-based content that displays only during specific time ranges of playback.

Use web-services to provide context-relevent information to your video.

Create your own on-screen controls or programming guide.

Use JSONP and make it interactive!

Create picture-within-picture viewing.

Use all those graphics and text APIs you know how to use from canvas, right on top of the video.

Use your location to deliver relevant advertising.

BULLET POINTS

- You can play video by using the <video> element with a few simple attributes.

- The autoplay attribute starts playback on page load, but use only when appropriate.

- The controls attribute causes the browser to expose a set of playback controls.

- The look and feel of controls differs among browsers.

- You can supply your own poster image with the poster attribute.

- The src attribute holds a URL to the video to be played.

- There are many "standards" for video and audio formats.

- Three formats are in common usage, WebM, MP4/H.264 and Ogg/Theora.

- Know your audience to know what formats you need to supply.

- Use the <source> tag to specify alternative video formats.

- Use fully specified types in your <source> tag to save the browser work and time.

- You can continue to support other video frameworks, like Flash, by adding a fallback <object> tag in the video element.

- The video object provides a rich set of properties, methods and events.

- Video supports play, pause, load, loop and mute methods and properties to directly control the playback of the video.

- The ended event can be used to know when video playback has ended (for instance, to implement a playlist).

- You can programmatically ask the video object if it can play a format with canPlayType.

- The canPlayType method returns empty string (no support for format), maybe (if it might be able to play the format) or probably (if it confidently thinks it can play the format).

- Canvas can be used as a display surface for video to implement custom controls or other effects with video.

- You can use a scratch buffer to process video before copying it to the display.

- You can use a setTimeout handler to process video frames; while it isn't linked directly to every frame of the video, it is the best method we have right now.

- You can use a URL as a video source to play network-based videos.

- Some browsers enforce a same origin policy on video so that you need to serve the video from the same origin as your source page.

- Errors are always possible, if not probable, with video, especily when a network is involved.

- The error event can be used to notify a handler when video retrieval, decoding or playback errors occur.

- The video element relies on progressively downloaded video. Currently there is no HTML5 standard for streaming, although the standards bodies are looking at HTTP-based streaming solutions.

- There is currently no standard way of protecting video delivered through the video element.

HTML5cross

Before you sit back and watch some more Webville TV, do a quick crossword to make it all stick. Here's your Chapter 8 crossword puzzle.

Across

2. Type of delivery the video element uses for video.
4. To provide several video options, use _____ source elements.
5. Kind of buffer we used canvas for.
7. Property to play your video over and over.
8. Starts a video as soon as it can.
11. The open source audio codec.
12. Used to display processed video.
13. When the show is over, this event is thrown.
14. I can play this type, can you?
15. Look and feel of browser controls _____.

Down

1. Use _____ if you want a built-in way to control video.
3. We saw '50s _____ films.
5. What you should do if an asteroid is going to hit the earth.
6. The Starbuzz CEO spills his _____.
9. What we processed on every setTimeout call.
10. Clint Eastwood would like this effects style.

Sharpen your pencil Solution

This book isn't really about video processing and effects, but it sure is fun. Below we've got the western and sci-fi effects. Look through the code and make notes on the right as to how each works. Oh, and we added an extra one—what does it do? Here's our solution.

```javascript
function western(pos, r, g, b, data) {
    var brightness = (3*r + 4*g + b) >>> 3;
    data[pos * 4 + 0] = brightness+40;
    data[pos * 4 + 1] = brightness+20;
    data[pos * 4 + 2] = brightness-20;
}
```

The Western filter emphasizes the red and green components of the pixel while de-emphasizing the blue component, to give the video a brownish tinge.

```javascript
function scifi(pos, r, g, b, data) {
    var offset =  pos * 4;
    data[offset] = Math.round(255 - r) ;
    data[offset+1] = Math.round(255 - g) ;
    data[offset+2] = Math.round(255 - b) ;
}
```

The scifi filter reverses the amounts of RGB components of each pixel. So if a pixel had a lot of red, it now has a little. If a pixel had a little green, it now has a lot.

```javascript
function bwcartoon(pos, r, g, b, outputData) {
    var offset =  pos * 4;
    if( outputData[offset] < 120 ) {
        outputData[offset] = 80;
        outputData[++offset] = 80;
        outputData[++offset] = 80;
    } else {
        outputData[offset] = 255;
        outputData[++offset] = 255;
        outputData[++offset] = 255;
    }
    outputData[++offset] = 255;
    ++offset;
}
```

The bwcartoon filter turns every pixel with a red component of less than 120 (out of 255) into black, and turns all other pixels into white, giving the video a weird cartoony-like B&W appearance.

VIDEO RECONNAISSANCE SOLUTION — TOP SECRET

iOS and Android devices (among others)

Video \ Browser	Safari	Chrome	Firefox	Mobile Webkit	Opera	IE9+	IE8	IE7 or <
H.264	✓	some		✓		✓		
WebM		✓	✓		✓			
Ogg Theora		✓	✓		✓			

Watch it! This will change fast! So check the latest support on the Web.

CASE FILE: VIDEO

HTML5cross Solution

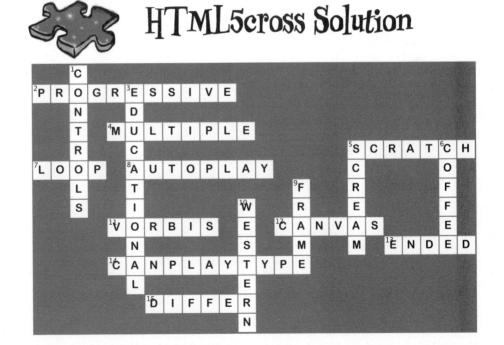

9 storing things locally

Web Storage

> I'm done with this small closet and wearing the same pantsuit over and over. With HTML5 I've got enough local storage to wear a new suit every day!

Tired of stuffing your client data into that tiny ~~closet~~ cookie? That was fun in the '90s, but we've got much bigger needs today with web apps. What if we said we could get you five megabytes on every user's browser? You'd probably look at us like we were trying to sell you a bridge in Brooklyn. Well, there's no need to be skeptical—the HTML5 Web Storage API does just that! In this chapter we're going to take you through everything you need to store any object locally on your user's device and to make use of it in your web experience.

How browser storage works (1995 - 2010)

Building a shopping cart? Need to store some user preferences for your site? Or just need to stash some data that you need to be associated with each user? That's where browser storage comes in. Browser storage gives us a way to persistently store data that we can use in building a web experience.

Up until now there's been one game in town—the browser cookie—for storing information on the browser. Let's see how cookies work:

Behind the Scenes

1 When your browser retrieves a web page, say from "pets-R-us.com," the server can send a cookie along with its response. Cookies contain one or more key and value pairs:

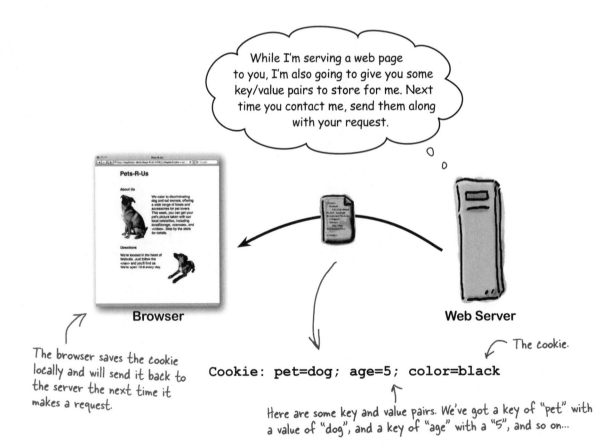

> While I'm serving a web page to you, I'm also going to give you some key/value pairs to store for me. Next time you contact me, send them along with your request.

Browser

Web Server

The browser saves the cookie locally and will send it back to the server the next time it makes a request.

The cookie.

`Cookie: pet=dog; age=5; color=black`

Here are some key and value pairs. We've got a key of "pet" with a value of "dog", and a key of "age" with a "5", and so on...

2 The next time the browser makes a request to "pets-R-us.com," it sends along any cookies that were sent previously:

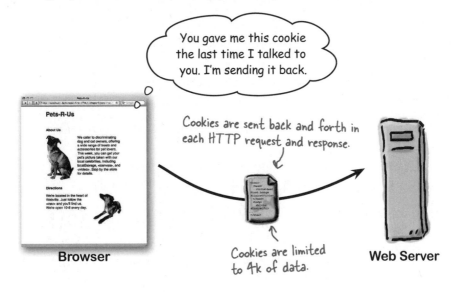

> You gave me this cookie the last time I talked to you. I'm sending it back.

Cookies are sent back and forth in each HTTP request and response.

Browser

Cookies are limited to 4k of data.

Web Server

---

3 The server can then use the cookie to personalize the experience, in this case promoting relevant items to the user, but there are many other ways cookies can be used too.

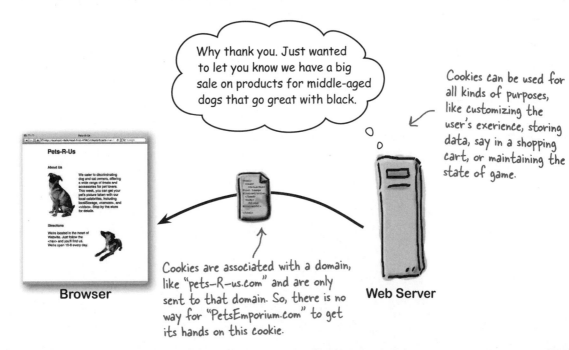

> Why thank you. Just wanted to let you know we have a big sale on products for middle-aged dogs that go great with black.

Cookies can be used for all kinds of purposes, like customizing the user's exerience, storing data, say in a shopping cart, or maintaining the state of game.

Browser

Cookies are associated with a domain, like "pets-R-us.com" and are only sent to that domain. So, there is no way for "PetsEmporium.com" to get its hands on this cookie.

Web Server

✹BRAIN POWER

Cookies have been with us a long time, but you might be able to think of some ways they could be improved on.

Check all the items below that you think make cookies problematic:

☐ There's only 4k to work with, my app needs more storage than that.

☐ Sending the cookie back and forth every time seems really inefficient, especially if I'm on a mobile device with not a lot of bandwidth.

☐ They sound like a good way to transmit viruses and other malware to my browser.

☐ I've heard the way the key/value pairs are done as part of the HTTP request is a pain to deal with in code.

☐ Aren't we potentially sending personal data back and forth every time we make a request?

☐ They don't seem well matched to all the client-side development we've been doing. They seem to assume everything in happening in the server.

For the record, and despite news reports to the contrary, cookies are quite safe and not a haven for virus writers.

I'm hoping that HTML5 provides a simple, client-side API to storage that is persistent, stored on the browser, offers more storage capacity, and is transmitted to a server only if I want it to be.

How HTML5 Web Storage works

HTML5 gives us a nice, simple JavaScript API in the browser for storing key/value pairs that are persistent. You're not limited to four stingy kilobytes of storage either; all browsers today will gladly offer you five to ten megabytes of storage in every user's browser. HTML5's local storage was also created with web apps (and mobile apps!) in mind—local storage means your app can store data in the browser to reduce the communication needed with the server. Let's check out how it works (and then we'll jump head first into the API):

Behind the Scenes

1 A page can store one or more key/value pairs in the browser's local storage.

2 And then later use a key to retrieve its corresponding value.

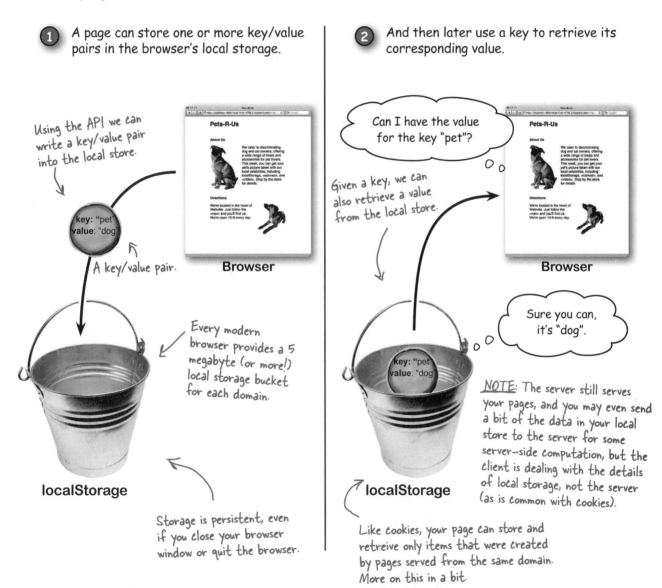

Using the API we can write a key/value pair into the local store.

key: "pet" value: "dog"

A key/value pair.

Browser

Every modern browser provides a 5 megabyte (or more!) local storage bucket for each domain.

localStorage

Storage is persistent, even if you close your browser window or quit the browser.

Can I have the value for the key "pet"?

Given a key, we can also retrieve a value from the local store.

Browser

Sure you can, it's "dog".

key: "pet" value: "dog"

NOTE: The server still serves your pages, and you may even send a bit of the data in your local store to the server for some server-side computation, but the client is dealing with the details of local storage, not the server (as is common with cookies).

localStorage

Like cookies, your page can store and retreive only items that were created by pages served from the same domain. More on this in a bit.

Note to self...

Need a system for getting things done? It's hard to improve on the old Post-it note system (more commonly known as *stickies*). You know how it works: you jot down your "to do" item, stick it somewhere, and once you've done the task, you throw the sticky in the trash (or recycle it).

How about we build one using HTML? Let's see, we need a way to store all those stickies, so we're going to need a server, and some cookies... oh, wait a second, back up the bus, we can do this with the HTML5 Web Storage API!

The Web Storage API is simple, fun and instantly gratifying. We promise!

Pick up dry cleaning

High-tech productivity tool.

No fooling around, we're going to jump right in and start using the local store. To do that you should create a simple html page with all the basics: a head, a body, and a script (or just use the starter file `notetoself.html` in the code examples). Follow along by typing the code into your <script> element (typing it in helps it stick):

1 There's not much more to a sticky than the text you write on it, right? So, let's start by storing a sticky for "Pick up dry cleaning":

We're starting simple, but before you know it, we'll have a whole Stickies app up and running.

The Web Storage API is available to you through the localStorage object. You'll find this already defined for you by the browser. When you use it you're making use of the underlying local storage system.

The setItem method takes two strings as arguments that act as the key/value pair.

You can only store items of type String. You can't directly store numbers or objects (but we'll find a way to overcome this limitation soon).

```
localStorage.setItem("sticky_0", "Pick up dry cleaning");
```

To store something, we use the setItem method.

The first string argument is a key that the item is stored under. Name it whatever you want as long as it is a string.

The second string is the value you'd like to store in local storage.

2 That was easy enough; let's add a second item to the local store:

```
localStorage.setItem("sticky_1", "Cancel cable tv, who needs it now?");
```

Another key. Like we said already, you can use any key you like as long as it is a string, but you can only store one value per key.

A value to go with our new key.

3 Now that we have two values stored safely in our browser's local storage, you can now use one of the keys to retrieve its corresponding value from localStorage. Like this:

We're getting the value associated with the key "sticky_0" from the local store...

...and assigning it to the variable named sticky.

```
var sticky = localStorage.getItem("sticky_0");
```

```
alert(sticky);
```
And to make this a little more interesting, let's use the alert function to pop the sticky note's value up on the screen.

Time for a test drive!

Make sure you've got all this code into your script element and load it into your browser.

Here's the result of our test drive:

There's our JavaScript alert, with the value of sticky_0 as the alert message.

What's cool about this is that this value was stored in and retrieved from the browser's localStorage! You could quit your browser, go on vacation to Fiji for a month, come back, and it will still be there waiting on you.

Okay, okay, we agree the example could have been a little more exciting, but work with us here, we're getting there...

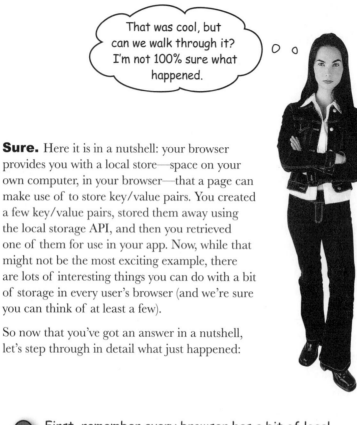

That was cool, but can we walk through it? I'm not 100% sure what happened.

Sure. Here it is in a nutshell: your browser provides you with a local store—space on your own computer, in your browser—that a page can make use of to store key/value pairs. You created a few key/value pairs, stored them away using the local storage API, and then you retrieved one of them for use in your app. Now, while that might not be the most exciting example, there are lots of interesting things you can do with a bit of storage in every user's browser (and we're sure you can think of at least a few).

So now that you've got an answer in a nutshell, let's step through in detail what just happened:

1 First, remember every browser has a bit of local storage that you can use to store key/value pairs.

Every modern browser has local storage behind the scenes ready for you to use to store key/value pairs.

localStorage

Browser

2 With that local storage you can take a key and a value (both in the form of strings) and you can store them.

```
localStorage.setItem("sticky_0", "Pick up dry cleaning");
```

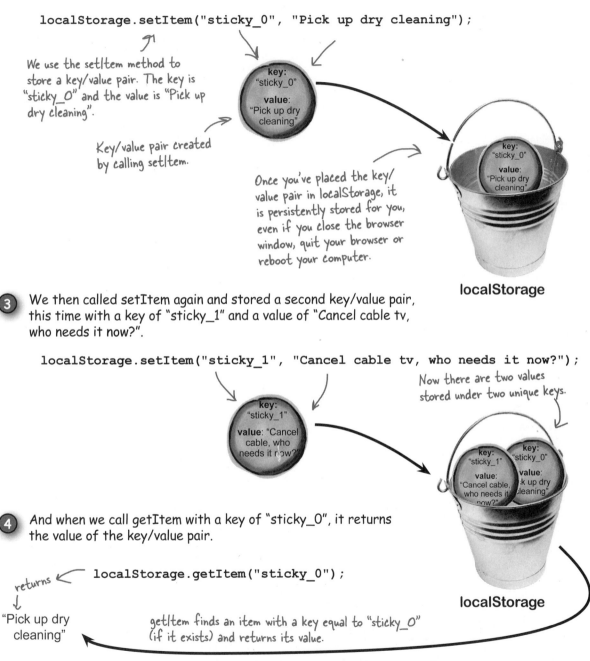

We use the setItem method to store a key/value pair. The key is "sticky_0" and the value is "Pick up dry cleaning".

key: "sticky_0"

value: "Pick up dry cleaning"

Key/value pair created by calling setItem.

Once you've placed the key/value pair in localStorage, it is persistently stored for you, even if you close the browser window, quit your browser or reboot your computer.

key: "sticky_0"

value: "Pick up dry cleaning"

localStorage

3 We then called setItem again and stored a second key/value pair, this time with a key of "sticky_1" and a value of "Cancel cable tv, who needs it now?".

```
localStorage.setItem("sticky_1", "Cancel cable tv, who needs it now?");
```

Now there are two values stored under two unique keys.

key: "sticky_1"

value: "Cancel cable, who needs it now?"

key: "sticky_1"

value: "Cancel cable, who needs it now?"

key: "sticky_0"

value: "Pick up dry cleaning"

4 And when we call getItem with a key of "sticky_0", it returns the value of the key/value pair.

```
localStorage.getItem("sticky_0");
```

returns

"Pick up dry cleaning"

getItem finds an item with a key equal to "sticky_0" (if it exists) and returns its value.

localStorage

Note that by getting an item we don't remove it from the store, it's still there. We're just getting the value for the given key.

<h1 style="text-align:center">there are no
Dumb Questions</h1>

Q: First you said "Web Storage" and then you started talking about "local storage." Are they the same?

A: The Web standard is named "Web Storage" but most people just call it local storage (in fact, the browsers even expose the API through the localStorage object). Web Storage is actually not the best name for the standard (because items are stored in your browser, rather than on the Web). But that said, we're stuck with it. You'll see us use the term local storage more than the standard name of "Web Storage."

Q: How widely supported is the Web Storage API? Can I count on it being there?

A: Yes; in fact it is one of the better supported APIs, even all the way back to IE8 and is now in most modern mobile browsers. There are a few caveats here and there, but we'll point them out as we go. In terms of counting on Web Storage, as always you should test before using APIs. Here's how you test for localStorage:

```
if (window["localStorage"]) {
    // your localStorage code here...
}
```

Notice that we test by checking to see if the window global object has the localStorage property. If it's there, we know the browser supports localStorage.

Q: At the very beginning of the chapter you mentioned 5MB of storage on each browser. Is that five megabytes total across all apps?

A: No, that is actually five megabytes per domain.

Q: You said the server didn't need to be involved, but then you started talking about domains.

A: Right, all the storage is managed in the client. The domain comes in because five megabytes is allocated to all the pages from the same domain for storage. Pet-R-Us.com gets five, PetEmporium.com gets five more, and so on, all on your machines.

Q: How does this compare to Google Gears [or insert your favorite proprietary local storage technology here]?

A: There's nothing wrong with other browser storage technology, but HTML5's local storage is now the standard (and Google, Apple, Microsoft and others now recognize Web Storage as the standard way to store content locally in the browser).

Q: What happens if I perform a `setItem` on the same key multiple times. Say I called setItem twice on `"sticky_1"`, what happens? Do I get two `sticky_1`'s in the local store?

A: No. Keys are unique in localStorage, so setItem will overwrite the first value with the second value. Here's an example; if you ran this code:

```
localStorage.setItem("sticky_1", "Get Milk");
localStorage.setItem("sticky_1", "Get Almond Milk");
var sticky = localStorage.getItem("sticky_1");
```

The value of sticky would be "Get Almond Milk".

Q: Who can see the data in my local store?

A: Local storage is managed according to the origin (you can just think of the origin as your domain) of the data. So, for instance, every page on wickedlysmart.com can see the items stored by other pages on that site, but code from other sites, say, google.com, can't access that storage (they can access only their own local storage items).

Q: When I'm loading a page from my computer, like we are in these exercises, what is my origin?

A: Good question. In that case your origin is known as the "Local Files" origin, which is great to use for testing. If you have access to server you could test your files there too, and then you'll be in your domain's origin.

Watch it!

Local Storage may not work properly in all browsers if you're using file://.

This is another case where some browsers require that you serve pages using localhost:// or a hosted server, rather than loading from a file. So if your stickies aren't working, try running from a server or try a different browser.

So, I can store strings in localStorage, but what if I want to store a number? I was thinking I might use localStorage to store integer item counts and floating point prices for a shopping cart app I want to write, is this the wrong technology?

Joel

You've got the right technology.

It's true, with `localStorage` you can only use strings as keys and values. But, that's not as restricting as it sounds. Let's say you need to store the integer 5. You can store the string "5" instead, and then convert it back to an integer when you retrieve it from the local store. Let's take a look at how you'd do this for integers and floats.

Say you want to store an integer with the key "numitems". You'd write:

```
localStorage.setItem("numitems", 1);
```

What? Didn't we just say we couldn't store integers?

Okay, it might look like you're storing an integer here, but JavaScript knows this needs to be a string, so it coerces the integer value into a string for you. What `setItem` actually sees is the string "1", not an integer. JavaScript isn't as smart when you retrieve a value with `getItem`:

```
var numItems = localStorage.getItem("numitems");
```

In this code, `numItems` is assigned the string "1", not an integer as we'd like. To make sure `numItems` is a number, you need to use the JavaScript function `parseInt` to convert a string to an integer:

We wrap the value in a parseInt call, which converts the string to an integer.

```
var numItems = parseInt(localStorage.getItem("numitems"));
numItems = numItems + 1;
localStorage.setItem("numitems", numItems);
```

We can add 1 to it because it's a number.

Then we store it again, with JavaScript taking care of the conversion again.

If you're storing floating point values, you'll want to use the `parseFloat` function when you get the price items from localStorage instead:

Same thing here, we store a float value which is coerced into a string.

```
localStorage.setItem("price", 9.99);
var price = parseFloat(localStorage.getItem("price"));
```

And we convert it back to a float with parseFloat.

Were Local Storage and the Array separated at birth?

Local storage has another side you haven't seen yet. Not only does `localStorage` provide the getter and setter methods (that is, `getItem` and `setItem`), it also allows you to treat the localStorage object as an associative array. What does that mean? Well instead of using the `setItem` method, you can assign a key to a value in the store like this:

```
localStorage["sticky_0"] = "Pick up dry cleaning";
```

Here, the key looks like an index for the storage array.

And here's our value sitting over here on the righthand side of an assignment statement.

We can also retrieve the value stored in a key this way too. Here's the syntax:

```
var sticky = localStorage["sticky_0"];
```

This works exactly like using the call to the getItem method.

Here we assign our variable sticky to...

...the value of the key "sticky_0" in the local store.

Not bad, huh? So, use either syntax, they are both valid. But if you are used to using associative arrays in JavaScript, this syntax may be more concise and readable for you.

But wait, there's more!

The localStorage API also provides two other interesting things: a property, `length`, and a method, `key`. The `length` property holds the number of items in the local store. You'll see what the `key` method does below:

Here we're iterating over each item.

The length property tells us how many items are in localStorage.

Big picture: we're using the length to iterate over the contents of localStorage (just like an array), and accessing each key (like "sticky_0") as we go. We can then use that key to extract its corresponding value.

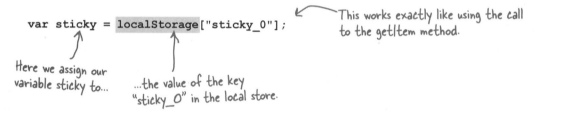

```
for (var i = 0; i < localStorage.length; i++) {
    var key = localStorage.key(i);
    var value = localStorage[key];
    alert(value);
}
```

For each item in the localStorage, the key method gives us the key (like "sticky_0", "sticky_1" and so on).

Go ahead give it a try...do you get an alert for each item?

Then with the key name we can retrieve the value.

there are no
Dumb Questions

Q: When I iterate through localStorage using localStorage.length and localStorage.key, what order are the items in? The same as the order I wrote them into the store?

A: Actually the order of the items isn't defined. What does that mean? It means you'll see every key/value in the store by iterating, but you shouldn't count on any specific order in your code. In fact, different browers may give you different ordering for the same code and items.

── The Shell Game ──

Ready to try your luck? Or should we say skill? We've got a game for you to test your command of localStorage, but you'll need to be on your toes. Use your knowledge of getting and setting key/value pairs in localStorage to keep track of the pea as it shifts from shell to shell.

Feel free to use this space to keep track of the state of localStorage.

```javascript
function shellGame() {
    localStorage.setItem("shell1", "pea");
    localStorage.setItem("shell2", "empty");
    localStorage.setItem("shell3", "empty");
    localStorage["shell1"] = "empty";
    localStorage["shell2"] = "pea";
    localStorage["shell3"] = "empty";
    var value = localStorage.getItem("shell2");
    localStorage.setItem("shell1", value);
    value = localStorage.getItem("shell3");
    localStorage["shell2"] = value;
    var key = "shell2";
    localStorage[key] = "pea";
    key = "shell1";
    localStorage[key] = "empty";
    key = "shell3";
    localStorage[key] = "empty";

    for (var i = 0; i < localStorage.length; i++) {
        var key = localStorage.key(i);
        var value = localStorage.getItem(key);
        alert(key + ": " + value);
    }
}
```

You can type it in to check your answer and see which shell the pea is in.

Which shell has the pea? Write your answer here:

Key	Value
shell1	
shell2	
shell3	

Fireside Chats

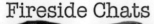

Tonight's talk: **Cookie and Local Storage**

Tonight we have the incumbent browser storage technology, the "Cookie" along with the new front runner, Local Storage.

Cookie:

There he is, the golden boy, Local Storage. I've been in this business for over a decade and you think you can come along like you know something. A little wet behind the ears, aren't you?

Do you have any idea how many pages I'm used on? Ever looked at your stats?

Hey, I'm ubiquitous, pervasive, everywhere! I don't think there is a browser on a desktop, device or mobile browser no matter how old, where you won't find me.

We'll see. Just what exactly do you think you offer over me? My storage works just fine.

I have no idea what you're talking about.

Local Storage:

Sure, you could look at it that way, or, you could say I was built from all the experience gained from your mistakes.

Give it a few years and take another look. The reality is I'm helping to enable a whole new generation of web applications in the browser. A lot of those pages you mention, are *just* pages.

I'm catching up fast. Of all the HTML5 technologies, I'm one of the best supported.

Well, I'm not sure I want to mention this in public, but you do have a size issue.

Hey, you started all this, not me. You know very well that you are limited to 4K of storage, I have over 1,200 times that!

Cookie:

Yeah, I'm light, nimble, we might even say agile.

Come on, I'm an open book, just pure storage to put whatever you want in.

Oh, and key/value pairs are some great innovation?

<Snicker> Oh yeah, and you store everything as a string! Nice work! </Snicker>

Yeah yeah, call me in ten years, we'll see if you've stood the test of time.

You'll see, you'll be calling me crying when they say "Haha, 5 megabytes, is that all you got?"

Local Storage:

Ha, that's rich. Have you ever talked to a web developer? You're anything but agile. Given you are Mr. Statistics, do you have the stats on the number of developer hours lost to stupid mistakes and misconceptions using cookies?

What you really mean is you essentially have no data format at all, so developers have to reinvent a new scheme for storing data in cookies.

We don't need great innovation on storage; key/value pairs work great, are straightforward and fit many computing applications.

You can get a lot of mileage out of strings, and if you need something more complex there are ways.

Oh you can bet on it. Face it, you were doomed from the start. I mean come on, who names their kid Cookie?

Getting serious about stickies

Now that you've had a little time to play with Web Storage, let's take this implementation further. We're going to create a Sticky Notes application so you can see your stickies and add new ones. Let's take a peek at what we're going to build before we build it.

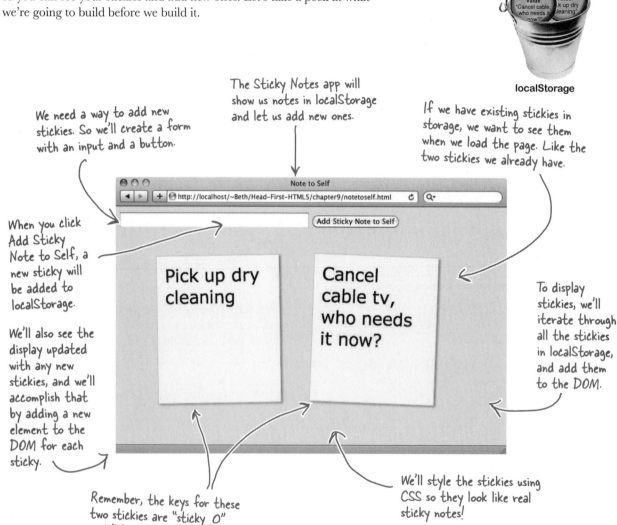

localStorage

The Sticky Notes app will show us notes in localStorage and let us add new ones.

We need a way to add new stickies. So we'll create a form with an input and a button.

If we have existing stickies in storage, we want to see them when we load the page. Like the two stickies we already have.

When you click Add Sticky Note to Self, a new sticky will be added to localStorage.

We'll also see the display updated with any new stickies, and we'll accomplish that by adding a new element to the DOM for each sticky.

To display stickies, we'll iterate through all the stickies in localStorage, and add them to the DOM.

We'll style the stickies using CSS so they look like real sticky notes!

Remember, the keys for these two stickies are "sticky_0" and "sticky_1". We're going to keep following our convention and create keys for stickies with incrementing integers, like sticky_2, sticky_3, and so on.

Creating the interface

To start, we need a way to enter the text of our sticky notes. And it would be great if we could see them in the page, so we need an element to hold all the notes in the page.

Let's work on some code to do that, starting with the HTML markup—take your existing HTML file and add a `<form>` element, the `<ul>` element and the CSS link to it, like below:

Here's our main HTML file.

```
<!doctype html>

<html>

<head>

<title>Note to Self</title>

<meta charset="utf-8">

<link rel="stylesheet" href="notetoself.css">

<script src="notetoself.js"></script>

</head>

<body>

    <form>

        <input type="text" id="note_text">

        <input type="button" id="add_button" value="Add Sticky Note to Self">

    </form>


    <ul id="stickies">

    </ul>

</body>

</html>
```

We've thrown in a little CSS to make things look a little more like real stickies. This book isn't about CSS, but feel free to check out the source!

We're going to move all our JavaScript to the file "notetoself.js".

We've added a form as a user interface to enter new stickies.

And we've got to have somewhere to place our stickies in the interface, so we're going to put them in a unordered list.

The CSS handles making each list item look a little more like a Post-it note.

Seriously!

Now let's add the JavaScript

We've got everything we need in the page now, and we've got a couple sticky notes in localStorage waiting to be displayed. Let's get them on the page by first reading them from localStorage and then placing them inside the unordered list element we just created. Here's how we do that:

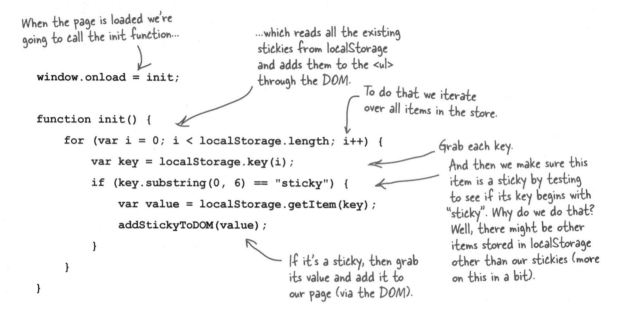

When the page is loaded we're going to call the init function...

...which reads all the existing stickies from localStorage and adds them to the <ul> through the DOM.

```
window.onload = init;

function init() {
    for (var i = 0; i < localStorage.length; i++) {
        var key = localStorage.key(i);
        if (key.substring(0, 6) == "sticky") {
            var value = localStorage.getItem(key);
            addStickyToDOM(value);
        }
    }
}
```

To do that we iterate over all items in the store.

Grab each key.

And then we make sure this item is a sticky by testing to see if its key begins with "sticky". Why do we do that? Well, there might be other items stored in localStorage other than our stickies (more on this in a bit).

If it's a sticky, then grab its value and add it to our page (via the DOM).

So now we need to write the addStickyToDOM function, which is going to insert the notes into the <ul> element:

```
function addStickyToDOM(value) {
    var stickies = document.getElementById("stickies");
    var sticky = document.createElement("li");
    var span = document.createElement("span");
    span.setAttribute("class", "sticky");
    span.innerHTML = value;
    sticky.appendChild(span);
    stickies.appendChild(sticky);
}
```

We're being passed the text of the sticky note. We need to create a list item for the unordered list and then insert it.

So, let's get the "stickies" list element.

Create a list element, and give it a class name of "sticky" (so we can style it).

Set the content of the span holding the text of the sticky note.

And add the span to the "sticky" li, and the li to the "stickies" list.

Time for another test drive!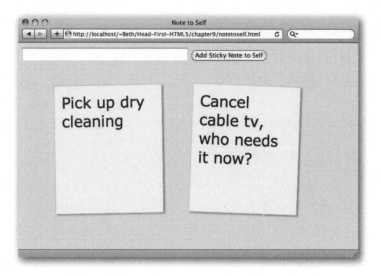

Go ahead and get this code into your script element and load it into your browser.

Here's what we got when we loaded the page in our browser:

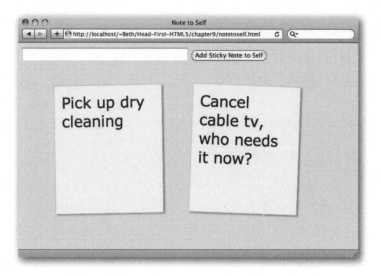

Completing the user interface

Now all we need to do is enable the form so we have a way to add new notes. To do that we need to add a handler for when the "Add Sticky Note to Self" button is clicked, and also write some code to create a new sticky. Here's our code to add a handler:

Add this new code to your init function:

```
function init() {
    var button = document.getElementById("add_button");
    button.onclick = createSticky;

    // for loop goes here
}
```

Let's grab a reference to the "Add Sticky Note to Self" button.

And add a handler for when it is clicked. Let's call the handler createSticky.

The rest of the code in init stays the same, we're saving a few trees by not repeating it here.

And the code to create a new sticky note:

When the button is clicked,
this handler is invoked.

It first retrieves the text in
the form text box.

```
function createSticky() {
    var value = document.getElementById("note_text").value;
    var key = "sticky_" + localStorage.length;
    localStorage.setItem(key, value);

    addStickyToDOM(value);
}
```

Then we need to create a unique key
for the sticky. Let's use "sticky_"
concatenated with the length of the
entire store; it will keep increasing, right?

Then we add a new sticky to
localStorage using our key.

And finally, we add the
new text to the DOM to
represent the sticky.

Yet another test drive!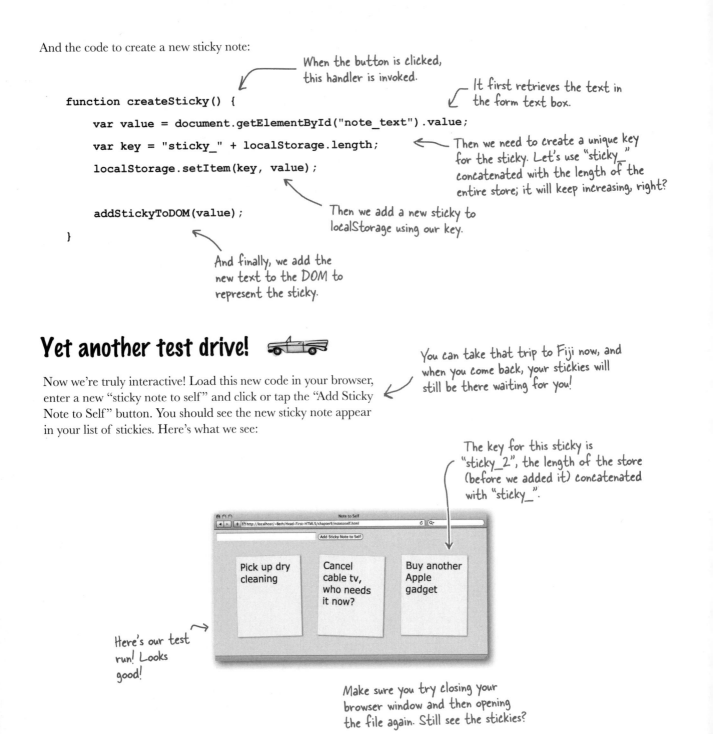

Now we're truly interactive! Load this new code in your browser, enter a new "sticky note to self" and click or tap the "Add Sticky Note to Self" button. You should see the new sticky note appear in your list of stickies. Here's what we see:

You can take that trip to Fiji now, and
when you come back, your stickies will
still be there waiting for you!

The key for this sticky is
"sticky_2", the length of the store
(before we added it) concatenated
with "sticky_".

Here's our test
run! Looks
good!

Make sure you try closing your
browser window and then opening
the file again. Still see the stickies?

there are no
Dumb Questions

Q: Why do we test to see if each item's key begins with the string "sticky"?

A: Remember that all the pages from one domain (like apple.com) can see every item stored from other pages in that domain. That means if we aren't careful about naming our keys, we could clash with another page that is using the same keys in a different way. So, this is our way of checking to make sure an item is a sticky (as opposed to say an order number or a game level) before we use its value for a sticky note to self.

Q: What if there are lots of items in localStorage, including lots of items that aren't stickies? Wouldn't it be inefficient to iterate through the entire set of items?

A: Well, unless you are talking about a very large number of items we doubt you'd notice a difference. That said, you're right, it isn't efficient and there may be better ways to approach managing our keys (we'll talk about some of them shortly).

Q: I'm wondering about using localStorage.length as the sticky number in the key. As in

```
"sticky_" + localStorage.length
```

Why did we do that?

A: We need some way to create new keys that are unique. We could use something like the time or generate an integer that we increase each time. Or, as we did, we can use the length of the store (which increases each time we add an item). If you are thinking this might be problematic, we'll come back to that. And if you hadn't thought about it being problematic, no worries, we'll still come back to it.

Q: I created a bunch of stickies in Safari and then switched to Chrome, and I don't see any of my stickies in Chrome. Why not?

A: Each browser maintains its own local storage. So if you create stickies in Safari, you will only see them in Safari.

Q: I just reloaded my page and now my stickies are in a different order!

A: When you add a new sticky note, we add the new sticky note item by appending it to the notes list, so it always goes at the end of the list. When you reload the page, the notes are added in the order they're found in localStorage (which, remember, isn't guaranteed to be in any particular order). You might think that the order would be the same order that the items were added to the store, or some other reasonable ordering, however, you can't count on that. Why? Well one reason is the spec doesn't specify an ordering, so different browsers may implement this in different ways. If your browser does appear to return items in an order that makes sense to you, consider yourself lucky, but don't count on that ordering because your user's browser may order your items another way.

Q: I often use the "for in" form of the for loop. Will that work here?

A: Sure will. It looks like this:

This will iterate through each key in localStorage. Very handy.

```
for (var key in localStorage) {
    var value = localStorage[key];
}
```

Q: What if I don't want a sticky any more? Can I delete stickies?

A: Yes, we can delete items from localStorage using localStorage.removeItem method. You can also remove items from localStorage directly using the browser console. We're going to show you both in this chapter.

 **BRAIN POWER**

Given the way stickies are implemented, there would be a problem with our naming scheme if a user could delete a sticky at will. Can you think of what the problem is?

We need to stop for a little scheduled service

Wouldn't it be great if there were a tool to directly view the items in your localStorage? Or a tool to delete items or even clear the whole thing out and start over when you are debugging?

Well, all the major browsers ship with built-in developer tools that allow you to directly examine your local store. As you might expect, these tools differ between browsers, so rather than covering them all here, we're going to point you in the right direction, and then you can dig in and figure out the specifics of your own browser. As an example though, let's see what Safari offers:

Today's Special, Flush your browser's localStorage

Not to mention new versions of the browsers are popping up faster than we can write pages!

We've clicked on the Resources tab to inspect localStorage.

Developer tools as they appear in the Safari browser.

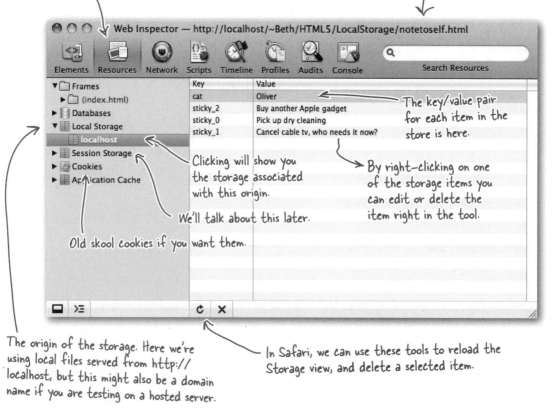

The key/value pair for each item in the store is here.

Clicking will show you the storage associated with this origin.

We'll talk about this later.

Old skool cookies if you want them.

By right-clicking on one of the storage items you can edit or delete the item right in the tool.

The origin of the storage. Here we're using local files served from http://localhost, but this might also be a domain name if you are testing on a hosted server.

In Safari, we can use these tools to reload the Storage view, and delete a selected item.

To enable or access the developer tools, as we said, you'll need to do different things for different browsers. Point your browser to http://wickedlysmart.com/hfhtml5/devtools.html to see how to do this on your specific browser.

Do-It-Yourself maintenance

There's another way to clear out your items (and as we we'll see in a bit, to
delete them one by one), which requires doing a little maintenance on your
own, right from JavaScript. The localStorage API includes a handy method,
`clear`, that deletes all items from your local store (at least, the ones from your
domain). Let's take a look at how we can use this call in JavaScript by creating
a new file named `maintenance.html`. Once you've done that, add the code
below, and we'll step through how it works.

This is a good tool
for your toolbox.

```
<!doctype html>
<html>
<head>
<title>Maintenance</title>
<meta charset="utf-8">
<script>
window.onload = function() {
    var clearButton = document.getElementById("clear_button");
    clearButton.onclick = clearStorage;
}

function clearStorage() {
    localStorage.clear();
}
</script>
</head>
<body>
    <form>
        <input type="button" id="clear_button" value="Clear storage" />
    </form>
</body>
</html>
```

We've added one button to
the page, and this code adds
a click handler for the button.

When you click the button, the
clearStorage function is called.

All this function does is call the
localStorage.clear method. Use with caution
as it will delete <u>all</u> the items associated
with the origin of this maintenance page!

And here's our button. Use this file
whenever you need to erase everything
in localStorage (good for testing).

Watch it!

This deletes all items in your domain!

If you've got a super valuable local store related to another project in the same domain, you'll lose all your items by running this code. Just sayin'...

After you've typed in the code, go ahead and load it in your browser.
It's safe (with regards to our Sticky Notes app) to go ahead and clear
your localStorage now, so give it a try! Make sure you've figured out
your developer tools first so you can observe the changes.

I've got an issue. While I've been doing the exercises in the book, I've also been using my knowledge to create our company's new shopping cart. My Sticky Notes app stopped working. When I look at localStorage with the Safari dev tools, I see that my sticky counts are all messed up, I have "sticky_0", "sticky_1", "sticky_4", "sticky_8", "sticky_15", "sticky_16", "sticky_23", "sticky_42".

I have a feeling this is happening because I'm creating other items in localStorage at the same time as the stickies. What the heck is going on?!

Ah, you've discovered a major design flaw.

Alright, it's time to come clean: we've built a great little app so far, and it should work perfectly for years to come *as long as you don't introduce any other items* into the localStorage (like Joel did with his shopping cart). Once you do that, our whole scheme of tracking stickies no longer works, or, at least, no longer works well. Here's why:

If you're willing to live with that, cool; otherwise you better keep reading.

First of all, our sticky notes are numbered from zero to the number of stickies (minus one):

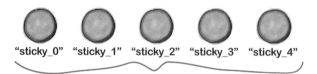

"sticky_0" "sticky_1" "sticky_2" "sticky_3" "sticky_4"

Five notes, labeled from zero to four.

To add a new sticky, we count the number of items in the local store and create our new key from that number:

```
var key = "sticky_" + localStorage.length;
```

"sticky_5"

And to display all the stickies, we iterate from zero to the length of the local store (minus one):

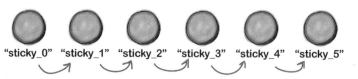

"sticky_0" "sticky_1" "sticky_2" "sticky_3" "sticky_4" "sticky_5"

Length is now six, so iterate zero to five, displaying each note from "sticky_0" to "sticky_5".

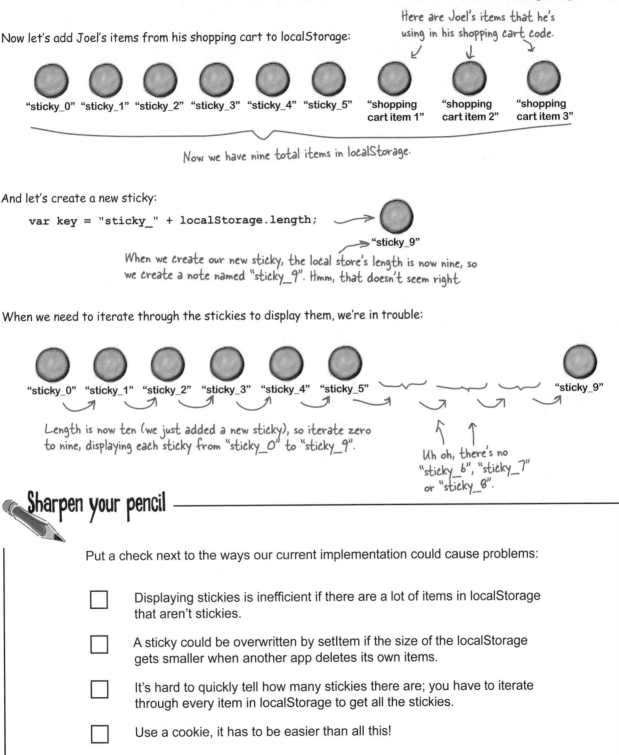

Now let's add Joel's items from his shopping cart to localStorage:

Here are Joel's items that he's using in his shopping cart code.

"sticky_0" "sticky_1" "sticky_2" "sticky_3" "sticky_4" "sticky_5"   "shopping cart item 1"   "shopping cart item 2"   "shopping cart item 3"

Now we have nine total items in localStorage.

And let's create a new sticky:

```
var key = "sticky_" + localStorage.length;
```

"sticky_9"

When we create our new sticky, the local store's length is now nine, so we create a note named "sticky_9". Hmm, that doesn't seem right.

When we need to iterate through the stickies to display them, we're in trouble:

"sticky_0" "sticky_1" "sticky_2" "sticky_3" "sticky_4" "sticky_5"   "sticky_9"

Length is now ten (we just added a new sticky), so iterate zero to nine, displaying each sticky from "sticky_0" to "sticky_9".

Uh oh, there's no "sticky_6", "sticky_7" or "sticky_8".

Sharpen your pencil

Put a check next to the ways our current implementation could cause problems:

☐ Displaying stickies is inefficient if there are a lot of items in localStorage that aren't stickies.

☐ A sticky could be overwritten by setItem if the size of the localStorage gets smaller when another app deletes its own items.

☐ It's hard to quickly tell how many stickies there are; you have to iterate through every item in localStorage to get all the stickies.

☐ Use a cookie, it has to be easier than all this!

If only I could store an array in localStorage. We could use it to hold all the keys of the stickies and we could also always easily know the number of stickies we're storing. But we all know localStorage stores only strings, so even though an array would be dreamy, I know it's just a fantasy...

We have the technology...

We haven't been lying, it is true that you can store only strings as the values of localStorage items, however that isn't the whole truth because we can always convert an array (or an object) into a string before we store it. Sure, it seems like cheating, but it's a totally legit way to store your non-String data types in localStorage.

We know you're dying to jump into the nitty-gritty of how to store arrays, but before we do, let's first step through how an array would actually solve our (and Joel's) problems.

Let's rewind and say we've got six stickies in localStorage:

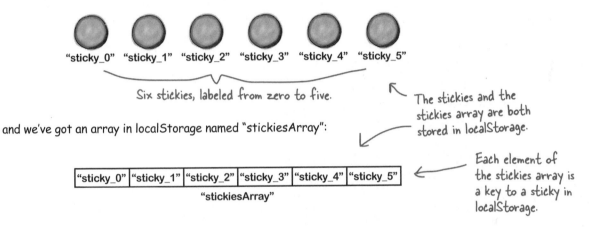

"sticky_0"   "sticky_1"   "sticky_2"   "sticky_3"   "sticky_4"   "sticky_5"

Six stickies, labeled from zero to five.

↖ The stickies and the stickies array are both stored in localStorage.

and we've got an array in localStorage named "stickiesArray":

"sticky_0"	"sticky_1"	"sticky_2"	"sticky_3"	"sticky_4"	"sticky_5"

"stickiesArray"

← Each element of the stickies array is a key to a sticky in localStorage.

Now let's add a new sticky. Let's call the sticky "sticky_815". Why such a crazy number? Because we're not going to care what it is called anymore as long as it is unique. So, to add the sticky, we just add "sticky_815" to the array and then store an item for the sticky, just like we have been. Like this:

We've got an extra sticky in localStorage.

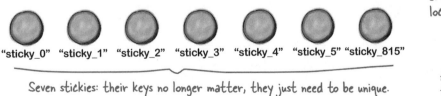

"sticky_0"   "sticky_1"   "sticky_2"   "sticky_3"   "sticky_4"   "sticky_5" "sticky_815"

Seven stickies: their keys no longer matter, they just need to be unique.

"sticky_0"	"sticky_1"	"sticky_2"	"sticky_3"	"sticky_4"	"sticky_5"	"sticky_815"

"stickiesArray"

And we've extended the stickies array by one value.

Reworking our app to use an array

Okay, we know roughly how we're going to keep track of our stickies using an array, but let's take this a little further and make sure we can iterate through and display all the stickies. In the current code we display all the stickies in the `init` function. Can we rewrite that using an array? We'll look at the existing code first, and then see how it changes (hopefully for the better) with an array. Don't type in this code yet; we're focusing on the changes we need to make for now and not making this code bulletproof. We'll bring on the bulletproof stuff in just a bit.

Before...

```
function init() {

    // button code here...

    for (var i = 0; i < localStorage.length; i++) {
        var key = localStorage.key(i);
        if (key.substr(0, 6) == "sticky") {
            var value = localStorage.getItem(key);
            addStickyToDOM(value);
        }
    }
}
```

Here's our old code that relies on the stickies having specific names, sticky_0, sticky_1, and so on..

Wow, this was messy, come to think of it.

As we now know, this might break because we can't depend on all stickies to be there if we're naming them based on the count of the items in localStorage.

New and improved

```
function init() {

    // button code here...

    var stickiesArray = localStorage["stickiesArray"];
    if (!stickiesArray) {
        stickiesArray = [];
        localStorage.setItem("stickiesArray", stickiesArray);
    }


    for (var i = 0; i < stickiesArray.length; i++) {
        var key = stickiesArray[i];
        var value = localStorage[key];
        addStickyToDOM(value);
    }
}
```

We're starting by grabbing the stickiesArray out of localStorage.

We need to make sure there is an array in localStorage. If there isn't one, then let's create an empty one.

We're iterating here through the array.

Each element of the array is the key of a sticky, so we're using that to retrieve the corresponding item from localStorage.

And then we add that value to the DOM just like we have been.

NOTE: you still don't know how to store and retrieve arrays in localStorage, so treat this as pseudo-code until we show you. We'll have to make a very small addition for this to work.

Exercise

We still need to figure out how to actually store an array in localStorage.

You might have already guessed that we can use JSON to create a string representation of an array and if so, you're right. And once you have that you can store it in localStorage.

Recall that there are only two methods in the JSON API: stringify and parse. Let's put these methods to work by finishing the init function (check the solution at the end of the chapter before moving on):

```
function init() {
    // button code here...
    var stickiesArray = localStorage["stickiesArray"];
    if (!stickiesArray) {
        stickiesArray = [];
        localStorage.setItem("stickiesArray", _____(stickiesArray));
    } else {
        stickiesArray = _____(stickiesArray);
    }
    for (var i = 0; i < stickiesArray.length; i++) {
        var key = stickiesArray[i];
        var value = localStorage[key];
        addStickyToDOM(value);
    }
}
```

We added this else clause because you'll need to do something if you get the array from localStorage (because it's a string not an array).

Converting createSticky to use an array

We've almost got this app covered. All we need to do is to rework the `createSticky` method, which, as you'll remember, just gets the text for the sticky from the form, stores it locally, and then displays it. Let's look at the curent implementation before changing it:

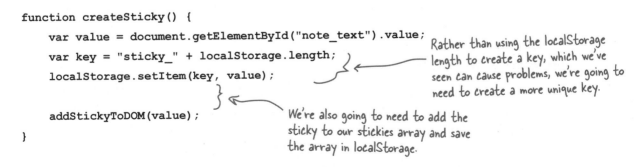

```
function createSticky() {
    var value = document.getElementById("note_text").value;
    var key = "sticky_" + localStorage.length;
    localStorage.setItem(key, value);

    addStickyToDOM(value);
}
```

Rather than using the localStorage length to create a key, which we've seen can cause problems, we're going to need to create a more unique key.

We're also going to need to add the sticky to our stickies array and save the array in localStorage.

What needs to change?

We have two things that need to change in `createSticky`.
First, we need a new way to generate a key for each sticky that
is unique. We also need to alter the code so that it stores the
sticky in the `stickiesArray` in localStorage.

 We need to create a unique key for the sticky

There are lots of ways to create unique keys. We could use the
date and time, or create fancy random 64-bit numbers, or hook
our app up to an atomic-clock API. Hmm, the date and time
sounds like a nice, easy way to do this. JavaScript supports a
date object that returns the number of milliseconds since 1970;
that should be unique enough (unless you're going to create
your stickies at a *really fast* rate):

*Create a Date object, then get
the current time in milliseconds.*

```
var currentDate = new Date();
var time = currentDate.getTime();
var key = "sticky_" + time;
```

*Our new
code to
create a
unique key.*

*And then create the key by
appending the milliseconds to
the string "sticky_".*

② **We need to store the new sticky in the array**

Now that we have a way to create a unique key, we need to
store the text of the sticky with that key, and add the key to the
`stickiesArray`. Let's work through how to do that, and then
we'll put all this code together.

Let's first grab the stickies array.

```
var stickiesArray = getStickiesArray();
localStorage.setItem(key, value);
stickiesArray.push(key);
localStorage.setItem("stickiesArray",
          JSON.stringify(stickiesArray));
```

*And store the array back in
localStorage, stringifying it first.*

*Rather than repeat all that code to get
and check the stickiesArray, just like we did
in init (on the previous page), we're going to
create a new function to do it. We'll get to
this in just a sec.*

*We then store the key with its value like
we always did (only with our new key).*

*We then use the array method
push, which appends the key onto
the end of the stickies array.*

---

there are no
Dumb Questions

Q: What are milliseconds since 1970?

A: You might already know a millisecond
is a 1000th of a second, and the `getTime`
method returns a count of milliseconds that
have occurred since 1970. Why 1970? That
behavior is inherited from the Unix operating
system, which defined time that way. While
it isn't perfect (for instance, it represents
times before 1970 with negative numbers), it
does come in handy when you need a unique
number or to track time in JavaScript code.

Q: Isn't all this parsing and stringifying
of JSON types rather inefficient? And if my
array gets really large isn't that also going
to be inefficient to store?

A: Theorectially yes on both counts. But
for typical web page programming tasks it
usually isn't an issue. That said, if you're
implementing a serious application with very
large storage requirements, you could see
issues using JSON to convert items to and
from strings.

Excellent, once I've got this working I'm going to rework my shopping cart the same way and these two apps are going to be able to work from the same origin without any problems. I also love using an array; it makes everything much simpler to keep track of!

Putting it all together

It's time to integrate all this new array-based code, including the `init` and `createSticky` functions. To do that we're first going to abstract a small bit of code that's needed in both functions—it's the code that retrieves the stickies array from localStorage. You've seen it in `init`, and we need it again in `createSticky`. Let's take that code and put it in a method called `getStickiesArray`—it should look familar to you given the code we've already walked through:

First we get the item "stickiesArray" out of localStorage.

```
function getStickiesArray() {

    var stickiesArray = localStorage.getItem("stickiesArray");

    if (!stickiesArray) {

        stickiesArray = [];

        localStorage.setItem("stickiesArray", JSON.stringify(stickiesArray));

    } else {

        stickiesArray = JSON.parse(stickiesArray);

    }

    return stickiesArray;

}
```

If this is the first time we've loaded this app, there might not be a "stickiesArray" item.

And if there isn't an array yet we create an empty array, and then store it back in localStorage.

Don't forget to stringify it first!

Otherwise, we found the array in localStorage, and we need to parse it to convert it to a JavaScript array.

In either case, we end up with an array, and we return it.

Putting it all together continued...

With `getStickiesArray` written, let's look at the simplified, final versions of the `init` and `createSticky` functions. Go ahead and type these in:

```
function init() {

    var button = document.getElementById("add_button");

    button.onclick = createSticky;


    var stickiesArray = getStickiesArray();


    for (var i = 0; i < stickiesArray.length; i++) {

        var key = stickiesArray[i];

        var value = localStorage[key];

        addStickyToDOM(value);

    }

}
```

Remember we also set up the button events here in the init method.

Next we grab the array with the stickies' keys in it.

Now we're going to iterate through the stickies array (not the localStorage items!).

Each item in the array is a key to a sticky. Let's grab each one.

And grab its value from localStorage.

And add it to the DOM just like we've been doing.

With `init` finished, we just have `createSticky` left:

```
function createSticky() {

    var stickiesArray = getStickiesArray();

    var currentDate = new Date();

    var key = "sticky_" + currentDate.getTime();

    var value = document.getElementById("note_text").value;

    localStorage.setItem(key, value);

    stickiesArray.push(key);

    localStorage.setItem("stickiesArray", JSON.stringify(stickiesArray));

    addStickyToDOM(value);

}
```

We start by grabbing the stickies array.

Then let's create that unique key for our new sticky.

We add sticky key/value to localStorage.

And add the new key to the stickies array...

And then we stringify the array and write back to localStorage.

Finally, we update the page with the new sticky by adding the sticky to the DOM.

Test Drive!

Get all this code in and clear out your localStorage to make a nice clean start. Load this code, and you should see exactly the same behavior as last time. Joel, you'll see your code working correctly now!

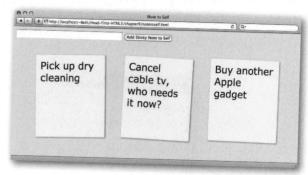

there are no Dumb Questions

Q: We're using "sticky_" as the prefix for our localStorage item names. Is there a convention for localStorage naming schemes?

A: There is no convention for naming localStorage items. If your web app is on a small site at a domain that you have control over, then naming shouldn't be an issue since you'll be aware of all the names being used by all the different pages at the site. We think it's probably a good idea to use a name that indicates the page or web app relying on that item. So "sticky_" helps us remember that those items are related to the Sticky Notes app.

Q: So if my sticky notes app is just one of many apps at a domain, I have to worry about potential conflicts right?

A: Yes. In that case, it would be a good idea for you (or someone who manages the web sites at the domain) to put together a plan for how to name items.

Q: If I have a lot of stickies, my stickiesArray is going to get very long. Is that a problem?

A: Unless you create thousands of stickies, it shouldn't be (and if you do create thousands of stickies, we want to know how you are so productive!). JavaScript is pretty fast these days.

Q: So just to be clear, we can store any object in localStorage, just by stringifying it first with JSON?

A: Right. JSON strings are simplified versions of JavaScript objects, and most simple JavaScript objects can be turned into a string using JSON and stored in localStorage. That includes arrays (as you've seen) as well as objects containing property names and values, as you'll see shortly.

> **Pick a naming scheme for your localStorage items that won't conflict with those of other applications at the same domain.**
>
> **If you need to store arrays or objects in localStorage, use JSON.stringify to create the value to store, and JSON.parse after you retrieve it.**

Be careful around
the sharp objects!

Deleting sticky notes

She's right, this app isn't going to be very successful if we can't remove stickies. We've already mentioned the `localStorage.removeItem` method in this chapter, but we haven't really talked about it. The `removeItem` method takes the key of an item, and removes that item from localStorage:

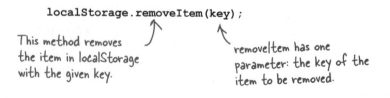

```
localStorage.removeItem(key);
```

This method removes
the item in localStorage
with the given key.

removeItem has one
parameter: the key of the
item to be removed.

That sounds easy enough, doesn't it? Ah, but if you think about it, there is more to removing an sticky note than calling the `removeItem` method—we also need to deal with `stickiesArray`...

Sharpen your pencil

Let's delete a sticky!

Below you'll see the contents of localStorage. You've got all the JavaScript you want along with the removeItem method. Using a pencil, sketch out what you need to do to remove `sticky_1304220006342` from localStorage. After you've sketched it out, go ahead and write some pseudo-code below to show how you're going to write your code.

"sticky_1304294652202" "sticky_1304220006342" "sticky_1304221683892" "sticky_1304221742310" "shopping cart item 1" "shopping cart item 2"

"sticky_1304294652202"	"sticky_1304220006342"	"sticky_1304221742310"	"sticky_1304221683892"

"stickiesArray"

← Your pseudo-code here

Sharpen your pencil
Solution

Let's delete a sticky!

Below you'll see the contents of localStorage. You've got all the JavaScript you want along with the removeItem method. Using a pencil, sketch out what you need to do to remove `sticky_1304220006342` from localStorage. After you've sketched it out, go ahead and write some pseudo-code below to show how you're going to write your code. Here's our solution.

localStorage.removeItem("sticky_1304220006342");

"sticky_1304294652202" "sticky_1304220006342" "sticky_1304221683892" "sticky_1304221742310" "shopping cart item 1" "shopping cart item 2"

"sticky_1304294652202"	"sticky_1304220006342"	"sticky_1304221742310"	"sticky_1304221683892"

"stickiesArray"

(1) Remove the sticky with the key "sticky_1304220006342" from localStorage using the localStorage.removeItem method.

(2) Get the stickiesArray.

(3) Remove element with key="sticky_1304220006342" from the stickiesArray.

(4) Write stickiesArray back into localStorage (stringifying it first).

(5) Find "sticky_1304220006342" in the DOM and remove it.

The deleteSticky function

You made a plan for how to delete the sticky notes, so let's take a look at the
`deleteSticky` function:

First, we remove the sticky note from localStorage using
removeItem, passing in the key of the sticky to delete.

```
function deleteSticky(key) {
    localStorage.removeItem(key);
    var stickiesArray = getStickiesArray();
    if (stickiesArray) {
        for (var i = 0; i < stickiesArray.length; i++) {
            if (key == stickiesArray[i]) {
                stickiesArray.splice(i,1);
            }
        }

        localStorage.setItem("stickiesArray", JSON.stringify(stickiesArray));
    }
}
```

We're using the getStickiesArray function to get
the stickiesArray from localStorage.

We make sure we have a stickiesArray
(just in case), and then iterate
through the array looking for the key
we want to delete.

When we find the right key, we delete
it from the array using splice.

splice removes elements from an array starting at the
location given by the first argument (i), for as many
elements as are specified in the second argument (1).

Finally, we save the
stickiesArray (with the key
removed) back to localStorage.

> I get the code, but I don't see
> how we're getting the key to pass to
> deleteSticky. Come to think of it, how
> is the user choosing the note to delete
> in the first place?

How do you select a sticky to delete?

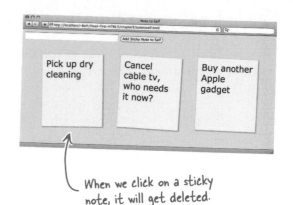

We need a way for the user to select a sticky note to delete. We could get all fancy and add a little delete icon to each note, but for our Sticky Notes app, we're going to do something much simpler: we're going to just delete the sticky note if the user clicks on it. That may not be the best implementation in terms of usability, but it's straightforward.

To implement this, we first need to change the stickies so that we can detect *when* a sticky is clicked on, and then we'll pass that along to the deleteSticky function.

A lot of this needs to happen in the addStickyToDOM function, let's see how:

> When we click on a sticky note, it will get deleted.

> Big picture: we're going to use the key of the sticky note, which, remember, is "sticky_" + time, to uniquely identify the note. We'll pass in this key whenever we call addStickyToDOM.

```
function addStickyToDOM(key, value) {

    var stickies = document.getElementById("stickies");

    var sticky = document.createElement("li");

    sticky.setAttribute("id", key);

    var span = document.createElement("span");

    span.setAttribute("class", "sticky");

    span.innerHTML = stickyObj.value;

    sticky.appendChild(span);

    stickies.appendChild(sticky);

    sticky.onclick = deleteSticky;

}
```

> We're adding a unique id to the <li> element that represents the sticky in the DOM. We're doing this so deleteSticky will know which sticky you clicked on. Since we already know the sticky's key is unique, we're just using that as the id.

> We're also adding click handler to every sticky. When you click on a sticky, deleteSticky will be called.

Exercise

Your job now is to update all the code so that everywhere we're calling addStickyToDOM, we're passing in the key as well as the value. You should be able to easily find these places. But after you've finished , check the solution at the end of the chapter to make sure.

> Don't skip this, or the upcoming test drive won't work!

How to get the sticky to delete from the event

We've now got an event handler on each sticky note listening for clicks. When you click on a sticky, `deleteSticky` will be called and an event object will be passed into `deleteSticky` with information about the event, like which element was clicked on. We can look at the `event.target` to tell which sticky was clicked on. Let's take a closer look at what happens when you click on a sticky note.

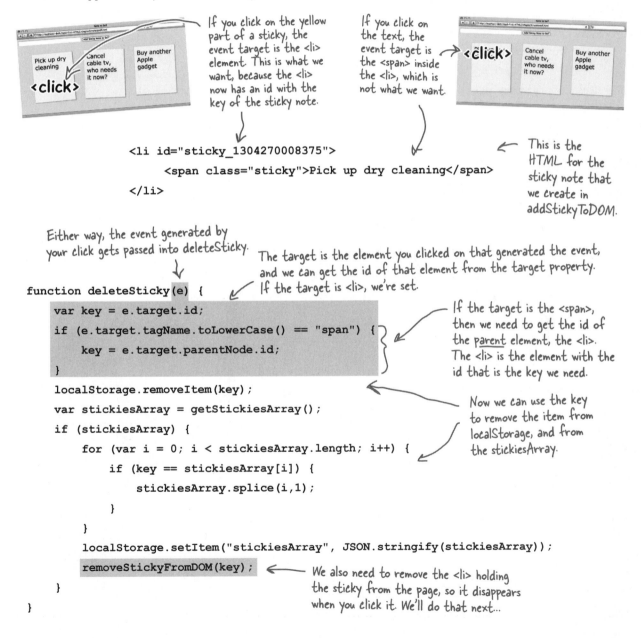

If you click on the yellow part of a sticky, the event target is the <li> element. This is what we want, because the <li> now has an id with the key of the sticky note.

If you click on the text, the event target is the <span> inside the <li>, which is not what we want.

This is the HTML for the sticky note that we create in addStickyToDOM.

```
<li id="sticky_1304270008375">
    <span class="sticky">Pick up dry cleaning</span>
</li>
```

Either way, the event generated by your click gets passed into deleteSticky.

The target is the element you clicked on that generated the event, and we can get the id of that element from the target property. If the target is <li>, we're set.

```
function deleteSticky(e) {
    var key = e.target.id;
    if (e.target.tagName.toLowerCase() == "span") {
        key = e.target.parentNode.id;
    }
    localStorage.removeItem(key);
    var stickiesArray = getStickiesArray();
    if (stickiesArray) {
        for (var i = 0; i < stickiesArray.length; i++) {
            if (key == stickiesArray[i]) {
                stickiesArray.splice(i,1);
            }
        }
        localStorage.setItem("stickiesArray", JSON.stringify(stickiesArray));
        removeStickyFromDOM(key);
    }
}
```

If the target is the <span>, then we need to get the id of the parent element, the <li>. The <li> is the element with the id that is the key we need.

Now we can use the key to remove the item from localStorage, and from the stickiesArray.

We also need to remove the <li> holding the sticky from the page, so it disappears when you click it. We'll do that next...

Delete the sticky from the DOM, too

To finish up the delete, we need to implement the removeStickyFromDOM function. You updated the addStickyToDOM function earlier to add the key of the sticky as the id of the <li> element holding the sticky in the DOM, so we can use document. getElementById to find the sticky in the DOM. We get the parent node of the sticky, and use the removeChild method to delete the sticky:

Pass in the key (also the id) of the
sticky element we're looking for.

We grab the <li> element
from the DOM...

```
function removeStickyFromDOM(key) {
    var sticky = document.getElementById(key);
    sticky.parentNode.removeChild(sticky);
}
```
<li> <ul> remove the child node <li>

... and remove it by first
getting its parentNode and
then using removeChild to
remove it.

Okay, test it...

Get all that code in, load the page, add and delete some stickies. Quit your browser, load it again, and give it a real run through!

We can delete
stickies now!

> Nice work! Now, can you give me a way to color code my stickies? You know yellow for urgent, blue for ideas, pink for backburner, that kind of thing?

But of course we can!

Come on, given your level of experience with this we're going to be able to knock this out. How do we do it? Well, we're going to create an object to store the text of the note and its color, and then we're going to store that as the value of the sticky item, using JSON.stringify to convert it to a string first.

Update the user interface so we can specify a color

Right now, all our notes are yellow. Wouldn't it be nicer if we could have a whole range of sticky note colors?

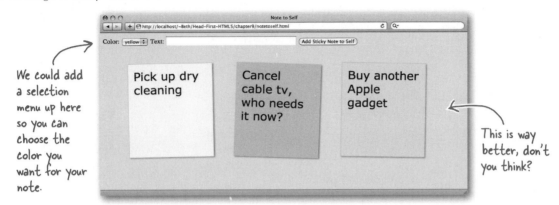

We could add a selection menu up here so you can choose the color you want for your note.

This is way better, don't you think?

Let's tackle the easy part first: updating the HTML so we have a selection menu of colors to choose from. Edit your `notetoself.html` file and update your form to add the colors like this:

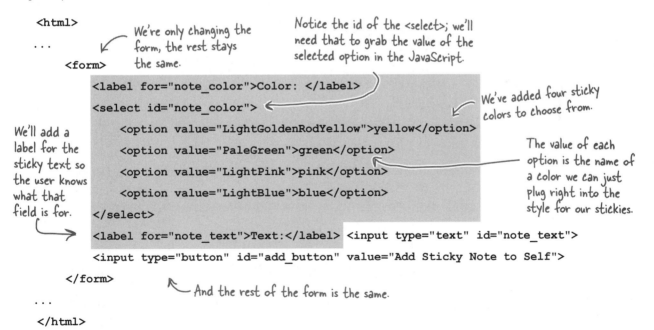

```
<html>
    ...
        <form>
            <label for="note_color">Color: </label>
            <select id="note_color">
                <option value="LightGoldenRodYellow">yellow</option>
                <option value="PaleGreen">green</option>
                <option value="LightPink">pink</option>
                <option value="LightBlue">blue</option>
            </select>
            <label for="note_text">Text:</label> <input type="text" id="note_text">
            <input type="button" id="add_button" value="Add Sticky Note to Self">
        </form>
    ...
</html>
```

We're only changing the form, the rest stays the same.

Notice the id of the <select>; we'll need that to grab the value of the selected option in the JavaScript.

We've added four sticky colors to choose from.

We'll add a label for the sticky text so the user knows what that field is for.

The value of each option is the name of a color we can just plug right into the style for our stickies.

And the rest of the form is the same.

We've been using CSS to define the default color for the notes. Now we want to store a note's color with the note itself. So, now the question is: how are we going to store the color for the sticky note in localStorage?

JSON.stringify, it's not just for Arrays

To store the color of the sticky with the text of the sticky, we can use the same technique we used for `stickiesArray`: we can store an object that contains the text and the color as the value for the sticky in localStorage.

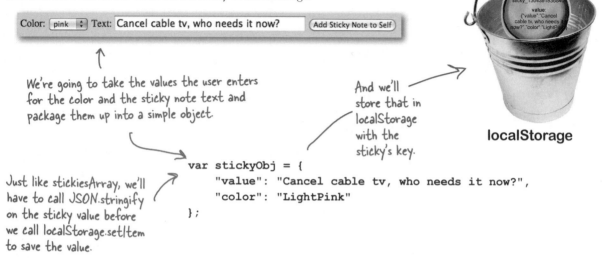

Color: [pink ⬍] Text: [Cancel cable tv, who needs it now?] (Add Sticky Note to Self)

We're going to take the values the user enters for the color and the sticky note text and package them up into a simple object.

And we'll store that in localStorage with the sticky's key.

localStorage

Just like stickiesArray, we'll have to call JSON.stringify on the sticky value before we call localStorage.setItem to save the value.

```
var stickyObj = {
    "value": "Cancel cable tv, who needs it now?",
    "color": "LightPink"
};
```

Let's rewrite the `createSticky` function to store the color with the sticky note text. To represent the text and the color, we'll use our handy object:

```
function createSticky() {
    var stickiesArray = getStickiesArray();
    var currentDate = new Date();
    var colorSelectObj = document.getElementById("note_color");
    var index = colorSelectObj.selectedIndex;
    var color = colorSelectObj[index].value;
    var key = "sticky_" + currentDate.getTime();
    var value = document.getElementById("note_text").value;
    var stickyObj = {
            "value": value,
            "color": color
    };
    localStorage.setItem(key, JSON.stringify(stickyObj));
    stickiesArray.push(key);
    localStorage.setItem("stickiesArray", JSON.stringify(stickiesArray));
    addStickyToDOM(key, stickyObj);
}
```

We do the usual thing to grab the value of the selected color option.

Then we use that color to create stickyObj: an object that contains two properties, the text of the sticky, and the color the user selected.

And, we JSON.stringify the stickyObj before we put it in localStorage.

Now, we're passing the object instead of a text string to addStickyToDOM. Which means you'll need to update addStickyToDOM too, right?

Using the new stickyObj

Now that we're passing stickyObj to addStickyToDOM, we need to update the
function to use the object instead of the string we were passing in before, and to set
the background color of the sticky. It's a fairly easy change though; let's take a look:

> We need to change the parameter here to be the stickyObj rather than the text value of the sticky.

```
function addStickyToDOM(key, stickyObj) {
    var stickies = document.getElementById("stickies");
    var sticky = document.createElement("li");
    sticky.setAttribute("id", key);

    sticky.style.backgroundColor = stickyObj.color;

    var span = document.createElement("span");
    span.setAttribute("class", "sticky");
    span.innerHTML = stickyObj.value;
    sticky.appendChild(span);
    stickies.appendChild(sticky);
    sticky.onclick = deleteSticky;
}
```

> We get the color from the stickyObj we're passing into addStickyToDOM.

> Notice that when we set the background color property in JavaScript, we specify it as backgroundColor, NOT background-color, like in CSS.

HTML element objects have a style property you can use to access the style of that element.

> And then we need to get the text value we're going to use in the sticky note from the object.

There is one other place we need to update the code, and that is in init, where
we are getting the stickies from localStorage and passing to addStickyToDOM
when we first load the page.

```
function init() {
    var button = document.getElementById("add_button");
    button.onclick = createSticky;

    var stickiesAray = getStickiesArray();

    for (var i = 0; i < stickiesArray.length; i++) {
        var key = stickiesArray[i];
        var value = JSON.parse(localStorage[key]);
        addStickyToDOM(key, value);
    }
}
```

> Now when we get the value of the sticky note from localStorage, we need to JSON.parse it, because it's an object, not a string anymore.

> And we pass that object to addStickyToDOM instead of the string (the code looks the same, but the thing we're passing is different).

Test drive sticky note colors

Before running the Note to Self app again, you'll need to clear out your localStorage first because the previous version of our stickies didn't have any color stored in them, and now we're using a different format for our sticky values. Before we were using strings, now we're using objects. So empty out your localStorage, reload the page, and add some stickies, selecting a different color for each one. Here are our stickies (and we'll also check out localStorage too):

> You can use your maintenance.html file to clear out your localStorage, or use the console.

> We picked yellow, pink, and blue for our sticky notes when we added them.

> Each sticky note's value is now a (JSON stringified) object containing the text value of the sticky and the color of the sticky.

> I was thinking, if we can store objects and arrays, why don't we just store all the notes in the array itself, why do we need all these other items? It seems to make it all complicated when it could just be embedded in one item in localStorage.

For some uses, that makes a lot of sense.

Knowing what we know now, we certainly could design the stickies so that they were objects embedded in an array. And going forward you might decide to do just that. It might also make sense for your shopping cart. The only downside is that the `JSON.stringify` and `JSON.parse` methods have to do a lot more work anytime you make a change, for instance to add a note we have to parse the entire set of notes, add the note, and then stringify all the notes again before writing them back in to the store. But, for the amount of data in Stickies, that shouldn't be a problem in general (although do think about mobile devices with limited CPUs and the effect of the CPU usage on battery life).

So whether you want to pack everything into one object or array in localStorage, really depends on how many data items you need to store, how big each one is, and what type of processing you're going to do on them.

While our implementation here may be a bit of overkill for a limited number of Stickies, we hope you agree it gave us a great way to think about the localStorage API and how to deal with items in it.

~~DON'T~~ TRY THIS AT HOME
(OR BLOWING UP YOUR 5 MEGABYTES)

We've told you that you have five whole megabytes of storage on every user's browser, but while five megabytes sounds like a lot, remember that all your data is stored in the form of a string rather than in a byte-efficient data format. Take a long number, say, the national debt—when expressed in floating point form it takes up very little storage, but when expressed in the form of a string, it takes up many times that amount of memory. So, given that, the five megabytes might not hold as much as you think.

So what happens when you use all 5MBs? Well, unfortunately this is one of those behaviors that isn't well defined by the HTML5 specification, and browsers may do different things when you exceed your limit—the browser may ask if you want to allow more storage, or it may throw a QUOTA_EXCEEDED_ERR exception, which you can catch like this:

Here's a setItem call in the middle of the try block; if anything goes wrong and setItem throws an exception, the catch block will be invoked.

```
try {
    localStorage.setItem(myKey, myValue);
} catch(e) {
    if (e == QUOTA_EXCEEDED_ERR) {
        alert("Out of storage!");
    }
}
```

A try/catch captures any exceptions that are thrown within the try block.

This is one JavaScript area we haven't covered, you might want to add it to your list of things to look into.

We're testing to see if this is a storage quota error (as opposed to some other type of exception). If so, we alert the user. You'll most likely want to do something more meaningful than just an alert.

Not all browsers are currently throwing the QUOTA_EXCEEDED_ERR exception. But they still throw a exception when you exceed your limit, so you may want to handle the general case of an exception occuring when you set an item.

DANGER
Explosive
Exercise

We don't see any reason not to push your browser to the limit, see what it's made of, see how far it can go, see what its behavior is under pressure. Let's write a little code to push your browser over its storage limit:

```html
<html>
<head>
<script>

localStorage.setItem("fuse", "-");
while(true) {
    var fuse = localStorage.getItem("fuse");
    try {
        localStorage.setItem("fuse", fuse + fuse);
    } catch(e) {
        alert("Your browser blew up at" + fuse.length + " with exception: " + e);
        break;
    }
}
localStorage.removeItem("fuse");
</script>
</head>
<body>
</body>
</html>
```

Let start with a one-character string, with the key "fuse".

And just keep increasing its size...

...by doubling the string (by concatenating it with itself).

Then we'll try to write it back to localStorage.

If it blows up, we're done! We'll alert the user and get out of this loop.

And let's not leave a mess, so remove the item from localStorage.

Go ahead and type this in, light the fuse by loading it, and have fun! Try this on a few different browsers.

If you have the nerve to run this, put your results here.

....

....

....

Use at your own risk!

Watch it! *Seriously, this code could crash your browser, which might lead to your operating system being unhappy, which could lead to you losing work. Use at your own risk!!!*

I've been beta testing my shopping cart app and users don't want their shopping cart sticking around in the browser. How can I remove all the shopping cart items when the user closes the browser? Did I choose the wrong technology?

No Luke, there is another Skywalker.

It turns out that localStorage has a sister, named sessionStorage. If you substitute the global variable `sessionStorage` everywhere you've used `localStorage` then your items are stored only during the browser session. So, as soon as that session is over (in other words, the user closes the browser window), the items in storage are removed.

The `sessionStorage` object supports exactly the same API as localStorage, so you already know everything about it you need to.

Give it a try!

WHO DOES WHAT?

At this point you've been through the localStorage API. Below you'll find all the main characters of the API sitting with their masks on. See if you can determine who does what. We've gone ahead and done one for you to get you started.

clear   Use me to store items for the long term.

sessionStorage   I take keys and values and write them into the localStorage. Now keep in mind if there's an item with that key already in the localStorage, I'm not going to warn you, I'm just going to overwrite it so you better know what you're asking for.

key   If you overstay your welcome in localStorage and use too much space you'll get an exception and you'll be hearing from me.

setItem   Need to knock off an item? I'll get the job done discreetly.

            Just give me a key and I'll go out and find the item with that key and hand its value to you.

removeItem   I'm a short term kinda guy, I'll store your stuff just as long as you have the browser open. Close your browser, and poof, all your stuff is gone.

length   When you've had it with all the items in your localStorage, I clean up all those items and throw them away, leaving you with a nice fresh and empty localStorage (keep in mind I can only clean up my own origin).

getItem   Need to know how many items are in your localStorage? That's me.

localStorage   Give me an index, and I'll give you a key from that index in localStorage.

QUOTA_EXCEEDED_ERR

Now that you know localStorage, how are you going to use it?

There are many ways to make use of localStorage—the Stickies app used them so we didn't need a server, but even with a server, localStorage can be quite helpful. Here's a few other ways developers are using them:

In my new Twitter client, I'm going to cache Twitter search results for efficiency with localStorage. When my users search, I'm going to check the local results first. That could really help my mobile users.

I'm going to store playlists with metadata for my users. They'll be able to store their favorite clips along with the timecode where they left off viewing.

I'm using sessionStorage for my new ecommerce library's shopping cart. If the user closes the browser, I want the shopping cart to go away.

I've got a really cool game that works in two different browser windows, and I'm using localStorage to synchronize state.

I'm storing lots of local data to make my clients' apps fast on their mobile devices. Having a large store on the client side is a huge win for me.

This gives me a new way to store user state. I used to need some kind of server-side based session and backend storage. Now I can just store my users' state locally, and bring in the server-side code only when I have to.

review of web storage

BULLET POINTS

- Web Storage is a store in your browser and an API you can use to save and retrieve items from the store.

- Most browsers provide at least 5 megabytes of storage per origin.

- Web Storage consists of local storage and session storage.

- Local storage is persistent, even if you close your browser window or quit the browser.

- Items in session storage are removed when you close your browser window or quit the browser. Session storage is good for temporary items, not longer term storage.

- Both local storage and session storage use exactly the same API.

- Web Storage is organized by origin (think domain). An origin is the location of the document on the Web (e.g., wickedlysmart.com or headfirstlabs.com).

- Each domain has a separate storage, so items stored in one origin are not visible to web pages in another origin.

- Use localStorage.setItem(key) to add a value to the store.

- Use localStorage.getItem(key) to retrieve a value from the store.

- You can use the same syntax as associative arrays to set and retrieve items to and from the store. Use localStorage[key] to do this.

- Use the localStorage.key() method to enumerate the keys in localStorage.

- localStorage.length is the number of items in localStorage at a given origin.

- Use the console in your browser to see and delete items in localStorage.

- You can delete items directly from localStorage by right-clicking on an item and choosing delete (note: may not work in all browsers).

- You can delete items from localStorage in code using the removeItem(key) method and the clear method. Note that the clear method deletes everything in localStorage at the origin where you do the clear.

- The keys for each localStorage item must be unique. If you use the same key as an existing item, you'll overwrite the value of that item.

- One way to generate a unique key is to use the current time in milliseconds since 1970, using the Date object's getTime() method.

- It is important to create a naming scheme for your web app that will still work if items are removed from the store, or if another app creates items in the store.

- Web Storage currently supports storing strings as values for keys.

- You can convert numbers stored in localStorage as strings back to numbers using parseInt or parseFloat.

- If you need to store more complex data, you can use JavaScript objects and convert them to strings before storing using JSON.stringify, and back to objects after retrieving using JSON.parse.

- Local storage may be particularly useful on mobile devices to reduce bandwidth requirements.

- Session storage is just like local storage, except that what's saved in the browser's store doesn't persist if you close the tab, the window, or exit the browser. Session storage is useful for short term storage, such as for a shopping session.

HTML5cross

Take some time to test your own local storage.

Across

3. When we used the _____ of localStorage to create key names, we ran into a problem: gaps in the names of our sticky notes.
4. Luke Skywalker's sister.
7. We have to _____ an object before we store it in localStorage.
8. Most browsers offer _____ megabytes of storage per origin.
9. We can detect which sticky note the user clicks on by looking at the event _____.
10. We store an item in localStorage with this method.
11. localStorage can store only _____.
12. We thought it would be just a fantasy to store an _____ in localStorage but it turns out you can, with JSON.
13. Use a try/_____ to detect quota-exceeded errors in localStorage.

Down

1. We used the _____ to hold the keys of all our stickies so we could easily find them in localStorage.
2. sessionStorage is just like localStorage except its not _____ if you close your browser window.
5. We create an _____ to store the sticky note text and its color in one localStorage item.
6. Use _____ to convert a string to an integer.
7. Cookie has a _____ issue.
8. If you store something in your browser and fly to _____ , it will still be there when you come back.

The Shell Game Solution

Ready to try your luck? Or should we say skill? We've got a game for you to test your command of localStorage, but you'll need to be on your toes. Use your knowledge of getting and setting key/value pairs in localStore to keep track of the pea as it shifts from shell to shell. Here's our solution.

```
function shellGame() {
    localStorage.setItem("shell1", "pea");
    localStorage.setItem("shell2", "empty");
    localStorage.setItem("shell3", "empty");
    localStorage["shell1"] = "empty";
    localStorage["shell2"] = "pea";
    localStorage["shell3"] = "empty";
    var value = localStorage.getItem("shell2");
    localStorage.setItem("shell1", value);
    value = localStorage.getItem("shell3");
    localStorage["shell2"] = value;
    var key = "shell2";
    localStorage[key] = "pea";
    key = "shell1";
    localStorage[key] = "empty";
    key = "shell3";
    localStorage[key] = "empty";

    for (var i = 0; i < localStorage.length; i++) {
        var key = localStorage.key(i);
        var value = localStorage.getItem(key);
        alert(key + ": " + value);
    }
}
```

Which shell had the pea?

Key	Value
shell1	empty
shell2	pea
shell3	empty

The pea is under shell2.

Exercise Solution

Your job was to update all the code so that everywhere we're calling addStickyToDOM, we're passing in the key as well as the value.

You should have updated all the calls to addStickyToDom in `init` and `createSticky`, to look like this:

```
addStickyToDOM(key, value);
```

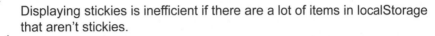

Sharpen your pencil
Solution

Put a check next to the ways our current implementation could cause problems:

- ☑ Displaying stickies is inefficient if there are a lot of items in localStorage that aren't stickies.

- ☑ A sticky could be overwritten by setItem if the size of the localStorage gets smaller when another app deletes its own items.

- ☑ It's hard to quickly tell how many stickies there are; you have to iterate through every item in localStorage to get all the stickies.

- ☐ Use a cookie, it has to be easier than all this!

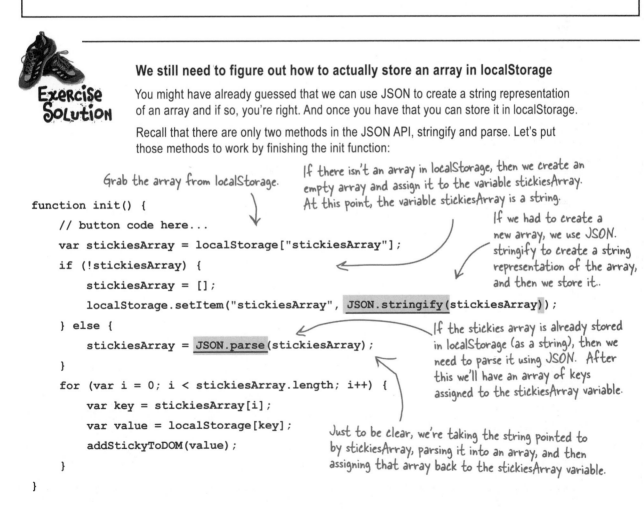

Exercise Solution

We still need to figure out how to actually store an array in localStorage

You might have already guessed that we can use JSON to create a string representation of an array and if so, you're right. And once you have that you can store it in localStorage.

Recall that there are only two methods in the JSON API, stringify and parse. Let's put those methods to work by finishing the init function:

Grab the array from localStorage.

If there isn't an array in localStorage, then we create an empty array and assign it to the variable stickiesArray. At this point, the variable stickiesArray is a string.

If we had to create a new array, we use JSON.stringify to create a string representation of the array, and then we store it.

```
function init() {
    // button code here...
    var stickiesArray = localStorage["stickiesArray"];
    if (!stickiesArray) {
        stickiesArray = [];
        localStorage.setItem("stickiesArray", JSON.stringify(stickiesArray));
    } else {
        stickiesArray = JSON.parse(stickiesArray);
    }
    for (var i = 0; i < stickiesArray.length; i++) {
        var key = stickiesArray[i];
        var value = localStorage[key];
        addStickyToDOM(value);
    }
}
```

If the stickies array is already stored in localStorage (as a string), then we need to parse it using JSON. After this we'll have an array of keys assigned to the stickiesArray variable.

Just to be clear, we're taking the string pointed to by stickiesArray, parsing it into an array, and then assigning that array back to the stickiesArray variable.

DON'T TRY THIS AT HOME
(OR BLOWING UP YOUR 5 MEGABYTES)

We've told you that you have five whole megabytes of storage on every user's browser, but while five megabytes sounds like a lot, remember that all your data is stored in the form of a string rather than in a byte-efficient data format. Take a long number, say, the national debt—when expressed in floating point form it takes up very little storage, but when expressed in the form of a string, it takes up many times that amount of memory. So, given that, the five megabytes might not hold as much as you think.

So what happens when you use all 5MBs? Well, unfortunately this is one of those behaviors that isn't well defined by the HTML5 specification, and browsers may do different things when you exceed your limit—the browser may ask if you want to allow more storage, or it may throw a QUOTA_EXCEEDED_ERR exception, which you can catch like this:

A try/catch captures any exceptions that are thrown within the try block.

```
try {
    localStorage.setItem(myKey, myValue);
} catch(e) {
    if (e == QUOTA_EXCEEDED_ERR) {
        alert("Out of storage!");
    }
}
```

Here's a setItem call in the middle of the try block; if anything goes wrong and setItem throws an exception, the catch block will be invoked.

We're testing to see if this is a storage quota error (as opposed to some other type of exception). If so, we alert the user. You'll most likely want to do something more meaningful than just an alert.

Not all browsers are currently throwing the QUOTA_EXCEEDED_ERR exception. But they still throw a exception when you exceed your limit, so you may want to handle the general case of an exception occuring when you set an item.

We don't see any reason not to push your browser to the limit, see what it's made of, see how far it can go, see what its behavior is under pressure. Let's write a little code to push your browser over its storage limit:

```html
<html>
<head>
<script>

localStorage.setItem("fuse", "-");
while(true) {
    var fuse = localStorage.getItem("fuse");
    try {
        localStorage.setItem("fuse", fuse + fuse);
    } catch(e) {
        alert("Your browser blew up at" + fuse.length + " with exception: " + e);
        break;
    }
}
localStorage.removeItem("fuse");
</script>
</head>
<body>
</body>
</html>
```

Let start with a one-character string, with the key "fuse".

And just keep increasing its size...

...by doubling the string (by concatenating it with itself).

Then we'll try to write it back to localStorage.

If it blows up, we're done! We'll alert the user and get out of this loop.

And let's not leave a mess, so remove the item from localStorage.

Go ahead and type this in, light the fuse by loading it, and have fun! Try this on a few different browsers.

Our results from Safari and Chrome.

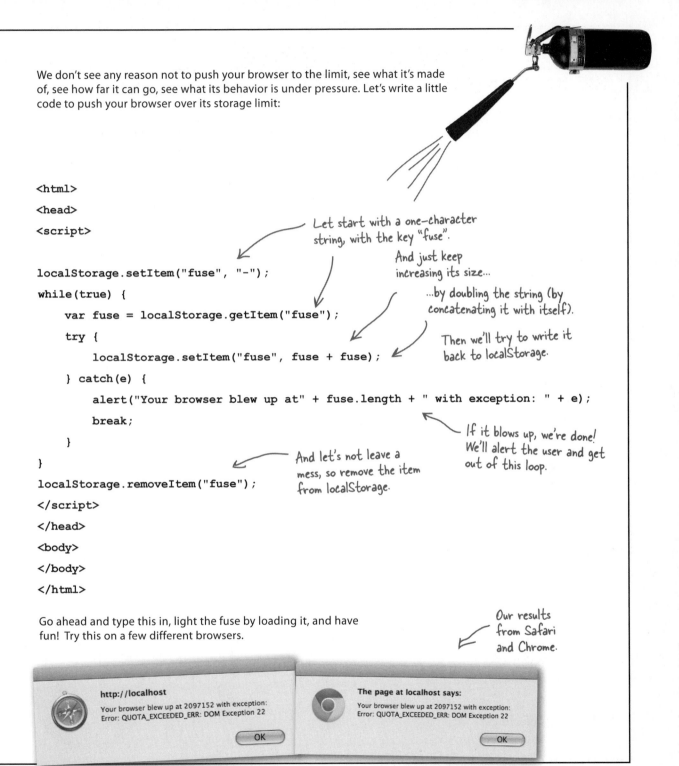

http://localhost
Your browser blew up at 2097152 with exception:
Error: QUOTA_EXCEEDED_ERR: DOM Exception 22
OK

The page at localhost says:
Your browser blew up at 2097152 with exception:
Error: QUOTA_EXCEEDED_ERR: DOM Exception 22
OK

WHO DOES WHAT? SOLUTION

At this point you've been through the localStorage API. Below you'll find all the main characters of the API sitting with their masks on. See if you can determine who does what. Here's our solution.

clear

sessionStorage

key

setItem

removeItem

length

getItem

localStorage

QUOTA_EXCEEDED_ERR

Use me to store items for the long term.

I take keys and values and write them into the localStorage. Now keep in mind if there's an item with that key already in the localStorage, I'm not going to warn you, I'm just going to overwrite it so you better know what you're asking for.

If you overstay your welcome in localStorage and use too much space you'll get an exception and you'll be hearing from me.

Need to knock off an item? I'll get the job done discreetly.

Just give me a key and I'll go out and find the item with that key and hand its value to you.

I'm a short term kinda guy, I'll store your stuff just as long as you have the browser open. Close your browser and, poof, all your stuff is gone.

When you've had it with all the items in your localStorage, I clean up all those items and throw them away, leaving you with a nice fresh and empty localStorage (keep in mind I can only clean up my own origin).

Need to know how many items are in your localStorage? That's me.

Give me an index, and I'll give you a key from that index in localStorage.

HTML5cross Solution

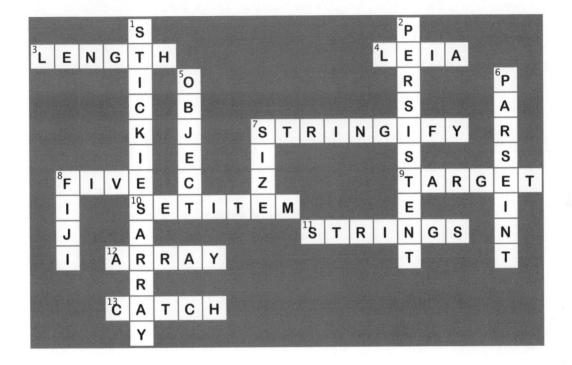

10 putting javascript to work

Web Workers

Okay I can't do EVERYTHING around here, this is going to require a little help.

How about some help into the elevator shaft?

Slow script—do you want to continue running it?

If you've spent enough time with JavaScript or browsing the Web you've probably seen the "slow script" message. And, with all those multicore processors sitting in your new machine how could a script be running *too slow*? It's because JavaScript can only do one thing at a time. But, with HTML5 and Web Workers, *all that changes*. You've now got the ability to spawn *your own* JavaScript workers to get more work done. Whether you're just trying to design a more responsive app, or you just want to max out your machine's CPU, Web Workers are here to help. Put your JavaScript manager's hat on, let's get some workers cracking!

this is a new chapter   **473**

The Dreaded Slow Script

One of the great things about JavaScript is it does only one
thing at a time. It's what we like to call "single-threaded." Why's
that great? Because it makes programming straightforward.
When you have lots of threads of execution happening at the
same time, writing a program that works correctly can become
quite a challenge.

The downside of being single-threaded is that if you
give a JavaScript program too much to do, it can get
overwhelmed, and we end up with "slow script" dialogs. The
other ramification of having only one thread is if you have
JavaScript code that is working really hard, it doesn't leave
a lot of computational power for your user interface or your
user's interactions, and your application can appear to be
sluggish, or unresponsive.

Slow Script
Safari is no longer responding because of a script on
the webpage "Fractal Explorer" (http://localhost/
~Beth/HTML5/MandelNoWW/fractal.html). Do you
want to stop running the script, or let it continue?

Stop   Continue

How JavaScript spends its time

Let's see what this all means by taking a look at how JavaScript
handles the tasks of a typical page:

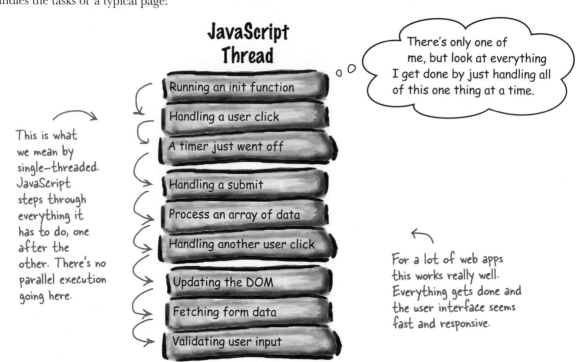

JavaScript Thread

Running an init function

Handling a user click

A timer just went off

Handling a submit

Process an array of data

Handling another user click

Updating the DOM

Fetching form data

Validating user input

This is what
we mean by
single-threaded.
JavaScript
steps through
everything it
has to do, one
after the
other. There's no
parallel execution
going here.

There's only one of
me, but look at everything
I get done by just handling all
of this one thing at a time.

For a lot of web apps
this works really well.
Everything gets done and
the user interface seems
fast and responsive.

When single-threaded goes BAD

It's true, for a lot of uses, this single-threaded mode of computing by JavaScript works great, and as we've said, it makes programming straightforward. But, when you've written code that is so "computationally intensive" it starts to impact JavaScript's ability to get everything done, the single-threaded model starts to break down.

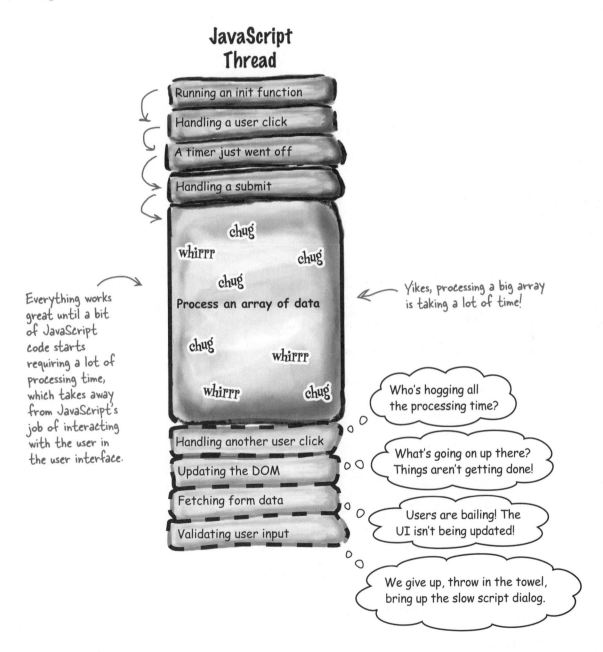

JavaScript Thread

- Running an init function
- Handling a user click
- A timer just went off
- Handling a submit

chug

whirrr   chug

chug

Process an array of data

chug

whirrr

whirrr   chug

- Handling another user click
- Updating the DOM
- Fetching form data
- Validating user input

Everything works great until a bit of JavaScript code starts requiring a lot of processing time, which takes away from JavaScript's job of interacting with the user in the user interface.

Yikes, processing a big array is taking a lot of time!

Who's hogging all the processing time?

What's going on up there? Things aren't getting done!

Users are bailing! The UI isn't being updated!

We give up, throw in the towel, bring up the slow script dialog.

Adding another thread of control to help

Before HTML5, we were stuck with one thread of control in our pages and apps, but with Web Workers we've now got a way to create another thread of control to help out. So, if you've got code that takes a long time to compute, you can create a Web Worker that will handle that task while the main JavaScript thread of control is making sure everything is good with the browser and the user.

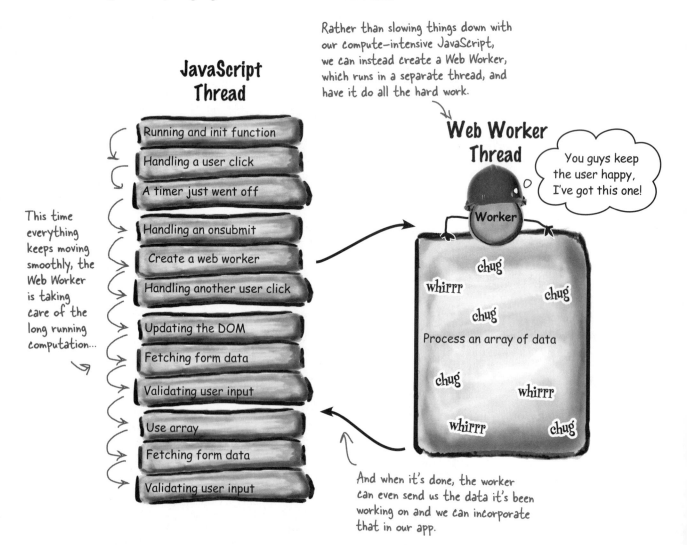

Rather than slowing things down with our compute-intensive JavaScript, we can instead create a Web Worker, which runs in a separate thread, and have it do all the hard work.

JavaScript Thread

- Running and init function
- Handling a user click
- A timer just went off
- Handling an onsubmit
- Create a web worker
- Handling another user click
- Updating the DOM
- Fetching form data
- Validating user input
- Use array
- Fetching form data
- Validating user input

This time everything keeps moving smoothly, the Web Worker is taking care of the long running computation...

Web Worker Thread

You guys keep the user happy, I've got this one!

Worker

chug
whirrr
chug
chug
Process an array of data
chug
whirrr
whirrr
chug

And when it's done, the worker can even send us the data it's been working on and we can incorporate that in our app.

Now, we've made a big deal out of the fact that one thread of control keeps things simple and easy to program, and that is true. But, as you're going to see, Web Workers have been carefully crafted to make sure things stay simple, easy and safe for the programmer. We'll see how in just a moment...

JavaScript Exposed (Again)

This week's interview:
Where JavaScript spends his time.

Head First: Welcome back JavaScript, great to have you.

JavaScript: Glad to be here, as long as we stick to my schedule, lots to do.

Head First: That is actually where I thought we might focus our time today. You're a super successful guy, you have so much going on—how do you get it all done?

JavaScript: Well, I have a philosophy: I do one thing at a time, and I do it really well.

Head First: How do you do only one thing at a time? To us it looks like you're retrieving data, displaying pages, interacting with the user, managing timers and alerts, and on and on...

JavaScript: Yes, I do all that, but whatever I'm doing, I do only that. So if I'm dealing with the user, that's all I do until I'm done with that.

Head First: How can that be true? What if a timer goes off, or network data arrives, or whatever, don't you stop and do that?

JavaScript: When an event occurs, like the ones you've mentioned, that event is added to a queue. I don't even look at it until I've finished whatever I'm working on. That way I do everything correctly and safely and efficiently.

Head First: Are you ever late getting to one of those tasks on the queue?

JavaScript: Oh it happens. Luckily I'm the technology behind browser web pages, so how bad can it be if I get a little behind? You should talk to the guys that have to run code for spacecraft thrusters or nuclear power plant controllers, those guys have to live by different rules—that's why they make the big bucks.

Head First: I've always wondered what's going on when I get the "Slow script, do you want to continue" dialog on my browser. Is that you taking a break?

JavaScript: Taking a break! Hah. That's when someone has structured their page such that I've got so much work to do, I can't do it all! If you write a bit of JavaScript that hogs all my time, then your interaction with your user is going to suffer. I can only do so much.

Head First: Sounds like you need some help.

JavaScript: Well thanks to HTML5, I have help now because that's where Web Workers come in. If you really need to write compute-intensive code, use Web Workers to offload some of the work—that way I can keep my focus, and workers can do some of the heavy lifting for me (without getting in my way).

Head First: Interesting, we'll look into that. Now, next question... Oh, wait, he's gone, looks like he's off to his next task. Serious guy, huh?

How Web Workers work

Let's take a look at a day in the life of a Web Worker: how workers are created, how they know what to do, and how they get results back to your main browser code.

To use Web Workers, the browser first has to create one or more workers to help compute tasks. Each worker is defined with its own JavaScript file that contains all the code (or references to code) it needs to do its job.

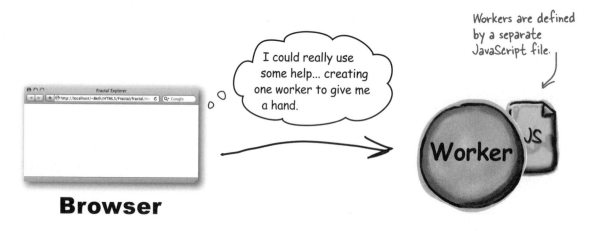

I could really use some help... creating one worker to give me a hand.

Browser

Workers are defined by a separate JavaScript file.

Worker

Now, workers live in a very restricted world; they don't have access to many of the runtime objects your main browser code does, like the DOM or any of the variables or functions in your main code.

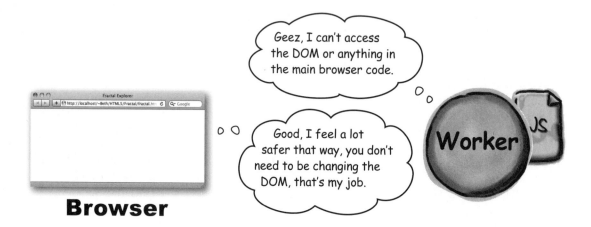

Geez, I can't access the DOM or anything in the main browser code.

Good, I feel a lot safer that way, you don't need to be changing the DOM, that's my job.

Browser

Worker

To get a worker to start working, the browser typically sends it a message. The worker code receives the message, takes a look at it to see if there are any special instructions, and starts working.

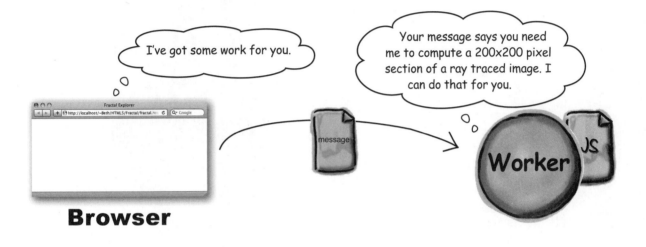

When the worker completes its work, it then sends a message back, with the final results of what it's been working on. The main browser code then takes these results and incorporates them into the page in some way.

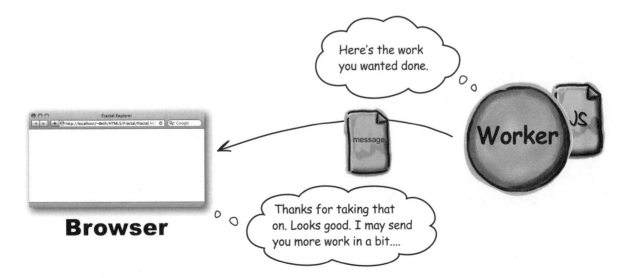

Why not allow workers to access the DOM? I mean this seems like a lot of trouble to pass messages back and forth when all of these workers are running in the same browser.

To keep things efficient.

One reason the DOM and JavaScript have been so successful is that we're able to highly optimize DOM operations because we have only one thread with access to the DOM. If we let multiple threads of computation concurrently change the DOM, then we'll seriously impact its performance (and browser implementors would have to go to great effort to make sure making changes to the DOM is safe). The truth is, allowing a bunch of changes to the DOM at the same time can easily lead to situations where the DOM is in an inconsistent state, which would be bad. Very bad.

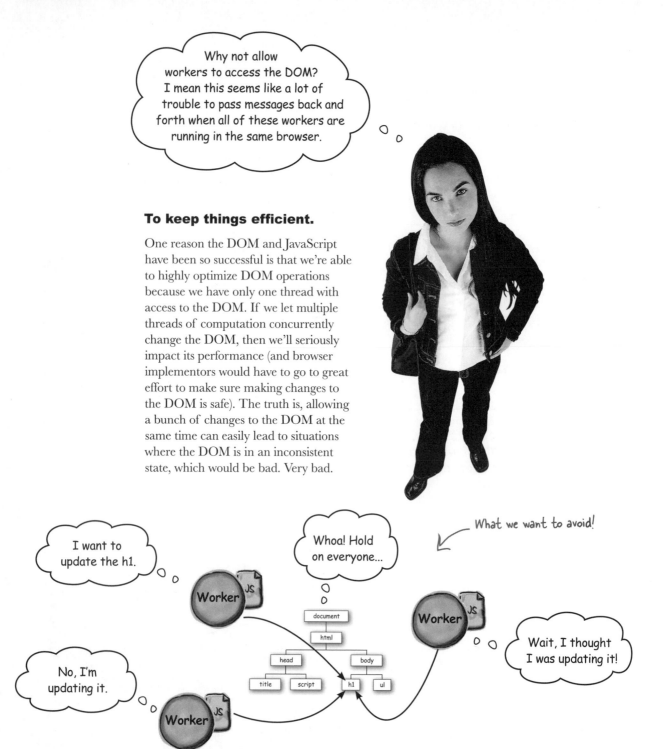

I want to update the h1.

Whoa! Hold on everyone...

What we want to avoid!

Worker

Worker

Wait, I thought I was updating it!

No, I'm updating it.

Worker

document
html
head
body
title
script
h1
ul

Sharpen your pencil

Take a look at all the potential uses for workers below. Which ones might improve the design and the performance of an app?

☐ Caching data for use in your pages.

☐ Processing large amounts of data in arrays or large JSON responses from web services.

☐ Managing a database connection along with adding and removing records for the main page.

☐ Automated race track betting agent.

☐ Analyzing video.

☐ ....

☐ ....

☐ ....

☐ Spell checking the page as the user types.

☐ Polling web services and alerting the main page when something happens.

☐ Image processing of data in a canvas.

☐ Code syntax or other language highlighting.

☐ Pre-fetching data based on what your user is doing.

☐ Managing advertising for your page.

☐ ....

☐ ....

☐ ....

Your ideas here!

All answers are good uses, although you could debate a couple: spell checking & syntax checking may be better done in the main page code; race track betting may be better not done at all. ;-)

Google's Chrome browser has some extra security restrictions that will prevent you from running Web Workers directly from a file. If you try, your page won't run and you'll get no indication of why (including no error messages telling you what's wrong!).

So, for these examples, we recommend either using a different browser, or running your own server and running the examples from http://localhost. Or you can upload them to a hosted server if you have access to one.

You can also use the Chrome runtime switch --allow-file-access-from-files, but we don't recommend this switch beyond just testing your code.

Almost all the modern browsers support Web Workers, but there is one exception: Internet Explorer 9. The good news is that for IE10 and later, you can count on Web Workers, but with IE9 and all the IE versions before it, you'll have to supply an alternative experience.

But rather than worrying about IE specifically, here's how you can easily check to see if any browser supports Web Workers:

If workers are supported, the property Worker will be defined in the global scope, window.

And if Worker isn't defined, then we've got no support in the browser.

```
if (window["Worker"]) {
    var status = document.getElementById("status");
    status.innerHTML = "Bummer, no Web Workers";
}
```

You'll want to handle that condition in a way that is appropriate for your app. Here, we're just letting the user know by putting a message in an element with id="status".

Your first Web Worker...

Let's get down to the business of creating a worker to see how this all works. To do that we need a page to put everything in. We'll go with the simplest HTML5 markup we can get away with; type this into `pingpong.html`:

```
<!doctype html>
<html lang="en">
    <head>
        <title>Ping Pong</title>
        <meta charset="utf-8">
        <script src="manager.js"></script>
    </head>
<body>
    <p id="output"></p>
</body>
</html>
```

> Have hard hat, will travel. Just point me to a JavaScript file with what you want me to do.

This JavaScript code is going to create and manage all the workers.

And we'll be putting some output from the worker here.

How to create a Web Worker

Before we start implementing `manager.js`, let's look at how you actually create a Web Worker:

To create a new worker, we create a new Worker object...

```
var worker = new Worker("worker.js");
```

And we're assigning the new worker to a JavaScript variable named worker.

... the "worker.js" JavaScript file contains the code for the worker.

Web Worker

So that's how you create one worker, but of course you don't have to stop there; you can create as many workers as you like:

```
var worker2 = new Worker("worker.js");
var worker3 = new Worker("worker.js");

var another_worker = new Worker("another_worker.js");
```

We can easily create two more workers that make use of the same code as our first worker.

We'll see how to use multiple workers together in a bit...

Or we can create other workers based a different JavaScript file.

Writing Manager.js

Now that you know how to create a worker (and how easy it is), let's start working on our `manager.js` code. We'll keep this code simple and create just one worker for now. Create a file named `manager.js` and add this code:

```
window.onload = function() {
    var worker = new Worker("worker.js");
}
```

— We'll wait for the page to fully load.

← And then create a new worker.

That's a great start, but now we want to get the worker to actually do some work. As we've already discussed, one way we tell a worker to do some work is by sending it a message. To send a message we use the worker object's `postMessage` method. Here's how you use it:

```
window.onload = function() {
    var worker = new Worker("worker.js");

    worker.postMessage("ping");
}
```

← And we're using the worker's postMessage method to send it a message. Our message is the simple string "ping".

→ Want to send more complex messages? Here's how...

↑ The postMessage method is defined for you in the Web Worker API.

postMessage Up Close

You can send more than just strings in `postMessage`. Let's look at everything you can send in a message:

```
worker.postMessage("ping");
worker.postMessage([1, 2, 3, 5, 11]);
worker.postMessage({"message": "ping", "count": 5});
```

← You can send a string...

← ... an array...

← ... or even a JSON object.

You **can't** send functions:

```
worker.postMessage(updateTheDOM);
```

← You can't send a function... it might contain a reference to the DOM allowing the worker to change the DOM!

Receiving messages from the worker

We're not quite done with our `manager.js` code yet—we still need to be able to receive a message from the worker if we're going to make use of all its hard work. To receive a worker's message we need to define a handler for the worker's `onmessage` property so that anytime a message comes in from that worker, our handler will be called (and handed the message). Here's how we do that:

```javascript
window.onload = function() {
    var worker = new Worker("worker.js");

    worker.postMessage("ping");

    worker.onmessage = function (event) {
        var message = "Worker says " + event.data;
        document.getElementById("output").innerHTML = message;
    };
}
```

Here we're defining a function that will get called whenever we receive a message from this worker. The message from the worker is wrapped in an event object.

The event object passed to our handler has a data property that contains the message data (what we're after) that the worker posted.

When we get a message from the worker we'll stuff it in a <p> element in the HTML page.

onMessage Up Close

Let's take a quick look at the message our `onmessage` handler is receiving from the worker. As we've said, this message is wrapped in an `Event` object, which has two properties we're interested in: `data` and `target`:

This is the object that is sent from the worker to the code in your page when the worker posts a message.

```javascript
worker.onmessage = function (event) {
    var message = event.data;
    var worker = event.target;
};
```

The data property contains the message the worker sent (e.g., a string, like "pong").

And the target is a reference to the worker that sent the message. This can come in handy if you need to know which worker it's from. We'll be using this later in the chapter.

Now let's write the worker

To get started on the worker, the first thing we need to do is to make sure the worker can receive messages that are sent from `manager.js`—that's how the worker gets its work orders. For that we're also going to make use of another `onmessage` handler, the one in the worker itself. Every worker is ready to receive messages, you just need to give the worker a handler to process them. Here's how we do that (go ahead and create a file `worker.js` and add this code):

```
onmessage = pingPong;
```

We're assigning the onmessage property in the worker to the pingPong function.

We're going to write the function pingPong to handle any messages that come in.

Writing the worker's message handler

Let's write the worker's message handler, `pingPong`, and we're going to start simple. Here's what it's going to do (you might have already guessed from the name `pingPong`): the worker's going to check any message it gets to make sure it contains the string "ping", and if it does, we're going to send a message back that says "pong". So, in effect, the work of the worker is just to get a "ping" and to answer with a "pong"—we're not going to do any heavy computation here, we're just going to make sure the manager and worker are communicating. Oh, and if the message doesn't say "ping", we're just going to ignore it.

So the function `pingPong` takes a message and responds with "pong". Go ahead and add this code to `worker.js`:

When the worker receives a message from the main code, the pingPong function will be called, and the message will be passed in.

```
onmessage = pingPong;
function pingPong(event) {
    if (event.data == "ping") {
        postMessage("pong");
    }
}
```

And if the message contains a string that says "ping", we'll send back a message that says "pong". The worker's message goes back to the code that created the worker.

Notice the worker uses postMessage to send messages, too.

Serving up a test drive

Make sure you've got `pingpong.html`, `manager.js` and
`worker.js` typed in and saved. Now keep those files open so
you can review them and let's think through how this works.
First, `manager.js` creates a new worker, assigns a
message handler to it, and then sends the worker
a "ping" message. The worker, in turn, makes sure
`pingPong` is set up as its message handler, and then
it waits. At some point, the worker receives a message
from the manager, and when it does it checks to see
that it contains "ping", which it does, and then the
worker does ~~a lot of~~ very little hard work and sends
a "pong" message back.

At this point the main browser code receives a
message from the worker, which it hands to the
message handler. The handler then simply prepends "Worker
says " to the front of the message, and displays it.

Now, our calculations here say the page should display
"Worker says pong"...okay okay, we know, you can't take the
suspense any more... go ahead and load the page already!

> Wait a sec, just thinking ahead...
> if we ever create more than one
> pong worker I may actually have
> to break a sweat.

BE the Browser

It's time to pretend you're the browser evaluating JavaScript. For each bit of code below, act like you're the browser and write its output in the lines provided. You can assume this code is using the same worker.js we just wrote:

← You can check the solutions at the end of the chapter.

```javascript
window.onload = function() {
    var worker = new Worker("worker.js");
    worker.onmessage = function(event) {
        alert("Worker says " + event.data);
    }
    for (var i = 0; i < 5; i++) {
        worker.postMessage("ping");
    }
}
```

....
....
....
....

```javascript
window.onload = function() {
    var worker = new Worker("worker.js");
    worker.ommessage = function(event) {
        alert("Worker says " + event.data);
    }
    for(var i = 5; i > 0; i--) {
        worker.postMessage("pong");
    }
}
```

....
....
....
....

```
window.onload = function() {
    var worker = new Worker("worker.js");            ..................................................
    worker.onmessage = function(event) {             ..................................................
        alert("Worker says " + event.data);          ..................................................
        worker.postMessage("ping");
    }                                                ..................................................
    worker.postMessage("ping");
}
```

Careful if you try these;
you might have to kill your
browser to escape...

```
window.onload = function() {
    var worker = new Worker("worker.js");
    worker.onmessage = function(event) {             ..................................................
        alert("Worker says " + event.data);          ..................................................
    }                                                ..................................................

    setInterval(pinger, 1000);                       ..................................................

    function pinger() {
        worker.postMessage("ping");
    }
}
```

Sharpen your pencil

While workers typically get their work orders through a message, they don't have to. Check out this nice, compact way to get work done with workers and HTML. When you know what it does, describe it below. You can check your solution with ours at the end of the chapter.

quote.html

```
<!doctype html>
<html lang="en">
    <head>
        <title>Quote</title>
        <meta charset="utf-8">
    </head>
<body>
    <p id="quote"></p>
    <script>
        var worker = new Worker("quote.js");
        worker.onmessage = function(event) {
            document.getElementById("quote").innerHTML = event.data;
        }
    </script>
</body>
</html>
```

quote.js

```
var quotes = ["I hope life isn't a joke, because I don't get it.",
              "There is a light at the end of every tunnel... just pray it's not a train!",
              "Do you believe in love at first sight or should I walk by again?"];
var index = Math.floor(Math.random() * quotes.length);
postMessage(quotes[index]);
```

Your description here:

Try typing in the code and running it!

....

....

....

Exercise

Let's add a couple of workers to our pingPong game. Your job is to fill in the blanks to complete the code so we have three pings sent to the workers, and three pongs back from the workers.

```
window.onload = function() {
    var numWorkers = 3;
    var workers = [];
    for (var i = 0; i < ....................... ; i++) {
        var worker = new ....................... ("worker.js");
        worker. ..................... = function(event) {

            alert(event.target + " says "
                                   + event. ............... );
        };
        workers.push(worker);
    }
    for (var i = 0; i < ....................... ; i++) {
        workers[i]. ..................... ("ping");
    }
}
```

We're creating three workers, and storing them in an array, workers.

Write your code in the blanks.

Here, we're adding the new worker to the workers array.

there are no Dumb Questions

Q: Can I just pass a function instead of a JavaScript file when I create the worker? That would seem easier and more consistent with how JavaScript usually does things.

A: No, you can't. Here's why: as you know, one of the requirements of a worker is that it not have access to the DOM (or to any state of the main browser thread for that matter). If you could pass a function to the Worker constructor, then your function could also contain reference to the DOM or other parts of your main JavaScript code, which would violate that requirement. So, the designers of Web Workers chose instead to have you just pass a JavaScript URL to avoid that issue.

Q: When I send a worker an object in a message, does it become a shared object between my main page and the worker?

A: No, when you send an object the worker gets a copy of it. Any changes the worker makes will not affect the object in your main page. The worker is executing in a different environment than your main page, so you have no access to objects there. The same is true of objects the worker sends you: you get a copy of them.

Q: Can workers access localStorage or make XMLHttpRequests?

A: Yes, workers can access localStorage and make XMLHttpRequests.

Exercise Solution

Let's add a couple of workers to our pingPong game. Your job was to fill in the blanks to complete the code so we have three pings sent to the workers and three pongs back from the workers. Here's our solution.

We use numWorkers to iterate three times and create three workers (feel free to change this variable to add more!)

```
window.onload = function() {
    var numWorkers = 3;
    var workers = [];
    for (var i = 0; i < numWorkers; i++) {
        var worker = new Worker("worker.js");
        worker.onmessage = function(event) {

            alert(event.target + " says "
                                + event.data);
        };
        workers.push(worker);
    }
    for (var i = 0; i < workers.length; i++) {
        workers[i].postMessage("ping");
    }
}
```

We set up the message handler in our main page code by using the onmessage property of the worker.

We use the data property to get the contents of the message.

We ping the worker with postMessage.

You could also use numWorkers here if you like.

Notice that no changes are needed to the worker code. Each worker is happy to do its thing independently.

You'll see this alert 3 times.

> http://localhost
> [object Worker] says pong
>
> OK

> I've been wondering how to include additional JavaScript files in my worker. I've got some financial libraries I'd like to make use of and copying and pasting them into my worker would result in a huge file that's not very maintainable.

Take a look at importScripts.

Web Workers have a global function named `importScripts` that you can use to import one or more JavaScript files into your worker. To use `importScripts` just give it a comma separated list of files or URLs you'd like to import, like this:

```
importScripts("http://bigscience.org/nuclear.js",
              "http://nasa.gov/rocket.js",
              "mylibs/atomsmasher.js");
```

Place zero or more comma-separated JavaScript URLs in importScripts.

Then when `importScripts` is invoked, each JavaScript URL is retrieved and evaluated in order.

Notice that `importScripts` is a full-fledged function, so (unlike `import` statements in a lot of languages) you can make runtime decisions about importing, like this:

```
if (taskType == "songdetection") {
    importScripts("audio.js");
}
```

Because importScripts is a function, you can import code as the task demands.

Virtual Land Grab

Explorers of the Mandelbrot Set have already grabbed areas of the virtual countryside and given them names like the lovely "Seahorse Valley," "Rainbow Islands," and the dreaded "Black Hole." And given the value of physical real estate these days, the only play left seems to be in the virtual spaces. So, we're going to build an explorer for the Mandelbrot Set to get in on the action. Actually, we have to confess, we already have built it, but it's slow—navigating around in the entire Mandelbrot Set could take a very long time —so we're hoping together we can speed it up, and we have a hunch Web Workers may be the answer.

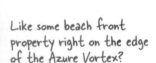

Like some beach front property right on the edge of the Azure Vortex?

Take a look around

Go ahead and fire up `http://wickedlysmart.com/hfhtml5/chapter10/singlethread/fractal.html` and you'll see a visualization of the Mandelbrot Set in the distance. Just click anywhere and you'll zoom into an area of the map. Keep clicking to explore different areas, or reload to start over. Watch out for areas with black holes, they tend to suck you in. We don't know about you, but while the scenery is beautiful, our viewer could be a little faster... ya think? It would be great to have enough performance to maximize the view to the entire browser window as well! Let's fix all that by adding Web Workers to the Fractal Explorer.

Mandel what?

Well, if you happen to be a mathematician

then you know the Mandelbrot Set is the equation:

$$z_n+1 = z_n^2 + c$$

and that it was discovered and studied by Benoit Mandelbrot. You also know that it's simply a set of complex numbers (numbers with a real part, and an imaginary part) generated by this equation.

If, on the other hand, you're not a mathematician, the best way to think about the Mandelbrot Set is as an infinitely complex fractal image—meaning an image that you can zoom into, to any level of magnification, and find interesting structures. Just look at some of the things you can find by navigating into the set:

And why are we so interested in it? Well, the set has a few interesting properties. First, it's generated by a very simple equation (the one above) that can be expressed in just a few lines of code; second, generating the Mandelbrot Set takes a fair number of computing cycles, which makes it a great example for using Web Workers. And finally, hey, it's cool and a trip to work with, and what a great app to end the book with, don't you think?

RIP Benoit Mandelbrot, who passed during the writing of this book. We were lucky to have known you.

How to compute a Mandelbrot Set

Let's take a look at how you'd typically structure your code to compute a Mandelbrot Set before we get workers involved. We don't want to focus much on the nitty-gritty of computing Mandelbrot pixel values; we've already got all that code taken care of, and we're going to give it to you in a sec. For now, we just want you to get sense of the big picture view of how to compute the set:

Note, our aim here isn't to teach you to be a numerical analyst (who can code equations with complex numbers); it's to adapt a compute intensive application to use Web Workers. If you are interested in the numerical aspects of the Mandelbrot Set, Wikipedia is a great place to start.

To compute the Mandelbrot Set we loop over each row of the image.

```
for (i = 0; i < numberOfRows; i++) {

    var row = computeRow(i);

    drawRow(row);

}
```

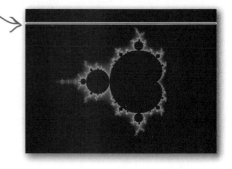

And for each row we compute the pixels for that row.

And then we draw each row on the screen. You can probably see the row-by-row display when you run the test code in your browser.

Now this code is just meant to be simple pseudo-code—when it comes to writing the code for real, there are a few more details we need to get into: for instance, to compute a row we need to know the width of the row, the zoom factor, the numerical resolution to which we want to compute it, and a few other small details. We can capture all those details in a task object like this:

width

The zoom factor

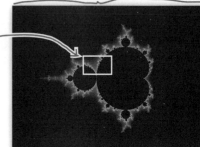

```
for (i = 0; i < numberOfRows; i++) {

    var taskForRow = createTaskForRow(i);

    var row = computeRow(taskForRow);

    drawRow(row);

}
```

And we pass taskForRow into computeRow, which returns the computed row.

The taskForRow object holds all the data needed to compute a row.

Level of precision to compute

Now the trick is going to be taking this and reworking it to divide up the computation among a number of workers, and then adding the code that handles giving tasks to workers, and handles dealing with the results when the workers complete the tasks.

How to use multiple workers

You already know how to create new workers, but how do you use them to do something a little more complicated, like computing the rows of the Mandelbrot Set? Or applying a Photoshop-like effect over an image? Or ray tracing a movie scene? In all these cases, we can break up the job into small tasks that each worker can work on independently. For now, let's stick with computing the Mandelbrot Set (but the pattern we're going to use can be applied to any of these examples).

To get started, the browser first creates a bunch of workers to help (but not too many—workers can be expensive if we create too many of them—more on this later). We'll use just five workers for this example:

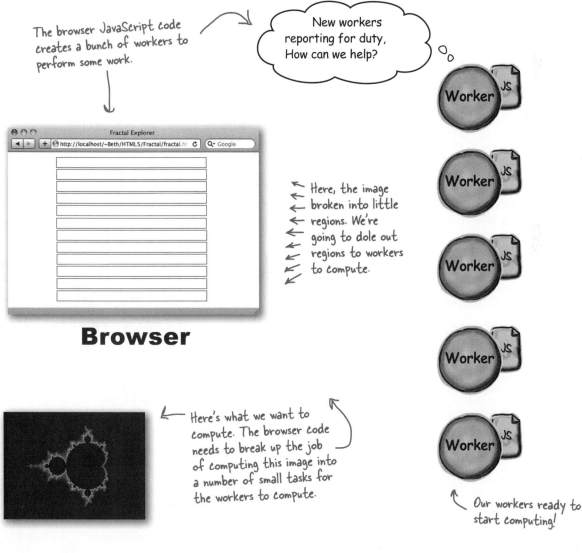

The browser JavaScript code creates a bunch of workers to perform some work.

New workers reporting for duty, How can we help?

Here, the image broken into little regions. We're going to dole out regions to workers to compute.

Browser

Here's what we want to compute. The browser code needs to break up the job of computing this image into a number of small tasks for the workers to compute.

Our workers ready to start computing!

Next, the browser code doles out a different part of
the image for each worker to compute:

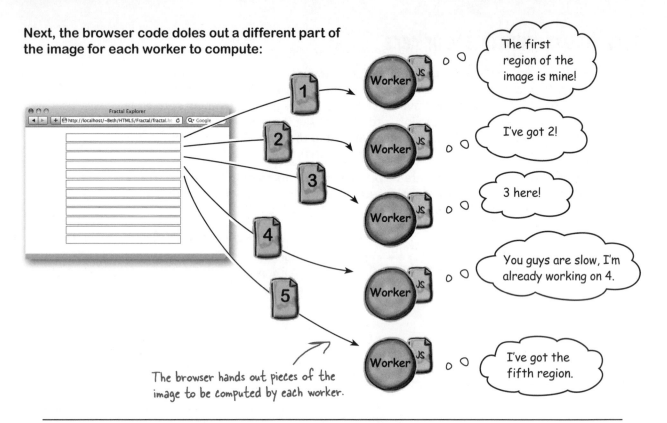

The browser hands out pieces of the
image to be computed by each worker.

Each worker works on its own piece of the image independently. As a
worker finishes its task, it packages up the result and sends it back.

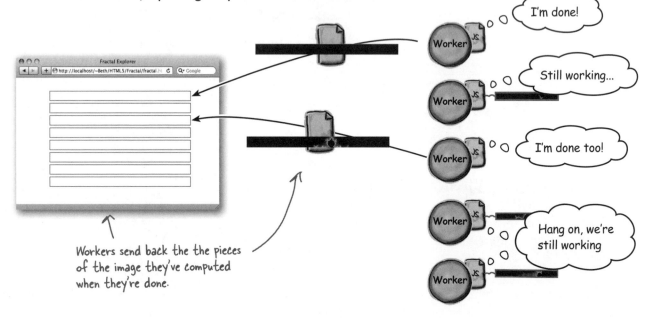

Workers send back the the pieces
of the image they've computed
when they're done.

As pieces of the image come back from the workers they are aggregated into the image in the browser, and if there are more pieces to compute, new tasks are handed out to the workers that are idle.

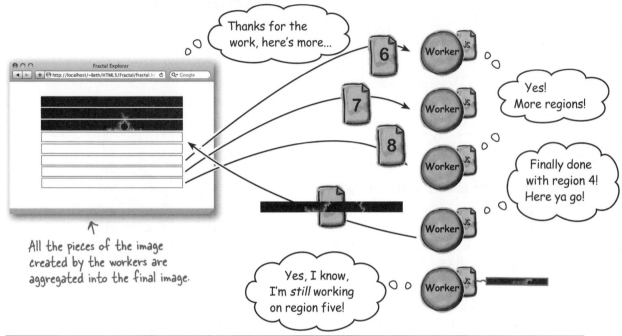

All the pieces of the image created by the workers are aggregated into the final image.

With the last piece of the image computed, the image is complete and the workers sit idle, until the user clicks to zoom in, and then it all starts again...

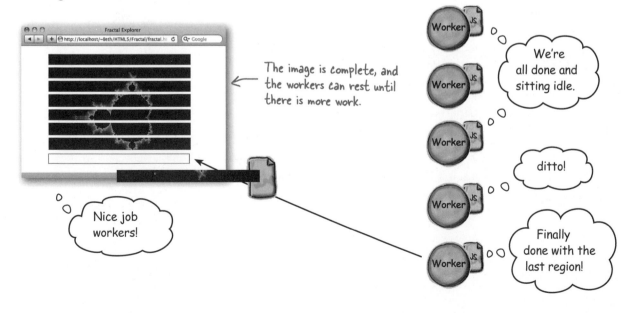

The image is complete, and the workers can rest until there is more work.

> What does it matter if I break up the task and distribute it to workers? I mean, my computer still has the same CPU, how could the computation get any faster?

It can be faster in two ways...

First consider an application that has a lot of "computing" going on that also has to be responsive to the user. If your application is hogging a lot of JavaScript time, your users are going to experience a sluggish interface that feels slow (again, because JavaScript is single-threaded). By adding workers to such an app you can immediately improve the feel of the app for your users. Why? Because JavaScript has a chance to respond to user interaction in between getting results from the workers, something it doesn't have a chance to do if everything's being computed on the main thread. So the UI is more responsive— and your app's just going to *feel* faster (even if it isn't running any faster under the hood). Don't believe us? Give it a try and put some real users in front of your app. Ask them what they think.

The second way *really is faster*. Almost all modern desktops and devices today are shipping with multicore processors (and perhaps even multiple processors). Multicore just means that the processor can do multiple things concurrently. With just a single thread of control, JavaScript in the browser doesn't make use of your extra cores or your extra processors, they're just wasted. However, if you use Web Workers, the workers can take advantage of running on your different cores and you'll see a real speedup in your app because you've got more processor power being thrown at it. If you've got a multicore machine, just wait, you're going to see the difference soon.

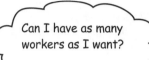

Can I have as many workers as I want?

In theory, not in practice.

Web Workers aren't intended to be used in large numbers—while creating a worker looks simple in code, it requires extra memory and an operating system thread, which can be costly in start-up time and resources. So, in general you'll want to create a limited number of workers that you reuse over time.

Take our Mandelbrot example: in theory you could assign a worker to compute every single pixel, which would probably be much simpler from a code design perspective, but given that workers are heavy-weight resources, we would never design our app that way. Instead, we'll use a handful of workers and structure our computation to take advantage of them.

Let's get a little further into the design of the Fractal Explorer and then we'll come back and play with the number of workers we're using to understand the performance implications.

BRAIN POWER

You've certainly got a lot of background now on building Web Worker apps, how to create and use workers, a bit about how you can solve big computations by breaking them down into small tasks that can be computed by your workers, and you even know a little about how Mandelbrot sets are computed. Try to put it all together and think through how you'd take the pseudo-code below and rewrite it to use workers. You might first assume you have as many workers as you need (say a worker for every single row), and then add the constraint that you have a limited number of workers (fewer workers than the number of rows):

```
for (i = 0; i < numberOfRows; i++) {

    var taskForRow = createTaskForRow(i);

    var row = computeRow(taskForRow);

    drawRow(row);

}
```

Here's our pseudo-code now, what do you need to do to add Web Workers?

Your notes go here:

Let's build the Fractal Explorer app

Here's what we need to do:

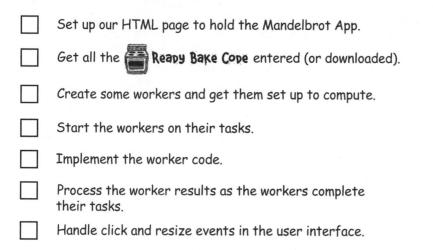

- [ ] Set up our HTML page to hold the Mandelbrot App.

- [ ] Get all the 🍲 Ready Bake Code entered (or downloaded).

- [ ] Create some workers and get them set up to compute.

- [ ] Start the workers on their tasks.

- [ ] Implement the worker code.

- [ ] Process the worker results as the workers complete their tasks.

- [ ] Handle click and resize events in the user interface.

Creating the Fractal Viewer HTML Markup

First we need to set up an HTML page to hold our app. You'll want to create an HTML file named `fractal.html` and add the following markup. Let's check it out:

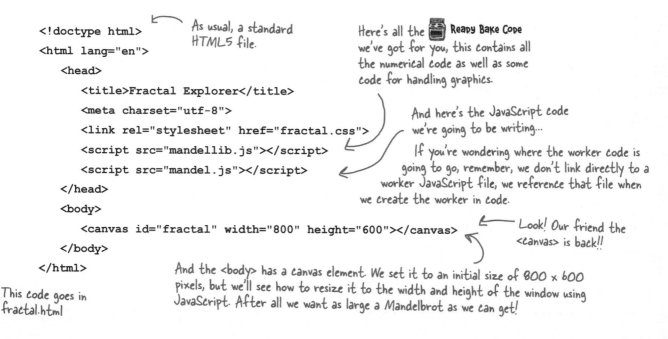

```
<!doctype html>
<html lang="en">
    <head>
        <title>Fractal Explorer</title>
        <meta charset="utf-8">
        <link rel="stylesheet" href="fractal.css">
        <script src="mandellib.js"></script>
        <script src="mandel.js"></script>
    </head>
    <body>
        <canvas id="fractal" width="800" height="600"></canvas>
    </body>
</html>
```

As usual, a standard HTML5 file.

Here's all the 🍲 Ready Bake Code we've got for you, this contains all the numerical code as well as some code for handling graphics.

And here's the JavaScript code we're going to be writing...

If you're wondering where the worker code is going to go, remember, we don't link directly to a worker JavaScript file, we reference that file when we create the worker in code.

Look! Our friend the <canvas> is back!!

This code goes in fractal.html

And the <body> has a canvas element. We set it to an initial size of 800 x 600 pixels, but we'll see how to resize it to the width and height of the window using JavaScript. After all we want as large a Mandelbrot as we can get!

Ready Bake Code

Reminder: you can download all the code from http://wickedlysmart.com/hfhtml5

We have to tell you we were planning on an entire chapter on the wonders of computing the Mandelbrot Set... we planned to explain it to you in detail, including a history of Benoit Mandelbrot, how he discovered it, all its amazing properties, pixel optimizations, color maps, and so on, but then we got the call from our editor—you know, THE CALL. I guess we were running a bit late on this book, so our apologies, but we're going to have to give you some Ready Bake Code code to do the low-level computation of the Mandelbrot graphics. Here's the good side though: we can focus on how to use Web Workers without spending the next couple of days on math and graphics. That said, we encourage you to explore those topics on your own!

Anyway, first we've got the code used to manage tasks and draw the rows for the fractal images. Start by typing this code into a file called "mandellib.js":

```
var canvas;
var ctx;
```

Notice our canvas and context are here.

```
var i_max = 1.5;
var i_min = -1.5;
var r_min = -2.5;
var r_max = 1.5;
```

These are the global variables the Mandelbrot graphics code uses to compute the set and display it.

```
var max_iter = 1024;
var escape = 1025;
var palette = [];

function createTask(row) {
    var task = {
        row: row,
        width: rowData.width,
        generation: generation,
        r_min: r_min,
        r_max: r_max,
        i: i_max + (i_min - i_max) * row / canvas.height,
        max_iter: max_iter,
        escape: escape
    };
    return task;
}
```

This function packages up all the data needed for the worker to compute a row of pixels, into an object. You'll see later how we pass this object to the worker to use.

This code goes in mandellib.js.

☑ Create HTML
☐ Ready Bake Code
☐ Create workers
☐ Start the workers
☐ Implement the workers
☐ Process the results
☐ User interaction code

Ready Bake Code Continued...

```javascript
function makePalette() {
    function wrap(x) {
        x = ((x + 256) & 0x1ff) - 256;
        if (x < 0) x = -x;
        return x;
    }
    for (i = 0; i <= this.max_iter; i++) {
        palette.push([wrap(7*i), wrap(5*i), wrap(11*i)]);
    }
}
```

makePalette maps a large set of numbers into an array of rgb colors. We'll use this palette in drawRow (below) to convert the value we get back from a worker to a color for the graphic display of the set (the fractal image).

drawRow takes the results from the worker and draws them into the canvas.

```javascript
function drawRow(workerResults) {
    var values = workerResults.values;
    var pixelData = rowData.data;
    for (var i = 0; i < rowData.width; i++) {
        var red = i * 4;
        var green = i * 4 + 1;
        var blue = i * 4 + 2;
        var alpha = i * 4 + 3;
        pixelData[alpha] = 255; // set alpha to opaque
        if (values[i] < 0) {
            pixelData[red] = pixelData[green] = pixelData[blue] = 0;
        } else {
            var color = this.palette[values[i]];
            pixelData[red] = color[0];
            pixelData[green] = color[1];
            pixelData[blue] = color[2];
        }
    }
    ctx.putImageData(this.rowData, 0, workerResults.row);
}
```

It uses this rowData variable to do it; rowData is a one-row ImageData object that holds the actual pixels for that row of the canvas.

Here's where we use the palette to map the result from the worker (just a number) to a color.

And here's where we write the pixels to the ImageData object in the context of the canvas!

This code should be familiar; it's similar to what we did in Chapter 8 with video and canvas.

This code goes in mandellib.js.

Ready Bake Code Continued...

setUpGraphics sets up the global variables used by all the graphics drawing code as well as the Mandelbrot computation.

```javascript
function setupGraphics() {

    canvas = document.getElementById("fractal");
    ctx = canvas.getContext("2d");

    canvas.width = window.innerWidth;
    canvas.height = window.innerHeight;

    var width = ((i_max - i_min) * canvas.width / canvas.height);
    var r_mid = (r_max + r_min) / 2;
    r_min = r_mid - width/2;
    r_max = r_mid + width/2;

    rowData = ctx.createImageData(canvas.width, 1);

    makePalette();
}
```

Here's where we grab the canvas and the context and set the initial width and height of the canvas.

These are variables used to compute the Mandelbrot Set.

Here, we're initializing the rowData variable (used to write the pixels to the canvas).

And here we're initializing the palette of colors we're using to draw the the set as a fractal image.

This code goes in mandellib.js.

Ready Bake Code Continued...

This Ready Bake Code is what the worker will use to do its mathematical computation of the Mandelbrot Set. This is really where the magic of the computation happens (and if you explore the Mandelbrot Set more deeply, this is where you'll want to focus). Type this code into "workerlib.js":

computeRow computes one row of data of the Mandelbrot Set. It's given an object with all the packaged up values it needs to compute that row.

```javascript
function computeRow(task) {
    var iter = 0;
    var c_i = task.i;
    var max_iter = task.max_iter;
    var escape = task.escape * task.escape;
    task.values = [];
    for (var i = 0; i < task.width; i++) {
        var c_r = task.r_min + (task.r_max - task.r_min) * i / task.width;
        var z_r = 0, z_i = 0;

        for (iter = 0; z_r*z_r + z_i*z_i < escape && iter < max_iter; iter++) {
            // z -> z^2 + c
            var tmp = z_r*z_r - z_i*z_i + c_r;
            z_i = 2 * z_r * z_i + c_i;
            z_r = tmp;
        }
        if (iter == max_iter) {
            iter = -1;
        }
        task.values.push(iter);
    }
    return task;
}
```

Notice that for each row of the display, we're doing two loops, one for each pixel in the row...

That's a lot of computation. Good!

... and another loop to find the right value for that pixel. This inner loop is where the computational complexity is, and this is why the code runs so much faster when you have multiple cores on your computer!

The end result of all that computation is a value that gets added to an array of named values, which is put back into the task object so the worker can send the result back to the main code.

We'll take a closer look at this part in a bit.

This code goes in workerlib.js.

Creating workers, and giving them tasks...

With the **Ready Bake Code** out of the way, let's now turn our attention to writing the code that is going to create and hand tasks to the workers. Here's how it's going to work:

1 We create an array of workers, initially all idle. And an image with nothing computed (nextRow = 0).

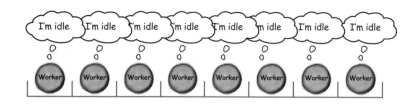

nextRow = 0

2 We iterate through the array, and create a task for each idle worker:

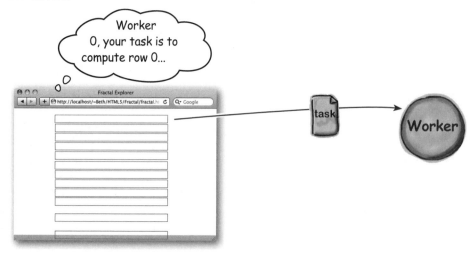

3 We continue to iterate, looking for the next idle worker to give a task to. The next one is nextRow = 1. And so on...

nextRow = 1

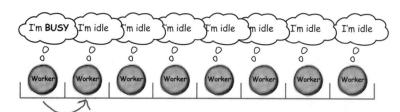

Writing the code

Now that we know how we're going to create and manage our workers, let's write the code. We really need an initial function for this, so let's create a function in `mandel.js` named `init`—we'll place a few other things in it as well, to get the app up and running (like making sure we have the graphics intialization out of the way):

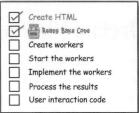

First let's define a variable that holds the number of workers we want. We're choosing 8, feel free to play with this when you've got the app working.

Why 8? Well, we happen to have a computer with 8 cores so it matches well with our compute power. But even if you don't have 8 cores, 8's a good number to try first.

```
var numberOfWorkers = 8;
var workers = [];
```

And here's an empty array to hold our workers.

```
window.onload = init;
```

Let's set up an onload handler that calls init when the page is fully loaded.

```
function init() {
    setupGraphics();
```

This function is defined in the Ready Bake Code and handles getting the canvas context, resizing the canvas to your browser's size, and a few other graphic details.

Now, iterate over the number of workers...

```
    for (var i = 0; i < numberOfWorkers; i++) {
        var worker = new Worker("worker.js");
```

...and create a new worker from "worker.js", which we haven't written yet.

```
        worker.onmessage = function(event) {
            processWork(event.target, event.data);
        }
```

We then set each worker's message handler to a function that calls the processWork function, and we'll pass it the event.target (the worker that just finished), and the event.data (the results from the worker).

```
        worker.idle = true;
```

One more thing... remember we are going to want to know which workers are working and which are idle. To do that we'll add an "idle" property to the worker. This is our own property, not part of the Web Worker API. Right now we're setting it to true since we haven't given the workers anything to do.

```
        workers.push(worker);
    }
```

And we add the worker we just created to the array of workers.

```
    startWorkers();
}
```

And finally, at some point we need to start these workers working. We'll put that code in a function named startWorkers, which we need to write.

This code goes in mandel.js.

Getting the workers started

Okay we've got a few things to knock out: we need to start the workers, we need to write the function that can process the work that comes back from the workers and, well, we need to write the code for the worker too. Let's start by writing the code to start the workers:

☑ Create HTML
☑ Ready Bake Code
☑ Create workers
☐ Start the workers
☐ Implement the workers
☐ Process the results
☐ User interaction code

We're adding two more global variables to mandel.js.

The first is nextRow, which keeps track of which row we're on as we work our way through the image.

```
var nextRow = 0;
var generation = 0;
```

Every time the user zooms into the Mandelbrot image we start a new image computation. The generation variable keeps track of how many times we've done this. More on this later.

```
function startWorkers() {
    generation++;
    nextRow = 0;
```

The startWorkers function is going to start the workers, and also restart them if the user zooms into the image. So, each tme we start the workers we reset nextRow to zero and increment generation.

How both of these are used will become clearer in a bit...

```
    for (var i = 0; i < workers.length; i++) {
        var worker = workers[i];
```

Now, we loop over all the workers in the workers array...

```
        if (worker.idle) {
```

... and check to see if the worker is idle.

```
            var task = createTask(nextRow);
```

If it is, we make a task for the worker to do. This task is to compute a row of the Mandelbrot Set. createTask is defined in mandellib.js, and it returns a task object with all the data the worker needs to compute that row.

```
            worker.idle = false;
            worker.postMessage(task);
```

Now, we're about to give the worker something to do, so we set the idle property to false (meaning, it's busy).

```
            nextRow++;
        }
    }
}
```

And here's where we tell the worker to start work, by posting a message containing the task. The worker is listening for a message, so when it gets this message, it will start working on the task.

And finally, we increment the row, so the next worker gets the next row.

This code goes in mandel.js.

Implementing the worker

putting javascript to work

☑ Create HTML
☑ Ready Bake Code
☑ Create workers
☑ Start the workers
☐ Implement the workers
☐ Process the results
☐ User interaction code

Now that we've got the code to get our workers started by passing each a task, let's write the worker code. Then all we need to do is come back and process the results from the worker, once the worker has computed its part of the fractal image. Before we write the code for the worker though, let's quickly review how it should work:

① Worker is handed a task with postMessage.

② The worker takes the task and passes it to a Ready Bake function to compute the row.

`computeRow( task );`

③ The computed row is completed and we need to send it back to the main page code.

④ Result is sent back from worker with another postMessage.

So let's implement this: go head and type the following code into your `worker.js` file.

We're using importScripts to import the workerlib.js
Ready Bake Code so the worker can call the computeRow
function defined in that library file.

All the worker does is set up the onmessage
handler. It doesn't need to do anything else,
because all it does is wait for messages from
mandel.js to start working!

```javascript
importScripts("workerlib.js");

onmessage = function (task) {

    var workerResult = computeRow(task.data);

    postMessage(workerResult);

}
```

It gets the data from the task, and passes
that to the computeRow function, which does
the hard work of the Mandelbrot computation.

The result of the computation, saved in the
workerResult variable, is posted back to the
main JavaScript using postMessage.

This code goes
in worker.js

A little pit stop...

That was a lot of code in just a few pages. Let's take a quick pit stop, and refuel our tanks and stomachs.

We also thought you might want to get a quick peek behind the scenes and see what the worker tasks and results look like (they look remarkably similar as we'll see). So, grab a bottle of sarsaparilla and let's take a look while you're resting...

 ## Close up on Tasks

So you've looked at the call to createTask and postMessage, which uses the task:

```
var task = createTask(nextRow);
worker.postMessage(task);
```

And you might be wondering what that task looks like. Well, it's an object made up of propeties and values, let's take a look:

```
task = {
    row: 1,
    width: 1024,
    generation: 1,
    r_min: 2.074,
    r_max: -3.074,
    i: -0.252336,
    max_iter: 1024,
    escape: 1025
};
```

Identifies the row we're creating the pixels value for.

Identifies width of the row.

Identifies how many times we've zoomed in. We'll see how this is used in a bit...

These define the area of the Mandelbrot we're computing.

And these control the precision of what we're computing.

The task contains all the values the worker needs to do its computation.

Close up on Results

And what about the results we get from computing the row in the worker?

```
var workerResult = computeRow(task.data);

postMessage(workerResult);
```

What does this look like? Remarkably similar to the task:

```
workerResult = {
    row: 1,
    width: 1024,
    generation: 1,
    r_min: 2.074,
    r_max: -3.074,
    i: -0.252336,
    max_iter: 1024,
    escape: 1025,
    values: [3, 9, 56, ... -1, 22]
};
```

This is all the same as the task. That's great because when we get it back from the worker we know everything about the task.

The worker takes the task passed to it and then adds a values property to it that contains the data needed to draw the row on the canvas.

Ah, but this is new. These are the values of each pixel, which still need to be mapped to colors (which happens in drawRow).

Time to get back on the road...

Thanks for taking some time with us to check out the tasks and results. You better take a last swig of that sarsaparilla—we're hitting the road again!

Back to the code: how to process the worker's results

Now that you've seen how the worker's results work, let's see what happens when we get them back from the worker. Recall that when we created our workers, we assigned a message handler named `processWork`:

```javascript
var worker = new Worker("worker.js");

worker.onmessage = function(event) {
    processWork(event.target, event.data);
}
```

Our message handler calls processWork, passing it the data from the worker, and also the target, which is just a reference to the worker that sent the data.

When a worker posts a message back to us with its results, it's the `processWork` function that's going to handle it. As you can see, it is passed two things: the target of the message, which is just a reference to the worker that sent it, and the data of the message (that's the task object with the values for a row of the image). So our job now is to write `processWork` (enter this code in `mandel.js`):

```javascript
function processWork(worker, workerResults) {
    drawRow(workerResults);
    reassignWorker(worker);
}
```

We hand the results to drawRow to draw the pixels to the canvas.

And our worker is all free, so we can reassign it to another task. To do that let's write a function reassignWorker.

We're almost there, so let's just knock out `reassignWorker` while we're at it. Here's how it works: we check the row we're computing by using our `nextRow` global variable, and as long as there's more to compute (which we can determine by looking at how many rows are in our canvas), we give the worker a new assignment. Otherwise, if there's no more work to do, then we just set the worker's idle property to true. Go ahead and enter this code in `mandel.js` too:

```javascript
function reassignWorker(worker) {
    var row = nextRow++;

    if (row >= canvas.height) {
        worker.idle = true;
    } else {
        var task = createTask(row);
        worker.idle = false;
        worker.postMessage(task);
    }
}
```

We're going to give this worker the next row that needs computing, so we get the row number from nextRow, and increment nextRow (so the next worker gets the next one).

If the row is greater than or equal to the height of the canvas, we're done! We've filled the entire canvas with results from the Mandelbrot Set workers.

Canvas is a global variable that was assigned when we called setupGraphics in our init function.

But if we've still got rows to do, we create a new task for the next row to do, make sure our worker's idle property is false, and post a message with the new task to the worker.

This code goes in mandel.js.

Psychedelic test drive

Enough code already! Let's road test this thing. Load the `fractal.html` file into your browser and see your workers going to work. Depending on your machine, your Fractal Explorer should run a little faster than before.

We haven't written any code to handle resizing your browser window, or clicking to zoom into the fractal for that matter. So, for right now, all you'll be able to see is the image on the right.

But, hey, so far so good, huh?

> There it is! Too bad we can't zoom, and too bad it doesn't fill the whole window yet, but we'll get to that...

Handling a click event

We've got our workers busy working to compute the Mandelbrot Set and returning results to us so we can draw them on the canvas, but what happens if you click to zoom in? Fortunately, because we're using workers to do the intense computation in the background, the UI should be snappy in dealing with your click. That said, we need to write a little code to actually handle the click. Here's how we do that:

☑ Create HTML
☑ Ready Bake Code
☑ Create workers
☑ Start the workers
☑ Implement the workers
☑ Process the results
☐ User interaction code

 1 The first thing we need to do is add a handler to take care of mouse clicks, and remember, the clicks are happening on our canvas element. To do that we just add a handler for the canvas's onclick property, like this:

```
canvas.onclick = function(event) {
    handleClick(event.clientX, event.clientY);
};
```

> If the canvas is clicked on, we call the function handleClick with the x and y position of the click.

Add this code below the call to setUpGraphics in the init function of "mandel.js".

2 Now we just need to write the handleClick function. Before we do let's think about this a second: when a user clicks on the canvas it means they want to zoom into the area they're clicking on (you can go back to the single-threaded version at `http://wickedlysmart.com/hfhtml5/chapter10/singlethread/fractal.html` to see this behavior). So when the user clicks, we need to get the coordinates of where they want to zoom, and then get all the workers working on creating a new image. Remember too, we've already got a function to assign new work to any idle workers: startWorkers. Let's give it a try...

handleClick is called when the
user clicks on the canvas to
zoom into the fractal.

We pass in the x, y position of
the click so we know where they
clicked on the screen.

This code resizes the area of the
fractal we are computing, with the
x, y position at the center of the
new area. It also makes sure the
new area has the same aspect ratio
of the existing one.

```javascript
function handleClick(x, y) {
    var width = r_max - r_min;
    var height = i_min - i_max;
    var click_r = r_min + width * x / canvas.width;
    var click_i = i_max + height * y / canvas.height;

    var zoom = 8;

    r_min = click_r - width/zoom;
    r_max = click_r + width/zoom;
    i_max = click_i - height/zoom;
    i_min = click_i + height/zoom;

    startWorkers();
}
```

This is where we set the global variables that
are used to create tasks for workers: the zoom
level determines how far zoomed in we are into
the fractal, which determines which values of
the Mandelbrot Set are being computed.

Now, we're ready to restart the workers.

This code goes
in mandel.js.

Nice! We can zoom, but
we still need to resize
the canvas to fit our
window fully.

Another test drive

Let's give those code changes a try. Reload
fractal.html in your browser and this time
click somewhere in the canvas. When you
do you'll see the workers start working on the
zoomed-in view.

Hey, you should be able to start exploring now!
After you've played around a bit, let's make a
few final changes to get this implementation all
the way there.

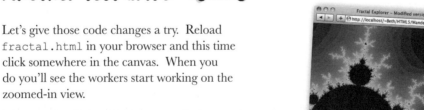

Fitting the canvas to the browser window

We said we wanted the fractal image to fill the browser window, which means we need to resize the canvas if the window size changes. Not only that, but if we change the canvas size we should also fire off a new set of tasks to the workers so they can redraw the fractal to fill up the new canvas size. Let's write the code to resize the canvas to the size of the browser window, and we'll also restart the workers while we're at it.

```javascript
function resizeToWindow() {
    canvas.width = window.innerWidth;
    canvas.height = window.innerHeight;
    var width = ((i_max - i_min) * canvas.width / canvas.height);
    var r_mid = (r_max + r_min) / 2;
    r_min = r_mid - width/2;
    r_max = r_mid + width/2;
    rowData = ctx.createImageData(canvas.width, 1);

    startWorkers();
}
```

resizeToWindow makes sure the canvas width and height are set to match the new width and height of the window.

It also updates the values that the worker will use to do its computation based on the new width and height (we make sure the fractal will always fit the canvas and maintain the aspect ratio of the window).

And once again, we restart the workers.

There's one administrative detail that uses a global variable we haven't told you about: rowData. rowData is the ImageData object that we're using to draw pixels into a row of the canvas. So, when we resize the canvas, we need to recreate the rowData object so that it is the same width as the new width of the canvas. Check the function drawRow in mandellib.js to see how we use rowData to draw pixels into the canvas.

Now we need to do one more thing: install `resizeToWindow` as a handler for the browser window's resize event. Here's how we do that:

```javascript
window.onresize = function() {
    resizeToWindow();
};
```

You'll want to place this code in the init function of `mandel.js`, just below the call to `setUpGraphics`.

This code goes in mandel.js.

The anal-retentive ~~chef~~ coder

There's just one more thing, and we could let this one go, but the code just doesn't seem correct without it. Think through this with us: you've got a bunch of workers happily working on their rows and all of the sudden the user has to go and click on the screen to zoom. Well isn't that great, because the workers have been working hard on their rows, and now the user wants to go and change the entire image, making all that work useless. Even worse, the workers have no knowledge that the user has clicked, and they're going to send back their results anyway. And far worse, the code in the main page is gladly going to receive and display that row! And not to get all doomsday and everything, but we've got exactly the same problem if the user resizes the window.

Note to Editor: Apologies for the little rant here, but, hey, after this many pages, well, it can get to you...

Now, you'd probably never notice any of this because there aren't that many workers, and the workers very quickly compute the same rows for the new image, overwriting the previous, incorrect rows. But hey, it just feels wrong. Not only that, it's so easy to fix we just have to.

Of course we have a little confession to make: we knew this was coming, and you might remember a little variable we stuck in named `generation`. Remember, every time we restart our workers we increase the value of `generation`. Also remember the results object that comes back from the worker: every result has its "generation" as a property. So we can use generation to know if we've got a result from the current or the previous visualization.

Let's look at the code fix, and then we can talk about how it works; edit your `processWork` function in `mandel.js` and add these two lines:

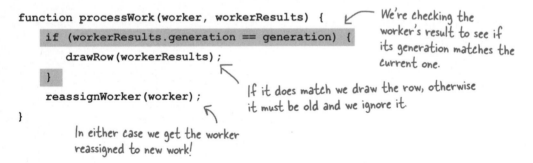

```
function processWork(worker, workerResults) {
    if (workerResults.generation == generation) {
        drawRow(workerResults);
    }
    reassignWorker(worker);
}
```

We're checking the worker's result to see if its generation matches the current one.

If it does match we draw the row, otherwise it must be old and we ignore it.

In either case we get the worker reassigned to new work!

So all we're doing here is checking to make sure the current generation we're working on matches the generation of the result that comes back from the worker. If it does, great, then we need to draw the row. If it doesn't, well that means it must be old, and so we just ignore it—it's too bad our worker wasted its time on it, but we don't want to draw an old row from the previous image on the screen.

So, really, that's it, we promise, it's time to make sure you have the changes above typed in, and get ready for...

Time for the final test drive!

That's it! You should be ready to go with all your code. Load the `fractal.html` file into your browser and see your workers going to work. This version should be faster and more responsive than the original, single-threaded version; if you've got more than one core on your computer, then it will be *a lot* faster.

Have fun... zoom in... explore. Let us know if you find any undiscovered "country" in the Mandelbrot Set (tweet your screenshots to **#hfhtml5** if you want!).

Resize your screen to any shape or size now!

Click, zoom, explore!

IN THE LABORATORY

If you're writing high performance code you'll want to check out how the number of workers can impact your app's runtime.

To do that, you can use the task monitor on either OS X or Windows. If we go back to our original version (the single-threaded one at `http://wickedlysmart.com/hfhtml5/chapter10/singlethread/fractal.html`) our performance looks like the graph on the right.

Our machine with eight cores. One core is maxed out and can't compute any harder. The other seven are doing nothing to help.

We have eight cores in our machine, and so in the Fractal Explorer with Web Workers, we're setting the number of workers to match that, with `numberOfWorkers = 8`. And you can see in our activity monitor, all 8 cores are being used to the max.

What do you think will happen if we set the number of workers to 2, or 4, or 16, or 32? Or something in between?

Give it a try on your machine and see what values work best for you.

Now our eight cores are really working hard, and our fractal computation is WAY faster.

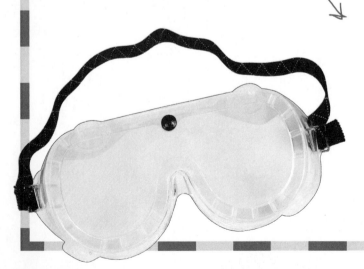

STAKE YOUR CLAIM!

You've done it! You've got a fully functional Fractal Explorer that's all ready for exploring the Mandbelbrot territory. So what are you waiting for—dig in and find your little slice of the virtual universe. Once you've found it, print it, paste it in here, and give your new little homestead a name.

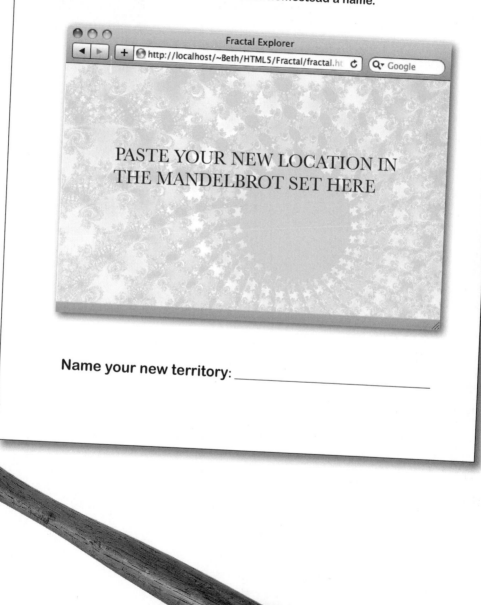

Name your new territory: _____

Now before you take off, would you believe there's even more to know about Web Workers? Check out the next couple of pages to see everything we didn't cover in this chapter.

Terminate a worker

You've created workers to do a task, the task is done, and you want to get rid of all the workers (they do take up valuable memory in the browser). You can terminate a worker from the code in your main page like this:

```
worker.terminate();
```

If the worker happens to still be running, the worker script will abort, so use with caution. And once you've terminated a worker you can't reuse it; you'll have to create a new one.

You can also have a worker stop itself by calling **close();** (from inside the worker).

Handle errors in workers

What happens if something goes terribly wrong in a worker? How can you debug it? Use the onerror handler to catch any errors and also get debugging information, like this:

```
worker.onerror = function(error) {
    document.getElementById("output").innerHTML =
        "There was an error in " + error.filename +
        " at line number " + error.lineno +
        ": " + error.message;
}
```

Use importScripts to make a JSONP request

You can't insert new `<script>` elements to make JSONP requests from workers,
but you **can** use importScripts to make JSONP requests, like this:

```
function makeServerRequest() {
        importScripts("http://SomeServer.com?callback=handleRequest");
}
function handleRequest(response) {
        postMessage(response);
}
makeServerRequest();
```

Remember your JSONP? Include your callback function in the URL query, and it will be called with the JSON results passed into the response parameter.

Use setInterval in your workers

You might have missed this (it went by fast, we used it in only one example), but you can use
setInterval (and setTimeout) in your workers to do the same task repeatedly. For instance you
could update the quotes worker (quote.js) to post a random quote every 3 seconds, like this:

```
var quotes = ["I hope life isn't a joke, because I don't get it.",
              "There is a light at the end of every tunnel...just pray it's not a train!",
              "Do you believe in love at first sight or should I walk by again?"];
function postAQuote() {
    var index = Math.floor(Math.random() * quotes.length);
    postMessage(quotes[index]);
}
postAQuote();
setInterval(postAQuote, 3000);
```

Move these two lines into a postAQuote function...

... call postAQuote to send a quote right away, and then set an interval to send more quotes, every 3 seconds.

Subworkers

If your worker needs help with its task, it can create its own workers. Say you're giving your
worker regions of an image to work on, the worker could decide that if a region is bigger
than some size, it will split it up among its own subworkers.

A worker creates subworkers just like the code in your page creates a worker, with:

```
var worker = new Worker("subworker.js");
```

Remember that subworkers, just like workers, are fairly heavy-weight: they take up memory
and are run as separate threads. So, be cautious about how many subworkers you create.

BULLET POINTS

- Without Web Workers, JavaScript is single-threaded, meaning it can do only one thing at a time.

- If you give a JavaScript program too much to do, you might get the slow script dialog.

- Web Workers handle tasks on a separate thread so your main JavaScript code can continue to run and your UI remains responsive.

- The code for a Web Worker is in a separate file from your page's code.

- Web Workers don't have access to any of the functions in the code in your page or the DOM.

- The code in your page and the Web Worker communicate via messages.

- To send a message to a worker, use postMessage.

- You can send strings and objects to a worker via postMessage. You can't send functions to a worker.

- Receive messages back from workers by setting the worker's onmessage property to a handler function.

- A worker receives messages from the code in your page by setting its onmessage property to a handler function.

- When a worker is ready to send back a result, it calls postMessage and passes the result as the argument.

- Worker results are encapsulated in an event object and placed in the data property.

- You can find out which worker sent the message using the event.target property.

- Messages are copied, not shared, between your main page code and the worker.

- You can use multiple workers for large computations that can be split into multiple tasks, such as computing a fractal visualization or ray tracing an image.

- Each worker runs in its own thread, so if your computer has a multicore processor, the workers are run in parallel, which increases the speed of the computation.

- You can terminate a worker by calling worker.terminate() from the code in your page. This will abort the worker script. A worker can also stop itself by calling close().

- Workers also have an onerror property. You can set this to an error handling function that will be called if your worker has a script error.

- To include and use JavaScript libraries in your worker file, use importScripts.

- You can also use importScripts with JSONP. Implement the callback you pass in the URL query in the worker file.

- While workers do not have access to the DOM or functions in your main code, they can use XMLHttpRequest and Local Storage.

HTML5cross

Wow, Chapter 10; you've done it. Sit back, relax and make it stick by working the rest of your brain a little. Here's your Chapter 10 crossword puzzle.

Across

4. You can pass _____ to workers using postMessage.
8. Capability of a processor to do more than one thing at a time.
9. The property used to register a handler to receive messages.
11. Workers can't access the _____.
12. Our first example used this game.
13. The most famous fractal.
14. _____/worker.
15. A lovely area of the Mandelbrot countryside is _____ Valley.
16. The guy who wrote the original version of Fractal Viewer.

Down

1. Workers can use XMLHttpRequest and access _____.
2. How to import additional code into a worker.
3. _____ of execution.
5. How to abort a worker.
6. Mandelbrot uses _____ numbers.
7. How to create a Worker.
10. The manager and workers communicate with these.

Okay we never told you this, it's James Henstridge.

BE the Browser Solution

It's time to pretend you're the browser evaluating JavaScript.

```javascript
window.onload = function() {
    var worker = new Worker("worker.js");
    worker.onmessage = function(event) {
        alert("Worker says " + event.data);
    }
    for (var i = 0; i < 5; i++) {
        worker.postMessage("ping");
    }
}
```

This sends five ping messages to the worker, which responds with five pongs, so we get five "Worker says pong" alerts.

```javascript
window.onload = function() {
    var worker = new Worker("worker.js");
    worker.ommessage = function(event) {
        alert("Worker says " + event.data);
    }
    for(var i = 5; i > 0; i--) {
        worker.postMessage("pong");
    }
}
```

This sends five pong messages to the worker, which ignores them since they aren't pings. No output.

```javascript
window.onload = function() {
    var worker = new Worker("worker.js");
    worker.onmessage = function(event) {
        alert("Worker says " + event.data);
        worker.postMessage("ping");
    }
    worker.postMessage("ping");
}
```

This sends a ping and then each time a pong comes back, sends another, so we get an infinite loop of pong alerts.

```javascript
window.onload = function() {
    var worker = new Worker("worker.js");
    worker.onmessage = function(event) {
        alert("Worker says " + event.data);
    }

    setInterval(pinger, 1000);

    function pinger() {
        worker.postMessage("ping");
    }
}
```

This sends a ping every second, so we get a pong back each time it sends a ping.

Sharpen your pencil
Solution

While workers typically get their work orders through a message, they don't have to. Check out this nice, compact way to get work done with workers and HTML. When you know what it does, describe it below:

quote.html

```html
<!doctype html>
<html lang="en">
    <head>
        <title>Quote</title>
        <meta charset="utf-8">
    </head>
<body>
    <p id="quote"></p>
    <script>
        var worker = new Worker("quote.js");
        worker.onmessage = function(event) {
            document.getElementById("quote").innerHTML = event.data;
        }
    </script>
</body>
</html>
```

quote.js

```javascript
var quotes = ["I hope life isn't a joke, because I don't get it.",
              "There is a light at the end of every tunnel….just pray it's not a train!",
              "Do you believe in love at first sight or should I walk by again?"];
var index = Math.floor(Math.random() * quotes.length);


postMessage(quotes[index]);
```

Your description here:

In our HTML, we have a script that creates a worker, which executes immediately. The worker chooses a quote randomly from the quotes array, and sends the quote to the main code using postMessage. The main code gets the quote from event.data and adds it to the page in the "quote" <p> element.

HTML5cross Solution

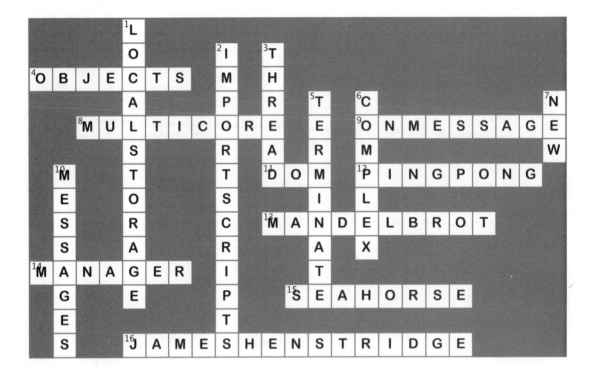

Wouldn't it be dreamy if this were the end of the book? If there were no bullet points or puzzles or JavaScript listings or anything else? But that's probably just a fantasy...

Congratulations!
You made it to the end.

Of course, there's still an appendix.

And the index.

And the colophon.

And then there's the web site...

There's no escape, really.

Appendix: leftovers

The Top Ten Topics (we didn't cover)

We've covered a lot of ground, and you're almost finished with this book. We'll miss you, but before we let you go, we wouldn't feel right about sending you out into the world without a little more preparation. We can't possibly fit everything you'll need to know into this relatively small chapter. Actually, we *did* originally include everything you need to know about HTML5 (not already covered by the other chapters), by reducing the type point size to .00004. It all fit, but nobody could read it. So, we threw most of it away, and kept the best bits for this Top Ten appendix.

This really *is* the end of the book. Except for the index, of course (a must-read!).

#1 Modernizr

One thing you've probably noticed in this book, is that when you want to detect browser support for an API, there is no uniform way of doing so; in fact, almost every API is detected in a different way. For geolocation, for instance, we look for the geolocation object as a property of the navigator object, while for web storage we check to see if localStorage is defined in the window object, and for video we check to see if we can create a video element in DOM, and so on. Surely there's a better way?

Modernizr is an open source JavaScript library that provides a uniform interface for detecting browser support. Modernizer takes care of all the details of the different means of detection, even factoring in all the edge cases around older browsers. You'll find the Modernizr home page at `http://www.modernizr.com/`

Modernizr has gained a lot of developer support so you'll see it used widely around the Web. We highly recommend it.

Including Modernizr in your page

To use Modernizr, you need to load the JavaScript library into your page. To do that you first visit the Modernizer site at `http://www.modernizr.com/download/`, which allows you to custom configure a library that contains just the detection code you need (or you can always grab everything while you're there). After you've done that, stash the library in a file of your choice and load it into your page (visit Modernizr's web site for addition tutorials and documentation on best practices for doing this).

How to detect support

Once you've got Modernizr installed, detecting HTML5 elements and JavaScript APIs gets a lot easier and more straightforward:

Here's an example of detecting for geolocation, web storage and video, all in a consistent manner.

Note: Modernizr goes far beyond simple API detection and can also detect support for CSS features, video codecs and many other things. So, check it out!

```
if (Modernizr.geolocation) {
    console.log("You have geo!");
}
if (Modernizr.localstorage) {
    console.log("You have web storage!");
}
if (Modernizr.video) {
    console.log("You have video!");
}
```

#2 Audio

HTML5 gives you a standard way to play audio in your pages, without a plug-in, with the `<audio>` element:

```
<audio src="song.mp3" id="boombox" controls>
   Sorry but audio is not supported in your browser.
</audio>
```

Look familiar? Yes, audio supports similar functionality as video (minus video, obviously).

In addition to the `<audio>` element, there is also a corresponding Audio API that supports the methods you'd expect, like `play`, `pause` and `load`. If this sounds familiar, it should, because the audio API mirrors (where appropriate) the video API. Audio also supports many of the properties you saw in the video API, like `src`, `currentTime` and `volume`. Here's a bit of audio code to get a feel for using the API with an element in the page:

```
var audioElement =
    document.getElementById("boombox");

audioElement.volume = .5;

audioElement.play();
```

Get a reference to the audio element, then lower its volume to 1/2 and start playing.

Also like video, each browser implements its own look and feel for player controls (which typically consist of a progress bar with play, pause and volume controls).

Despite its simple functionality, the audio element and API give you lots of control. Just like we did with video, you can create interesting web experiences by hiding the controls and managing the audio playback in your code. And with HTML5, you can now do this without the overhead of having to use (and learn) a plug-in.

A Standard for Audio Encodings

Sadly, like video, there is no standard encoding for audio. Three formats are popular: mp3, wav and Ogg Vorbis. You'll find that support for these formats varies across the browser landscape with different levels of support for the various formats in each browser (as of this writing, as of this writing, Chrome is the only browser that supports all three formats).

#3 jQuery

jQuery is a JavaScript library that is aimed at reducing and simplifying much of the JavaScript code and syntax that is needed to work with the DOM, use Ajax and add visual effects to your pages. jQuery is an enormously popular library that is widely used and expandable through its plug-in model.

Remember, Ajax is just a name for using XMLHttpRequest, like we did in Chapter 6.

Now, there's nothing you can do in jQuery that you can't do with JavaScript (as we said, jQuery is just a JavaScript library), however it does have the power to reduce the amount of code you need to write.

jQuery's popularity speaks for itself, although it can take some getting used to if you are new to it. Let's check out a few things you can do in jQuery and we encourage you to take a closer look if you think it might be for you.

A working knowledge of jQuery is a good skill these days on the job front and for understanding others' code.

For starters, remember all the window onload functions we wrote in this book? Like:

```
window.onload = function() {
    alert("the page is loaded!");
}
```

Here's the same thing using jQuery:

```
$(document).ready(function() {
    alert("the page is loaded!");
});
```

Just like our version, when the document is ready, invoke my function.

Or you can shorten this even more, to:

```
$(function() {
    alert("the page is loaded!");
});
```

This is cool, but as you can see it takes a little getting used to at first. No worries, it becomes second-nature fast.

So what about getting elements from the DOM? That's where jQuery shines. Let's say you have an anchor in your page with an id of "buynow" and you want to assign a click handler to the click event on that element (like we've done a few times in this book). Here's how you do that:

So what's going on here? First we're setting up a function that is called when the page is loaded.

```
$(function() {
    $("#buynow").click(function() {
        alert("I want to buy now!");
    });
});
```

Next we're grabbing the anchor with a "buynow" id (notice jQuery uses CSS syntax for selecting elements).

And then we're calling a jQuery method, click, on the result to set the onclick handler.

That's really just the beginning; we can just as easily set the click handler on *every anchor* on the page:

```
$(function() {
    $("a").click(function() {
        alert("I want to buy now!");
    });
});
```

To do that, all we need to do is use the tag name.

Compare this to the code you'd write to do this if we were using JavaScript without jQuery.

Or, we can do things that are much more complex:

```
$(function() {
    $("#playlist > li").addClass("favorite");
});
```

Like find all the <li> elements that are children of the element with an id of playlist.

And then add them to the class "favorite".

Actually this is jQuery just getting warmed up; jQuery can do things much much more sophisticated than this.

There's a whole 'nother side of jQuery that allows you to do interesting interface transfomations on your elements, like this:

```
$(function() {
    $("#specialoffer").toggle(function() {
        $(this).animate({ backgroundColor: "yellow" }, 800);
    },function() {
        $(this).animate({ backgroundColor: "white" }, 300);
    });
});
```

This toggles the element with an id of specialoffer between being yellow and 800 pixels wide, and white and 300 pixels wide, and animates the transition between the two states.

As you can see, there's a lot you can do with jQuery, and we haven't even talked about how we can use jQuery to talk to web services, or all the plug-ins that work with jQuery. If you're interested, the best thing you can do is point your browser to `http://jquery.com/` and check out the tutorials and documentation there.

And, check out Head First jQuery too!

#4 XHTML is dead, long live XHTML

We were pretty tough on XHTML in this book, first with the "XHTML is dead" discussion, and then later with "JSON versus XML". The truth is, when it comes to XHTML, it is only XHTML 2 and later that has died, and in fact, you can write your HTML5 using XHTML-style if you want to. Why would you want to? Well, you might need to validate or transform your documents as XML, or you might want to support XML technologies, like SVG (see #5), that work with HTML.

Let's look at a simple XHTML document and then step through the high points (we couldn't possibly cover everything you need to know on this topic, as with all things XML; it gets complicated, fast).

```
<!DOCTYPE html>
<html xmlns="http://www.w3.org/1999/xhtml">
    <head>
        <title>You Rock!</title>
        <meta charset="UTF-8" />
    </head>
    <body>
        <p>I'm kinda liking this XHTML!</p>
        <svg xmlns="http://www.w3.org/2000/svg">
            <rect stroke="black" fill="blue" x="45px" y="45px"
                width="200px" height="100px" stroke-width="2" />
        </svg>
    </body>
</html>
```

← Same doctype!

This is XML, we need a namespace!

All elements have to be well formed; note the trailing /> here to close this empty element.

We're using SVG to draw a rectangle into our page. Check out #5 (next page) for more on SVG.

We can embed XML right in the page! Kinda cool.

Now here's a few things you need to consider for your XHTML pages:

Closing all your elements, quotes around attribute values, valid nesting of elements, and all that.

- Your page must be well formed XML.

- Your page should be served with the `application/xhtml+xml` MIME type, for this you'll need to make sure your server is serving this type (either read up on this or contact your server administrator).

- Make sure and include the XHTML namespace in your `<html>` element (which we've done above).

Like we said, with XML there's a lot more to know and lots of things to watch out for. And, as always with XML, may the force be with you...

#5 SVG

Scalable Vector Graphics, or SVG, is another way—aside from canvas—of including graphics natively in your web pages. SVG has been around a while (since 1999 or so) and is now supported in all the current versions of major browsers, including IE9 and later.

Unlike canvas, which, as you know, is an element that allows you to draw pixels into a bitmap drawing surface in your page with JavaScript, SVG graphics are specified with XML. "XML?" you say? Yes, XML! You create elements that represent graphics, and then you can combine those elements together in complex ways to make graphic scenes. Let's take a look at a very simple SVG example:

We're using the XHTML-style HTML5 because we're using SVG, which is XML-based.

```
<!DOCTYPE html>
<html xmlns="http://www.w3.org/1999/xhtml">
<head>
  <title>SVG</title>
  <meta charset="utf-8" />
</head>
<body>
  <div id="svg">
    <svg xmlns="http://www.w3.org/2000/svg">
      <circle id="circle"
              cx="50" cy="50" r="20"
              stroke="#373737" stroke-width="2"
              fill="#7d7d7d" />
    </svg>
  </div>
</body>
</html>
```

We're using an <svg> element right in our HTML!

Our SVG is simple: it contains only a circle that is located at position x=50, y=50 and has a radius of 20...

... a stroke that is 2 pixels wide and colored dark grey...

... and is filled with a medium grey.

You can grab this circle element just like any other element from the DOM and do stuff with it... for instance you could add a click handler and change the circle's fill attribute to "red" when the user clicks on the circle.

SVG defines a variety of basic shapes, like circles, rectangles, polygons, lines, and so on. If you have more complex shapes to draw, you can also specify paths with SVG—of course, at that point things start getting more complex (as you already saw with paths in canvas). However, there are graphical editors that will let you draw a scene and export it as SVG, saving you the headache of figuring out all those paths yourself!

What's so great about SVG? Well, one nice aspect of SVG is that you can scale your graphics as big or small as you want and they don't pixellate, like a jpeg or png image would if you scaled it. That makes them easy to reuse in different situations. And because SVG is specified with text, SVG files can be searched, indexed, scripted and compressed.

We've barely scratched the surface of what you can do with SVG, so explore more if this topic interests you.

#6 Offline web apps

If you've got a smartphone or tablet, you're probably accessing the Web on the go, and with WiFi and cellular networks, you're connected almost all the time. But what about those times when you're not? Wouldn't it be great if you could keep on using those great HTML5 web apps you've been building for yourself?

Well, now you can. Offline web applications are supported by all modern desktop and mobile browsers (with one exception: IE).

So how do you make your web application available offline? You create a *cache manifest* file that contains a list of all the files your app needs to work, and the browser will download all those files, and switch to the local files if and when your device goes offline. To tell your web page that it has a manifest file, you simply add the filename of the cache manifest file to your `<html>` tag, like this:

```html
<html manifest="notetoself.manifest">
```

With offline web apps, you can use your favorite web apps when you're not connected!

Here's what the `notetoself.manifest` file contains:

```
CACHE MANIFEST        ←——— Every cache manifest file
CACHE:                      must start with this.
notetoself.html  ⎫
notetoself.css   ⎬←——— List all the files you want to cache
notetoself.js    ⎭       in the CACHE section: html, css,
                         javascript, images, etc.
```

This file says: when you visit the web page that points to this file, download all the files listed in the `CACHE` section of the file. You can also add two other sections to the file, `FALLBACK` and `NETWORK`. `FALLBACK` specifies what file to use if you try to access a file that isn't cached, and `NETWORK` specifies files that should never be cached (for example, visit tracking resources).

Now, before you run off to go play with this, you need to know two things: first, you need to make sure your web server is set up to serve the mime type for cache manifest files correctly (just like we had to do for video files in Chapter 8). For example, on an Apache server, add this line to your `.htaccess` file at the top level of your web directory:

```
AddType text/cache-manifest .manifest
```

The other thing you need to know is that testing offline web applications is tricky! We recommend checking out a good reference on the topic and reading the HTML5 offline web applications specification.

Once you've got basic caching working, you can use JavaScript to be notified of cache events, such as when a cache manifest file is updated and the status of the cache. To be notified of events, you add event handlers to the `window.applicationCache` object, like this:

```javascript
window.applicationCache.addEventListener("error", errorHandler, false);
```

Implement the errorHandler to be notified if there's an error with the cache.

#7 Web Sockets

We looked at two ways of communicating in this book: XMLHttpRequest and JSONP. In both cases we used a request/response model based on HTTP. That is, we used the browser to make a request for the initial web page, CSS and JavaScript, and each time we needed something else, we made another request using XMLHttpRequest or JSONP. We even made requests when there was no new data for us, which happened sometimes in the Mighty Gumball example.

Web Sockets is a new API that allows you to keep an open connection with a web service so that any time new data is available the service can just send it to you (and your code can be notified). Think of it like an open phone-line between you and the service.

Here's a high-level overview of how you use it: first, to create a web socket we use the web socket constructor:

```
var socket = new WebSocket("ws://yourdomain/yourservice");
```

Notice this URL uses the ws protocol, not the http protocol.

And remember you or someone else is going to have to write the server code so you have something to talk to!

You can be notified as soon as the socket is open with the open event, which you can assign a handler for:

```
socket.onopen = function(){
    alert("Your socket is now open with the web service");
}
```

Here we supply a handler that is called when the socket is fully opened and ready for communcation.

You can send a message to the web service with the postMessage method:

```
socket.postMessage("player moved right");
```

Here's we're sending the server a string; binary is coming but not widely supported yet.

And to receive messages you register another handler, like this:

```
socket.onmessage = function(event) {
    alert("From socket: " + event.data);
};
```

By registering a handler, we receive all messages, which are contained in the event's data property.

There's a little more to it than this, of course, and you'll want to check out some tutorials online, but there's not much more to the API. This API has been lagging behind some of the other HTML5 API development, so check out the latest browser compatibility guides before you undertake a major project.

#8 More canvas API

We had fun with the canvas in Chapter 7, building our TweetShirt startup. But there are lots of other fun canvas-related things you can do and we wanted to touch on a few more of them here.

We mentioned very briefly that you can `save` and `restore` the canvas context. Why would you want to do that? Let's say you've set some properties of the context, like the `fillStyle`, `strokeStyle`, `lineWidth` and so on. And you want to then temporarily change those values to do one thing, like draw a shape, but not have to reset them all to get back to the property values you had previously. You can use the `save` and `restore` methods to do that:

```
context.fillStyle = "lightblue";

    . . .

context.save();

context.fillStyle = "rgba(50, 50, 50, .5)";

context.fillRect(0, 0, 100, 100);

context.restore();

    . . .
```

We set up a bunch of properties in the context and do some drawing.

Now, we save the context. All those properties are saved safely. We can change them...

... and then get them all back to where they were when we saved them simply by calling the restore method! At this point, all our properties are what they were before we saved.

These methods come in particularly handy when you want to *translate* or *rotate* the canvas to draw something and then put it back to its default position. What do the `translate` and `rotate` methods do? Let's take a look...

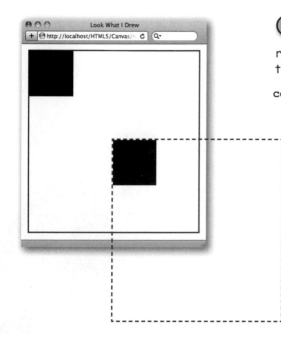

① We've got a 400x400 canvas in the page. If we draw a black rectangle at x=0, y=0, it is drawn in the top left corner, like you'd expect.

```
context.fillRect(0, 0, 100, 100);
```

② Now, we'll pick up the canvas and move it 200 pixels to the right, and 200 pixels down. If we draw another rectangle at x=0, y=0, the rectangle is drawn 200 pixels right and down from the other rectangle. We've just translated the canvas.

```
context.translate(200, 200);

context.fillRect(0, 0, 100, 100);
```

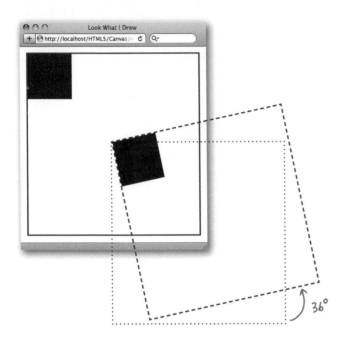

③ What if we rotate the canvas before we draw the rectangle? The canvas rotates around its top left corner (by default), and since we just moved the top left corner to 200, 200, that's the position where the canvas rotates.

```
context.translate(200, 200);
context.rotate(degreesToRadians(36));
context.fillRect(0, 0, 100, 100);
```

↑ When you translate or rotate the canvas, it's moved on a grid that's positioned with respect to the top left corner of the browser window. If you've positioned your canvas using CSS, those values are taken into account. Try it!

Now let's put all that together! You can use the `translate` and `rotate` methods together to create some interesting effects.

```
var canvas = document.getElementById("canvas");

var context = canvas.getContext("2d");

var degrees = 36;

context.save();

context.translate(200, 200);

context.fillStyle = "rgba(50, 50, 50, .5)";


for (var i = 0; i < 360/degrees; i++) {

    context.fillRect(0, 0, 100, 100);

    context.rotate(degreesToRadians(degrees));

}

context.restore();
```

We're saving the context here so we can easily restore it to its normal grid position after we're done.

← We translate our canvas by 200, 200.

We're drawing 10 rectangles by rotating the canvas 36 degrees before drawing a rectangle at 0, 0 each time through the loop.

← Now our canvas is back at its original position!

And here's the result. Fun!

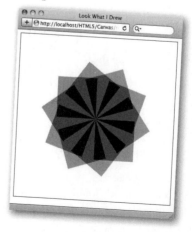

Combine these simple transformations with other, even more powerful (and complex!) methods like compositing and transforms, and the possibilities for creating graphic art with canvas are endless.

#9 Selectors API

You already know how to select elements from the DOM using `document.getElementById`; we've used it throughout this book as a way to get HTML and JavaScript working together. You've also seen how to use `document.getElementsByTagName` (this method returns an array of all elements that match a tag), and there's even a `getElementsByClassName` method (returning, you guessed it, all elements that are in a given class).

With HTML5, we now have a new way of selecting elements from the DOM, inspired by jQuery. You can now use the same selectors you use in CSS to select elements for styling in your JavaScript to select elements from DOM with the `document.querySelector` method.

Let's say we have this simple HTML:

```
<!doctype html>
<html lang="en">
<head>
  <title>Query selectors</title>
  <meta charset="utf-8">
</head>
<body>
  <div class="content">
    <p id="avatar" class="level5">Gorilla</p>
    <p id="color">Purple</p>
  </div>
</body>
</html>
```

Take a close look at the structure of this HTML. We're going to use the selectors API to select elements from the page.

We've got a `<div>` element with the class "content", and two `<p>` elements, each with their own ids, and one with the class "level5".

Now, let's use the selectors API to ask for the "avatar" `<p>` element:

```
document.querySelector("#avatar");
```

That's essentially the same thing as `document.getElementId("avatar")`. Now let's use the element's class to select it:

```
document.querySelector("p.level5");
```

Now we're using the tag name and the class to select it.

We can also select a `<p>` element that is a child of the `<div>` element, like this:

```
document.querySelector("div>p");
```

or even like this:

```
document.querySelector(".content>p");
```

Here, we're using a child selector to select a `<p>` element that is a child of the `<div>`. It selects the first one, by default.

And, if what we really want is *all* the `<p>` elements in the `<div>`, we can use the other method in the selectors API, `querySelectorAll`:

```
document.querySelectorAll("div>p");
```

Now we get all the child `<p>` elements of the `<div>`!

`querySelectorAll` returns an array of elements, just like `getElementsByTagName`. And that's it! Those are the only two methods in the API. The selectors API is small, but adds powerful new functionality for selecting elements.

#10 But, there's even more!

Okay, we really wanted to keep it to the ten things we didn't tell you, but it looks like we've got a ways to go, and instead of standing between you and your reading of the index, we're going to give you a bunch more in a single page. Here they are (keep in mind some of these areas are still evolving, but we knew you'd want to know about them for future reference):

Indexed Database API and Web SQL

If you're looking for something more industrial than the Web Storage API to store your data locally, keep an eye on the web database space. Two competing visions are out there right now: Web SQL and IndexedDB. Ironically, Web SQL is the more widely supported of the two, but was recently deprecated by the standards bodies (meaning they don't recommend adopting it as a standard, and you probably shouldn't base your next startup on it). IndexedDB, on the other hand, isn't widely implemented yet, but has support from Google and Firefox. IndexedDB provides fast access to a large collection of indexed data, while Web SQL is a small SQL engine that runs in the browser. Keep an eye out for where these technologies go; they are changing fast!

Drag and Drop

Web developers have been doing drag and drop with jQuery for a while now, and now this functionality is native in HTML5. With the HTML5 Drag and Drop API, you specify something to drag, where you can drop it, and JavaScript handlers to be notified of the various events that occur while dragging and dropping. To make an element draggable, just set the `draggable` attribute to true. Just about any element can be dragged: images, lists, paragraphs, and so on. You can customize the dragging behavior by listening for events like `dragstart` and `dragend` and even change the style of an element to look like you want while it's being dragged. You can send along a little bit of data with your dragged element using the `dataTransfer` property; access this through the `event` object to know if, say, the element is being moved or copied. As you can see, there are lots of great opportunities to build new UI interactions with HTML5 Drag and Drop.

Cross-document Messaging

In chapter 6, we used a communication pattern known as JSONP to get around the cross-domain communication issues with XMLHttpRequest. There's another way you can communicate between documents—even documents in different domains. The Cross-document Messaging API specifies that you can post a message to a document you've loaded using an `iframe` element. This document could even be at a different domain! Now, you wouldn't want to load just *any* document into your `iframe`; you'll want to make sure it's from a domain you trust and set it up to receive your messages. But the upshot is that this is a way to get messages back and forth between two HTML documents.

And we could go on...

The exciting thing about HTML5 is that there are so many new capabilities being developed at a fairly fast pace; there's even more we could put on the this page, but we're out of room. So keep up to date with us on the Web at `http://wickedlysmart.com` for all the latest developments in HTML5!

I can't believe the book is almost over. Before you go, we've got a little parting gift for you from the City of Webville; it's the guide to the HTML5 elements (and what's new in CSS3) that we promised you. Isn't Webville great?!

The HTML5 Guide to New Construction

Here in Webville we've recently made a few additions to our building codes and we've prepared a handy guide to any new construction you might be considering. In particular we've added a bunch of new new semantic elements that give you even more power to architect your pages. Now, our guide isn't exhaustive; rather, our goal here is to give you, the experienced builder, enough to be familiar with the new HTML5 elements and CSS3 properties so you can use them in the web applications you're learning how to build in this book when you're ready. So if you need a quick tutorial on the semantic additions to HTML5, take one—they're FREE (for a limited time only).

Webville Guide to HTML5 Semantic Elements

Here in Webville we've made some recent changes to our building code and we've prepared a handy guide for all your new construction. If you've been using <div>s for common construction like headers, navigation, footers, and blog articles, then we have some new building blocks for you. So make sure you're up to code.

<section>

A <section> is a "generic document". You could use <section> to mark up, oh, say a Guide to HTML. Or to enclose the HTML for a game. A <section> is *not* a generic container—that's <div>'s job. And remember, use <div> if you're just grouping elements together for styling purposes.

<article>

An <article> is a self-contained chunk of content that you might want to share with another page or web site (or even your dog). Perfect for blog posts and news articles.

<header>

<header> is for the tops of elements like <section> and <article>. You might also use <header> at the top of the body to create the main header for your page.

<footer>

<footer> is for the bottoms of things. Things like <section>s, <article>s and <div>s. You might think you're only allowed one on a page; in fact, you can use it whenever you need footer content on a section of your page (like a bio or references for an article).

<hgroup>

This one can be tricky. Unlike <header>, which can contain any elements related to a header, <hgroup> is specifically for grouping headings (<h1>...<h6>) together inside a <header>. Good for outlines.

Webville Guide to HTML5 Semantic Elements

`<nav>`

<nav> is navigation and for links, of course. But not just any links: use <nav> when you have a group of links, like navigation for your site, or a blogroll. Don't use it for single links in paragraphs.

`<aside>`

<aside> is handy for all kinds of things that are chunks of content outside the main flow of your page, like a sidebar, a pull quote, or an after-thought.

`<time>`

Finally! It's about time. You can mark up your times with <time>. No need to rush; take your time and do it right—you'll need to study up a bit on the valid formats for <time>.

`<progress>`

Almost done? Yes, we're making progress through these HTML5 elements...<progress> represents how far along you are in completing a task. Use with a little CSS and JavaScript for some nice effects.

`<abbr>`

Hey Mr., make sure you use an abbreviation for that long word! Great for search, because search engines aren't always as smart about abbreviations as we are.

`<mark>`

Use <mark> to mark words, for highlighting or editing, say. A good one to use with search engine results.

Adding style to your new construction with CSS3

Webville Guide to CSS3 Properties

Now that you've got your new building blocks into place, it's time to think about some interior design. You'll want to make all your new construction look good, right?

New properties

There are quite a few new properties in CSS3, many of which do what web page authors have been doing for years with various contortions of HTML, images, and JavaScript. Examples:

```
opacity: 0.5;
```
← Makes an element 50% opaque

```
border-radius: 6px;
```
← Creates a rounded effect with a 6px curvature on each corner

```
box-shadow: 5px 5px 10px #373737;
```
← A shadow 5px long, 5px high, a blur of 10px and a dark grey color.

New layouts

There are a couple of powerful new ways to lay out your page with CSS that go beyond positioning and are much easier to use. Examples:

```
display: table;
display: table-cell;
```
} This gives you a table layout without the HTML tables.

```
display: flexbox;
flex-order: 1;
```
← With flexbox you have greater control over how the browser flows boxes, like <div>s onto the page.

New animations

With animations, you can animate between property values. For instance you can make something disappear by transitioning the opacity from opaque to translucent:

```
transition: opacity 0.5s ease-in-out;
```
← The transition property specifies a property to transition into and out of, (in this case opacity), how long to take to do the transition and the easing function, so it's gradual.

```
opacity: 0;
```
← By setting opacity to 0, say on a hover event, we can create a disappear/reappear animation.

New selectors

There are a whole slew of new selectors, including nth-child, which lets you target specific child elements enclosed in an element. Finally, you can set the background color of alternating rows in a list without going crazy.

```
ul li:nth-child(2n) { color: gray; }
```
This means: select every other list item and set the background color to gray.

Index

Symbols

E

effectFunction
> calling to apply video filter 397
> used as variable to hold video filter function 391

effects 410
> applying to videos 389–391
> choice of, video booth 378
> creating using canvas context translate and rotate methods 541
> writing special effects for video 399–404

element objects 158
> returned by getElementById method 160

elements
> accessing with getElementById 59
> adding to the DOM 100
> creating 99
> getting with getElementById method 114, 157
> getting with getElementByTagName method 154
> getting with getElementsByClassName method 154
> getting with getElementsByTagName method 269
> setting attributes with setAttribute method 267

else clauses in if statements 50

empty strings
> assigning as value to variable 26
> checking for 95
> comparing variables to 108

enableHighAccuracy option 198, 201

encoding your own video 360

ended event, video 365
> adding event listener for 386
> writing handler for 367

endedHandler function (example) 386

enumerating properties of an object 133

error handlers
> for cache errors 538
> Geolocation API 190, 207
>> for getCurrentPosition 174, 177–179
>> for watchPosition 194
> video errors 406
> in workers 522

error property, video object 405

errors
> browsers overlooking small errors in HTML files 9
> Geolocation API
>> timeout error 200
>> types of errors 178
> handling errors with video playback 371
> JavaScript syntax 44
> localStorage, quota exceeded 458
> no XMLHttpRequest errors, 200 response code 239
> video error types 405

event handling 89
> addEventListener method, registering event handler 367
> button click handler 102
> clearWatch event handler 195
> creating handler and assigning it to button onclick property 91
> handler alerting user that button was clicked 92
> handleRefresh function 265
> handler for ended video event 386
> handlers for video booth buttons 377
> handler to make image of canvas drawing 347
> HTTP request handler 221
> onclick event handler
>> createSticky (example) 431
>> deleteSticky (example) 450
> onclick event handler to zoom in on canvas in Fractal Viewer 515
> onload event handler for twitter bird image (example) 333
> onload event handler function for Mighty Gumball (example) 229
> onload handler as anonymous function 156
> onmessage event handler for Web Sockets 539
> onmessage event handler for worker 485
> onopen event handler for Web Sockets 539
> previewHandler function (example) 302
> review of important points 108
> reworking handleButtonClick to obtain song title typed into form by user 96
> types of events handled by JavaScript 95

event object
> data and target properties 485
> dataTransfer property 543
> target property 451

F

M

Mac
Apache server, configuring MIME types 371
setting up server on 231
task monitor on OS X 520
makeImage function (example) 347
makeServerRequest function (example) 523
Mandelbrot, Benoit 495
Mandelbrot Set. *See also* Fractal Explorer application,
building
computing 496
equation 495
explorer for 494
ready-baked code for computing 504–507
using multiple workers to compute 497–500
mapOptions object 184
mapping your position 182
maps
adding markers to 186, 204
adding to a page 183
displaying on your page 184
testing map display on your page 185
<mark> element 547
markers, adding to map 186, 204
controlling frequency of new markers 209
optimizing marker usage 206
markup, new 16, 533
Math.floor function 70, 304, 319
Math library 73, 75
Math.PI 317
Math.random function 70, 304, 319
x, y, and width of squares drawn on canvas 308
maximumAge option 199, 201
message handler, writing for worker 486
messages
data that can be sent 484, 491
receiving by Web Worker 486
receiving from Web Workers 485
sending and receiving using Web Sockets 539
sending from Web Worker 486
sending to Web Workers 484

messaging, cross-document 543
<meta> tags 31
omitting 9
specifying in HTML5 4
methods 142, 160
code reuse and 146
converting functions to 143
functions versus 151
this keyword, how it works 149
Microsoft. *See also* Internet Explorer; Windows systems
Smooth Streaming 404
Web Platform Installer 231
Mighty Gumball application (example) 214–218
browser cache, watching out for 272
displaying sales 230
improving the display 235
making JSONP dynamic 264–271
moving to live server 237–246
options to circumvent cross-origin request problems 247–251
removing duplicate sales reports 273
reviewing the specs 228
reworking code to use JSON 236
testing locally 230, 234
updating code to use JSONP 256–263
updating JSON URL with lastreporttime 275
writing onload handler function 229
milliseconds since 1970 442
MIME types
application/xhtml+xml 536
making sure server is serving video files with correct type 371
of video files 359, 369
mobile browsers 20
HTML5 support 18
mobile devices
browser support for offline web apps 538
canvas on 335
testing geolocation code 179
Modernizr library, JavaScript 532
movements, tracking 192–198
form to start and stop tracking 193
moveTo method, canvas context 311
.mp3 audio 533

src attribute
    \<script\> element 53, 218, 249
        updating with setAttribute 267
    \<source\> element 358, 359
    \<video\> element 353, 354
src property
    audio object 533
    image object 333
    video object 370
startWorkers function (example) 509, 510
statements 37
    ending with semicolon 39
stickies application (example) 418, 428
    adding "Add Sticky Note to Self" button 431
    adding JavaScript code 430
    converting createSticky to use an array 441
    creating interface 429
    deleting sticky from DOM 452
    deleting sticky notes 446
    design flaw 436
    integrating array-based code 443
    rewriting to use an array 440
    selecting sticky note to delete 450
    updating user interface to specify color 453–456
streaming video 403
    technologies for 404
string concatenation operator (+) 26, 45
string expressions 43
stringify method. *See* JSON.stringify method
strings
    accessing and enumerating object properties 133
    in arrays 71
    as associative array indexes 424
    conversions to numbers in expressions 45
    converting objects to JSON string format 226
    converting to floats with parseFloat function 423
    converting to integers with parseInt function 423
    creating string representation of an array 441, 467
    key/value pairs stored in local storage 418
    as objects 159
    primitive type in JavaScript 40
    receiving from Web Workers with onmessage in event.
        data property 485
    sending to Web Workers with postMessage 484

stroke method, canvas context 312
strokeText method, canvas context 328
structure 35, 545
\<style\> element
    adding border to canvas 288
    CSS is style standard 9, 31
style property 455
subworkers 523
success handler, Geolocation API 174, 175, 190
SVG (Scalable Vector Graphics) 537

T

table and table-cell layouts 548
target property, event object 451, 485
task monitor on OS X or Windows 520
tasks, sending and receiving data from Web Workers
    (Fractal Explorer example) 512
terminate method, worker object 522
textAlign property, canvas context 328
    aligning tweet text in t-shirt design app (example) 331
textBaseline property, canvas context 329
text, drawing on canvas 325–332, 338
    displaying HTML entities 335
    drawText function 345
    splitting it into lines 335
    text methods and properties in canvas API 328
text \<input\> element, value property 94
    checking whether user entered input 96
Theora video format 357
third-party hosting services 230, 232
this (keyword) 144
    adding to movie object (example) 145
    questions and answers about 151
    using with constructors 147
    using with method calls 149, 151
threading. *See also* Web Workers
    adding another thread of control 476
    single-threaded model, JavaScript 474
    with Web Workers 478, 524

W

Colophon

All interior layouts were designed by Eric Freeman and Elisabeth Robson.

Kathy Sierra and Bert Bates created the look & feel of the Head First series. The book was produced using Adobe InDesign CS and Adobe Photoshop CS. The book was typeset using Uncle Stinky, Mister Frisky (you think we're kidding), Ann Satellite, Baskerville, Comic Sans, Myriad Pro, Skippy Sharp, Savoye LET, Jokerman LET, Courier New and Woodrow typefaces.

Interior design and production all happened exclusively on Apple Macintoshes—two Mac Pros and two MacBook Airs to be precise.

Writing locations included: Bainbridge Island, Washington; Portland, Oregon; Las Vegas, Nevada; Port of Ness, Scotland; Seaside, Florida; Lexington, Kentucky; Tucson, Arizona; and Anaheim, California. Long days of writing were powered by the caffeine fuel of Honest Tea, GT's Kombucha, and the sounds of Sia, Sigur Ros, Tom Waits, OMD, Phillip Glass, Muse, Eno, Krishna Das, Mike Oldfield, Audra Mae, Devo, Steve Roach, Beyman Brothers, Pogo, all the people at turntable.fm, and a heck of a lot more 80s music than you'd care to know about.

This isn't goodbye

Bring your brain over to
wickedlysmart.com